Thomas William Marshall

Christian missions

Their agents, their method, and their results Vol. 3

Thomas William Marshall

Christian missions
Their agents, their method, and their results Vol. 3

ISBN/EAN: 9783741198717

Manufactured in Europe, USA, Canada, Australia, Japa

Cover: Foto ©Lupo / pixelio.de

Manufactured and distributed by brebook publishing software (www.brebook.com)

Thomas William Marshall

Christian missions

CHRISTIAN MISSIONS:

THEIR AGENTS,
THEIR METHOD, AND THEIR RESULTS;

BY

T. W. M. MARSHALL.

A FRUCTIBUS EORUM COGNOSCETIS EOS.
S. MATT. VII, 16.

VOL. III.

LONDON,
BURNS AND LAMBERT, 17, PORTMAN STREET,
PORTMAN SQUARE.

BRUSSELS,
H. GOEMAERE, RUE DE LA MONTAGNE, 52.

1862
The right of translation is reserved.

CHAPTER IX.

MISSIONS IN AMERICA.

PART I.

SOUTH AMERICA.

The gifts and promises of God, it has been said, have travelled from East to West, from the rising to the setting sun. To each tribe of the human family in turn the Angel of the Covenant has delivered the message of peace, then passed on his way. In the appointed hour he crossed the great sea, with his face westwards. Then, for the first time, the Name of Jesus was proclaimed in that mighty continent which stretches almost from pole to pole, and within whose boundless plains a new chapter of man's history has found its scenes and its actors. Here, among many tribes, and nations of various tongues, the ministers of light and darkness have long contended together for the mastery. When we have read the story of their conflict, we may close our book. Earth has nothing more to offer us. We shall have visited in turn all her provinces; and having started from the remote eastern sea which beats against the long coasts of China, we shall stand at length on the opposite frontier of man's narrow home, the western limit of his wanderings, and may once more look across the ocean to the land from which we commenced our journey.

No portion of the earth presents on a larger scale, none in more vivid colours, the contrast which it has been the business of these volumes to trace, than that whose religious history we are about to review. When nature divided the great American continent into two parts, she seems to have prepared by anticipation a separate theatre for the events of which each was to be the scene, and for the actors who were destined to perform in either a part so widely dissimilar. The one was to be the exclusive domain of the Church, the other the battle field of all the Sects.

A thousand writers have related, with sympathy or regret, but otherwise with unvarying uniformity, the historical results of a distribution which all seem to have noticed, and in which may be traced, on the broadest scale, and with a clearness and precision which exclude even the risk of error, all the characteristic marks which have distinguished in every age the City of God from the City of Confusion. The races of the South, we shall see, have derived both their religion and their civilization from the missionaries of the Cross; the tribes of the North, doomed to swift destruction, have been abandoned to teachers of another school, and to prophets of another faith. And these have been the results of the unequal partition. In the *South*, the Church has united all, of whatever race, and in spite of the ignorance or the ferocity of the barbarians, in spite of the follies or the crimes of some of her own children, into one household and family. In the *North*, the original heirs have been banished or exterminated, without pity and without remorse, that the sects might build up in the desert which they had created a pandemonium of tumult and disorder, so full of division and discord, that the evil spirits might well congregate here from all the « dry places » of the earth, and deem that they had found at last their true home. Let us introduce at once a few of the witnesses whom we are hereafter to hear, that we may understand what is the history upon which we are about to enter, and what are the facts which it will disclose to us.

The contrast which we are going to trace is thus indicated, with frank outspoken candour, by men who had analysed all its features. « More than a million and a half of the pure aboriginal races, » says the author of the Natural History of Man, « live in *South* America in the profession of Christianity. »(1) « The history of the attempts to convert the Indians of *North* America, » says the annalist of Protestant missions, « is a record of a series of failures. » (2) This is the first great fact, in its broad outlines, which will be presented to our notice; and it is

(1) Prichard, section 44, p. 427.
(2) Quoted in *Monthly Review*, vol, LXXXIV, p. 143.

one, as an eminent English ethnologist observes, « which must be allowed to reflect honour on the Roman Catholic Church, and to cast a deep shade on the history of Protestantism. » (1)

A second and equally impressive fact, which has excited the attention of a multitude of writers of all nations, is thus expressed by a prejudiced traveller, who had lived amongst the tribes of the equinoxial regions. « Far from being diminished, *their* number has considerably increased. A similar increase has taken place *generally* amongst the Indian population in that part of America which is within the tropics... the Indian population *in the missions* is constantly augmenting. » On the other hand, — « In the neighbourhood of the United States, on the contrary, the Indians are fast diminishing in numbers... in the United States, as civilization advances, the Indians are constantly driven beyond its pale. » (2) We shall trace this contrast hereafter in all its details.

Finally, a third feature of the prodigious contrast which we are about to examine is this, — that while the innumerable native tribes who have been converted to Christianity between the thirtieth parallel of north and the thirty-fifth of south latitude, through a tract of more than four thousand miles in length and nearly three thousand in breadth, have never departed from the Catholic faith, and, as Protestant writers will assure us, cleave to it at this day as obstinately as ever; — within the wide territories

---

(1) Prichard, ubi supra.
(2) *Journal of a Residence in Colombia*, by Captain Charles Stuart Cochrane, vol. I, ch. III, pp. 218, 233.

of the United States, where the Indian has only been corrupted or destroyed, nominal Christians of the Anglo-Saxon race have themselves become divided and subdivided into such a chaos of jarring sects, that, as their own leaders declare, with a sorrow which comes too late, there is nothing like it in the history of the world. « In the western world, » says a Protestant minister, « religion is made to appear too often as a source of contention rather than as a bond of union and peace. » (1) Already, at the close of the 17th century, the English governor of New-York reported of that province, that it swarmed with men « of all sorts of opinions, and the most part of none at all ; » and a hundred years later, an English clergyman could still describe the inhabitants of his own district as « people of almost all religions and sects, but the greatest part of no religion. » (2) In our own day, it has even become necessary to adopt a new nomenclature, in order to classify divisions and subdivisions which had elsewhere neither a form nor a name. « Two grand divisions of the Baptists, » one of the innumerable offshoots from the Anglican Establishment, who already possess more than five thousand churches, are known, Mr Olmsted says, « as the Hard Shells and the Soft Shells ; » and even such titles are perhaps no greater outrage upon the religion of the Gospel than many which are daily uttered, with quiet complacency, in our own land. The relations of

(1) *The Western World Revisited*, by the Revd Henry Caswall; ch. i, p. 9 ; ch. xii, p. 316.

(2) *Documentary History of New York*, vol. I, p. 186 ; vol. III, p. 1,113.

these cognate tribes to one another, Mʳ Olmsted adds, are marked by « an intense rivalry and jealousy » as « persistent » as that which subsists between Druses and Maronites, between the followers of Ali and the disciples of Omar. (1) « The dearest and warmest friends of the Republic, » we are told, « look with fear and trembling on her sectional divisions, her party jealousies,... the strange and anomalous divisions, sub-divisions, and minor sub-divisions of her interminable and contending religious denominations. » (2) « Churches are divided, » observes another Protestant writer, « Presbyteries are divided, Synods are divided, the General Assembly is divided ; » and this is due, he considers, to « extreme looseness in doctrine and practice on the one hand, and a violent attempt to coerce it into orthodoxy on the other. » (3) « The continual splitting of the numerous sections of Protestantism, » Dʳ Schedel remarks, in 1858, still recording the unwelcome phenomena to which the disciples of the Reformation feel that *they* can apply no remedy, and using them as an argument in favour of rationalism, « has had the effect of producing a deep impression of its danger for religion. » (4) Lastly, — for there is no need to multiply testimonies to a fact which no one disputes, or to the real nature of a religion of which these are so invariably the fruits, that its own pro-

(1) Olmsted, *Our Slave States.*
(2) *Statesmen of America*, by S. Maury, p. 483.
(3) Colton's *Thoughts on the Religious State of the Country*, p. 66.
(4) *The Emancipation of Faith*, by H. E. Schedel, M. D. ; vol. II, p. 410. (N. York, 1858).

fessors now regard all unity as chimerical, except the diabolical unity of evil, — Dr Stephen Olin, a respectable Wesleyan preacher, exclaims once more; « Twenty years of observation have produced in my mind a deliberate conviction, that the sorest evil which presses upon the American Churches, the chiefest obstacle to their real progress in holiness and usefulness, is the spirit of sectarianism. » (1)

But even these three facts do not illustrate the whole contrast, which we are about to trace in America after proving it for every other land, between the work of the Church and the work of the Sects. The first has won a thousand tribes to the Cross; has seen them increase and multiply on every side under her gentle rule; and has preserved them for two hundred years, in spite of many calamities, in unbroken unity of faith. The second have not gained so much as a single tribe, have destroyed without mercy the races which they could not convert, and have themselves become a proverb to the whole earth of religious division and discord. Yet this also does not exhaust all the facts of the contrast.

It would have been something if the Sects could have pleaded that at least they had done their best, and only failed after earnest and courageous effort. Even this is a praise which they have not cared to earn, and which their own advocates refuse to allow them. We shall see presently what Protestant writers say of the dauntless courage and sublime patience of the men who converted South America; of

(1) *Works*, vol. II, p. 451.

their own friends they speak as follows. « The pious men of America, » says Möllhausen, with pardonable irony, « look with indifference on the heathens before their own doors, but send out missionaries to preach Christianity in the remotest parts of the world! When, through the covetousness of the white civilised races, the free inhabitants of the steppes shall have been ruined and exterminated, Christian love will find its way *to their empty wigwams*, and churches and meeting-houses rise over the graves of the poor victimised owners of the green prairies. » (1) They leave *them* to perish with indifference, says another German Protestant, who, like Möllhausen, had lived amongst them, because « there are no territories to be won, there are no natives to be enticed into building comfortable houses for the Christian teachers, they would have to lead a wild life with *them*, no further profit in view as is the case with the South Sea Islands, but only the prospect of being driven with their pupils from one place to another, living on grubs, acorns, and other indigestible things; while, on the other hand, a comfortable life and a good income look far more inviting. » (2) Such language need not surprise us, for we have seen many examples in the course of these pages both of the contempt which the more enlightened Protestants feel for their own missionaries, and the indifference with which they avow it.

Dr Moritz Wagner, another German Protestant,

(1) *Journey from the Mississipi to the Coasts of the Pacific*, vol. I, ch. XI, p. 220. Ed. Sinnett.
(2) Gerstaecker, *Journey round the World*, vol. I, ch. VI, p. 350.

who also had lived among American missionaries,
has already told us, in the same tone of honest
reprobation, that « America's evangelical apostles,
who have never yet raised their voices against the
hunting down the poor red-skins, pay many hundred
thousand dollars to support their useless missions in
the East » — not because they love the orientals
more, but simply, as Dr Livingstone intimates with
respect to South Africa, because they cannot bear to
be anticipated or excluded by the restless activity of
rival sects. Mr Buckingham also, an English writer,
who had dwelt amongst them, notices the characteristic fact, that while an American religious society
voted by acclamation thousands of dollars at once to
Persia, Siam, or the Sandwich Islands, which
demanded nothing from them and only asked to be
left alone; they allotted, as if in derision, « for North
American Indians, » perishing at their own doors,
the modest sum of two hundred! (1) And even when
their cautious emissaries, moved by the attractions
which alone prevail with such men, venture to follow
the native to his forest home, it is only to abandon
after a brief space the unprofitable labour; so that
Humboldt did not scruple to say, that the relics of
the aboriginal races of North America, who have
come into contact with the agents of English or
American religions, are « sinking into a *lower* moral
state than they occupied before. » (2)

« And this heavy reproach is repeated, in still
more emphatic language, even by American Protest-

---

(1) *America*, by J. S. Buckingham Esq., vol. I, ch. x.
(2) *Preface* to Möllhausen's *Journey*, p. XIII.

ants. « While the Pequods and other northern tribes, » says Judge Hall, of Cincinnati, « were being extirminated, or sold into slavery, the more fortunate savage of the Mississippi was listening to the pious counsels of the Catholic Missionaries. *They exercised, of choice, an expansive benevolence, at a period when Protestants, similarly situated, were bloodthirsty and rapacious.* » (1) « The Jesuit mission-farms, » says Mr Law Olmsted, in 1857, « are an example for us. Our neighbourly responsibilities for the Lipans » — a tribe on the Texan frontier — « is certainly more close than for the Feejees, and if the glory of converting them to decency be less, the expence would certainly be in proportion. » (2) Lastly, Mr Melville, also one of their own countrymen, noticing the vaunt that paganism is almost extinct in the United States, thus rebukes the hollow and impious boast. « The Anglo-Saxon hive have extirpated Paganism from the greater part of the North American continent, *but with it they have likewise extirpated the greater portion of the Red race.* » (3)

Such, by German, English, and American testimony has been the work of Protestantism. On the other hand, a modern French naturalist, who visited in person thirty-nine existing nations of pure American race in the Southern continent, and collected statistics from which we shall borrow hereafter, declares, that he found indeed, scattered through the

(1) *History of the Religious Denominations of the United States*, by J. D. Rupp, p. 163.
(2) *Journey Through Texas*, p. 298.
(3) *The Marquesas Islands*, ch. XXVI, p. 217.

regions which he so painfully explored, 94, 197 pagans; but that he counted also, within the same district, 1,590,930 *native* Christians. And then he relates, speaking rather as a man of science than as a Christian, that these poor Indians, often robbed of their pastors and almost always wronged by their rulers, exhibit the same astonishing inflexibility of faith, even in cases where they have been enfeebled by ignorance or superstition, of which we have already seen so many examples; so that, as M. d'Orbigny observes, « they push their profession of the Catholic religion even to fanaticism. » (1) Mendoza could say, at an earlier date, and in language more worthy of the subject, that « the natural people of South America, never since they were converted, have been found in any heresy, nor in any thing contrary to the Roman faith; » (2) and living Protestants will presently assure us, not only that all attempts to shake their faith are equally vain at the present day, but that in many parts of South America, and notably in Chili, where the emissaries of the English Bible Society have made their appearance, « the life of an Englishman is in danger among the peasantry, » so vehement is their dislike of heresy, and of those who recommend it to them. (3) Finally, for we must not anticipate evidence which will claim our attention later, Sir James Mackintosh thus attests the memorable contrast which had not escaped

(1) *Voyage dans l'Amérique Méridionale*, par Alcide D'Orbigny, tome IV, p. 252.
(2) *Historie of the Kingdome of China*, vol. II, p. 224. Ed. Hakluyt Society.
(3) *Travels in Chili*, by John Miers, vol. II, ch. xix, p. 223.

his philosophical review, and of which the fact noticed by Mendoza is not the least instructive portion. « The natives of America, who generally felt the comparative superiority of the European race only in a more rapid or a more gradual destruction, and to whom even the excellent Quakers dealt out little more than penurious justice, were, under the paternal rule of the Jesuits, » — he might have added, under that of the Franciscans, the Dominicans, and many more, — « reclaimed from savage manners, and instructed in the arts and duties of civilised life. » (1) Such, in its leading features, is the history of which we are now going to trace the outlines.

In attempting to follow the course of events of which the details have filled hundreds of volumes, and which had for their theatre the whole extent of the vast American continent, — in the North, from California to the Gulf of Florida, and from the banks of the St. Laurence to those of the Gila and the Colorado; in the South, from Carthagena to Buenos Ayres, and from the Andes to the mouths of the Amazon, the Orenoco, and the Plata; it is not a history which the reader will expect to find, hardly even a sketch, of a warfare which has filled the world with envy or admiration, which lasted more than two centuries, and in which the Church poured out like water the sweat and the blood of her children; while even her enemies have celebrated its final issue with an enthusiasm which the most inveterate prejudice could not silence, as one of the most aston-

---

(1) *Review of the Causes of the Revolution*, works, vol. II, p. 251. (1846).

ishing of her many triumphs. The story of American Missions includes names as venerable as any in the long catalogue of apostles, and tells of the deeds of a whole army of martyrs and confessors; — of Anchieta and Rodriguez, of Vieyra and d'Almeida, of D'Aguilar and Vénégas, of Herrera and Ugarte, of Betanzos and Las Casas, of Bracamante and Portillo, of Lopez and Barzana, of the Blessed Peter Claver and St. Francis Solano; — of the martyrs Suarez and Figuerroa, Baraza and Lizardi, Richter and Lucas Cavellero; of Aranda and Montalban, of Azevedo whom the Huguenots cut in pieces and Henri de la Borde whom the English ensnared and then cruelly murdered; of Jogues and de Brébœuf, of Lamberville and Lallemand, and a thousand more — for, as M. Cretineau Joly observes, « the number of missionaries who fell is really incalculable; » — of that multitude of apostolic warriors of whom even American Protestants of our own day have said, that their monuments wil yet be raised by the free people to whom they bequeathed examples of heroism which Americans know how to admire; who laboured, as Mr Washington Irving confessed, « *with a power which no other Christians have exhibited;* » (1) who excelled all others, » as Mr Schoolcraft admits, « in boldness, zeal, and indomitable efficacy; » (2) and who more than justified, as Professor Walters of Philadelphia remarks, whatever applause the admiration of mankind has lavished « upon their daunt-

---

(1) *Knickerbocker*, June 1838.
(2) *Notes on the Iroquois*, by Henry R. Schoolcraft, ch. xii, p. 403. (1847).

less courage and their more than human charity and zeal. » (1)

It is of such men, and of their work, that we are now to speak — not fitly, but according to the measure of our capacity. It is a comparison of their life and death, of their labours, sufferings, and conquests, with the sterile career of men of another order, but ostensibly busy in the same calling, which will furnish the last but not the least instructive example of the contrast of which we have already produced so many illustrations; and to which the Prophet pointed when he proposed this very contrast as the infallible test by which men should be able to distinguish, throughout the whole Christian era, between true and false apostles, between the work of the Church and the work of the Sects.

Let us begin with South America, and the world-famed Missions of Brazil and Peru, of Chili and Paraguay. A little later we shall traverse Mexico in our way to the north, enter California and Oregon, visit the lakes of the northern continent and the plains of Canada, and trace the decay of the unhappy races whom the Saxon, unable to convert them to God, has pushed from their homes, or violently swept from the earth, that he might people after his own fashion the regions from which they have been banished for ever.

We shall use, according to our custom, and as far as it is available, the testimony of Protestant writers. They have served us in all our former journies, and will not refuse to aid us in this. Let us

(1) Rupp, *Hist. of Religious Denominations*, etc., p. 119.

begin with their account of Catholic Missions in Brazil. Mr Southey—of whose sentiments towards the Catholic Church we shall presently see abundant tokens, and who did not hesitate to tell his countrymen, « I deprecate what is called Catholic Emancipation » — has diligently compiled whatever relates to the history of Brazil. He will be our principal guide.

It was in 1549 that John III of Portugal, solicitous, as Mr Southey observes, « for the souls of his Brazilian subjects, « resolved to despatch to their aid missionaries of the Society of Jesus. Brazil was not the only land which owed eternal gratitude to the Christian zeal of that vigorous and enlightened monarch, who received from his contemporaries more honour than Mr Southey is willing to allow him. « He was superstitious to the lowest depth of degradation, » says this English historian, with that quiet composure which his countrymen usually display in judging such men. In spite of this defect, « he was truly and righteously anxious to spread his religion, such as it was, among the heathen. » (1) So he sent Father Emanuel de Nobrega, and five others, chosen by St. Ignatius himself for this difficult mission; and it was under their auspices that the new city of St. Salvador, hitherto only a fortified camp, began to assume the dimensions which made it afterwards the capital of northern Brazil. « The Jesuits, » says Mr Southey, for Providence employs such men to proclaim the truths which they wish to hide, » im-

(1) *History of Brazil*, by Robert Southey, vol. I, ch. VIII, p. 214. (1817).

mediately began that system of beneficence towards the natives from which they never deviated till their extinction as an order. » From that hour the native of South America was to find, in every forest where he had made his home, and by the banks of every river on which his frail bark could float, a friend, a father, and a guide; who would save him from himself and from his oppressors, and teach him to love a religion which could move such as them to abandon home, country, and kinsfolk, in order to make such as him a partaker in its promises, its joys, and its rewards.

The attempt was bold, but not too bold. The missionaries, says Mr Southey, had to encounter « obstacles great and numerous, » and of these the almost universal practice of cannibalism was not the least formidable. But the children of St. Ignatius, like those of St. Francis and St. Dominic, who shared this field with them, knew how to combat the enemy, whatever form he might assume. They succeeded, therefore, in rooting out canibalism. It was their first victory; but Mr Southey, who will presently tell us how they did it, was so displeased with their proceedings, that he could only find relief by exclaiming, — « Nothing is too impudent for the audacity of such a priesthood, nothing too gross for the credulity of their besotted believers. » (1) Mr Southey, however, will inform us hereafter, that when missionaries of another faith attempted to instruct the same savage disciples, it was contempt, and not credulity, which they excited among them.

(1) Ch. viii, p. 230.

Happily, like the rest of his class, this historian is not rigorously consistent. « These missionaries, » he says, only a few pages later, « were every way qualified for their office. They were zealous for the salvation of souls; they had disengaged themselves from all the ties which attach us to life and were therefore not merely fearless of martyrdom, but ambitious of it. » (1) How such a temper, and such self-annihilation, were consistent with the grave demerits imputed to them by Mr Southey, he does not explain. « They believed the idolatry which they taught, » he says, as if he wished to excuse them as far as possible, « and were themselves persuaded that by sprinkling a dying savage, and repeating over him a form of words which he did not understand » — it is Mr Southey who says so — « they redeemed him from everlasting torments... Nor can it be doubted that they sometimes worked miracles upon the sick; for when they believed that the patient might be miraculously cured, and he himself expected that he should be so, faith would supply the virtue in which it trusted. » (2)

This singular explanation of their supernatural power, which seems to have satisfied Mr Southey, has one inconvenience; it leaves the missionaries under the reproach of idolatry, but it makes God their accomplice. Voltaire once said, with more them his usual wit and not more than his usual profaneness, « Si Dieu a fait l'homme à son image, l'homme le lui a bien rendu. » The ductile divinity imagined

(1) P. 252.
(2) P. 253.

by Mr Southey, who was so easily persuaded to work miracles even at the risk of propagating « idolatry, » had suffered not a little from that process, and was evidently fashioned after a human type. The infirmities of such a god disqualify him for ruling over Christians. But perhaps we may accept Mr Southey's admission that the Catholic missionaries « worked miracles upon the sick, » without adopting his explanation of the fact. Let us enquire of him, in the next place, how they extirpated cannibalism.

« All efforts at abolishing this accursed custom, » he says, « were in vain. One day Nobrega and his companions heard the uproar and rejoicing of the savages at one of these sacrifices; they made their way into the area, just when the prisoner had been felled, and the old women were dragging his body to the fire; they forced the body from them, and in the presence of the whole clan, who stood astonished at their courage, carried it off. The women soon roused the warriors to revenge this insult. By the time the Fathers had secretly interred the corpse, the savages were in search of them. » The barbarians were swift and eager in pursuit, but by the aid of the Portuguese authorities, the missionaries escaped their fury; and such was the impression which their intrepidity produced upon them, that « it was not long, » says our historian, « before these very savages came to solicit their forgiveness, and promised not to repeat these feasts. »

But Mr Southey has more to tell us. « One of the Jesuits, » he says, « succeeded in effectually abolishing cannibalism among some clans by going through them and flogging himself before their doors till he was covered with blood, telling them he thus tormented himself to avert the punishment which God would otherwise inflict upon them for this crying sin. *They could not bear this,* confessed what they had done was wrong, and enacted heavy punishments against any person who should again be guilty. »(1) It was thus that the missionaries rooted out cannibalism. It is true that the process involved pain and suffering, and that they encountered every day the risk of death in its most intolerable forms; but, as Mʳ Southey has remarked, « they were not merely fearless of martyrdom, but ambitious of it. »

With more remote tribes, over whom they had not as yet acquired the personal influence which they were afterwards to exert throughout the whole country, the Fathers, we are told, « thought themselves fortunate in obtaining permission to visit the prisoners and instruct them in the saving faith, before they were put to death. » It was a perilous ministry, which only such men would have accepted; and on these occasions, in order to escape the observation of the savages, while they complied with the divine precept which makes baptism a condition of salvation, « they carried with them wet handkerchiefs, or contrived to wet the skirt of their sleeve or habit, that out of it they might squeeze water enough upon the victim's head », to administer the sacrament of baptism. In recounting this proceeding, which excites his vehement disapprobation, Mʳ Southey adds; « What will not man believe, if

(1) P. 254.

he can believe this of his Maker!» As it was his Maker who taught him the lesson, why should man be blamed for believing it?

When at length, by inexhaustible patience and intrepid valour, living the while on the roots of the earth and sharing the rude cabin of the savage, these men of gentle birth and cultivated tastes had laboriously won some ferocious tribe from its foul superstitions, taught them to pronounce with reverence the sweet names of Jesus and Mary, and planted in them the first rudiments both of faith and civilization, « they made the converts erect a church in the village, which, however rude, fixed them to the spot; and they established a school for the children, whom they catechised in their own language... They taught them also to read and write, using, says Nobrega, the same persuasion as that wherewith the enemy overcame man,' Ye shall be as gods, knowing good and evil;' for this knowledge appeared wonderful to them, and they eagerly desired to attain it.» And then Mr Southey, unmoved even by the touching picture which he himself had drawn, haughtily exclaims; « Good proof how easily such a race might have been civilized!» More humane and candid writers will presently tell us, — indeed he will tell us himself, in a later volume, when he had forgotten these hasty words, — that they *were* civilised, and that this was the very process by which the arduous change was effected. Mr Southey adds, that « reading, writing, and arithmetic were taught them; they were trained to assist at Mass,» — that is, to do an act which in itself is no mean education, — « and to sing the church service.» Here was a beginning at least

of « civilization; » and it was so complete in its later
effects, so abiding in its influence, that three hundred
years after we shall find even English writers
not only celebrating the agricultural and economical
results still visible in the Christian Missions, but
contrasting the courtesy and dignity, as well as the
spiritual fervour, of these children of the forest, with
the boorish coarseness and animal instincts of their
own countrymen.

Mr Southey, however, was not satisfied, in this
early portion of his work, with the efforts of the
missionaries to civilize the natives of Brazil. Yet
even he could understand, and he expresses the
conviction in eloquent words, that « a ritual worship
creates arts for its embellishment and support; habits
of settled life take root as soon as a temple is founded,
and the city grows round the altar. » The Brazilians
anticipated Mr Southey in appreciating this important
fact, and he will trace for us hereafter, in spite of
himself, the prodigious work of civilization accomplished
among races even more barbarous than these
by the apostles of the Church; while others will tell
us, that if to « assist at Mass, » and to « sing the
church service » were the chief, they were not the
only lessons which they taught, — though they
taught these so well, that exactly three centuries after
Emanuel de Nobrega landed in Brazil, M. d'Orbigny,
who had listened with admiration to the
ecclesiastical music sung by the Indians in the mission
of San Xavier, confesses, « I could not but
admire the labours of the Jesuits, when I reflected
that previous to their arrival the Chiquitos, still in
the savage state, were scattered through the recesses

of the forest! » During twelve generations they have handed down, from father to son, the lessons which the Jesuits taught them; and d'Orbigny adds, that though they martyred the earlier missionaries, « once Christian, they have persevered, and at this day nothing would induce them to return to the life of the woods. » (1) To what extent they were really civilized, we shall learn hereafter, by the testimony of Protestant writers, including Mr Southey himself.

The first missionaries in Brazil, to whom we must now return, had to contend not only with the ignorance and ferocity of its native tribes, but with the profound immorality of the reckless adventurers who had deserted Portugal to try their fortunes in the new world. In Brazil, as in Mexico, it was from men of this stamp, — self-banished, and stained with many a crime, yet retaining even in their fall the faith which Catholics so rarely lose, — that the missionaries experienced the most obstinate and formidable opposition. Seeking only the goods of this world, they resented the admonitions of men who valued only those of the next. « As the Jesuits stedfastly opposed their cruelties, » we are told by two Protestant ministers, « the Portuguese resorted to every means of annoyance against them... As the Indians were driven back into the wilds of the interior, through fear of the slave-hunters, the Jesuits sought them out, and carried to them the opportunities of Christian worship and instruction. » (2) Hence the implacable warfare which the Portuguese merchants

(1) *Voyage*, etc., tome IV, p. 250.
(2) *Brazil and the Brazilians*, by Kidder and Fletcher, ch. xx, p. 368.

waged against the missionaries. But this was only an additional motive with the latter for deeds of charity towards their enemies. With uncompromising firmness but with gentle speech they admonished them of their errors, refusing the sacraments to all who maltreated their slaves or set them an unchristian example. « Many were reclaimed, » says Mr Southey, « by this resolute and Christian conduct. » The immorality of professing Christians was vanquished, then, by the same fervent apostles before whose presence idolatry had already begun to flee away.

In 1553, a reinforcement of seven Fathers arrived in Brazil, the number already in the field being wholly unequal to a work which was destined to assume such vast proportions, and to require the cooperation of so great a multitude of labourers, that the day arrived when the Jesuits alone in South America numbered seventeen hundred, out of the *thirteen thousand* who, at the same moment, were preaching the Faith to the heathen in every part of the globe. Amongst the new comers was one of that privileged order in whom the effects of the first transgression seem to be almost effaced, and who are admitted, while still in the flesh, to that intimate union with God which the rest of the elect only attain in another life. Joseph Anchieta was in his twentieth year when he arrived in Brazil. Here, during forty-four years, he was to display before the eyes of Christians and Pagans a new example of those astonishing virtues which confirm the one in the obedience of the faith, and attract the other, by the force of their irresistible fascination, to put on its easy yoke. But as we have now to enter a region in which such guides will decline to follow us, we must separate for a while from Mr Southey, and take for our companions men who do not start aside with instinctive repugnance from the presence of a saint, nor strive to reduce all the creatures of God to their own level, nor believe that the supernatural and the impossible are one and the same thing. We shall hear indeed what such men say of Anchieta, as we have already heard what they say of St. Francis, and de Nobili, and their kinsmen in grace; but we must leave them for a moment, lest they disturb us in our contemplation of one to whom even nature, it is said, was sometimes obedient; whom the beasts of the forest attended as companions, forgetting their instincts of carnage; in whose presence the very heathen held their breath, amazed at the works which God wrought by his hand; and who renewed on the other side of the Atlantic the triumphs of that divine ministry which had so often united heaven and earth in many a province of the old world. (1)

It was to a people among whom the graces of man's original state were so completely obliterated, that they were hardly raised above the brute creation, — « utterly devoid of modesty, without any clothing, and so gross and inhuman as actually to devour one another, » — that Anchieta, confiding only in the omnipotence of the weapons with which the Church arms her apostles, announced the law of Christ. A saint was needed for such a task, and a saint was at hand.

(1) The Life quoted is the Oratorian edition of 1849.

Employed at first in teaching Latin in the school which de Nobrega had founded at Piratininga, Anchieta spent his earlier years in patience, humility, and obedience; yearning for the hour when he might proclaim the Holy Name to the tribes of Brazil, but waiting in silence for the permission which he was too meek to anticipate. Meanwhile, he composed a Brazilian Grammar, which became afterwards a text book in Portugal for all who were destined for the American mission. A little later, he produced a dictionary of the same dialect; then an exposition of the whole body of Christian doctrine; and soon after, a multitude of canticles and devout songs, in four different languages, in order to replace the profane or indecent songs which were in use among the people. His compositions « were continually sung day and night, » says his biographer, « in the streets and thoroughfares, so that the praises of the Christian doctrine everywhere resounded. »

At length, having been admitted to the priesthood, he commenced the special work of a missionary. Alone, and with naked feet, fearing neither the pangs of hunger, nor the viper's sting, nor the jaw of the wild beast, he would penetrate the vast forests of this tropical land. On one occasion, having entered a wood, « without any conscious motive, and as if guided by another, » he found an aged Indian supported against a tree, who greeted him with the assurance that he had for some time been expecting his arrival. He had journied from a remote province, on the borders of the distant Plata, and could only explain that he had been guided by an impulse which he could not resist to that spot, where, he was told, "he should be taught the right path." When Anchieta, who comprehended that a special grace had brought to him this unexpected neophyte, had unfolded the chief mysteries of the Catholic faith, he replied; "It is thus that I already received, but I knew not how to express them." A little rain water, lodged in the leaves of some wild thistles, sufficed to baptize him; and when Anchieta returned to his companions, and related what had passed, he added, that he had just buried him, with his own hands, according to the rites of the Church.

But it was not always with such Indians as this that his apostolic journies bronght him in contact. The tribe of the Tamuyas, one of the fiercest and most warlike in Brazil, resenting the gradual advance of the Portuguese, and perhaps dreading the new power of which they might one day become the victims, fell suddenly on the colony of St. Vincent, massacred the white population, and ravaged the whole district with the blind and sanguinary fury of barbarians. Father de Nobrega, touched with compassion for the misery of these Christians, who were already preparing to abandon the country, conceived a project which only the heart of a true missionary could have entertained. Taking with him Anchieta, fitting companion for so perilous a mission, he boldly entered the territory of the Tamuyas. Received at first with unexpected reverence, the ambassadors hastened to propose terms of peace. Two months elapsed in fruitless negotiations, when de Nobrega was suffered to depart, in order to concert new measures at St. Vincent, leaving Anchieta as a hostage in the hands of the savages. As they parted at this critical moment, « Anchieta manifested to Father Nobrega three different circumstances which had been revealed to him in the same night, God then beginning to treat him as His familiar friend, and disclosing to him the hidden secrets of His Divine Providence. » The first was, that the town of Biritioca, at the entrance of St. Vincent, from which they were distant at that moment about seventy miles, was already in possession of the savages; the second, that a person well known to Nobrega had been crushed to death; the third, that a Portuguese vessel, laden with supplies, was on the point of entering the port of St. Vincent. On the arrival of Nobrega, the two first statements were immediately confirmed; a little later, the third received its welcome fulfilment.

Meanwhile, Anchieta was alone with the savages, as calm and unmoved as if he had been in the company of little children. Outraged by their intolerable indecency, and his life perpetually menaced by their capricious fury, he had recourse to the usual weapons of apostles, prayer and mortification. » The continence of these fathers, » says Mr Southey, to whom we may return for a moment, « had occasioned great admiration in their hosts, and they asked Nobrega how it was that he seemed to abhor what other men so ardently desired. He took a scourge out of his pocket, and said that by tormenting the flesh he kept it in subjection. » Anchieta, he adds, « who was in the prime of manhood, made a vow to the Virgin that he would compose a poem upon her life, trusting to preserve his own purity by thus fixing his thoughts upon the Most Pure. » Yet Mr Southey, true to his instincts, could elsewhere call the prudent austerities of Catholic missionaries, « the frantic folly of Catholicism. »

In spite of the difficulties of his position, Anchieta ceased not to preach the Gospel to his hosts, till « many of them were so well instructed, that he would have admitted them to the Sacrament of baptism, if he had not feared their want of constancy, and deemed it prudent to leave the gathering of this harvest to his companions. » But the more violent members of the tribe, irritated by the failure of the negotiations, and disappointed in their hope of plunder, resolved to put him to death without further delay. They announced to him, therefore, that he was to die at a certain hour, and that afterwards they should feast on his body. With perfect composure of soul and countenance he replied, that they would certainly not kill him at the time appointed; and when they asked him in amazement how he could display such assurance, he answered, — that he had learned from the Mother of that God whom he had preached to them that he was not yet to die. His confidence was justified, and after a captivity of three months, a treaty of peace was established, and Anchieta was once more embraced by his fellow missionaries at St. Vincent.

A few words will indicate his and their mode of life. They had not often a house to live in, and when they had, it was such as Anchieta describes in a letter to St. Ignatius, written from Piratininga, while he acted as professor under Manuel de Paiva. « Our house is composed of a number of long poles, of which the interstices are filled up with clay. The principal apartment, which is fourteen feet in length by ten in width, is at once our school, infirmary, dormitory, refectory, kitchen, and store-room. » In fact, it was a cabin with one room, in which twenty-six inmates were lodged. « Yet all our brothers are delighted with it, nor would they exchange this hut for the most magnificent palace. They remember that the Son of God was born in a stable, where there was but little space, and died on a cross, where there was still less. » Even Mr Southey acknowledges that the only food they had was « what the Indians gave them, » which was chiefly *mandioc* flour; and Anchieta himself, a man of noble birth, alluding to their rude manner of life, says jestingly; « We may be pardoned for not using napkins at a table on which there is nothing to eat. »

It was in the midst of privations which they hardly deemed worthy of notice that these first apostles of Brazil prosecuted their work. Anchieta was one of them, and here is a description of his life. « Barefooted, with no other garment than his cassock, his crucifix and rosary round his neck, the pilgrim's staff and his breviary in his hand, and his shoulders laden with the furniture requisite for an altar, Anchieta advanced into the interior of the country. He penetrated virgin forests, swam across streams, climbed the roughest mountains, plunged into the solitude of the plains, confronted savage beasts, and abandoned himself entirely to the care of Providence. All these fatigues, and all these dangers, had God alone for witness; he braved them for no other motive than to conquer souls. As soon as he caught sight of a man, Anchieta quickened his pace; his bleeding feet stain the rocks and sands of the desert, but he still walks onwards. As he approached the savage, he stretched out his arms towards him, and with words of gentleness strove to retain him beneath the shadow of the cross, which to him was the standard of peace. Sometimes, when the savages rejected his first overtures, he threw himself at their knees, bathing them with his tears, pressing them to his heart, and striving to gain their confidence by every demonstration of love. At first the savages made small account of this abnegation, but the Jesuit was not discouraged. He made himself their servant, and studied their caprices like a slave; he accompanied them in their wanderings, entered into their familiarity, shared their sufferings, their labours, their pleasures.» And the result of such a ministry, in which thousands were engaged at the same moment, from Lake Huron to Paraguay, and from Brazil to California, was this. « By degrees he taught them to know God, revealed to them the laws of universal morality, and prepared them for civilisation after he had formed them to Christianity. The whole country of Brazil was the theatre of Father Anchieta's ardent zeal; but amidst those vast solitudes, that of Itanoia, the land of stones, was his spot of predilection. It was so uncultivated, so rocky, that the very animals seemed to shun it; yet it was here that Anchieta, while toiling for the salvation of this ill-fortuned country, sought repose from the other dangers of his apostleship. » (1) We might refuse to believe that a man like ourselves could sustain such a life, and such labours, during more than forty years, but that

(1) *Life of Auchieta*, p. 175.

every other land presents to us, during the last three centuries, a thousand examples of the same virtues and the same victories.

In 1597 Anchieta died. The six Jesuits who landed with Nobrega had already increased to one hundred and twenty in Brazil alone, and a hundred more now hastened to fill the place of Anchieta, and to continue the work which he had begun. Before we pursue the history of their labours, let us notice briefly, as we have done in former cases, what Protestant writers relate of the men who had now departed.

Of Emanuel de Nobrega, even Mr Southey says, that he died, « worn out with a life of incessant fatigue. The day before his death, he went abroad, and took leave of all his friends, as if about to undertake a journey. They asked him whither he was going, and his reply was, ' *Home to my own country.* ' No life could be more actively, more piously, or more usefully employed : » (1) — and then Mr Southey, who, like all his class, would undertake to pronounce judgment at any moment on saints and angels, on principalities and powers, adds condescendingly, « the triumphant hope with which it terminated was not the less sure and certain, because of the errors of his belief. » Singular belief, to which alone God imparts the virtues and the victories of the apostolic life, while he unaccountably forgets to purify it from its « errors; » singular contradiction, which makes God, in every age, the unintelligent ally of a « corrupt » religion, — so corrupt, in the judgment of its adversaries, that if, as an American

(1) Ch. x, p. 310.

Protestant ingeniously observes, their estimate of it were true, « decomposition and the last stages of decay had long ago been passed. » (1)

Yet this Anglican historian adds, under an impulse which even he could not resist, — « So well had Nobrega's system been followed by Anchieta and his disciples, that, in the course of half a century, *all the nations along the coast of Brazil,* as far as the Portuguese settlements extended » — that is, through a range of more than two thousand miles — « were collected in villages under their superintendance. » (2) Never in the history of missions had so marvellous a triumph been obtained, except by the same class of men in the other provinces of America which we are still to visit. It is from Protestant writers alone that we can receive the evidence of that unparalleled triumph, since only by their testimony will it appear credible to their co-religionists. Nobrega died at the close of the 16th century, and « in the beginning of the 17th , » as Ranke observes, « we find the proud edifice of the Catholic Church completely reared in South America. There were five archbishoprics, twenty-seven bishoprics, four hundred monasteries, and innumerable parish churches. » And even this does not represent the whole work accomplished in a land which had been tenanted, only a century earlier, by savages who had little more of the nature of man than his external form. « Magnificent cathedrals had sprung up, of which the most splendid of all was,

(1) *North American Review*, July 1858, p. 283.
(2) Ch. XIII, p. 389.

perhaps, that of *Los Angeles*. The Jesuits taught grammar and the liberal arts; a complete system of theological discipline was taught in the universities of Mexico and Lima..... Conquests gave place to missions, and missions gave birth to civilisation. The monks, who taught the natives to read and to sing, taught them also how to sow and to reap, to plant trees and to build houses; and, of course, inspired the profoundest veneration and attachment. » So that Ranke might well exclaim, « Catholicism produced a mighty effect in these countries. » (1)

It was the contemplation of the same almost unexampled work, of which we shall better appreciate the character and extent when we have traced it in many provinces, which led Lord Macaulay to observe, in more emphatic phraseology; « The acquisitions of the Catholic Church in the New World have more than compensated her for what she has lost in the Old. » (2)

Of Anchieta —, the companion of Nobrega, and partner of his apostolic toils, — whose supernatural life has occasioned still greater perplexity to Protestant historians, they speak in such words as the following. « His self-denial as a missionary, » we are told by two American preachers, who vainly endeavoured to persuade even a solitary Brazilian to exchange a divine religion for a human one, « his labour in acquiring and methodizing a barbarous language, and his services to the State, were sufficient to secure to him an honest fame and a precious memory. » And

---

(1) Book VII, vol. II, p. 91.
(2) *Essay on Ranke's History of the Popes.*

then they exhaust all the resources of invective upon his biographers, by whom, they are not ashamed to say, « his real virtues were made to pass for little, » that they might magnify « his pretended miracles.» (1) If they had really read any history of the saint, they would have found, that his miracles are noticed simply as incidents in the life of one whose virtues were more wonderful than his miracles, and perhaps more difficult to imitate.

Mr Southey, as might he expected, uses similar language. « That Anchieta could work miracles, » he says, « was undoubtedly believed both by the Portuguese and by the natives, each according to their own superstition. The former sent volumes of attestations to Rome after his death.... the Tamuyas said there was a power in him which withheld the hands of men, *and this opinion saved his life.* » In other words, both Pagans and Christians were constrained to acknowledge a power of which they continually witnessed the exercise, and which multitudes, of all ranks and classes, solemnly attested on oath. It is Protestants alone, of all mankind, who deride the supernatural as the dream of superstition or the trick of the impostor; because they alone refuse to believe in the sanctity which they know to be unattainable by themselves, and believe to be impossible to others. » When Dr Horsley, a Protestant bishop of no mean repute, exhorted the English House of Lords to discourage all attempts to convert the Hindoos, because « the religion of a country is connected with its government, » this Anglican prelate consist-

---

(1) Kidder and Fletcher, ch. VII, p. 115.

ently added, that the apostolic power of working miracles having ceased, « he doubted whether the commission had not ceased also. » And most of his co-religionists appear to agree with him. « One circumstance, » say their representatives, « which must make all sensible and unprejudiced persons suspect very much the veracity of the Jesuits in general, is the account they give of miracles pretended to be wrought in the scenes of their several missions. » (1) Yet these men profess to worship Him who said to the first Missionaries, « *Ye shall do greater things than these!* » When did He who gave that promise recall it, or when did He first begin to send forth apostles without the gifts of apostles? And what new God is this, who has neither the will nor the power to interfere in human affairs, and who is as hopelessly fettered by the « laws of nature » as a plant or an insect? Is He, like the god of Baal, « asleep, » or is he « on a journey, » that he should forget to take note of man and his works? Or have Protestants agreed to accept the definition of the Creator which Kolben says was current among the Hottentots, who considered Him « an excellent man, who dwells far beyond the moon, and does no harm to any one? »

One thing is worthy of remark, — that a religion which professes to be founded on reason should despise all the laws of evidence; and that students of the Bible should scoff at miracles of which the sacred pages contain, according to human belief, some of the least credible examples. If Elias, « a man passible

(1) Lockman's *Travels of the Jesuits*, preface, p. XIV.

like unto us, » forbid dew or rain to descend on the earth save at his word, in order to admonish a guilty king, the tale is venerable and true; if St. Francis Solano bring forth water in the deserts of Chili to save a perishing multitude, and to this hour the miraculous stream is called « the fountain of St. Solano, » it is an execrable imposture. If the Eternal « stopped the mouths of lions » lest they should harm his prophet, let us marvel and adore; if the panther crouched by the side of His servant Anchieta as he prayed at midnight in the forest, or the viper dared not sting his naked foot when he trod upon it in the noonday, it is an impudent invention. If iron float at the bidding of Eliseus, though only to save a woodman's axe, let us fall down and magnify the Lord ; if Anchieta is upheld on the waters of the San Francisco, that an apostle might not perish out of the earth, we should scorn the superstition which believes the fact, and the impostor who relates it. If a dead man spring to life again, as the Scripture affirms, because his corpse touched the bones of a saint whom it was the will of God to honour, (1) who will refuse to praise and admire? If St. Augustine record the same fact of the bones of St. Stephen, in his own church, and before the very congregation who witnessed it, let us smile at the despicable fraud. If Agabus foretell a famine over the whole earth, « which came to pass in the days of Claudius, » (2) we should honour the prophet, though only a man like ourselves; if the blessed Anchieta

---

(1) IV Kings, XIII, 21.
(2) Acts, XI, 28.

predict a coming storm when the sky had been cloudless for six months, and a vast multitude witness the miraculous rain-fall which ensued, let us be sure it was only the crafty jugglery of a priest, or the gross credulity of a besotted crowd. If divine wisdom employ the voice of an ass to convey a warning to the rebellious prophet, let us accept without surprise both the messenger and his message; if divine power command the jaguar to stop in full career at the feet of St. Francis Solano, and humbly kneel before the servant of the Most High, let us welcome the improbable tale with a shout of derision. If Elias raise the dead from corruption, though only to comfort a sorrowing widow, it shall be the text of our songs and our meditations; if St. Francis Xavier open a grave, in the presence of thousands, to show a whole nation what the God of Christians can do, it is a pitiable fiction. If Elias is fed by ravens or by angels, and then fast forty days and nights, let no man doubt either his eating or his abstinence; if de' Nobili or de Britto instruct thousands unto righteousness by a whole life of austerity and mortification, it is only « the frantic folly of Catholicism. » If the face of St. Stephen shone with glory, so that all who stood by « saw his face as it had been the face of an angel,» let us acknowledge that grace can illuminate even this mortal body; if the blessed Peter Claver was transfigured before the eyes of a hundred witnesses, who saw the light play round his head, and covered their eyes with their hands, let us pity the degrading superstition which can accept the wretched tale. If a « hand-kerchief » or an « apron, » which had only touched the body of St. Paul, could heal diseases and put demons to flight, (1) what more natural than that the Most High should thus sanction, before men and angels, the Catholic use of relics? If the same thing be told of St. Bernard or St. Philip Neri, of Anchieta or St. Francis Regis, let us rend the heavens with our cry of anger, or stop our ears in indignant scorn.

Perhaps the true explanation of the inconsistency which accepts the one class of miracles without question, and rejects the other without enquiry, is found in the fact, that very few Protestants have any more real faith in the one than in the other. They would deal in precisely the same manner with both, but that they have no pressing reason to reject the first, while they have an urgent personal motive for denying the last. Yet even the Hindoo and the Mahometan, witnesses against the credulous incredulity of modern sects, have manifested, with all their faults, a deeper insight than they into the mystery of holiness; and have confesssd, in every age, that a god who ceased to display the power which he had once exerted, or to bestow the gifts which he had once conferred, would be only an impotent divinity, unworthy to reign over immortal men, and from whose palsied hand it would be lawful to pluck the feeble and useless sceptre. The instincts of the human heart, of the Pagan as well as of the Christian, reject such a god as Protestantism has invented; and the only race of men on earth who deny the wonder-working might of the True and Holy One in His saints and apostles, are they who acknowledge in

---

(1) Acts, xix, 12.

their inmost soul, without shame and without regret, that it never has been, and never can be, manifested in themselves. Who dreams of an Anglican miracle, or a Wesleyan prophet, or a Presbyterian saint? Who can imagine Middleton bidding a stream spring forth in the plains of Bengal? or Buchanan respected by panthers? or Judson transfigured? or Heber raising the dead?

This is no place to discuss at large the credibility of miracles. To the Christian, who is wisely familiar with Holy Scripture, and comprehends that the miracles of the New Testament are not isolated and abnormal but typical and characteristic facts, proper to the whole Dispensation which they adorn and illustrate, their cessation would be more inexplicable than their continuance. If they are rejected, it is by men who know neither God nor themselves; who, in spite of their profession of religion, have an instinctive fear and hatred of the supernatural; and who would rather believe that God is eternally silent, than confess that it is in the Church alone that He deigns to speak. They would not, indeed, believe a miracle, even if they saw one; but what they *fear* in them is their exhibition of Divine power, what they *hate* is their testimony to the Catholic faith. (1)

Yet modern science, not always hostile to revealed truth, has lately protested, by the voice of one of its

(1) « Image parfaite de Notre Seigneur Jésus-Christ, l'Église est en butte aux persécutions du monde, non pas parce que le monde oublie les prodiges qu'elle opère, ... mais tout au contraire parce que le monde *a en horreur* ces témoignages, ... *ces miracles qui le condamnent.* » Donoso Cortes, *Œuvres*, tome III, p. 128. (Ed. Veuillot.)

greatest adepts, against this irrational scepticism. A well known English mathematician, refuting by a scientific process the infidel *formula* of Hume, has declared, and elaborately proved, that however that *formula* be applied, it will *always* be false. Hume had said, that no amount of evidence can prove the truth of a miracle. Mr Babbage, testing the proposition by a purely analytical method, arrives at exactly the opposite conclusion. « If independent witness can be found, » he says, « who speak truth more frequently than falsehood, » — surely no intolerable postulate, — « it is *always* possible to assign a number of independent witnesses, the improbability of the falsehood of whose concurring testimony shall be *greater* than that of the miracle itself. » (1) Yet the shallow incredulity of the sects, though it annuls all the laws of evidence, and sets aside the most rigorous conclusions of science, affects to be a protest on behalf of the human intellect against the thraldom of superstition!

If now we continue the history of missions in Brazil, and take Mr Southey once more as our guide, we shall come to a new order of events. Hitherto we have seen men gradually converting the savages of half a continent by the display of supernatural virtues; and, except in a few instances which we have not staid to notice, as in the case of the martyrs Soza and Correa who fell in the very beginning of this apostolic warfare, accomplishing their work without even the customary tribute of blood. But that sacred debt was sure to be paid sooner or later,

---

(1) *Ninth Bridgewater Treatise*, app. p. 202; note E.

and we are about to witness the martyrdom of sixty-eight missionaries at once, massacred, not by pagan savages, but by more merciless heretics, whose fury no virtues could disarm, and who, in many a land, have made a compact with the heathen to slay the missionaries of the Cross.

In 1570, Father Ignatius Azevedo, by the nomination of St. Francis Borgia, conducted thirty-nine Fathers of the Society of Jesus from Madeira to Brazil. Thirty more started at the same moment from Lisbon, in two other vessels, as well as a number of postulants who had still to prove the strength of their vocation. The day after the ship which carried Azevedo sailed from Madeira, four French vessels, under the command of the Huguenot Jacques Sourie, bore down upon it. Sourie, says Mr Southey, « was a man as little disposed to show mercy to any catholic priests, as they would have been to show it towards him,.... and he did by the Jesuits as they would have done by him and all of his sect — put them to death. One of the novices escaped, being in a lay habit, the rest where thrown overboard, some living, some dying, some dead. » So smoothly does this English historian relate a tale which does not even provoke from him any other comment than this, that « when the tidings reached Madeira, the remaining Missionaries celebrated the triumph of their comrades, a triumph which many of them were yet to partake. » But this singular festival only inspired the mirth of Mr Southey, who considers that the *Te Deum* chanted in honour of martyrs by men who in a few days were to be martyrs themselves, « was as much the language of policy as of fanaticism. » St. Philip Neri would rather have said, as he was wont to say to the priests departing from Rome for the English mission, « *Salvete flores martyrum!* » St. Paul would have added, in his solemn accents, « *Quibus dignus non erat mundus!* »

A few days later, « one English and four French cruisers, » according to the tranquil narrative of Mr Southey, who does not mention that this time it was the Calvinist Capdeville who commanded, fell upon the remainder of the missionary fleet, and did their work so effectually, that « of sixty-nine Missionaries whom Azevedo took out from Lisbon, only *one*, who was left behind at one of the ports where they touched, arrived at Brazil. »

The blood of sixty-eight martyrs could hardly fail to win new graces for Brazil, and from that hour the work of conversion advanced with tenfold success. It was said, as Mr Southey records with indignation, that supernatural incidents accompanied this holocaust of martyrs, whose fires the waves of the deep sea could not extinguish. « After Azevedo was killed, the heretics, » Mr Southey merrily observes, « could not force out of his hand a picture of the Virgin, » which the martyr held in his dying grasp, and which, the English historian adds, with an appropriate and well-timed jest, « was a copy more miraculous than its miraculous original. » This picture, found still in his embrace by the crew of another ship which sailed over the spot where his body had been flung into the ocean, « was shown, » adds Mr Southey, « by the Jesuits at St. Salvador, with heroic impudence, with the print of Azevedo's bloody fingers upon it; »

but « ecclesiastical historians, » he remarks, « enlarge as they go on, because every one adds his lie to the heap. » If a martyrology were composed by demons, it is perhaps thus that they would write it.

Sixty years after the martyrdom of Azevedo and his companions, when their successors had reaped the full harvest of which the early seeds had been fertilised by their blood, a second drama of the same kind was enacted, and once more the knife and the axe were wielded by Protestants. This time it was the Dutch Calvinists who made war on defenceless missionaries, and here is Mr Southey's narrative of their operations.

The unconverted natives of the district of Rio Grande had carried devastation into the territory of Pernambuco, and though chastised by the troops under the command of Manuel Mascarenhas, were still planning in their forests new expeditions. Soldiers could not reach these swift-footed marauders, but there were men in Brazil of the school of de Nobrega and Azevedo who could. Mr Southey will tell us who they were. With no armour but prayer, and no weapon but the cross which they bore on their bosom, they advanced without fear into the retreats of the barbarians. « The Jesuits pacified them, » says the Protestant annalist, « and brought *a hundred and fifty hordes* into alliance with the Portuguese. » So true is that saying of Sir Woodbine Parish, who lived long in South America, that « the labours of the Jesuits were eventually more successful than all the military forces, » and that, in every province of the land, on both sides of the Andes, and by the banks of all the rivers which flow from them, « these indefatigable missionaries reduced one tribe after another to a state of comparative civilization. »

But the savage of the north-eastern provinces was now to find an ally more fierce and cruel than himself, and by whose example he was to learn, that if there were Chistians who were valiant only to suffer, to labour, and to bless, there were others who made religion itself the pretext of crimes from which even the savage would have shrunk. It was on Good Friday, in the year, 1633, that the Dutch Protestants, passing at midnight through the smoking ruins of Olinda, attacked Garassu in the early morn, while the inhabitants were assembled at the celebration, proper to that sorrowful day, of the Mass of the Presanctified. The moment was skilfully chosen. No ignorant Tamuya or Chiquito, no blundering Mohawk or Oneida, could have matched the Calvinist in his craft; no bloodhound could have torn his prey with more pitiless cruelty, when once he had fastened his fangs upon it. « The men who came in their way, » says Mr Southey, « were slaughtered, the women were stripped, and the plunderers with brutal cruelty tore away ear-rings through the ear-flap, and cut off fingers for the sake of the rings which were upon them. Having plundered and burnt the town, they set out on their return, taking with them as prisoners some Franciscans, whom for their profession they especially hated, and driving in mockery before them the priest in his vestments, just as they had forced him from the altar. » (1) It was thus they celebrated Good Friday.

(1) Vol. I, ch. XV, p. 486.

The next year they attacked Paraiba, apparently because « it contained a Misericordia, a Benedictine Convent, a Carmelite, and a Capuchin. » The inhabitants had capitulated, after a gallant defence, on the express promise of « free exercise of the Catholic religion and peaceable enjoyment of their property. » « The most atrocious cruelties, » says Mr Southey, for once taking part with the victims, « were exercised upon these brave people by the conquerors, and they who possessed any property were *tortured* till they paid the full sum which was demanded as a life-ransom. By these means the Dutch raised 28,000 crowns, and it is by such means that they have rendered their history as infamous, and their names as detestable, in the East and in the West, as in their own country their deeds have been glorious. » (1)

Yet these men professed to be exponents of the « reformed religion, » and missionaries of the gospel. It is true that even Mr Southey admits, that it was only « for the sake of raising sugar and tabacco » that they invaded Brazil; but they carried their religious ideas with them, and so, in the words of another historian, « from assassins they transformed themselves into missionaries. » They were more successful in the first character than in the last. « They sent out preachers, and controversial books in the Spanish language were circulated; » but, Mr Southey shrewdly adds, « if the Brazilians hated their conquerors as heretics, they hated heresy still more because it was the religion of their oppressors. The Dutch have

(1) P. 509.

always been a cruel people,... and there is no nation whose colonial history is so inexcusably and inexpiably disgraceful to human nature. » He had perhaps read their history in Japan and Ceylon.

The Dutch were not destined to triumph in Brazil, either as soldiers or missionaries, but they were not finally ejected till a later period. Meanwhile, they continued to exhibit a new example of the nature and influence of Protestant missions, a new proof that they are everywhere, as we have said, the worst impediment to the conversion of the heathen, not only because they obstruct the ministry of the true apostles, but because their agents teach the barbarian to despise a religion of which *they* are the professors. In 1637, in all the districts under their rule, « the Catholics were ordered to confine their processions within the walls of the churches; no new church was to be built without permission from the senate; no marriage celebrated until the bans had been published after the Dutch manner; » etc. There was even a certain refinement of ingenuity in some of their cruelties. Taking advantage of well known customs which piety had consecrated in Brazil, they ordered, « that those persons who, when they created new sugar-works, chose to have them blessed, were to have the office performed » — by a Protestant minister! The Count of Nassau, who was their supreme ruler, « received orders to restrict toleration within the narrowest bounds, and the reformed clergy were calling upon him to enforce these imprudent orders. »

In 1639, « Dutch missionaries laboured, » we are still quoting Mr Southey, « to teach a Lutheran instead of a Popish creed. » They failed indeed, but this was only, Mʳ Southey considers, because « implements of conversion were wanting; » that is, « Lutheran theology had nothing wherewith to supply the deficiency of saints, images, beads, crosses, etc. » The explanation seems to fall below the gravity of history. Lutheran theology, which the Brazilians rejected so decisively, does not appear to produce happy results even among those who profess to admire it. In Lutheran Prussia, where there is no deficiency of crosses and other symbols, it has all but extirpated Christianity; in Brazil, as we learn from two Protestant ministers in 1857, its results have been of the same unpleasant character. In « the Lutheran community at Nova Fribourgo, » a colony of German settlers, they report that « there was but little Christian vitality; Lutherans of the old church and state school are among the very last men to propagate the gospel. » (1) We need not wonder, then, that the Dutch failed to propagate such a gospel in Brazil.

But if they could not convert, they could destroy. In spite of every menace, and of unceasing cruelty and exactions, the people still clung to their old pastors. There was only one remedy for this obstinacy, and the Dutch adopted it. « The members of every monastic order were commanded within the space of a month to quit the Dutch possessions on the continent. The needful measure, » it is Mʳ Southey who speaks, « was carried into effect with brutal cruelty. The Dutch stripped them of their habits, and turned them ashore in their shirts and drawers, in such

(1) Kidder and Fletcher, ch. xv, p. 297.

remote situations that most of them perished. » (1)

When, in 1642, the Portuguese rose at last against the assassins, and re-captured Maranham, « those who were spared owed their lives, » says our historian, « to the interference of a Priest. » He had asserted not long before that any priest « would have put all the sect to death, » but now he relates that « he had borne the Crucifix before his comrades as a standard beneath which they were to march to victory, and he stretched out that Crucifix *to protect his enemies* now when the victory was won. » But with all his efforts he could only save the other foreigners, because « a Catholic feeling incensed the conquerors against the Dutch, more hated for their heretical opinions than for their cruelty and perfidiousness. » But we have heard enough of the Dutch, and it is time to return to the labours of a different order of missionaries.

In the middle of the seventeenth century, when the triumph of Christianity was already assured in Brazil, Portugal gave to this favoured mission another of those apostolic workmen of whom in that age she produced so many. Father Antonio Vieyra, the friend of kings and the counsellor of statesmen, who had rejected all the honours of the world, and had told his admiring sovereign, when he entreated him to accept a bishopric in Europe, that he would not exchange the lowly habit of a missionary « for all the mitres in the Portuguese monarchy, » had now entered Brazil. During many years this accomplished gentleman « ministered among the Indians and Ne-

(1) Vol. II, ch. xx, p. 65.

groes, for which purpose he made himself master, not only of the Tupi, but also of the Angolan tongue. » He was one, as Mr Southey confesses, who « must ever hold a place, not only amongst the greatest writers, but amongst the greatest statesmen of his country. » It is nothing new in the history of apostles that such a man should choose to devote his life to Indians and Negroes. The Catholic religion, in every age, has been able both to inspire and to reward such sacrifices. Once he wrote to the young prince of Portugal, who loved and honoured him as a father, to send fresh labourers to Brazil; and he added, — « I ask no provision for those who come, God will provide; what I ask is, that they may come, and that they may be many, and filled with zeal. »

It is curious to see what the malice of heresy could force even a scholar and a poet to say of such a man as this, — who was not only scholar and poet, but philosopher, orator, and statesman. « His devotion, » says Mr Southey, « had its root in superstition and madness. » Festus estimated in the same manner the devotion of St. Paul, because he, like the English writer, could not understand an apostle. Yet he adds immediately, contradicting himself at every page, — « Vieyra proceeded diligently with projects worthy of his order and of himself. » Fifty Indian villages were organised by his labours to the north of Maranham, « along an extent of four hundred leagues of coast. » So wonderful was the success of his labours, that on the 15th of August, 1658, he celebrated a solemn Mass of thanksgiving in commemoration of a treaty then concluded, « in the name of Jesus

Christ, » with the chiefs and representatives of more than *one hundred thousand natives*. (1)

Such a victory might have contented even apostolic ambition, but for Vieyra it was only a motive for fresh exertions. He now resolved, therefore, says our historian, « to pursue the same system of civilisation up the great rivers, and in the islands in the mouth of the Orellana. » Two Jesuits were sent up the river of the Tocantins, a perilous journey of nine hundred miles « to reduce a tribe of Topinambazes, » famous for their courage and ferocity. « They were old enemies of the Para settlers, » which increased tenfold the perils of the mission, but this did not daunt the companions of Vieyra, animated with his own spirit; and the Protestant historian is obliged to confess, that « these very enemies followed the Missionaries; and agreed to send deputies back with them, who should treat concerning peace, and arrange measures for their conversion. » More than a thousand of these hitherto irreclaimable barbarians, « of whom three hundred were warriors, » returned with the Fathers to the camp of their hated foes; and when the Governor, Vidal,—a man of such qualities that Vieyra wrote to the king, « if *he* had been in India, it would never have been lost to Portugal, » — saw this multitude of neophytes approaching, « stern and inexorable as he was in war, he is said to have wept for joy at beholding this wild flock brought within the fold of Christ. » Vieyra himself, though he might have been sitting in the courts of princes, started immediately to bring in the remainder of the tribe.

(1) Cretineau Joly, tome V, p. 114.

In every direction similar expeditions were undertaken, and always with the same results. No river was so broad or swift as to check their rapid march, no forest so dark or impenetrable as to bar their way. Whatever man, aided by the might of God, could do, they did. And the Indians, dazzled by their fortitude and valour, could resist neither the heroic courage which far surpassed their own, nor the patience which subdued and wore out their frowardness, nor the charity which they admired before they understood it. Everywhere and always, even by Protestant testimony, these apostles were the same. Take a few examples out of thousands. When the military expedition of Coelho against the people of the Sierra de Ibiapaba had completely failed, « and led to his own disgrace, » the missionaries, says Mr Southey; « prepared a peaceable expedition in the hope of reducing and civilising its inhabitants. These mountains extended about eighty leagues in length, and twenty in breadth; they rise in waves, one towering above another... To ascend them is the hard labour of four hours, in which hands and knees, as well as feet, must frequently be exerted. » And when the missionaries, often men delicately nurtured, and of gentle lineage, had surmounted these first difficulties, they found themselves in presence of the Tapuyas, « the oldest race in Brazil, » and so inconceivably barbarous, that « they ate their own dead as the last demonstration of love. »(1) They had repulsed the soldiers of Portugal, but were vanquished by a few unarmed Jesuits.

(1) Southey, ch. XIII, p. 377.

In 1603, Father Rodriguez conducted another apostolic band to the territory of the cannibal Aymores. « The people ridiculed his project, » says the Protestant historian, « thinking it impossible, that the Aymores, fleshed as they were with human meat, could be reclaimed from their habits of cannibalism. » Yet the savages themselves said of him and his companions, when they afterwards recounted their own submission; « The fathers were good men who had neither bows nor arrows, nor ever did wrong to any one, and nothing which they requested was to be denied. » And so « two villages were soon formed, the one containing twelve hundred Aymores the other four; and the Captaincy, which had hitherto with difficulty been preserved from utter destruction by the help of frequent succours from Bahia, was effectually delivered from its enemies. »(1)

In 1657, Fathers Emanuel Pires and Francis Gonsalvez were the first to ascend the Rio Negro, as Father Samuel Fritz was the first to trace the course of the Orellana, converting the Omaguas on the way — « a people, » as Southey observes, « so famous in the age of adventure, and still, in his day, the most numerous of all the river tribes: thirty of their villages are marked upon his map. » Before him, Fathers Christoval d'Acuna and Andres de Artieda, the one rector of a college, the other professor of theology at Quito, had accomplished an equally perilous mission at the request of the viceroy; for even the military adventurers of that age dared not accept, and refused to attempt, undertakings which the mis-

(1) P. 388.

sionaries alone, in the interests of religion and science, could be persuaded to embrace, since *they* « were not merely fearless of martyrdom, but ambitious of it. » We shall see hereafter how many found the crown which they sought. After a voyage of fifteen months, amid privations which we need not attempt to describe, Pires and Gonsalvez returned, bringing with them between six and seven hundred disciples; but Gonsalvez died of his fatigues. A little later, two others, who had taken another route, came back in their turn, followed by more than two thousand Indians, « who had consented to accept Christianity and civilisation. (1)

In every province, and in each successive year, the same arduous apostolate continued. In 1662, Father Raymond de Santa Cruz perished by violence in the waters of the Pastaza. « His was truly a noble and well spent life, » says an English Protestant. « His usual dress consisted of an old battered hat, a coarse cotton shirt, and a pair of sandals; » — this was the « gorgeous ceremonial » by which Catholic missionaries, we are told, gain their converts; — « and his mode of life was more simple than that of the Indians who surrounded him... but it should be remembered that there were many other intrepid and devoted men on the banks of these rivers, at the same time, who were equally zealous in preaching to the Indians, and who generally, like Father Raymond, met with a violent death, as the welcome reward of their exertions. » (2)

(1) Southey, p. 517.
(2) *Expeditions into the Valley of the Amazons*, by Clements R. Markham, F. R. G. S., Introd., p. xxx.

As early as 1663, the fruits of these patient toils were so abundant, that, as Mr Markham notices, even on the banks of the Upper Maranon « there were fifty-six thousand baptized Indians; » and from 1640 to 1682, no less than thirty-three different Christian settlements had been established in that region by this company of martyrs and apostles. (1)

In 1695, Henry Richter obtained the crown of martyrdom. « The most heroic devotion, » says Mr Markham, « could alone have enabled him to face the difficulties which surrounded him. During twelve years he performed forty difficult journies, through dense forests, or in canoes on rapid and dangerous rivers. He never took any provisions with him, but wandered bare-footed and half-naked through the tangled underwood, trusting wholly to Providence for support. His efforts were rewarded with success, and having learnt some of the Indian languages, he at last surrounded himself with followers. »

Such were the men, and such the toils, which won all South America to the cross. If sometimes they failed, or seemed to fail, it was only for a brief space. When Soto Mayor, one of the most valiant of this band of heroes, was rejected by a tribe which refused to be converted, he left with them his Crucifix, assuring them, with accents of patient love, that the God whom it represented would yet incline their hearts to truth. And when he was gone, their souls were stirred within them by the memory of his apostolic words; and one day they arrived in solemn procession, asking to be admitted to baptism, and

---

(1) *Expeditions*, etc., Introd., p. xxx.

bringing back with all reverence the Crucifix, of which Mr Southey, true to his instincts, observes, — « *this Idol* was deposited in the church of the Jesuits' College, where it was long venerated with especial devotion. »

In 1661, the corrupt Portuguese traders, whose traffic in slaves had been well nigh ruined by Vieyra and his companions, stirred up an insurrection, and cast the Fathers into prison. Vieyra himself, says the Protestant historian, « though treated more cruelly than any of his companions, betrayed not the slightest mark of irritation or impatience... an heroic mind, a clear conscience, and an enthusiastic sense of duty, produced in him that peace which passeth all understanding. » They were dragged on board ship, and despatched to Portugal, with a memorial to the king, setting forth their misdemeanours, and charging them with having ruined the prosperity of the colony. They were re-instated by a royal edict in the following year, with a sharp admonition to their accusers, but from that hour their enemies took counsel together to accomplish their destruction.

In 1676, Brazil being now divided into the three dioceses of Bahia, Pernambuco, and Rio de Janeiro, the first colony of Franciscan Nuns arrived. « Such institutions, » observes Mr Southey, who records the arrival of these ladies, and the establishment of their convent, « are better receptacles than Bedlam for the largest class of maniacs. » (1) Presently, as if the expression pleased his taste, he calls even An-

(1) Vol. II, ch. xxviii, p. 571.

chieta, D'Almeida, and Vieyra, — men adorned with every highest gift, both of nature and grace, which the Creator bestows on His creature, — « harmless maniacs. » If we quote such language, it is only to show how educated Protestants judge the men whom they cannot comprehend, and the works which they dare not imitate.

In reading words now almost habitual with Protestant critics, and of which we have seen too many examples in these pages, we are involuntarily reminded of the formidable sentence of Holy Writ which announces the final lot both of the accused and their accusers. When the former, we are told, shall have received their crown, the latter, « seeing it, shall be troubled with terrible fear, and shall say within themselves, repenting, and groaning for anguish of spirit : These are they whom we had sometime in derision, and for a parable of reproach. *We fools esteemed their life madness,* and their end without honour. Behold, how they are numbered with the children of God, and their lot is among the saints. » (1)

In 1696, Vieyra died, at the age of ninety. He had been seventy-five years a Jesuit, and Mr Southey remarks, with real or affected surprise, that « his vows were never repented. » He adds also, that « he had outlived the vexations as well as the joys of life; his enemies were gone before him to their account, and his virtues and talents were acknowledged and respected as they deserved. » (2)

(1) *Wisdom*, V, 2-5.
(2) Vol. III, ch. xxxi, p. 34.

We must hasten to an end. Twenty provinces still claim our attention, and we have barely glanced at the history of one. A hundred names might be added to those of Nobrega and Anchieta, of D'Almeida and Vieyra, but we have no space to recount them. They will pardon our silence. They are our fathers and kinsmen, but who can number all the links in such a genealogy? We have spoken only of the Fathers of the Society of Jesus, yet the children of St. Francis and St. Dominic, to whom America owes so much, might well have claimed the tribute of our respectful homage. « The Franciscans, » says Mr Clements Markham, though he appreciates their courage rather than the religion which inspired it, « continued during a century and a half to send devoted men into the forests, who preached fearlessly, explored vast tracts of previously unknown land, and usually ended their days by being murdered by the very savages whom they had come to humanize. » (1) In 1701, two Franciscan Fathers were martyred by the Aruans. Mr Southey relates what befell their mutilated bodies. « They found them in a state of perfect preservation, although they had lain six months upon the ground, exposed to animals, insects, and all accidents of weather, and although their habits were rotten. » It was no miracle, he adds, for he did not believe in miracles, « but fraud cannot be suspected. » The evidence was so conclusive, that even he could not venture to reject it. « The whole city of Belem, » he says, saw the bodies, which were ultimately interred in the Franciscan Church in that town.

(1) *Valley of the Amazons*, Introd., p. XXI.

CHAPTER IX.

Finally, if we ask what signs there are at this hour in Brazil of the presence of the apostolic workmen of whose toils we may not offer here a more minute account; if we enquire how far, in this case, the promise has been fulfilled which declared of old, « *They* shall known their seed among the Gentiles, and their offspring in the midst of peoples; » it is au American Protestant who informs us, in 1856, that there are still, after all the calamities which have befallen that empire, « *eight hundred thousand domesticated Indians,* » who call upon the name of Jesus, and invoke the protection of His Mother. (1)

Before we add a few words, in order to complete the narrative, upon the present state of Brazil, the fate of her earlier apostles claims a moment's attention. For two centuries they had toiled, with results which perhaps none but the Franciscans had ever rivalled, and having won the approval of God were now to receive their usual reward from man. St. Ignatius had dared to ask, it was his latest prayer, that his children « might be always persecuted. » The petition, we know, has been heard. In 1753, the brother of the Marquis de Pombal was made Captain General of Para and Marauham, and from that hour the fate of the Jesuits was sealed. By this man the requisite pleadings were prepared, and they were accepted with eagerness by the conspirators at Lisbon, as even Mr Southey observes, « notwithstanding their falsehood and palpable inconsistency. » (2) « A true statesman, » says the same

---

(1) *Life in Brazil,* by Thomas Ewbank, ch. xxxviii, p. 432.
(2) Vol. III, ch. xl., p. 510.

writer, singular witness in such a cause, « would assuredly have thought that the Jesuits in America were worthy of his especial favour, protection, and encouragement. » But Pombal, envious of a greatness which he could not share, had resolved to crush them. He knew that the Brazilian merchants would approve his design, for the Jesuits, as Mr Southey remarks, « were the only unpopular order, because they were the only Missionaries who uniformly opposed the tyranny of the Portuguese. » Of the charges brought against them, the same unsuspicious witness says, — « *all that are not absolutely false, are merely frivolous.* » (1) But Pombal was willing to suborn false witnesses, and if these had not been forthcoming, would have done without them. And so the decree went forth that the Jesuits should be banished.

Twice already they had been expelled from Brazil, and twice they had been restored amid the acclamations of the people. This time their exile was to last nearly a century. From Para *one hundred and fifteen* Fathers were deported, from Bahia *one hundred and sixty eight*, from Rio Janeiro *one hundred and forty five* — in all five hundred and twenty-eight; from this province alone. « The number expelled from all the Spanish Indies amounted to 5,677. » (2) We shall see hereafter what befell the Fathers in the other provinces. And this was the manner of their deportation. « They were stowed as closely as Negro-slaves, » says Mr Southey, whom we will quote to the last, and confined below decks on the voyage to

---

(1) P. 518.
(2) Southey, vol. III, ch. XLII, p. 614.

S. Luiz. » Yet, as even he observes, « they were men whose innocence and virtue must most certainly have been known. » And then he adds, his better nature triumphing for once over the instincts of heresy and unbelief, « they were treated with extreme cruelty upon the voyage; when they were suffering the most painful thirst, the captain would not allow, even to the dying, an additional drop of water to moisten their lips, nor would he permit them the consolation of receiving the last sacrament in death. Five of them died (in one ship) under this inhuman usage. »

And when at last this company of apostles reached Europe, followed by the sighs and tears of a whole continent, for eighteen weary years they languished in prison, till M. de Pombal passed to his account, with the horrible jest on his lips, « that the Jesuits were the longest lived body of men he ever knew. » But they followed him to the judgment, for, as the historian relates, « in a few years they were almost extinguished. »

Pombal had disappeared for ever, but not so the Society of Jesus. In 1817, the revolted Spanish colonies of South America, justifying their separation, reproached their former mistress in these earnest words. « You arbitrarily deprived us of the Jesuits, to whom we owe our social state, our civilisation, all our instruction, and services with which we can never dispense. » In 1834, the Argentine republic recalled them with acclamation; in 1842, Columbia solicited their return; in 1843, they were re-established in Mexico; in Chili, they are once more the model and the admiration of their brethren. And where are their persecutors? When the Jesuits returned to the province of Coimbra in 1832, more than one of them hastened to the town of Pombal, in order to offer in secret the suffrages of charity over the grave of the Marquis. To their amazement they found that the once imperious statesman had been so completely forgotten by all but them, that his body, covered with a ragged cloth, had remained without sepulture from 1782! But there is nothing in this fact to surprise us. The world, which pursues them with its heartless applause, abandons its heroes when the sword or the staff falls from their nerveless hands; and the Church alone, more tender than friends, more compassionate than kinsfolk, is found weeping over the tombs of her enemies, and praying for the pardon of their sins.

And now let us see what were the results of their expulsion. Only twenty-five years after their departure, the noblest colony which Portugal had ever possessed was in ruins. « Decay and desolation, » as Mr Southey confesses, had succeeded « the prosperity which had prevailed in the time of the Missionaries; houses falling to pieces; fields overgrown with wood; grass in the market places; the limekilns, the potteries, the manufactories of calico » — for the Jesuits had introduced all these — « *in ruins.* »

Pombal, says the same writer whom we have so often quoted, while affecting to care for the welfare of the Indians, « removed the only persons who could have co-operated with him for this end; the only persons who would have exerted themselves disinterestedly to promote the improvement and happiness of the Indians; the only persons who, for the love of God, would have devoted themselves dutifully, cheerfully, and zealously, to the service of their fellow creatures. In their place, such men as would undertake the office for the love of gain, were substituted; and the immediate consequences were injurious in every way. The laws in favour of the Indians » — the Missionaries had procured the abolition of slavery — « were infringed more daringly; the Directors themselves had an interest in oppressing them, because their profits were in proportion to the work performed; they had the power of compelling them to work, and they had neither authority, influence, nor inclination to check those vices which certainly were not practised under the moral discipline of the *Aldeas* » — the Jesuit Reductions. « That process of civilisation which had been going on so rapidly, and with such excellent effect » — in an earlier volume Mr Southey had scoffed at this civilisation — « was stopped at once and for ever; and a rapid depopulation began, because free scope was now given to drunkenness and to every other vice, and because many of the Indians fled into the wilderness, when they found that their state of filial subjection was exchanged for a servitude which had nothing either to sanctify or to soften it. » (1) And it is Mr Southey who writes this undesigned panegyric of Catholic Missionaries!

But Mr Southey is not the only writer of his class who makes these confessions. Dr Kidder and Mr Fletcher, two Protestant ministers, whose eager libels on the Catholic religion would perhaps excite our indignation if it were possible to treat them seriously, admit that the virtues of the Jesuits proved their

(1) P. 534.

ruin. « Their benevolence, and their philanthropic devotedness to the Indians, brought down upon them the hatred of their countrymen the Portuguese. » (1) « Centuries will not repair the evil done by their sudden expulsion, » says a candid English traveller;.... They had been the protectors of a persecuted race, the advocates of mercy, the founders of civilisation; and their patience under their unmerited sufferings forms not the least honourable trait in their character. » (2) Prince Adalbert of Prussia, though apparently insensible to apostolic virtues which he seems to have only contemplated with dull apathy or peevish dislike, confesses that « decay commenced with the expulsion of the Jesuits. » (3) Prince Maximilian of Wied-Neuwied, another modern traveller in Brazil, who observes that at Villa Nova, which he visited, « the Jesuits had collected six thousand Indians, » adds; « but most of them were driven away by the hard service exacted by the crown, and by the slavish manner in which they were treated. (4) M[r] Gardner also, who speaks, like these German Princes, from actual observation, says; « It is handed down from father to son, particularly among the middle and lower classes of Brazil, that the destruction of the Jesuitical power was a severe loss to the well-being of the country. There are of

---

(1) Ch. xx, p. 368.

(2) *Journal of a Voyage to Brazil*, by Lady Calcott, pp. 13, 36; (1824).

(3) *Travels in Brazil*, etc., by H. R. H. Prince Adalbert of Prussia, vol. II, p. 149. Ed. Schomburgh.

(4) *Travels in Brazil*, by Prince Maximilian of Wied-Neuwied, ch. vi, p. 150. (1820).

course but few alive now (1846) who have personal recollections of the excellent men who formed the Company of Jesus, but the memory of them will long remain; I have always heard them spoken of with respect and with regret. » (1) Lastly, for we need not multiply testimonies which we shall find to be identical for every province of America, another vehement Protestant goes a step further, and contrasts the Jesuits, as Lord Macaulay was wont to do, with the worldly and covetous missionaries of his own creed. « The early Missionaries who ventured into the prairies and savannahs of America gave many indications of being animated by an apostolic spirit... Destitute themselves, *they* had no lucrative employments to offer, in the shape of subaltern offices in a richly endowed missionary establishment, to tempt the natives to enlist as retainers in the household of Christianity. *They* did not practise the simony of buying converts. » (2) « They », says another English traveller, « have brought nearly the whole of the Indian population of South America into the bosom of their church. Notwithstanding the numerous church and sectarian missionaries sent from England, I never met with one Indian converted by *them*. » (3) Thus, according to the words of our Lord, when He noticed the judgments of men upon Himself and His disciples, » is wisdom justified of all her children. »

(1) *Travels in the Interior of Brazil*, by George Gardner, F. L. S.; ch. III, p. 81. (1846).
(2) *Asiatic Journal*, vol. IX, p. 3.
(3) *Nine months Residence in New Zealand*, by Augustus Earle, p. 171.

Before we finally quit Brazil, to pursue elsewhere the same enquiry, let us add, according to our custom, a brief account of the character and fortunes of Protestantism in that empire. The Huguenots of France, the Calvinists of Holland, and the Episcopalians of England, have all made attempts to acquire influence in Brazil. It would be impossible to say which class has failed most signally. It has often been observed, that heresy always presents itself under one of two aspects; when it does not act a tragedy, it performs a comedy; when it is not ferocious, it is ludicrous. The Dutch made the Brazilians groan, the English have only made them smile.

Of the Dutch Protestants, « whose colonial history is so inexpiably disgraceful to human nature, » we have heard more than enough. They were driven out, and went home to receive the condolence of their friends. The French Huguenots had scarcely a more brilliant destiny. Here is their sorrowful history, narrated by Protestant writers.

« Rio Janeiro, » we are told by Messrs Kidder and Fletcher, who always affect this florid style, « is fraught with interest to the Protestant Christian, as that portion of the New World where the banner of the Reformed religion was first unfurled. » As it was torn from its staff as soon as it was unfurled, these gentlemen were hardly prudent in calling public attention to this ill-starred banner. It was in 1556 that Villegagnon, himself an apostate, and who had once conducted Mary Stuart in safety through the English cruisers from Leith to France, landed at Rio with an *avant corps* of fourteen Calvinists, who seem to have been too much compromised in their own country to regret their forced emigration to another. It was their object, as Prince Adalbert sympathisingly observes, to form « the establishment of an asylum for Huguenots beyond the seas. » This « interesting band, » as the English historian of the London Missionary Society calls them, tried to introduce Calvinism among « the benighted savages; » but « it does not appear, » Dr Morison adds, « that any of them were savingly wrought upon by the truth; (1) indeed he presently confesses that they were bent chiefly on finding an « asylum, » and that « the conversion of the heathen was a secondary object. » Attacked by the Portuguese, who wisely objected to the presence of these seditious adventurers, their « banner » was speedily lowered. Villegagnon, recanting his errors, was reconciled to the Church, and left his companions to their fate. It was not likely that thirteen Protestant preachers would long « dwell together in unity; » and accordingly, as the Rev. Dr Walsh relates, « weakened by their intestine dissensions, » (2) they became an easy prey. « Their squabbles, » says Mr Ewbank, « and the bitterness of spirit accompanying them, ruined all. » (3) And so they came to a bad end; French Protestantism finally collapsed, and Brazil declined, once for all, to become « an asylum for Huguenots beyond the seas. »

The English have hardly been more successful. Dr Walsh, a minister of their established church, a

(1) *The Fathers of the London Missionary Society*, vol. I, p. 60.
(2) *Notices of Brazil*, by Revd R. Walsh, L. L. D., vol. I, p. 153. (1830).
(3) *Life in Brazil*, ch. VIII, p. 83.

gentleman whose integrity and kindly temper it is impossible not to admire, was honoured by the friendship of the Bishop of Rio, « the excellent José Caëtano da Silva-Coutinho, than whom a more learned or, I believe, a more amiable man does not exist. » This prelate, Dr Walsh says, « fasts all the year on one meal a day; » and he adds, perhaps with unintentional exaggeration, « he studies all night. » In 1810, this excellent Bishop was consulted by the civil authorities about a demand which the English residents in Rio had made for a public chapel in that city. He advised that it should be conceded, and for this reason. « The English have really no religion, but they are a proud and obstinate people; if you oppose them, they will persist, and make it an affair of infinite importance : but if you concede to their wishes, the chapel will be built and nobody will ever go near it. » « The Brazilians say he was right, » adds Dr Walsh in 1830, « for the event has verified the prediction. » The chapel, whose history the Bishop had so sagaciously predicted, « had an air of dirt and neglect, » says this clergyman, « quite painful to contemplate, and the congregation seemed to take no interest in it when it was built, notwithstanding their zeal to have it established. » (1) Twenty-six years later, in 1856, to bring the history down to the present hour, Mr Ewbank relates, that « the British chapel *never* received a native convert, while monks have drawn members from it. » (2)

One more anecdote may close the history of Angli-

(1) Vol. I, p. 328.
(2) Ch. xx, p. 238.

canism in Brazil. Dʳ Walsh had observed during his
residence « the deep impression of rational piety »
among the Brazilians, and that « the great body of
the people are zealously attached to their religion; »
and then he attests, with surprising candour, the
supreme but good-humoured contempt which they
manifested for Protestantism. « An English merchant
and his wife, » he says, « had incurred the wrath
of the Brazilians, » by sneering at their processions
in Passion Week, which these fervent islanders
loudly condemned as « popish idolatry. » The people
of Rio only replied, says Dʳ Walsh, by adding to the
images of Pilate, Judas Iscariot, and other malefact-
ors, « two figures that exactly resembled the merchant and his wife — nothing could be more correct
than the likeness. » (1)

Finally, in 1856, an American Protestant — evidently an amiable man, though he calls St. Francis
of Assisi « an Italian devotee of the 12th century, »
and looks upon the Catholic religion only as an
incomprehensible mystery which defies analysis and
baffles criticism — thus announces his view of the
actual prospects of Protestantism in Brazil. « The
more I see of this people » — whom he lauds as
« hospitable, affectionate, intelligent, and aspiring »
— « the more distant appears the success of any Protestant missions among them.... The people avoid a
missionary as one with whom association is disreputable, and they entertain a feeling towards him bor-
dering on contempt, arising from a rooted belief in
his ignorance and presumption. » (2)

(1) Vol. II, p. 398.
(2) Ubi supra.

If now we quit for a time the empire of Brazil at its northern frontier, we shall find, between the Amazon and the Orenoco, on the eastern coast, three narrow territories which acknowledge respectively the dominion of England, France, and Holland. Of the Dutch proceedings we have already heard more than enough, but a few words may be allowed with respect to the English and French.

British Guyana has found a capable historian in Dr Dalton. Two or three sentences from that candid writer will suffice to prove the contrast which we might have confidently anticipated, and which is not less conspicuous in this obscure region than in the wider fields which we have already visited. Of the Negroes under the patronage of English missionary societies, he says; « Puritans in profession, they are liberals in practice » — that is, as he explains, « they appeared to think that faith alone was necessary, and that good works were superfluous. » And them he gives one more example of the real influence of Protestant bibles. « The lazy, the dissolute, and the dis-affected, met every rebuke and remonstrance by *some scriptural phrase,* or religious expression. » Of the natives, he says; « After all, » that is after the usual enormous and perfectly useless expenditure, « the native Indian afforded but poor encouragement in the arduous task of Christianisation. » (1)

The negro appears to have profited as little by the presence of the English emissaries. His teachers have been aided during many years by the power and

---

(1) *History of British Guiana,* by Henry G. Dalton, M. D.; vol. II, ch. IV, pp. 146, 8.

wealth of England, but with so little fruit, as an English writer notices in 1860, that though he considers the Guyana Protestant negro « somewhat superior to his brother in Jamaica, » he thus describes the final influence of the teaching which he has received. « It seems to me that he never connects his religion with his life, never reflects that his religion should bear upon his conduct. » Mr Trollope adds, that his information was mainly derived « from clergymen of the Church of England, » whose unusual candour is perhaps due to the fact, that most of these singular « converts » had rejected their more tranquil ceremonies for the exciting harangues of the Baptist or Wesleyan preacher — whose sects have, as usual, accompanied the Church of England to Guyana. « They sing and halloa and scream, and have revivals. They talk of their ' dear brothers ' and ' dear sisters, ' and in their ecstatic howlings get some fun for their money. » (1) And this is all which the English have done in Guyana.

« The implements of conversion, » as Mr Southey speaks, appear to have been wanting; and Dr Dalton does not conceal that all the English efforts were only costly failures. On the other hand, this Protestant writer generously observes of the Catholic missionaries in British Guyana, who do not receive much aid from patrons of any sort, and least of all from the Government, — « all are respected for their piety and zeal. The number of Roman Catholics in the Colony is about 10,000. »

(1) *The West Indies and the Spanish Main*, by Anthony Trollope, ch. XII, p. 199.

In speaking of the French mission in Guyana, we are obliged, for the first time, to use Catholic evidence, in default of any other. In 1860, the Spanish missionary Sala, in company with another Dominican Father, entered this province, but both were immediately martyred. In 1643, the French Capuchins repeated the attempt with the same result. Four years earlier, the Jesuits entered the country at another point, under Fathers Méland and Pelleprat, and evangelised the savage tribe of the Galibis; whose ferocity they appear to have disarmed by their contempt of suffering and danger, and whose obedience they won by patient wisdom and charity. In 1653, Father Pelleprat pubished a grammar and dictionary of their language. In 1654, Fathers Aubergeon and Gueimu, after converting many pagans, were martyred, the one after twenty, the other after fifteen years of religious life. At this time the Dutch seized Cayenne, and when they were cast out, it was found, that « Jews and Protestants had everywhere thrown down the crosses, the emblem of our salvation. » (1) This was the only effect of their presence. At length, after the due proportion of martyrdoms, the work of conversion in French Guyana was so effectually accomplished, in spite of the peculiar difficulties of such a mission, and the impracticable character of the natives, that in 1674, Fathers Grillet and Béchamel started from Cayenne for the interior, with the intention of renewing in its dis-

(1) *Mission de Cayenne et de la Guyane Française*, par M. F. de Montézou, de la Compagnie de Jésus; Introd. p. x. (1857).

tant solitudes the same patient apostolate. Here, after fifteen years of prodigious toil, surmounting a thousand disgusts and disappointments occasioned by the inconstancy or the brutality of the savages, the celebrated Father Aimé Lombard was able to erect the first christian church at the mouth of the river Kourou. For twenty-three years he had laboured among these barbarians, and at last could report to his friend de la Neuville, in 1733, in these words. « Acquainted as you are with the levity of our Indians, you will no doubt have been surprised that their natural inconstancy should at length have been overcome. It is religion which has effected this prodigy, and which every day fixes its roots deeper in their hearts. The horror with which they now regard their former superstitions, their regularity in frequently approaching the sacraments, their assiduity in assisting at the divine office, the profound sentiments of piety which they manifest at the hour of death, these are indeed effectual proofs of a sincere and lasting conversion. » (1)

Such were the fruits of the blood and the toil of men in whom even the most degraded races of the earth, hitherto unconscious of either truth or virtue, detected the presence of God. And this was only a part of their work. Along both banks of the Oyapoch, throughout its course, missions were established by apostles who seem to have been almost exempt from human infirmity; and who, as a French historian relates, « formed the gigantic project, which had no terrors for the courage of these intrepid missionaries,

(1) P. 328.

of uniting by a chain of evangelical posts both extremities of Guyana. »

Already, in 1711, M. de la Motte-Aigron, Lieutenant of the King, could report; « It has at length pleased God to reward by a success almost incredible the constancy of His servants. » Fourteen years later, Father Arnaud d'Ayma, conspicuous for dauntless valour even among the one hundred and eleven Jesuits who laboured in this difficult field, had fought his way to the remotest of all the known tribes; and in that distant spot, amongst the nation of the Pirioux, — « lodged in a miserable cabin, living like the savages, spending his day in prayer, in the study of their language, or the instruction of their children, » — he so won the hearts of the barbarians, that at length « they resolved to follow him whithersoever he wished to lead them. » And then he founded the mission of St. Paul, on the Oyapoch, where he collected the Pirioux and the whole nation of the Caranes; as a little later Father d'Ausillac gathered by the banks of the Ouanari the tribes of the Tocoyenes, the Maourioux, and the Maraones.

In 1762, the evil day arrived for Guyana, as for every other land, and the madness of an hour put back the conversion of the heathen world to a future and unknown period. Once more the enemy triumphed; and there was a sound of mourning by the banks of the Oyapoch and the Ouanari, as by those of the Parana and the Paraguay.

In 1763, the Duc de Choiseul, imitating his compeer the Marquis de Pombal, formed the project of a grand scheme of colonisation in Guyana, perhaps in order to show that he also could do without the missionaries of the Cross. Fourteen thousand persons were persuaded by magnificent promises to emigrate to this province, where Choiseul bade them surpass, by the aid of a sounder political economy, the triumphs of the Jesuits. They began by expelling the venerable Father O'Reilly, the last survivor and sole representative of the Company of Jesus, and the Christian Indians fled before them. Two years later, the Chevalier de Balzac could report to Europe, occupied in admiring its own wisdom and enlightenment, that only 918 of the colonists remained alive. More than thirteen thousand dupes of M. de Choiseul, who proposed to eclipse the Jesuits in their own triumphs, had perished in two years! In the following year, 1766, M. de Fiedmond, governor of Cayenne, wrote thus to the Duc de Praslin, who was probably as indifferent to this catastrophe as to the acts of which it was a suitable sequel. « I have already informed the Duc de Choiseul how necessary it is to send priests to this colony. » And then he describes the destruction of the once flourishing Missions, the flight of the Indians, the growth of crime amongst the Negroes deprived of their pastors, and the rapid ruin of the colony. Finally, this officer adds, « religion is dying out among the whites, as well as amongst the coloured races. » (1)

For ten years he reiterated the complaint, but always in vain. How should « philosophers » condescend to entreat humble missionaries to repair the evils of which they had been themselves the authors? How should men in whom the light of faith had gone

(1) P. 335.

out, and whose intelligence was enfeebled by arrogant self-love, confess that the wide-spread ruin was the work of their own hands? At length the good king Louis XVI, himself destined to be a sacrifice to the impiety which had already devoured so many victims, sent three Jesuits—Fathers Padilla, Mathos, and Ferreira — who had been banished with the others from Brazil; and then was seen a touching spectacle, which has been described in the Journal of Christophe de Murr. « The poor savages, beholding once again men clothed in the habit which they had learned to venerate, and hearing them speak their own language, fell at their feet, bathing them with tears, and promised to live once more as good Christians, since they had restored to them the Fathers who had begotten them to Jesus Christ. »

In 1852, the Jesuits were once more in Cayenne. It was not the first time that a member of the family of Napoleon had understood, that if the *impossible* was to be accomplished, it was the Fathers of the Society of Jesus who must be asked to attempt it. Between June 1853, and September 1856, eleven Jesuits died in the swamps of Cayenne of yellow fever. « Oh! how many souls has he delivered from hell! » was the exclamation of a poor French outcast over the body of one of them. But they have cheerfully accepted this « crucifying mission, » as Father D'Abbadie called it; there were broken hearts to be comforted, and they asked no more. « Why do you weep, » said D'Abbadie to his brethren as they stood round his death bed in 1856; « I am going to heaven. » And it was always by the aid of the glorious and all-powerful Mother of God that he and his companions recovered the unhappy souls committed to their care. « What led you, » said one of the Fathers to an aged criminal who had obtained the grace of a happy death, « to seek at last the succours of religion? » « I have done nothing but evil during my whole life, » he replied; « one thing only I have never failed to do, and that I owe to the counsels of my mother : every day I have said the *Salve Regina*, in honour of the Holy Virgin. » And that Blessed One, by her mighty protection, had saved him at last.

It is time to leave Guyana, where the same works are in progress at this hour, and where missionaries who have sacrificed all for the love of God, and do not repent the sacrifice, still display the apostolic virtues which forced not long ago from the French governor of Cayenne this cry of admiration;— « You are happier than we; death itself has no terrors for such as you. » (1)

If now we continue our hasty journey through the provinces of South America, and traverse Venezuela, without halting by the banks of the Cayuni or the Apuré, so often trodden by the messengers of peace, we shall enter New Grenada, and at Carthagena we shall find the traces of one whom the Church has already presented to the homage of the faithful, under the title of the Blessed Peter Claver.

Born towards the close of the sixteenth century, an age in which the most prodigious graces of Heaven were poured out on every side, as if to counterpoise the irreparable calamities to which it also gave birth, this offspring of an illustrious Catalonian race

(1) P. 460.

displayed even in infancy the gifts with which he was to be more abundantly favoured in his after career. In 1602, he was admitted as a postulant into the Society of Jesus, at Tarragona. In 1610, he left Seville, at the bidding of Claude Aquavivà, for the land in which he was to spend thirty-nine years of what has been truly called « a perpetual martyrdom. » In 1615, he celebrated his first Mass at Carthagena, of which it was the will of God that he should become the apostle.

« Do every thing for the greater glory of God, » was one of the rules found in a book containing his secret thoughts, and a second was this; « Seek nothing in this world but what Jesus Himself sought — to sanctify souls, to labour, to suffer, and if necessary to die for their salvation, and all for the sake of Jesus ! » In these two rules, as Fleuriau observes, his whole life was comprised. »

At his solemn profession, he added to the customary engagements the special vow, « to be until death the slave of the Negroes. » How well he kept it, they know who have read the story of his life. As soon as a ship load of Negroes arrived from the coast of Africa, — from Congo, Guinea, or Angola, — « his pale emaciated face assumed a hue of health quite unusual to it. » It was he who first hurried to the shore to greet the captives, astonished to receive such a welcome; who consoled them with loving words of peace, and poured into their seared hearts the balm of hope. It was he who followed them with a father's love to their wretched homes, that by sharing their sufferings he might teach them how to bear them, how to unite them with the sufferings of

Christ. And then, in words of more than human wisdom, he spoke to them of Him whose name he could rarely mention without shedding tears. But who can describe that angelic ministry, unless filled with his own spirit? who can bear to contemplate the terrible austerities with which it was accompanied, and of which, in an age like this, one can hardly venture even to speak?

Clothed in a hair shirt from his neck to his feet, and presenting such an aspect as St. John the Baptist when he came out of the desert, to preach by his own example the doctrine of mortification, the man of God would sit during the long hours of the tropical day in the tribunal of penance, fainting with heat and with the fetid stench of the poor Africans who thronged round this physician of souls; and when evening came at last, and nature having given way they were obliged to carry him home in their arms, his only refreshment, we are told, was to spend hours in mental prayer. Even some of his companions, though members of that Society which has faced all trials and braved all dangers, sometimes lost their consciousness in the presence of sights upon which he calmly looked, both in the huts of the Negroes, and in the hospitals of St. Sebastian and St. Lazarus. It was he who ministered to the most loathsome diseases, and even kissed the hideous wounds which they had traced in bodies half devoured by scrofula or gangrene... (1) And in the midst of such scenes,

(1) « Malattia ordinaria è una certa specie di lebbra, che loro impiaga orribilmente la bocca e le gingive; indisi stende a comprendere tutte le membra e farne una sola piaga putrida e verminosa. » *Compendio della Vita del B. Pietro Claver*, p. 25.

at which angels are daily present in their invisible ministry, the spirit of God within him would sometimes break forth, so that the reflected glory of his Master shone around him. Once, at St. Sebastian's, the Archdeacon of Carthagena, who had gone to the hospital to distribute alms, « found him in the midst of the sick, with the look of a Seraph, his face shining like the sun, and a circle of light round his head. » More than once, a company returning home in the darkness of the night thought the house of the Saint was on fire, but discovered on approaching, as they afterwards attested on oath, that is was filled, like the temple of old, « with the glory of the Lord, » and saw him suspended in the air, and as it were transfigured before them. *Mirabilis est Deus in sanctis ejus!* (1)

There is no need to describe at length the works of this apostle, nor their marvellous fruits. How should *such* a missionary not succeed? It was the Mahometan Negroes from Guinea who gave him the greatest trouble. Yet he never ceased to pursue them with his cheerful pleasant speech, or sometimes with terrible menaces; — as once when he held up his crucifix before a dying and obstinate unbeliever, and exclaimed in accents which reached even that obdurate soul, « Behold the God who is about to judge you! » Multitudes of Turks and Moors owed their salvation to his ministry, for there was in him a power which few could resist. Once a ship containing more than six hundred English prisoners was captured in the Bay of Carthagena. Among the cap-

(1) Fleuriau, livre III.

tives was an Anglican dignitary, with his wife and family. Fleuriau calls him an « archdeacon, » and Boero a « bishop. » Touched as the latter relates, by the « squisita affabilità e amorevolezza » of Claver, and rejecting the Catholic Faith, like many of his sect, rather through ignorance and prejudice than from the malice of a disobedient heart, he strove in vain to resist the Saint; then he would promise to abandon his errors at some future period, declare « that he was in heart a Catholic, » that there was no need for precipitation, « that if he were reconciled to the Roman Church he would be deprived of his revenues and his numerous family of their subsistence. » But grace was too strong for him, and he died not long after in Father Claver's arms, rejoicing that he had escaped from delusious which still darken in our own day many a generous heart; and exulting in the light of that truth which had first dawned upon him in captivity. Almost all the other prisoners were converted in their turn, including one who had been accustomed to revile the Saint, and had called him to his face « a hypocrite and an impostor. »

Such was this servant of God, and such his work. It was especially among the Negroes that he laboured, and with results which have disposed for ever of the popular notion that this race is incapable of true conversion. « The authority he had gained over their minds, » says one of his biographers, « and their affection for him, made them obey without reply or hesitation; the mere sight of him would check the most unruly, and even the vicious, when they met him, knelt down to ask his blessing. » Finally, the number whom he gathered into the fold of Christ, either from Paganism or Mahometanism, was so great as to be incredible, if it were not certified by competent witnesses. « A religious questioned him on this subject shortly before he died, to whom he answered, that he thought he had baptized more than three hundred thousand; but as humility always led him to diminish the number of his good works, it has been asserted by persons likely to be well informed, that he had baptized at least four hundred thousand. »

In his last mission, Father Claver penetrated for the first time to the dangerous country between the Magdalena and the Cordilleras, « where the ferocity of the Indians had hitherto prevented the entrance of Christianity. » In 1654, he died. Three years later, his tomb was re-opened; when Dr Bartholomew Torrez, an experienced physician, affirmed on oath — that although the very coffin, and every thing in it, was completely rotten and decayed, « the body, with all its skin, nerves, and other parts, was sound and healthy, notwithstanding the quantity of lime which had covered it. »

It is not a formal history of Missions which we are writing, and for this reason we have not attempted to exhaust the facts which illustrate that history, even in a single province of the earth. Our purpose has been only to trace, in all lands, the contrast between the work of the Church and the work of the Sects; to show that God and His gifts have been ever with the first, never with the last; and to prove, by testimony so various, impartial, and harmonious, that neither pride nor anger shall be able to gainsay it, that Catholic and Protestant missions have differed so enormously both in their agents and their results, as to exclude all doubt in the mind of even the least thoughtful observer, of every man in whom the instincts of a Christian still survive, which were divine and which human. We are not obliged, therefore, to trace with minute detail the missions of Peru and Chili, which exactly resemble, in every feature, those which have been already reviewed.

A few words will suffice with reference to the two famous provinces whice lie between the Andes and the Ocean. In 1590, fifty-seven years after the last Inca perished in the city of Cassamarca, by the order of Pizarro — Fathers Antony Lopez and Michael Urrea were martyred in Peru. In 1593, eight Jesuits entered Chili. Aranda and Valdiva won to the faith the fierce and cruel Araucanians, but a little later, continuing their intrepid apostolate, Vecchi, Aranda, and Montalban were martyred; and when the Spaniards proposed to revenge their death, it was Valdiva who dissuaded them from this act of human justice, and afterwards established, by his own unaided ministry, four new missions in Chili. Vainly the trained soldiers of Spain tried to penetrate into the interior, where every forest concealed a hostile army, and every river must be forded in the midst of a storm of darts and arrows. And then these men of war had recourse to another order of warriors, bolder than themselves, because fighting in a nobler cause, and « missionaries were employed, » as an English writer observes, « to penetrate into the retreats of the Indians, in order to civilise them by converting them to Christianity. In these attempts, rendered doubly hazardous by the exasperation of the Indians, many of the ministers of religion fell victims to their zeal. » (1) But the work was never suspended. In 1598, de Medrano and de Figueroa had already penetrated the recesses of the Cordilleras. In 1604, a college had been founded at Santa Fé. Imperiali, D'Ossat, de Gregorio, and others carried the faith to one tribe after another, sometimes falling under the clubs or the arrows of the savages, but never crying in vain for new apostles to complete the work which they had left unfinished. In the single year 1614, fifty-six Fathers of the Society of Jesus arrived in Peru, to replace those who had fallen. At a still later date, Father Stanislas Arlet had traversed the most inaccessible forests and mountains of Western America, and gathered six nations into one family. Tucuman had become a Catholic province. The Dominicans were spread chiefly through the northern districts, the Franciscans were scattered at one time from Bogota to Buenos Ayres. The Jesuits were everywhere.

« From a corner of this department of Peru, » says Dr Archibald Smith, — candid and generous in spite of the prejudices of country and education, — « the voice of Christianity has penetrated into vast regions of heathen and savage tribes, and reached the unsettled wanderers among the thickest entanglements of the woods, which occupy a great portion of the widely extended missionary territory of Peru From Ocopa issued forth those zealous, persevering, self-denying, and enduring men, the great object of

(1) Stuart Cochrane, vol. I, ch. III, p. 219.

whose lives it has been, in the midst of danger, and in the name of the Saviour, to add to the faith of the Church, and to civilised society, beings whose spirits wera as dark as the woods they occupied. » (1) « All South America, » observes Mʳ Walpole, recording the same facts, « was explored under their direction. Overcoming every difficulty, surmounting toils, braving unheard of and unknown dangers, smiling at and glorying in wounds, hardships, death itself, these zealous men spoke of Jesus and His love and mercy in the remotest nook of this vast continent. » (2) Yet neither of these Protestant travellers, nor any of their class, — differing in this respect from the more discerning savages, who were converted by such apostles, because even they could recognise the presence of God in them, — appear to have been in any degree impressed by the truths which they eloquently narrate, or to have derived the slightest admonition from them.

We may not stay to notice one by one the men who evangelised the Peruvian races, redeeming the violence and cupidity of the soldiers of Spain, and winning the love and reverence of the native tribes in spite of the injuries which they had received from Europeans; but there is one of their number whom it is impossible not to mention, because to him was given, in a special manner, the title of Apostle of Peru. It was in 1589 that Francis de Solano sailed

(1) *Peru as it is*, by Archibald Smith, M. D. ; vol. II, ch. IV, p. 114.
(2) *Four Years in the Pacific*, by the Hon. F. Walpole, vol. II, ch. I, p. 25.

for America, designing to labour in the province of Tucuman, which lies between the Cordilleras and Paraguay, « because there he might hope to find the greatest dangers, and to suffer most for the glory of God. » Father Louis Bolanos, also a Franciscan, had preceded him, and having set out from Lima had travelled many a weary league on both banks of the Plata; but a greater than he was now to enter the same regions.

Perfectly conversant, like most of his order, with the dialects of the barbarous tribes whom he resolved to win, St. Francis Solano threw himself into the combat with all the ardour of an apostle. Already he had gathered thousands into the fold of Christ, when the remoter eastern tribes, who wandered through the country between the Dulce and the St. Tomé, came down in vast numbers, breathing fury and slaughter against their converted brethren, and threatening the most cruel torments to all who had become Christians. The neophytes began to fly in terror, and the new mission seemed to be menaced with swift and hopeless destination. Then Solano went forth alone, confiding in the protection of the Mother of God, to meet the advancing multitude. He was a servant of Him who had said, « the good shepherd giveth his life for the sheep. » The hour was come to die, and he would die as becomes an apostle. But he was only to be a martyr in desire; and « having by supernatural power arrested the advance of the barbarians, he addressed to them so moving a discourse on the Passion of our Divine Lord, and exhorted them with such burning words to embrace His holy religion, that in that single day more than nine thousand were converted. » (1)

After this he went through the land, preaching everywhere « Jesus Christ crucified; » and every where he was accompanied, like the primitive Missionaries, by « signs following. » Even the wild beasts, as multitudes were able to testify, rendered him homage after their kind. And no marvel, — for as one of his biographers observes, « It is a principle of theology, that the revolt of irrational creatures against man is only a consequence of man's rebellion against his Maker. » « The pre-eminence of our Blessed Lord over inanimate matter, and much more over the animal creation, » says a living authority, is the true cause that « as His saints advance in holiness and in likeness to Himself, the animals obey their words, revere their sanctity, and minister to their wants. » (2)

In 1610, St. Francis Solano died. Three hundred and four witnesses, of all ranks and classes, were examined on oath, and attested the prodigies which they had witnessed, and the heroicity of the virtues which had transformed a desert into a garden. Through a tract of two thousand miles he was numbered among the patrons and defenders of the faithful, and a hundred tribes burned lamps day and night in his honour, and called upon him to advocate their cause in Heaven. Then Urban VIII, by his famous decree of 1631, peremptorily forbade all public devotion till the claims of the Saint had been further examined, and refused even to allow the pro-

---

(1) See his life by Courtot, ch. VIII.
(2) F. Faber, *The Blessed Sacrament*, book IV, § 2, p. 433.

cess to continue until the apostolic edict was obeyed.
For twenty years, the grateful Indians, who had
loved their father with all their hearts, refused to
submit; till they comprehended at length, that it
was not by disobeying the Vicar of Christ that they
could honour one of His apostles. And so, with heavy
hearts, they brought in all the lamps which they had
kindled in his honour; and in 1656, his body was
removed from its shrine, and carefully hidden from
their sight. Nineteen years later the decree of Beati-
fication was pronounced, and in 1726 he was can-
onised.

The faith which St. Francis Solano preached is
still, in spite of many disasters, and of the crimes
and follies of successive rulers, the light and the
glory of Peru. Here, as in every other province
evangelised by the sons of St. Ignatius, St. Francis,
and St. Dominic, neither neglect nor oppression
have been able to undo that mighty work, unparalleled since the first ages of Christianity, by which it
was the will of God to replace the apostate millions
of Sweden, Germany, and Britain by a multitude of
new believers in China, India, and America. We
have seen that in the two former countries persecution and suffering have only confirmed the faith
planted in other days by the missionaries of the
cross; and it is time to show, once more by Protestant testimony, that in Brazil and Colombia, in Chili
and Peru, the same astonishing stability attests at
this hour by Whose power these nations were won
to the service of Christ, by Whose protection they
have been maintained in it.

In Brazil, where de Nobrega and Anchieta once

laboured, 800,000 domesticated Indians, as we have said, represent, even at this day, the fruits of their toil. Deprived during sixty years of their fathers and guides, and too often scandalized by the example of men who were Christians only in name, the native races have not only preserved the faith through all their sorrows and trials, but have everywhere rejected the bribes and the caresses of heresy. And now, after their long trial, a better day has dawned for them, and once more they listen to the loving counsels of wise and gentle guides; though the government of Brazil — imitating the pagan philosophy of European statesmen, and adopting the political atheism which in the old world has well nigh destroyed the foundations of social order, — has rather impeded than encouraged the work of regeneration. Even Protestant writers, in spite of violent and incurable prejudices, do justice to the generous virtues of this people. D*r* Walsh, an Anglican minister, frankly confesses, as we have seen, the « deep impression of rational piety, » and « zealous attachment to their religion, » which he noticed during his long residence among them. Drunkenness and blasphemy, he says, were unknown; though once he heard « on Sunday evening at Rio a desperate riot of drunken blasphemers, but they all swore *in English*. » (1) M*r* Gardner also observes, in 1846, after pursuing during some years his scientific researches in these tropical climes; « It was on a Sunday morning that I arrived in Liverpool from Brazil, and during the course of that day I saw in the streets a

(1) *Notices of Brazil*, vol. I, p. 381.

greater number of cases of intoxication than, I believe, I observed altogether among Brazilians, whether black or white, during the whole period of my residence in the country. » (1)

Before England had begun to educate her heathen masses, Brazil had inaugurated an elaborate system of public instruction. Dr Walsh notices, not only the universality of primary education in Brazil, but the still more remarkable fact, that many of the coloured races have been conspicuous for their success in various branches of knowledge. Speaking of the great public library at Rio, and the affluence of students of all ranks, he asks; « Is it not most unjust to accuse the Catholics as enemies to knowledge? Here is a noble and public literary institution, filled with books on all subjects, » — and with Bibles in almost every language, — « founded by a rigid Catholic monarch, and superintended and conducted by Catholic ecclesiastics, on a plan even more liberal, and less exclusive, than any similar establishment in our own Protestant country. » (2)

It would be too long to quote his interesting account of the *irmandades*, or religious brotherhoods; which « consist entirely of the laity, » and whose objects are to build and repair churches, found and maintain hospitals, bury the deceased poor, and to do, cheerfully and well, whatsoever else Christian charity can suggest. « It is quite inconceivable, » he says, « to an Englishman, what immense sums of money these lay brothers annually expend in what

(1) *Travels in the Interior of Brazil*, ch. I, p. 18.
(2) Vol. I, p. 438.

they conceive to be pious and charitable uses. » Even Messrs Kidder and Fletcher, though less capable than most of their countrymen of appreciating such works, and despising the Brazilians because they refused to exchange the doctrine of St. Paul for the crude inventions of New England Protestantism, speak with reluctant admiration, in 1857, of « the philanthropy and practical Christianity embodied in the hospitals of Rio and Janeiro; » while they are obliged to confess that « the devoted Italian Capuchins seem to be ever on errands of mercy, through tropic heats and rains. » (1) And then they console themselves with coarse abuse of the « greasy friars. » Yet Dr Walsh, a man of purer instincts, commends the virtues even of the native clergy, some of whom, owing to the want of ecclesiastical training, and the mistaken policy of the government towards the seminaries, are the least edifying of their class. « I really cannot find, » he says, « that the Brazilian clergy deserve the character imputed to them. From what I have seen myself and heard from others, they are, generally speaking, temperate in their diet, observant of the rules of their Church, assiduous in attending the sick, and charitable as far as their limited means permit. » (2)

Lastly, in spite of the gold of England and America, not a solitary Brazilian, white or black, has ever been induced to profess Protestantism; and Mr Ewbank has informed us, no doubt with regret, that « the people avoid a missionary as one with whom

(1) Ch. vii, p. 111.
(2) P. 374.

association is disreputable, » and regard him with sovereign contempt « from a rooted belief in his ignorance and presumption. »

Perhaps the reader may be disposed to ask himself at this point, in the presence of facts so remarkable, what that Power can be, everywhere exerted by one class of teachers and by one only, which even in the souls of negroes and savages has produced results at once so deep and so lasting? By what mysterious influence have they, in all lands, subdued such natures to the law of Christ; by what spell have they engrafted on them that supernatural faith which sixty years of utter abandonment could not weaken, nor evil example obliterate, nor bribes seduce, nor even ignorance corrupt?

In that vast region which stretches from the mouth of the San Francisco to the Isthmus of Panama, watered by the mightiest rivers of our globe, and including the district of the Amazon with its « forty-five thousand miles of navigable water communication,» the natives, who still find shelter in its forests, or guide their barks over its myriad streams, « push their profession of the Catholic religion, » we have been told, « even to fanaticism. » Yet it is a kind of marvel, considering their past history, that they should have any religion at all. A less grievous trial sufficed utterly to destroy the apostolic churches of Asia; but it seems to have been the special privilege of those founded in the 16th century, that no power should prevail against them. Of the modern Indian population, and the existing missions among them, many Protestant writers speak with admiration; though evidently perplexed by their obstinate adherence to the faith, in spite of their long calamities. Prince Maximilian notices the new mission at Belmonte, where he found « a race of civilised Indians converted to Christianity, » who « have abandoned entirely their ancient mode of life, and are now quite reclaimed. » (1) Prince Adalbert, though he writes in a more worldly and frivolous tone, speaks of meeting canoes on the river Xingu, all adorned with flags « bearing an image of the Virgin Mary » — sufficient evidence of the Christian instincts of this people. Where She is honoured, how should religion perish? How should even the untaught Indian lose the faith delivered to his fathers, so long as he is devout to Her who is both « the joy of heaven and the exultation of earth; » « the glory of the human race and the ornament of the universe; » « the gate by which the Creator entered into His own creation; » « the Word's eternal choice, whom to love exceedingly was to become one of His chiefest graces, one of the greatest of all His human perfections? » What marvel if piety still linger in tribes who rejoice to be Mary's children, and confide in her protection whom highest angels honour with lowly reverence, as at once, by a prodigy of election and grace, the Mother, the Daughter, and the Spouse, of the Everlasting God?

From other Protestant travellers in these regions we learn, that respect for the ministers of religion, as well as for the mysteries which they dispense, is also a characteristic of the same race.

Messrs Smyth and Lowe, two British officers, who

(1) *Travels in Brazil*, ch. x, p. 277.

travelled by water from Lima to Para, from the Pacific to the Atlantic, repeatedly attest the powerful influence of the Franciscans at the present day. Thus, at Saposoa, on the river Huallaga, « the priest is treated by the people with great respect. » On the banks of « the magnificent Ucayali, » the only Europeans they met were « those excellent persons whose aim had been to rescue its inhabitants from the most miserable and horrid state of barbarism, » in spite of the criminal indifference of « what is pleased to call itself a liberal government. » At Sarayacu, they are hospitably entertained by a Spanish missionary, and remark « the great influence his paternal care, during the long space of thirty-four years, gave him over the minds of all the civilized Indians, and his knowledge of their various languages. » They add that, « during the long interval of nine years, » through the *incuria* of the government, « he had not received any salary. » (1)

Mr Wallace, another English traveller, notices, in 1853, similar facts. Thus, at Javita, on the Rio Negro, « the girls and boys assemble morning and evening at the church to sing a hymn or psalm » — a practice which is not usual in English villages. On the Amazon he meets Negroes, who « all join in the responses with much fervour, » but unfortunately, according to Mr Wallace, « without understanding a word. » He does not say how he ascertained the fact; but he relates immediately, that some of them had just returned from a three days journey to have a child baptized, which encourages us to believe that

(1) *Narrative of a Journey from Lima to Para*, ch. IV, p. 194.

he was mistaken. Elsewhere he shows how religion enters into and colours the daily life of the Indians, so that at their frequent *festas*, « which are always on a Saint's-day of the Roman Catholic Church, » they will make a long tour to the various Indian villages, « carrying the image of the saint... » Like the natives of China and Ceylon, they willingly spend their substance also in token of their piety. « The live animals are frequently promised beforehand for a particular saint; and often, when I have wanted to buy some provisions, I have been assured ' that this is St. John's pig,' or ' that is ', etc. » (1) It is evident that, in spite of their misfortunes, their religion is still a reality. The English peasant does not refuse to sell his pig because it is promised to St. John, and would probably feel little respect for such self-denial, even if he knew who St. John was.

Mr Campbell Scarlett relates the same characteristic anecdotes, and displays the same incapacity to appreciate them. « At least four nights out of seven,» he says, speaking of the Indians of Panama, — for they are everywhere the same, — « I am indulged with a superstitious if not idolatrous ceremony. » It was one which he might have witnessed in many a hamlet of Austria, Bavaria, or Spain, and even of France or Belgium, with the approval of men not much addicted to idolatry, and as remarkable for intellectual vigour as any in Europe; for it was simply a harmless procession which disturbed Mr Scarlett's repose, wherein Christian Indians

(1) *Travels on the Amazon and Rio Negro*, by Alfred R. Wallace, ch. IV, p. 93; ch. IX, p. 270. (1853).

marched, « having on their heads a gorgeous image of the Virgin, under a canopy. » But the same obnoxious spectacle, in which simple hearts displayed their filial affection towards the Mother of Jesus, met him everywhere. « Mummeries disgraceful to Christianity, « he angrily observes, « occur in these countries so frequently, that they appear to occupy the greater part of every body's time and attention : »(1)— good proof of their being interested in Christianity, though it might perhaps be offensive to an English gentleman only anxious to sleep in peace.

In every region of the continent, the same spontaneous piety seems to manifest itself. Mr Markham goes to Canete, in Peru, and in that tranquil valley meets this phenomenon. « Early in the morning, one is roused by the voices of the young girls and women, when they all repair to the door of the chapel before going to work, and chaunt a hymn of praise upon their knees. This is repeated at sunset, when the day's work is concluded. » Presently he is at Cuzco, where he finds the devout population « showering scarlet salvias » over a crucifix which was being borne in procession. Like Mr Scarlett, he is offended, and gravely remarks, as if the occasion required a solemn protest, that « such exhibitions supply the place of the worship of the Sun. It is a question which is the most idolatrous. » (2) Yet this gentleman is indignant with the Spaniards for having, as he says, « *polluted* the altars of the Sun ! »

(1) *South America and the Pacific*, by the Hon. P. Campbell Scarlett, vol. II, ch. IX, p. 204.
(2) *Cuzco and Lima*, by Clements R. Markham, F. R. G. S.; ch. II, p. 27; ch. V, p. 155.

When Mr Mansfield, also an English traveller, sees « the Peons and *Chinas* (the Guarani women) all fall on their knees in the street, » at Corrientes, as Mr Markham saw others do at Yanaoca, he exclaims with solemn complacency, « It is sad to see such a power of devotion thrown away! » (1) It is true that he had detected, with the unerring sagacity of his countrymen, that these apparently devout people were in the habit of « worshipping a doll. » When educated Englishmen undertake to criticise Christian devotion, they not unfrequently attain, as in these cases, the uttermost limits of un-reason. Yet there are many of them who seriously marvel, when they are told that, in all which relates to religion, they are a proverb and a jest among all races of men; and this, as Mr Ewbank has candidly informed us, « from a rooted belief in their ignorance and presumption. »

Another English traveller, this time a Protestant missionary, far surpasses even Mr Scarlett, Mr Markham, and Mr Mansfield, in his repugnance to such manifestations of religious feeling. After observing that « the name of God is seldom long out of the mouth of any central American, » and sternly rebuking « a profane imitation of the Saviour riding upon an ass, » he reveals unconsciously in these curious words the temper which makes Protestants shrink from such exhibitions. « Who can compute the amount of positive evil which must result from *familiarising* the eye of a whole people with such objects

---

(1) *Paraguay, Brazil*, etc., by C. B. Mansfield Esq., M. A.; ch. IX, p. 265.

as these? » (1) That persons whose religion is not divine faith, but simply emotion, and who, like the Protestant visitors at Jerusalem, are only « scandalized » by familiarity with holy places and things, should dread any shock to their capricious and sentimental belief, is perhaps natural; but Catholics can bear to approach, and even to represent by sensible signs, the divine mysteries which God has taught them both to know and to love.

Another Protestant christian, also a witness to the devotion which he could not comprehend, after noticing the fervour displayed at a similar religious ceremony in Mexico, relates that he quitted the scene in disgust, and relieved his intelligent piety by an immediate visit to some Aztec ruins. « I contemplated the old Aztec god, » he says, « and *could not but regret the change* that had been imposed upon these imbecile Indians. » (2) This gentleman is at least perfectly candid in the exhibition of his sympathies.

On the river Magdalena, whose banks were once trodden by the Blessed Peter Claver, Captain Stuart Cochrane, who never mentions the Catholic religion without a jest or a curse, discovers the same offensive piety. « Every time (the native crew) stopped to take their meals, one of them uttered a prayer, and invoked not only the Virgin and all the Saints in the calendar, » which must have singularly protracted the repast, but some, he is quite sure, « of their own invention. » This is a practice, Captain Cochrane

---

(1) *The Gospel in Central America*, by Rev[d] F. Crowe; p.278.
(2) *Mexico and its Religion*, by Robert A. Wilson; ch. XXI, p. 231.

naively adds, « which they would think it wrong to omit, and which no doubt originated in piety. » When the meal was over, before they resumed their journey, they always « recited a prayer for the prosperity of our voyage » — a habit which might have taught this English gentleman a useful lesson, but which he only found « highly diverting. » (1) He confesses, however, that education was spreading universally in Colombia, « not only in the capital, but in the most remote villages of the republic. »(2)

Everywhere the same facts, illustrating impressively the undying ministry of the first apostles of America, are recorded by Protestant travellers, though usually without any comprehension of their significance. On the Lake of Nicaragua and in the quicksilver mines of southern California, two of the most unpromising places in the world, Mr Julius Froebel finds American Indians displaying the same generous and trustful piety. « I shall never forget, » he says, « the impressions of one night and morning on the San Juan river. Our boat had anchored in the midst of the stream... In the morning, a song of our boatmen addressed to the Virgin roused me from my sleep. It was a strain of plaintive notes in a few simple but most expressive modulations. The sun was just rising, and as the first rays, gilding the glossy leaves of the forest, fell upon the bronze-coloured bodies of our men, letting the naked forms of their athletic frame appear in all the contrast of light and

(1) *Journal of a Residence in Colombia*, vol. I, ch. III, pp. 143, 150.
(2) Vol. II, ch. IX, p. 15.

shade, while accents, plaintive and imploring, strained forth from their lips, I thought to hear the sacred spell by which, unconscious of its power, these men were subduing their own half-savage nature. At once the same song was repeated from behind a projecting corner of the bank, and other voices joined those of our crew in the sacred notes. Two canoes, covered from our view, had anchored near us during the night. The song at last died away in the wilderness. A silent prayer — our anchor was raised, and, with a wild shout of the crew, twelve oars simultaneously struck the water. » (1) Can any one imagine such a scene on the Thames or the Clyde?

At another time, it is in the mines of New Almaden that he finds « fifteen or twenty men calling down the blessing of Heaven on their day's work in the interior of the mountain, before a little altar cut out of the natural rock ; » and singing the same hymn to the Mother of Jesus, to the same air, at a distance of nearly two thousand miles. In both cases the only « spell » was that mysterious gift of faith which can illumine the darkness even of the Negro and the Indian, and both furnished an illustration of the truth imperfectly avouched by a travelled Protestant, when he exclaimed; « Catholicism has certainly a much stronger hold over the human mind than Protestantism. The fact is visible and undeniable. » (2)

It is the *universality* of this fact which gives to it its deep significance. No race of men to whom the

(1) *Seven Years Travel in Central America*, by Julius Froebel; ch. II, p. 20 ; ch. x, p. 585.
(2) Laing, *Notes of a Traveller*, ch. XXI, p. 430.

incomparable gift has once been imparted, however lowly their social or intellectual position, fail to bear witness to its marvellous power; and whilst millions of Englishmen, Swedes, and Germans, who have never received it, have sunk almost to the level of animals, have less apprehension of divine things than the very pagan, and neither know nor care « whether there be any Holy Ghost, » (1) the whole life of the untutored Indian is an unceasing manifestation of the *supernatural* principle within him. Peru is no exception to this rule. « The devotion of the population to Catholicism, » says a well-meaning Protestant missionary, after he had abandoned his hopeless undertaking, « is manifested in almost daily processions. » (2) So vehement is the repugnance of the Peruvians to heresy, a sentiment which could have no existence without deep religious conviction, that Dr Archibald Smith mildly complains, «these good people believed we were but Jews. » And then he relates that at Lima, on the death of a certain Englishman, « the good natured Bishop yielded his sanction to let the corpse have Christian burial; but subsequently to this permission, a mob was collected in the night, and the body was cast out from the church into the middle of the street. » (3) Such facts, even if they be deemed to indicate excessive zeal, are at least incontrovertible evidence of the power which religion exerts over the hearts of these various races, and afford an instructive contrast to the dull apathy,

(1) *Acts*, XIX, 2.
(2) *A Visit to the South Seas in the U. S. Ship Vincennes*, by S. Stewart, A. M.; vol. I, p. 197.
(3) *Peru as it is*, vol. I, ch. VII, p. 165.

or cheerless unbelief, of the same class in our own country. And though we have been told that « the life of an Englishman is in danger among the peasantry, » because he has made himself odious by his shallow and presumptuous bigotry; yet even Protestant writers confess « the kindness and hospitality » (1) of these races to all who know how to conduct themselves with modesty and good sense. Even Captain Cochrane says, « John Bull may certainly improve his manners by imitating those of the peasants of South America; » (2) Mr Kendall and Mr Olmsted repeatedly attest the universal charity and kindliness of the Indians of Mexico; Mr Markham celebrates the unbounded hospitality of the Peruvians, and not only acknowledges that the upper classes are « highly educated, » but that « many *Indians*, too, have distinguished themselves as men of literary attainments; » while Mr Froebel, contrasting « the unaffected kindness, good breeding, and politeness of the Mexican country people » with the manners of his own nation, declares, « In almost every respect they are superior to our German peasants. »

The only additional fact, in illustration of the enduring influence of religion over the Peruvian Indian, which we need notice here, has been recorded by Mr Clements Markham. Beyond the lofty range of the Yquicha mountains lies the almost inaccessible home of the tribe of Yquichanos. « Distinguished by their upright gait, independent air, and handsome features, » — « true lovers of liberty, » — « an

(1) Gerstaecker, vol. I, ch. x, p. 188.
(2) Vol. II, ch. xii, p. 150.

honour to the Indian races of South America, » in the words of M*r* Markham, they have twice vanquished the military forces of the Peruvian republic, and persisting in their loyalty to the Spanish crown, have defied every effort to subdue their independence. « No tax-gatherer, » he says, « dares to enter their country. » But while this « most interesting people, » in the words of the same Protestant writer, « refuse to submit to the capitation or any other tax, *they punctually pay their tithes to the priests* who come amongst them, and treat a single stranger with courteous hospitality. » (1)

In Chili, — as in Brazil, Colombia, and Peru, — a hostile witness reports, in 1840, that « education is certainly advancing; » (2) and he fully explains the progress when he adds, in 1847, « the influence of the Jesuits is gradually increasing. » (3) Two years later, M*r* Walpole praises the « many excellent schools, » and notices that those « attached to the various convents teach free of expence. » There is even, he adds, at Santiago a normal school for the training of teachers, « who are afterwards sent into the provinces. » « The priests, » he says, « mostly taken from the higher classes, are educated at the university, and are a well-informed order of men. » (4)

Of the people we are told, by various Protestant

(1) *Cuzco*, etc., ch. III, p. 71.
(2) *A Visit to the Indians of Chili*, by Captain Allen F. Gardiner, ch. VI, p. 172.
(3) *A Voice from South America*, ch. I, p. 14.
(4) *Four Years in the Pacific*, vol. I, ch. VIII, p. 165; ch. X, p. 349.

writers, that, both by their industry and piety, they are worthy of their teachers. Dr Smith declares that « the Christianised Indians of the Inca dynasty are truly hard labourers. » Major Sutcliffe relates that spiritual retreats for this class « are held yearly on many of the large haciendas, » at which they practice severe mortifications, using the discipline with such vigour that this gentleman, who judged the operation with the feelings of an Englishman and a Protestant, observes; « I frequently heard them, and wondered how they could stand such a self-flogging. » (1) They must at all events have been in earnest.

Of their invincible dislike of heresy Mr Miers offers an explanation, when he relates the answer of the principal author of the modern constitution of Chili to the objection, apparently urged by an Englishman, that religious toleration was unknown in Chili. « Toleration cannot exist in Chili, » he replied, in accounting for the absence of that word from the civil code, « because this presupposes a necessity for permitting it; but here we neither have any other, nor know any other religion than the Catholic. » (2) Finally, a French traveller, busy only with economical and financial questions, but filled with admiration of the resources and the prosperity of this profoundly Catholic people, exclaims; « What an immense future is in store for this nation, which, to wise institutions and a prudent liberty, adds all the resources of an incomparable soil! » (3)

(1) *Sixteen Years in Chili and Peru*, ch. IX, p. 320. (1841).
(2) *Travels in Chili and La Plata*, vol. II, p. 219.
(3) *Notice sur le Chili*, p. 42. (1844).

Yet Protestant missionaries, chiefly English or Scotch, careless of the fact, which their own experience has so often attested, that they only succeed in provoking the repugnance of this people towards themselves, their employers, and their opinions, continue to waste, year after year, the enormous sums imprudently entrusted to them, in efforts which always terminate in failure, and in operations which only excite ridicule. We have seen that, owing to such proceedings, the life of an Englishman is precarious in these regions, while his dead body is flung into the highway. It is certainly a grave question for the inhabitants of the British Isles, whether the annual expenditure of vast revenues in all parts of the world, with no other result than to kindle the contempt of every pagan, the disgust and indignation of every Christian nation, is a course of action likely to promote their own interests, or worthy of their proverbial sagacity. If England is abhorred, as is unhappily the case, by all races of men, from the White Sea to the Indian Ocean, and is even at this moment in considerable peril from the gradual accumulation of that universal hatred which may one day crush her, it is in no small degree to her foolish and offensive missions, and especially to the complacent vanity and ignorance of which they are only one of the manifestations, that the evil is due.

The Argentine Republic, in spite of the crimes of its rulers, and the perpetual disorders of its social state, still remains so immutably Catholic, that all the overtures of opulent missionaries, whether English or American, have only been greeted with derision. Dr Olin has told us, that the mission to Buenos

Ayres was such a signal failure, that it suggested even to his ardent mind only motives of despair. The experiment, he says, « was formally given up in 1841-2, after an unsuccessful attempt to make some impression on the native Catholic population of that country. » « No Protestant missions, » he remarks, « have hitherto yielded so little fruit as those set on foot for the conversion of Roman Catholics; » and then this Wesleyan minister adds the suggestion already quoted, « We will trust that it will inspire the Board with great caution in entertaining new projects for missions among Catholics. »

The same discouraging conclusion is adopted by a well meaning English traveller, who endeavoured to introduce Protestantism in the wide plains which stretch from the shores of the Plata and the Uruguay to the foot of the Cordilleras, but with such disastrous results that he also was constrained to recognise the hopelessness of the attempt. « The Protestant missionary under the present arbitrary system, » — this is his way of describing the good-humoured contempt of the people, — « appears to have little prospect of extending his ministerial labours beyond the members of his own church, either American or English. » (1)

Such are the testimonies of Protestants, of different nations and sects, still more astonished than mortified at the peremptory rejection of their various religions by all the South American races and tribes. Even the Carib and the Araucanian, the Peruvian and the Chilian, the vigorous Guacho who spurs his wild

--
(1) Captain Gardiner, *Visit*, etc., p. 24.

horse over the Pampas, and the milder Indian who urges his canoe over the swift waters of the Guaviare or the Ucayali, only laughs at the pretentious of a doctrine which outrages all his instincts of the holy and the true; which has banished every mystery, and, as far as the exuberance of divine mercy will permit, suspended every grace; which displays itself only in words which awaken no echo, and in emotions which die away with the words; and whose salaried and effeminate preachers, all contradicting themselves and one another, so little resemble the saints and martyrs from whom his fathers received the faith which he still prizes more than life itself, that far from recognising them as teachers of a divine religion, he is accustomed to ask in surprise, like his fellows in other lands, « whether they profess any religion whatever? »

Before we enter the last province which remains to be visited in South America, let us notice a few additional examples, not unworthy of a moment's attention, of the language in which Protestant travellers speak of *modern* missionaries in this land. It is well to learn from such witnesses that they have not degenerated from their fathers.

A British officer, who effected a few years ago the descent of the Amazon, had for a companion during a part of his voyage a Spanish Franciscan, who, by the toils of thirty-four years, had, « founded many new missions, » without aid from any human being, and whose career included the following incident.

A little to the north-east of Sarayacu, on the river Ucayali, dwelt the Sencis, a fierce and warlike tribe, still unconverted, whose solitary virtue was dauntless courage. With a courage greater than their own, Father Plaza, the Franciscan to whom our tale refers, resolved to enter their territory. He was seized at the frontier, as he had anticipated and desired, and then was enacted the following drama. « They asked him, » says the English traveller, « whether he was brave, and subjected him to the following trial. Eight or ten men, armed with bows and arrows, placed themselves a few yards in front of him, with their bows drawn and their arrows directed to his breast; they then, with a shout, let go the strings, but retained the arrows in their left hands, which he at first did not perceive, but took it for granted that it was all over with him, and was astonished at finding himself unhurt. » The savages had taken a captive who could give even them a lesson in fortitude : but they had another trial in store for him. « They resumed their former position, and approaching somewhat nearer, they aimed their arrows at his body, but discharged them close to his feet. » The narrator adds, and perhaps no other comment could be reasonably expected from a Protestant, that « if he had shown any signs of fear, he would probably have been despatched; » but that, « having, in his capacity of missionary, been a long time subjected to the caprices of the Indians, he had made up his mind for the worst, and stood quite motionless during the proof. » Finally, « they surrounded him, and received him as a welcome guest. » (1) We can hardly be surprised that such a missionary

(1) Lieut. Smyth, ch. xii, p. 227.

— whom even Mr Markham calls « a great and good man, » whose « deeds of heroism and endurance throw the hard-earned glories of the soldier far into the shade, » — should be able to « found many new missions, » even in this 19th century.

But there are at this hour many such as Padré Plaza in the South American missions, as even the most prejudiced travellers attest. He himself, having recently finished his apostolic career as Bishop of Cuença, was succeeded at Sarayacu by Father Cimini and three other missionaries, who ruled « about 1350 souls, consisting chiefly of Panos Indians. »(1)« The brave and indefatigable Father Girbal, » was a hero of the same order; and through every Catholic province of America, English and American travellers have discovered apostles who are ready to do in the 19th century what their predecessors did in the 17th and 18th. In Columbia, even Captain Cochrane applauds « the excellent Bishop of Merida. » Mr Gilliam, a consular agent of the United States, names « the celebrated and beloved Bishop of Durango.»(2) Dr Walsh has assured us that « a more learned or a more amiable man than the Bishop of Rio does not exist. » Mr Markham celebrates, in 1859, « Don Pedro Ruiz, the excellent Bishop of Chachapoyas, » in Peru. Sir George Simpson visits Monterey, and says, « Father Gonzalez is a truly worthy representative of the early missionaries. » (3) Mr Stewart is

(1) Markham, ch. VIII, p. 257.
(2) *Travels in Mexico*, by Albert M. Gilliam, ch. XVI, p. 288. (1846).
(3) *Narrative of a Journey round the World*, vol, I, ch. VII, p. 334.

at Lima, and meets Padré Arrieta, « in extensive
repute for piety and learning. » (1) Mr Forbes is at
San Luis Rey, where he sees Father Antonio Peyri,
who, « after thirty-four years of incessant labour, »
had finished his career by « voluntary retirement in
poverty to spend his remaining days in pious exercises. » (2) M. de Mofras is on the Pacific shore,
and finds Father Estenéga « teaching his neophytes
how to make bricks; » and Father Abella, at sixty
years of age, sleeping on a buffalo skin, and drinking
out of a horn, refusing to retire, and declaring that
« he will die at his post. » (3) Mr Walpole is in
Chili, and meets one of whom he says, « If amenity
of manners, great power of conversation, infinite
knowledge of men and countries, could have won,
his must have been a successful ministry. There was
a soft persuasion, a seeming deep serenity in his
words, very difficult to withstand. » (4) Mr Markham hears at Andahuaylas « the famous Chilian
preacher, Don Francisco de Paula Taforo, » and
finds him escorted by « one continued triumphal
procession; » while at Lima-tambo he makes the
acquaintance of the Franciscan Father Esquibias,
« whose good deeds it was refreshing to hear from his
parishioners; » and at San Miguel that of « the excellent
Father Revello, the true hearted and devoted missionary of the Purus, » the body of whose companion,
a young monk from Cuzco, « Revello found pierced

(1) Vol. I, p. 190. *Letter V.*
(2) *California*, ch. v, p. 229.
(3) *Exploration du territoire de l'Orégon*, par M. Duflot de
Mofras, tome I, ch. vii, pp. 352, 380.
(4) Ch. x, p. 218.

with nine arrows, one of them passing right through his chest. » (1) At El Paso, many a league to the North of Peru, Mʳ Kendall, an American Protestant, encounters « the incomparable Ramon Ortiz, » whose « charity and manly virtues adorn the faith which he professes and illustrates by his life. » (2) Lieut. Herndon is on the upper course of the Amazon, and finds in that remote solitude a Franciscan whom he thus describes. « Father Calvo, meek and humble in personal concerns, yet full of zeal and spirit for his office, was my beau ideal of a missionary monk. » (3) Mʳ Wallace is on the Rio Negro, and meets Padré Torquato, « a very well educated and gentlemanly man, who well deserves all the encomiums Prince Adalbert has bestowed on him. » (4) Lieut. Smyth is at Chasuta, where he finds Padré Mariana de Jesus, and notes in his journal, not only « the devotion of the Indians, » but that « their submissive obedience to the Padré, and the attention they show to the worship of the Church to which they have been converted, reflect great credit on their worthy pastor. » (5) And this docility, he says, is the more remarkable, because « they seem to consider themselves on a perfect equality with every body, showing no deference to any one but the Padré. » Lastly, Mʳ Cleveland is at Guadalupe, in the Pacific, and observes; « The more intimately we became acquaint-

---

(1) Ch. ιv, p. 92; ch. vιιι, p. 275.
(2) *Narrative of the Texan Santa Fé Expedition*, vol. II, ch. ιι, p. 41.
(3) *Valley of the Amazon*, ch. x. p. 205.
(4) *Ubi supra*, ch. vι, p. 160.
(5) *Ubi supra*, ch. xι, p. 213.

ed with Padré Mariano, the more we were convinced that his was a character to love and respect. He appeared to us of that rare class, who, for piety and the love of their fellow men, might justly rank with a Fenelon or a Cheverus. » (1) We shall hear a little later exactly the same language applied, by the same class of writers, to living missionaries in North America; let us close the list for the present with this reflection, — that every where Catholic missionaries are found having the graces and virtues of their calling, and every where Providence employs Protestant travellers to bear witness to both.

One province only remains to be visited, before we complete our rapid survey, and turn our faces towards the North. Between the Parana and the Colorado, and stretching from Santa Cruz de la Sierra in Upper Peru to the Straits of Magellan, and from the frontier of Brazil to Chili, lies the vast region which gave a name to perhaps the noblest Mission which the Christian religion ever formed since the days of the Apostles. Here was accomplished, amidst races so barbarous and cruel that even the fearless warriors of Spain considered them « irreclaimable, » one of those rare triumphs of grace which constitute an epoch in the history of religion. Here one tribe after another, each more brutal than its neighbour, was gathered into the fold of Christ, and fashioned to the habits of civilized life. Here lived and died an army of apostles, who seem to have been raised up at that special moment,

(1) *A Narrative of Voyages*, by Richard J. Cleveland, ch. xiv, p. 57. (1842).

when whole nations were lapsing into apostasy, as if to show that the very hour which *they* chose for departing from the Church was marked in Heaven as a season for pouring out upon her a flood of new graces. Here, as Muratori could say without exaggeration, amid a people so lately the sport of demons « the sublimest virtues of Christians are become, if the expression may be used, common virtues. » (1) Here, as even Voltaire confessed, was perfected a work which « seemed to be in some respects the triumph of humanity. » (2) Here, as Sir Woodbine Parish declares in our own day, in spite of the prejudices of his class, — « If we look at the good which (the Catholic missionaries) did, rather than for the evil which they did not, we shall find that, in the course of about a century and a half, *upwards of a million of Indians* were converted to Christianity by them, and taught to be happy and contented under the mild and peaceful rule of their enlightened and paternal pastors — a blessed lot when contrasted with the savage condition of the unreclaimed tribes around them. » (3) Such was the Mission of Paraguay, of which we are now to attempt to speak, though when we have said all which we know how to say, not the hundredth part will be told.

It was in 1586, as Charlevoix relates, that Don Francisco Victoria, the first Bishop of Tucuman, who had long laboured like the humblest missionary, but hitherto almost alone in the formidable diocese

---

(1) *Relat. delle Missioni*, p. 3.
(2) Ap. Cretineau Joly.
(3) *Buenos Ayres*, etc., ch. XVII, p. 260.

committed to his oversight, implored the Society of Jesus to come to his aid. (1) He was himself a Dominican, « and this shows, » observes Mr Southey, whose evidence we shall once more use, « how highly the Jesuits were at that time esteemed. » From the province of Peru, Barsena and Angulo were despatched; from Brazil, of which Anchieta was at that moment the provincial, five fathers were sent to Tucuman by way of Buenos Ayres, of whom the most celebrated, Manuel de Ortega, was to be associated with Barsena in that famous apostolate with which the names of these two heroes of the Cross are inseparably connected. The ship which carried Ortega and his companions was attacked in the Bay of Rio by the English, — at that time rivals of the Dutch in the war against Catholic missionaries, — and the Fathers, after being treated with the usual indignities, were carried out to sea, and finally flung into a boat, without either oars or provisions, and abandoned to the mercy of the waves. The boat drifted to Buenos Ayres, a distance of more than seven hundred miles, and when her passengers had returned thanks to Him who had saved them by so wonderful a providence, they crossed the Pampas to Tucuman, where they met the Fathers from Peru. (2)

It was Barsena and Ortega who commenced the celebrated Guarani Mission, and afterwards that of the Chiquitos, a nation composed of about thirty tribes, speaking more than twenty different lan-

(1) Charlevoix, *Histoire du Paraguay*, tome I, liv. IV, p. 278.
(2) *Ibid.*, p. 287.

guages, all radically different from the primitive Guarani dialect. Mʳ d'Orbigny observes that, at the present day, the Guarani has become the almost universal language of the natives inhabiting these regions; and an English historian of Brazil notices « the perfection with which the Jesuits spoke the Guaranitic idiom, » (1) of which they published grammars and dictionaries, and which perhaps owes its prevalence to their influence. Barsena spoke also the Tupi, a cognate dialect of the Guarani, and the Toconoté, of which he composed a grammar. Among the innumerable works, of which M. Crétineau Joly says « it would be impossible to number even the titles, » which the Jesuits produced in the department of philology, was a dictionary of the language of the Chiquitos, in three volumes; of which Mʳ d'Orbigny, « the chief authority, » as Dʳ Latham allows, has lately declared, « nothing more complete exists in any American language. » But such works were hardly more than relaxations amid their other toils.

We do not propose to follow Barsena, Ortega, and their companions through all the incidents of their apostolic career, which a few examples will sufficiently illustrate. They find a pestilence raging in the country around Asumpçion, and fling themselves at once according to their custom, into the midst of the danger. Six thousand Indians are baptized, and even Mʳ Southey pauses to acknowledge « the zeal and the intrepid charity with which they sought out the infected, and ministered to the

(1) Henderson's *History of Brazil*, ch. vi, p. 135.

dying.» Barsena, worn out by labour as much as by age, died at Cuzco in 1596, his last missionary work being to convert the sole remaining prince of the family of the Incas of Peru, with whom he shortly after departed to his true home.

For Ortega, many a year of toil, many an hour of danger and suffering, were still in store. Some of the incidents of his laborious life may be compared with any thing which history records, or romance has invented, in the field of perilous adventure. On one occasion, travelling in a plain between the Parana and the Paraguay, with a company of neophytes, they were overtaken by one of those sudden floods with which the lowlands of South America are sometimes devastated. They climbed into trees, but the flood rose higher and higher. They were without food; wild beasts and monstrous serpents, surprised by the deluge, disputed with them their retreat. For two days they remained between life and death. In the middle of the second night, Ortega perceived an Indian swimming towards him. He had volunteered to carry tidings to the Father that three of his catechumens and three Christians, lodged in the branches of a neighbouring tree, were at their last gasp; the first implored baptism, the others absolution. Binding his catechist, who shared his own refuge, more tightly to the branch which he had no longer strength to embrace, and having received his confession, Ortega leaped into the flood. A branch pierced through his thigh, inflicting a wound from which he never recovered, and which remained open for twenty-two years; but he swam on, baptized the three Indians, and saw them fall one after another into the gulf. Their struggle was over, but the three Christians still remained. Exhorting them, amidst the darkness of the night and the rushing of the waters, to fervent acts of contrition, which he recited with them, he saw two of them devoured in their turn by the flood. He had done all that charity could inspire or heroism perform, and returned to his own tree, in time to find his catechist with the water up to his neck. Hoisting him up by a final effort to a higher branch, he watched with him during the remaining hours of the night. On the morrow the flood abated, and the survivors pursued their way.

Ortega was now lamed for life, yet so little did he regard this additional obstacle, that on one occasion he performed a missionary journey of nine hundred miles at once. Every trial which could test his virtue befell him, and in all he was victorious. At Lima, the Holy Office of the Inquisition, to the amazement of the whole country, condemned him to prison. Ortega did not even ask what was his crime. He had been slanderously charged, though he knew it not, with revealing a confession. As he never opened his lips, his silence was accepted as an evidence of guilt. When he had been five months incarcerated, without a murmur or a question, his accuser died; and on his death-bed confessed, that it was Ortega's refusal to give him absolution which tempted him to invent the hateful calumny. Released from prison, with every mark of admiration and reverence, he resumed his apostolic career; and having brought multitudes into the Church, he died in 1622, surviving his companion Barsena by thirty years.

But he was only one in an army of soldiers as valiant as himself. We cannot even name the half of them; let it suffice to attempt a brief record of a few, and of their works. So like were they in their fortitude, their boundless zeal, and inexhaustible charity, that in describing one, we describe all.

Gaspard de Monroy, baffled in one of his journies by the obstinate ferocity of an Omagua chief, who not only rejected the Gospel himself, but threatened the most horrible death to the missionaries and to all who should embrace their doctrine, formed one of those sublime resolutions of which the world applauds with enthusiasm the feeble imitation in its own selfish heroes, but refuses to praise the execution in warriors of a nobler class. He set out alone, and alone he entered the hut of the savage. « You may kill me, » said the Father with a tranquil air, as soon as he stood in the presence of the barbarian, « but you will gain little honour by slaying an unarmed man. If, contrary to my expectation, you give me a hearing, all the advantage will be for yourself; if I die by your hand, an immortal crown awaits me in heaven. »(1) Astonishment disarmed the savage, and admiration kept him silent. Then, with a kind of reluctant awe, he offered to his unmoved visitor a drink from his own cup. A little later, he and his whole tribe were converted.

In 1604, Marcel Lorençana, a friend of Monroy, and Joseph Cataldino, are wrecked in the Paraguay, and only saved by the daring of the Christian Indians. It was Lorençana, — « who was rightly con-

(1) Charlevoix, liv. IV, p. 322.

sidered, » says Mʳ Southey, « an accomplished missionary, » — who obtained permission to go to the Guaranis, when their caciques had publicly announced, — « that they would never be satisfied till they had drank the blood of the last Mahoma, » a recently converted tribe, « out of the skull of the oldest missionary. » The Guaranis became afterwards, as we shall see, a proverb for their christian virtues.

But who shall estimate the toils by which these ferocious savages were converted into men and christians? « The Guarani race, » says a prejudiced English traveller in 1852, — 250 years after Lorençana had dwelt amongst them, « are a noble set of fellows — Roman Catholic the creed. » (1) It was no human power which wrought a change so marvellous and so enduring. « I was informed at Quito, » says the celebrated navigator Ulloa, « that the number of towns of the Guarani Indians in the year 1734 amounted to thirty-two, supposed to contain between thirty and forty thousand families, and that from the increasing prosperity of the Christian religion, they were then deliberating on building three other towns. »(2) From 1610 to 1768, 702,086 Guaranis were baptized by the Jesuits alone, besides those who were admitted into the Church by the Franciscans. (3)

It was Lorençana, for they were the same in all trials, who threatened the judgments of heaven

(1) *Paraguay, Brazil,* etc., by C. B. Mansfield Esq., M. A.; preface p. 9.
(2) Ulloa, *Voyage to S. America*; Pinkerton, vol. XIV, p. 636.
(3) Dobrizhoffer, *Account of the Abipones,* vol. III, p. 417. (1822).

against the Spaniards for their cruelty and avarice; and when commanded by an official of the church in which he was preaching to be silent and leave the pulpit, « immediately obeyed, without the slightest emotion of anger. » « It is said, » observes Southey, ¶ that this moderation affected the Treasurer so much, that he went into the pulpit, and with a loud voice confessed his fault, for having insulted a good man in the discharge of his duty. » A few days after the Treasurer came to a miserable end.

In 1605, Diego de Torrez, arrived in Peru as Provincial of Chili and Paraguay, bringing with him seven Fathers. In 1615, when his term of office expired, his successor de Onate found that the seven had become one hundred and nineteen. In 1617, thirty-seven more entered the field under the conduct of Viana. In 1628, forty-two arrived under Mastrilli. In 1639, thirty came with Diaz Tàno. And so to the last hour they were recruited, more than five thousand Jesuits from Spain alone finding here their cross and their crown.

In 1623, Juan Romero, superior of the Mission of Asumpcion, accepted a task which the viceroy had vainly proposed to his soldiers — that of tracing the Uruguay to its source. « None but a Jesuit, » says Mr Southey, « could make the attempt with any hope of safety » — because they alone were not solicitous about safety. Escorted by a few Indians, he had already advanced a hundred leagues, when he was forced back to Buenos Ayres, unable to communicate his own intrepidity to his followers. It was Romero who replied to some Christians who wished to punish the murderers of Father Gonzalvez, « the blood of martyrs is not to be avenged by blood. » In 1634, after a long life of apostolic toil, he was himself martyred.

Almost every year, from the beginning of this Mission to its close, was consecrated by a martyrdom. Let us notice at least a few of these glorious dates. Gonzalez, a man of illustrious birth, was one of the first. Often he had presented himself alone to the fiercest tribes, and when they lifted the bow or the club, he would say,— « this cross which you see me carry is more powerful than the arms of the Spaniards, and it is my only defence; » and the club would fall harmless to the ground, the arrow would be withdrawn from the bow. In 1615, he was ascending the Parana without any companion. « No European, » said an Indian cacique, who met him on his way, « has ever trodden this shore without dying it with his blood. » « Think not, » answered Gonzalez, « to alarm me with your threats. I am a servant of the only true God, whose ministers count it the greatest happiness which can befall them to shed their blood for Him. » A hundred times he encountered, and survived, the same perils, but his hour came at last. In 1628, on the 15th of November, just as he had finished the Holy Sacrifice, and had quitted the church, the savages rushed upon him; « one blow from a *macana* laid him lifeless upon the ground, and a second beat out his brains. » (1) Father Rodriguez, running out of the church at the cry of the savages, found the same end; and two days later, del Castillo, the companion of both, was also martyred.

(1) Southey, II, 294.

M' Southey, who recounts these events, after Charlevoix and other historians, admits that the barbarians were « impressed with astonishment, » not only by the miracles which are said to have followed the triple sacrifice, but especially by « the public rejoicings in which all classes of men partook, » in celebration of the triumph of the martyrs. « Nor could they contemplate, » says the English writer, « without astonishment the conduct of the Jesuits, their disinterested enthusiasm, their indefatigable perseverance, and the privations and dangers which they endured for no earthly reward. » They became anxious, he adds, « to see these wonderful men, » — as of old the people of Lystra and Derbe thronged round Paul and Barnabas, « saying, in the Lycaonian tongue, the gods are come down to us in the likeness of men, » (1) — and when they « once came within the influence of such superior minds, » even they discerned *Whose* messengers they were, and from murderers became disciples.

Montoya, whom Southey calls one of the most learned men of his age, and who was the author of a grammar of the Guarani language, was a missionary of the same class as Gonzalez and Rodriguez. A Guarani chief, Tayaoba, « who had long been the dread of the Spaniards, » and whose tribe were some of the fiercest of their race, had resolved to kill him. The nation of which this man was the leader was so ferocious in its habits, that « their arrows were headed with the bones of those whom they had slain, and in weaning their children the

(1) *Acts*, XIV, 10.

first food which was substituted for the mother's milk was the flesh of an enemy. » To this tribe, with the more than human intrepidity which marked his order, Montoya presented himself; and when he told them that he had come to teach them how they might be saved from eternal torments, « they replied that he was a liar if he said they were to be eternally tormented, and then let fly a volley of arrows upon him and his attendants. » Seven of the latter were killed, but Montoya, who seems to have been on this occasion miraculously preserved, retired with the rest; and when the savages had devoured the seven, « they expressed their sorrow that they had not tasted priest's flesh at the feast, and had the Jesuit's skull for a cup. » Another chief, Pindobe, « laid in wait for Montoya, for the purpose of eating him. » Yet even Tayaoba and his horrible crew were so impressed, as Mr Southey relates, with the astonishing valour and dignity of the missionaries, that « this fierce warrior sent two of his sons secretly to the Reduction of St. Francis Xavier, to see whether what he had heard of these establishments was true. » A little later, Tayaoba was instructed and baptized by Montoya, « with twenty-eight of his infant children. » (1)

We have mentioned Cataldino, the companion of Lorençana, and the friend of Montoya. In 1623, he was one day superintending the erection of a forest church, when Montoya suddenly appeared before him with the announcement, that a tribe of hostile savages were at his heels. « The will of God be done,

(1) Southey, p. 290.

my dear Father, » said Cataldino, and then quietly resumed his work, without even turning his head towards the yelling crowd, who were rushing upon him. Amazed at his calm indifference, or restrained by an unseen power, they gazed upon him for a while, and then disappeared in the forest.

In 1632, Christoval de Mendoza, the grandson of one of the conquerors of Peru, was martyred by a tribe to whom he had been preaching. « It was his hope and faith, » we are told by Mr Southey, « that his life and death might atone for the offences of his ancestors against those Indians for whose salvation he devoted himself. » « He is said, » observes Dobrizhoffer, « to have baptized ninety-five thousand Indians. » In 1634, Espinosa, who had been the companion of Montoya, Suarez, and Contreras, in all their toils, and whose own life had been a long series of dangers and sufferings, was martyred by the Guapalaches. He was on his road to Santa Fé, whither he was going to beg food and to buy cotton for his neophytes, suffering from the barbarity of the unconverted Indians. He knew his danger, but the famine was urgent, and he hurried on to fall into the snare which the savages had laid for him.

In 1636, Osorio and Ripario, who had founded a new Reduction in the country of the Ocloias, were tortured to death by the Chiriguanes. The former appears to have received a revelation of the death by which he was to glorify God, since he had himself announced it beforehand in a letter to the celebrated Cardinal de Lugo. (1)

(1) Charlevoix, liv. IX, p, 377.

In 1639, Alfaro gained in his turn the crown of martyrdom; and the death of so many victims had already been so prolific, according to the law of Christian Missions, in graces to the heathen, that even at this early date there were already twenty-nine separate Reductions in the two provinces of Parana and Uruguay, in which more than three hundred thousand Indians had learned to practise all the virtues of the Christian life.

Let us pass at once to the close of the seventeenth century, and take up the narrative from the year 1683, in which Ruiz and Solinas, accompanied by a secular priest, Don Ortiz de Zaraté, who aspired to the crown of martyrdom, entered the mountain region of Chaco. Already they had formed a new Reduction, under the title of St. Raphael, in which four hundred families were assembled, and Ruiz had departed for Tucuman, when Solinas and Zaraté were attacked by the Tobas and Macobis, and on the 17th of March, 1686, fell under their arrows and clubs.

In 1690, Mascardi and Quilelmo, who had penetrated almost to the southern extremity of the continent, were martyred by the Patagonians, that so the blood of apostles might sanctify the land throughout its length and breadth; while Father Joseph Cardiel « was reduced to such straits as to be obliged to feed on grass, unless he preferred dying of emptiness. » (1)

In 1694, some of the best and bravest of this company of preachers, — de Arce, Centeno, Hervas, de Zéa, d'Avila, and others, — formed new Reductions on every side, amid perils which had no terrors for

(1) Dobrizhoffer, p. 150.

such men, though most of them were destined to lose
their lives in the work. Twice de Arce attempted in
vain to subdue the fierce Chiriguanas, « one of the
most numerous and formidable of all the South
American nations. » They are supposed, Mr Southey
relates, to have killed in the course of two centuries
« more than one hundred and fifty thousand Indians.»
When the missionary sought to arrest their attention
by warning them of the fire of hell, they replied
disdainfully, « that they should find means of putting
it out. » So his superiors removed him for a time,
and sent him with Ignatius Chomé, « one of the
most intelligent and most meritorious of the Jesuits,»
to the Chiquitos. Chomé had composed a grammar
and a dictionary of both the Zamuco and Chiquito
tongues; had translated Thomas à Kempis into the
latter; and written a history of their nation. It is a
circumstance worthy of remark, that of the seven
companions who accompanied de Arce in this attempt, not two were of the same race. They were a
Sardinian, a Neapolitan, a Belgian, an Austrian, a
Bohemian, a Biscayan, and a Spaniard of La Mancha.
« So curiously, » says Mr Southey, « was this extraordinary Society composed of men of all nations.
And what a pre-eminent knowledge of mankind must
the Jesuits have possessed from this circumstance
alone; this knowledge, of all others the most difficult
of acquisition, was thus acquired by them as a
mother tongue, and they were fitted for missionaries
and statesmen almost without study. » Yet this gentleman, intoxicated with self-love, thought himself
qualified to pass sentence upon them all, and to
rebuke their « superstition » and « idolatry ! »

De Arce was now amongst the Chiquitos. Abandoned to the most extraordinary and eccentric superstitions, which it would be unprofitable to describe in detail, and brutalised by almost perpetual intoxication, they had killed the first missionaries who went amongst them, and flattered themselves that they were now delivered for ever from their importunate presence. But they were saved by the very blood which they had shed, as Saul owed his conversion to the martyrdom of St. Stephen. « From their first establishment, » says the English historian, « the Chiquito Missions were uniformly prosperous in all things. Here, as in other parts of America, the Jesuits were usefully, meritoriously, and piously employed; ready, at all times, to encounter sufferings, perils, and death itself, with heroic and Christian fortitude. » And so they converted the whole nation; and with such lasting results, that as M. d'Orbigny observes, the Chiquitos, « happier than other tribes, all live to this day in the Missions, under the old form of government established by the Jesuit Fathers. » (1) It was amongst the Chiquitos that this traveller heard the ecclesiastical music which filled even his fastidious ear with admiration.

De Arce, to whom we must return for a moment, aspiring after new dangers and more arduous toils, now entered for the third time the territory of the Chiriguanas. It was almost certain death, but he was one of those missionaries who can say with St. Paul, who finished his career by martyrdom as they did,

(1) Tome IV, p. 260.

« The charity of Christ constraineth me. » We have no space to relate his labours and tribulations, which were so fruitful, that when, at a later period, the enemies of these apostolic warriors came to count the final results of their warfare, they found forty thousand Chiriguanas, now fervent and docile Christians, collected together in a single Mission. De Arce died as he had lived, and as it was fitting that such a man should die, martyred by the Payaguas, in 1717, together with his fellow missionaries, Maco, Sylva, and de Blende.

Lucas Cavallero, also destined for martyrdom, was labouring at the same time amongst the Puraxis. Unable to resist his fearless charity, and captivated by his preaching and example, they also are won to Christianity and civilization. It would have been reasonable that he should have reposed, at least for a time, amongst these now peaceful neophytes; but he was willing to postpone thoughts of ease to another life, and once more plunged into the thick of the battle. In vain the Puraxis implore him not to expose himself to the fury of the barbarians. He leaves them his blessing, and confiding them to other pastors, hastens to the Manacicas. They also are subdued by his word, and he is next among the Sibacas. Everywhere he is victorious; and as the Quiriquicas had now become the most implacable enemies of his neophytes, and were thirsting for his own blood, he presents himself among them. Such were the simple tactics of these soldiers of the Cross. They ask where danger is to be found, only to confront it. Four other tribes in succession are evangelised by the same indomitable missionary, and still he survives. But such a career could not last for ever. His brethren, who knew how to judge apostolic gifts, were accustomed to say of him, « that St. Francis Xavier had no more perfect imitator than Lucas Cavallero. » On one occasion he was saluted by a shower of arrows, but they inflicted no wound, though they rained on him from every side. At length his hour arrived, and he found amongst the Puyzocas, in 1711, the crown of martyrdom for which he had so long and so patiently laboured.

Let us notice also Father Falconer, an English Jesuit, « of great skill in medicine, » who succeeded in founding a mission in the Pampas, which he called Nuestra Senora del Pilar, and whose manner of life is thus described by the writer from whom Maria Theresa of Austria used to delight to hear such narratives, when he had been banished from America. « Wandering over the plains with his Indians to kill horseflesh, having no plate, either of pewter or wood, he always, in place thereof, made use of his hat, which grew at length so greasy, that it was devoured while he slept by the wild dogs with which the plains are over-run. » (1)

Cyprian Baraza, says Mr Southey, « was perhaps the most enlightened Jesuit that ever laboured in South America. » (2) He had set out from Lima with the martyr del Castillo, and ascended in a canoe the river Guapay. For twelve days they urged on their frail boat, till they reached the camp of the

(1) Dobrizhoffer, p. 145.
(2) Vol. III, ch. xxxiv, p. 198.

tribe whom they sought. It was among the Moxos, in the country to the south of the Portuguese territory of Mato Grosso, that Baraza was destined to toil for twenty-seven years. Recalled for a moment to Santa Cruz by his superiors, in consequence of a fever which had reduced him to what appeared incurable debility, he spent the long days of his convalescence in learning the art of weaving, that he might introduce it among his future disciples. At length he was able to resume the apostolate which had been interrupted, and found himself amongst a people so ignorant and barbarous that they had not even any chiefs, lived only for rapine and murder, and hunted men instead of beasts for food. Among these degraded savages this man of profound learning and elegant tastes consented to spend his life; sharing their filthy lodging; studying all their caprices; imitating their habits; and descending himself almost to the condition of a savage, in order to raise them to the dignity of Christians. And this life, for the love of God, he led for more than a quarter of a century; till on the 16th of September, 1702, being then in his sixty-first year, he was martyred by the Baures, whom he had visited in the hope of converting them, and who by his death were won to Christ.

Like all his fellows, he had not only planted but reaped, even in this rugged soil. At his death, fifteen colonies of Christian Moxos had been formed, from twenty to thirty miles apart from each other. « With his own hand, » observes Mr Markham, « he baptized 110,000 heathens. He found the Moxos an ignorant people, more savage and cruel than the wild beasts, and he left them *a civilised community*, established in villages, and converted to Christianity. » (1) The churches, of which he was often himself the architect, « were large, well built, and richly ornamented, » says M* Southey. The Moxos, once so barbarous, had become, as the same writer relates, not only excellent workmen, but even skilful artists. « Cotton was raised in all the settlements, » an active commerce created, and habits of intelligent industry formed. « More comforts, » says M* Southey, « were found in the Missions of the Moxos and Baures than in the Spanish capital of Santa Cruz de la Sierra. » (2) And the apostle who had accomplished this amazing work, and who, during many years, had permitted himself no other couch than the bare ground or the steps of his church, was deemed happy and glorious by all his companions, because in his old age he attained to martyrdom, and after devoting all his faculties for forty years to the service of his Master, was beaten to death by the clubs of savages.

A century after his martyrdom, they were still, says M* Markham, « a thriving, industrious people; *famous* as carpenters, weavers, and agriculturists; » and an Anglo-Indian writer, alluding in 1857 to this prodigious and lasting work of civilisation throughout the whole southern continent, asks how it can be explained that even « the slaves and mestijos of S. America should be able to purchase of one single class of English manufactures, *twenty four times as*

---

(1) *Introd*. p. XLI.
(2) Vol. III, ch. XLII, p. 606.

much as the free, enlightened, and happily guided
Hindus ! » (1)

Such as Baraza, and Cavallero, and Espinosa, they
continued to the end. Dobrizhoffer, the apostle of
the Abipones, « was contented, » says M*r* Southey,
though he hated and reviled the very men whom he
was forced to applaud, « to employ, in labouring
among these savages, under every imaginable circumstance of discomfort and discouragement, talents
which would have raised him to distinction in the
most enlightened parts of Europe. » Hénart, once
a page of honour in the court of Henri IV, was a
man of the same school, and « chose the riches of
Christ » before the favour of the most popular of
earthly kings; and Herréra, in whom the most
learned men of Europe would have recognised a
master, but whom the Abipones slew; and Hervas,
who died of fatigue, after all his immense labours,
by the banks of an obscure stream ; and d'Aguilar,
who governed the Reductions of the Parana, and at
the head of seven thousand Christian Indians saved
Peru to the crown of Spain; and Martin Xavier, a
kinsman of St. Francis, who, with Father Balthasar
Sena, was cruelly starved to death; and Sylva and
Niebla, both martyred by the Payaguas; and Arias
and de Arenas, who won the same crown; and
Ugalde, whom the Mataguyos killed. Not inferior to
these were Machoni and Montijo, the apostles of the
Lulles; and Julian de Lizardi, who was martyred
by the Chiriguanes, his body being found pierced
with arrows, and his breviary lying open by his side

(1) Mead, *The Sepoy Revolt*, ch. xxvii, p. 347.

at the office for the dead, as if he had chaunted his own Requiem; and Castanarez, who converted the Zamucos, when they had martyred Albert Romero, and was slaughtered himself, in 1744, by the Mataguyos, after forty years of toil; and Joseph de Quiroga, one of the most famous seamen of Spain before he put on the habit of St. Ignatius; and Juan Pastor, who at seventy-three years of age presented himself alone in the camp of the Mataguyos; and Juan Vaz, perhaps a kinsman of that other Vaz of whom we heard in Ceylon, who died in old age of pestilence while ministering to the sick; and Alvarez, who dwelt alone among the fierce Caaïquas, whom the Spaniards could never reduce, and dared not provoke; and Philip Suarez, the martyr; and Altamirano, and Bartholomew Diaz, and a thousand more, whom we can neither name nor praise, — whom God made what they were, who did all their works for His sake alone, and who found in Him their eternal reward.

We have still to show, in conclusion, and we shall be able to do so by the testimony of enemies, what were the actual and final results accomplished in Paraguay by the labours at which we have now glanced. But first let it be permitted to add a word upon the men themselves, of whom we have noticed only an inconsiderable number, because their lives sufficiently represent and illustrate those of their companions, and because thousands in that age left no other memorial on earth by which their passage may now be traced than the multitude of disciples, from Canada to China, and from Paraguay to Abyssinia, who by their ministry were « renewed in the spirit of their minds, » and gathered into the fold of Christ.

It would be a mere indiscretion to suggest reflections which the deeds of this great company of apostles, who will be imitated by Catholic missionaries to the end of time, will awaken in every Christian soul, and which they kindled even in the breast of the cannibal savage, half beast and *half idiot, who* wandered by the banks of the Parana and *the Uru*guay, guided only, till these men stood before him, by the instincts of an animal, and the passions of a demon. But it is well to observe, in contemplating the supernatural virtues of which we have witnessed the action, that they were the natural fruit of gifts and graces which were not only fair to look upon, and mighty to subdue the arts of the wicked one, and to unbind in every land the fetters of his victims; but which had a yet deeper and more awful significance, as even the barbarians of Asia and America understood, inasmuch as they revealed the immediate and intimate Presence of God, as surely as the golden-fringed cloud tells of the great orb behind, whose rays it obscures but cannot hide. These men were mighty, but evidently not by their own strength; valiant, because they feared nothing but sin; patient, for they walked in the steps of the Crucified; and wise, beyond the wisdom of the children of Adam, because to them it had been said, by Him who once gave the same assurance to earlier Missionaries, « It is not you that speak, but the Spirit of your Father that speaketh in you. » (1)

Yet it was at the very moment in which the loving

(1) S. Matt. x, 20.

Providence of God was sending forth into all lands, from the crowded cities of the furthest East to the solitudes of the unknown West, such a multitude of apostles as the world had never before seen; and that His Spirit, with a mighty inspiration, was filling thousands at once with such graces, and leading them to such victories, as men had almost begun to reckon among the impossible glories of an earlier age; that a people of Saxon origin, newly separated from the Church to which they owed all their past happiness, all their noblest institutions, all their knowledge, and all their civilisation, were filling the air with imprecations against the very religion upon which the Almighty was once more impressing, before the face of the Gentiles now entering into *their* forfeited inheritance, the seal of His august sanction. It was at this time, when every pagan land was being newly fertilised with the blood of apostles, who died for the name of Jesus, and would have died, — as More, and Fisher, Campion and Parsons, and many more, died in England, — as joyously and exultingly, for the Church which He illumined with His presence, or for the least of her doctrines; that the founders and promoters of the Anglican schism, less discerning than the pagans of India or China, more blind and perverse than the savages of Brazil and Paraguay, were blaspheming the faith which the Hindoo and the Omagua could no longer resist, when they had once heard the more than human wisdom which proclaimed it to them. It was in the very age in which St. Francis began that immortal apostolate, and those stupendous labours, which were to be continued during two centuries, and in which his brethren and kinsmen were to win to the Church more souls than all the powers of hell were about to snatch from her; that Cranmer, in language which none but an apostate could use, was stirring up the English against the Church which he called « the cursed synagogue of Antichrist; » (1) that Ridley was reviling her, with the accents of an energumen, as « the Beast of Babylon, that devilish drab, whore, and beast; » (2) that Becon, the intimate of Cranmer, was shrieking like a maniac against « the pestiferous and damnable sect of the papists; » and declaring, in hideous words, that « the Sacrifice of the Mass came from hell; » (3) that Jewel, as if the powers of darkness used his mouth for a trumpet, was calling the Vicar of Christ, « the Man of Perdition; » (4) that Grindal, who was called « Archbishop of Canterbury, » was commanding all the altars in England, upon which the Adorable Sacrifice of the New Law had once been offered, » to be utterly taken down, broken, defaced, *and bestowed to some common use;* » (5) that Sandys, who was styled « Archbishop of York, « was raving like one possessed against « that synagogue of Satan, that man of sin, that triple-crowned beast, that double sworded tyrant, that thief and murderer, that adversary unto Christ; » and lastly, that the Anglican Church, the

---

(1) *Against Transubstantiation*, book, II, p. 238, ed. Parker Society.
(2) *Piteous Lamentation*, p. 50; *Letters*, p. 409.
(3) *The Jewel of Joy*, p. 449; Cf pp. 264, 380.
(4) *Zurich Letters*, pp. 33, 47.
(5) *Remains*, p. 134; App. p. 480.
(6) *Sermon* xx, p. 389.

creation of these very men, was exhorting all her ministers diligently to teach the people of England, whether they would hear or no, that, till Cranmer and Beza arose, « *the whole world* had been sunk in the pit of damnable idolatry by the space of nine hundred years and odd! » (1)

We have heard the blasphemy, and have seen how God rebuked it. It was at this moment, long expected by the heathen world, that He resolved to create twice ten thousand apostles in the same hour, who should gather from East and West, from lands hitherto unknown, a new company of guests to that divine banquet which « they who were invited. » (2) might never more taste, and preach in His name to nations lying in the shadow of death the mystery of salvation which England was now rejecting. And that all men might surely know whose messengers they were, He clothed them in armour brought out of the innermost sanctuary of Heaven, and endowed them with gifts which the Seraphim might have consented to share. Once again the world saw an army of apostles, filled with the zeal of St. Paul, the tenderness of St. Peter, and the charity of St. John; austere as the Baptist, who fed on locusts and wild honey, yet merciful to the weak and infirm; ready to die, like St. Stephen, at the word of their Master, and rewarded in death with the same beatific vision which consoled his agony and theirs. England had begun, for the first time in her history, to invoke maledictions on the Church, and this was God's answer.

(1) *Homily on Peril of Idolatry.*
(2) S. Luke. xiv, p. 24.

It is time to bring our account of the missions of Paraguay to a close. In estimating the actual fruits of those missions, it is not the evidence of Catholic writers which we shall interrogate. Protestant authorities, many of whom would read with sympathy, even if they hesitated to repeat, the horrible language of the authors of their religion, will tell us what the Missionaries really effected in South America, and even, as far as such men could understand them, by what means they obtained their success. Mr Southey, who uses such, « intemperate language, » as an English protestant remarks, that « the general circulation of his book is rendered impossible; » (1) who declares that Vieyra, and Baraza, and Cavallero, and the rest, « never scrupled at falsehood when it was to serve a pious purpose; » who relates that Paraguay exhibited « the naked monstrosity of Romish superstition; » and who describes the sacred mysteries of the Christian Altar in terms which it would be profanation to repeat, and which the evil spirits would not dare to employ, because *they* « believe and tremble; » will be our most appropriate witness. Here is his summary of the labours of the Missionaries, as respects their geographical limits.

« A chain of Missions had now been established in all parts of this great continent. Those of the Spaniards from Quito met those of the Portuguese from Para, » thus connecting the Pacific with the Atlantic. « The Missions on the Orenoco communicated with those of the Negro and the Orellana. The

(1) *Voyage to Brazil*, by Lady Calcott, p. 13.

Moxo Missions communicated with the Chiquito, the Chiquito with the Reductions in Paraguay, and from Paraguay the indefatigable Jesuits sent their labourers into the Chaco, and among the tribes who possessed the wide plains to the South and West of Buenos Ayres. Had they not been interrupted in their exemplary career, by measures equally impolitic and iniquitous, it is possible that ere this they might have completed the conversion and civilisation of all the native tribes; and probable that they would have saved the Spanish colonies from the immediate horrors and barbarizing consequences of a civil war. » (1)

Let us hear next what he says of their converts, who once wandered naked through the woods, fed on human flesh, and had almost lost the instincts of humanity. « At the close of the eighteenth century, the Indians of these reductions were *a brave, an industrious, and comparatively a polished people.* They were good carvers, good workers in metal, good handicrafts in general, and the women manufactured calico of the finest quality, etc. etc. » (2)

Again. « Considerable progress had been made both in the useful and ornamental arts. Besides carpenters, masons, and blacksmiths, they had turners, carvers, painters, and gilders; they cast bells and built organs... They were taught enough of mechanics to construct horse-mills, enough of hydraulics to

---

(1) Vol. III, p. 372. « In fatto non v'ha in tutta l'America meridionale terra alcuna, dove non sieno penetrati i missionarii, e quasi nessuna tribù, a cui non sia stato bandito il Vangelo. » *Storia Universale delle Cattoliche Missioni*, vol. I, cap. IV, p. 162.

(2) P. 842.

raise water for irrigating the lands, and supplying their public cisterns. A Guarani » — we know what he had been in his unconverted state — « however nice the mechanism, could imitate any thing which was set before him. »(1)

Once more. So universal was the industry of these populous communities, once disdainful of all toil but that of the chase, that the commerce of South America received a development, under the prudent direction of their paternal guides, which even the political economists of our own day might contemplate with admiration, — if such philosophers could applaud a state of society in which none were poor and none rich; in which each worked for all; where there was labour without hardship, and obedience without oppression ; and in which was exhibited, on a vast scale, that wonderful spectacle which made even Mr Southey exclaim,— « Never has there existed any other society in which the welfare of the subjects, temporal and eternal, has been the sole object of the government ! » — and which forced from such a man the confession, that « the inhabitants, for many generations, enjoyed a greater exemption from physical and moral evil *than any other inhabitants of the globe.* »(2)

We might stop here, dismissing all further details as superfluous, at least in such a sketch as this; but the educational and religious aspects of these communities claim also a moment's attention. « In every Reduction, » says Mr Southey, not only was the

(1) Vol. II, ch. xxiv, p. 350.
(2) *Ibid.*, p. 360.

knowledge of reading, writing, and arithmetic literally universal, « but there were some Indians who were able to read Spanish and Latin as well as their own tongue. » And as at Carthagena, at the other extremity of the continent, a university was founded under the immediate sanction of the Sovereign Pontiff; so at Cordoba, as Mr Southey observes « the university became famous in South America. »

Lastly, the influence of religion among this vast population of converted savages was so powerful and all-pervading, so utterly was vice in all its forms banished from among them, that in 1721, the Bishop of Buenos Ayres, Don Pedro Faxardo, could report to Philip V of Spain; « Their innocence is so universal, that I do not believe a mortal sin is committed in these Reductions in the course of a year. » (1)

Mr Southey offers an explanation, after his manner, of this almost fabulous innocence. « Few vices, » says this gentleman with apparent seriousness, « could exist in such communities. Avarice and ambition were excluded; there was little room for envy, and little to excite hatred and malice. » He forgets that there was human nature, with all its frailties; and that the enemy of man, who found an entrance even into Paradise, had probably free access to Paraguay. « Drunkenness, » he continues, in order to prove that even the virtues of these Catholic Indians were not merits, « was effectually prevented by the prohibition of fermented liquors. » Yet he relates in his next volume, forgetting, as such witnesses are apt to do, what he had previously said, that « the In-

(1) Charlevoix, liv. V, p. 94.

dians of these Reductions cultivated the cane, both for sugar *and rum;* and *distilleries,* which in most places produce little but evil, may be regarded with complacency there, because the moderate use of ardent spirits appears to counteract the ill effects of marshy situations. » (1)

Finally, as the absence of avarice, ambition, envy, and drunkenness, were perfectly natural in vast communities of many thousand persons, recently recruited from utter barbarism, and cannot reasonably be deemed Christian virtues; so the crowning grace of purity was also, according to this Protestant authority, a mere result of « precaution, » and of « the spirit of monachism.» Besides, as he gravely observes, « their idolatry came in aid of this precautionary system; » which means, it appears, that « no person who had in the slightest degree trespassed against the laws of modesty could be deemed worthy to be accounted among the servants of the Queen of Virgins. » And so, in all these great communities, thanks to « monachism » and « idolatry, » the law of chastity was kept inviolate.

And now we have heard enough. For two hundred years this work had been in progress, and these were its fruits. Once more the promise had been fulfilled which said of the apostles of the Church, « *They* shall build the places that have been waste from of old. And they shall know their seed among the Gentiles, and their offspring in the midst of peoples. » Once more the Missionaries of the Cross had glorified their Master by one of those victories, of which

(1) Ch. XLIV, p. 842.

the philosophers and the philanthropists of this world are always dreaming, always announcing the future promise to their credulous disciples, but always abandoning in impotent despair. Once more the Church had perfected one of those seemingly impossible triumphs which man may never compass or achieve by his own power; and of which all the stages — the first conception, the gradual progress, and the final execution — are traversed only by the succour and the inspiration of the Most High. But even the Church does not always triumph, or how would she imitate the life of her Lord? Like Him, to day she is saluted with Hosannahs, to morrow she puts on the Crown of Thorns. It was now the enemy's turn to triumph. Here, as in other lands, he understood, that if he would scatter the sheep, he must first smite the shepherds. While they watched the fold, no irreparable evil could befall the flock. Often, during those two hundred years, the evil one had tried to force an entrance. At one time, his agents massacred the pastors who kept such careful watch, but a moment after their place was supplied by others as vigilant and undaunted. At another, he employed corrupt Europeans — filled with jealousy and malice, furious because the Indian had found a refuge from their oppression, or smarting with the shame of baffled cupidity — to plot their destruction. In the single year 1630, the infamous Paulistas — Portuguese and other slave traders, of various nations — carried off by force fifteen hundred Indians from the Reductions. Fathers Mansilla and Manceta, as M*r* Southey relates, « had the courage to follow them as close as they could, trusting to what they might find in the woods for subsistence, and administering such consolation as they could to the dying, with whom the road was tracked. » But these ravages, formidable as they were, could not mar the work of the Missionaries; who during two centuries were affectionately supported in all their conflicts by the sovereigns of Spain and Portugal, and often led their Indian soldiers to victory against the enemies of religion and monarchy, when no other power in America could have saved either. The day was now at hand when the same troops would have fought with equal valour to save their Fathers from outrage, if the latter had not refused to use in their own defence the forces which they had constantly employed with success in that of others. « Upwards of a hundred thousand civilized Indians, » says a Protestant author, « were ready to take arms in defence of their spiritual leaders, and it was only by their own earnest entreaties to their flocks that tranquillity was preserved. » (1)

We have seen in the earlier chapters of this history how the Christian Missions, just when they seemed about to embrace the whole heathen world, were suddenly overthrown in every land; not by the failure of apostolic labourers, — who were never so numerous as at that hour, — but by a conspiracy which had its agents in every court of Europe, and which enlisted the eager sympathies of statesmen, philosophers, and infidels, who attacked the Church through the Society of Jesus, and who despaired of executing the selfish or criminal projects which they

(1) Mansfield, p. 443.

had formed, so long as they were confronted on all sides by an army of indomitable warriors — more sagacious than the statesmen, more subtle than the philosophers, more courageous than the infidels — whom they could neither divide by policy, nor bribe by favour, nor terrify by threats. And so these puritans of a pantheistic civilisation, invoking with cynical hypocrisy the names of liberty justice and progress, and despairing of victory by any other means over their patient and accomplished adversaries, had recourse at last to vulgar and ignoble violence, the strategy of the bandit, and the craft of the highwayman. It was the only weapon in their armoury, and they used it without remorse.

« The Jesuits were hurried into exile, » says Mr Southey, « with circumstances of great barbarity; » and then he shows, that even aged men, who had grown infirm in the work of the Missions, actually died in the arms of the soldiers, as they were dragged along the road. And the same scenes occurred in every part of America. « Throughout Chili, » says another English Protestant, « in deep midnight, the military governor of every town, attended by a military guard, took possession of every convent. The manner of performing the act was disgraceful to those who ordered its execution; it bore the appearance of performing an act of which they were ashamed. » (1) Out of thirty, who were despatched in one vessel from Buenos Ayres, « only five, » says Dobrizhoffer, « reached Cadiz half alive. » (2)

(1) Miers. vol. II, ch. XVIII, p. 208.
(2) Vol. III, p. 415.

Let us add, in conclusion, a few additional testimonies from Protestant writers, who have honestly confessed not only the virtues of the Missionaries, but the iniquity of the charges brought against them, the malignity of the treatment which they received, and the woful results of their exile.

They were charged with amassing riches, and even Southey says, — « that the Jesuits accumulated nothing from Paraguay is most certain. » They were libelled for excluding the Spanish language from the Missions, and Southey observes, — « malice has seldom been more stupid in its calumnies. » They were taunted with making converts « by violence, » though they were every hour at the mercy of their own disciples, and the same unfriendly writer replies, — « persuasion was their only weapon. » They were accused of seeking to form a « principality, » and of governing it independently of Spain, and of their own Order in Europe, and even Mr Southey answers ; « The charge will in itself appear incredible to those who reflect upon the character and constitution of the Company. » They were all linked together, he observes, by « perfect unity of views and feelings; » whereas the very design imputed to them, « if successful, would in its inevitable consequences have separated the province from the general system, and deprived the Jesuits there of those supplies without which their Order in that country would in one generation have been extinct. They had their root in Europe; and had the communication been cut off, it would have been barking the tree. » (1)

(1) Vol. III, ch. xx, p. p. 501.

Yet a respectable Anglican clergyman, reviving the very calumnies which even a Southey despised, and which the remorse of their original authors long since retracted and disavowed, was not ashamed to say a few years ago before the University of Oxford, as if sure of the sympathetic applause of such an audience, that « *it was not the Church* that was planted among the natives of Paraguay, » though that Mission was governed by Bishops and constituted by an Ecclesiastical Council, « but a *principality* of Jesuits! » (1) So true it is that, in our days, the clergy of this particular school, living only for their own theories and loving only their own inventions, abandoning even the pretence of reverence which they once affected for the Mother of Saints, and surpassing in intemperance the most thoughtless of their sect, have been willing, out of hatred to the Church which has only compassion for them, to catch up the abandoned weapons of the infidels of the 18th century, of the very men upon whose malignant fables the contempt of civilised Europe has long ago done justice.

Let us continue the chain of testimony which this digression has interrupted. « The King of Spain, » says M* Prichard, « yielding to the advice of the enemies of religion and of monarchy, ordered their expulsion from Paraguay, and left 120,000 converts from one single aboriginal nation destitute of the advice and guidance of their spiritual and temporal instructors. » (2)

(1) Grant's *Bampton Lectures*, v, 152.
(2) Section 47, p. 466.

Sir Woodbine Parish, who ridicules, like M⁁ Southey, the hollow pretexts of their enemies, and eloquently describes the true aim and character of the Missions, says ; « This was that *imperium in imperio* which once excited the astonishment of the world, and the jealousy of princes. How little cause they had to be alarmed by it was best proved by the whole fabric falling to pieces on the removal of a few poor old priests. A more inoffensive community never existed. » And then he generously adds, — « It was an experiment on a vast scale, originating in the purest spirit of Christianity, to civilise and render useful hordes of savages who otherwise would, like the rest of the aborigines, have been miserably exterminated in war or slavery. » He even confesses, that « its remarkable success excited envy and jealousy, and caused a thousand idle stories to be circulated as to the political views of the Jesuits in founding such establishments; » and that these very rumours, invented by malice, and propagated by selfish cupidity, « contributed, there is no doubt, to hasten the downfall of their Order. » (1)

« It is not easy, » is the confession of a more prejudiced writer, « to find a parallel in history to the act of gigantic self-abnegation, so to speak, by which the Order renounced without a blow a dominion so vast, and seemingly so firmly founded, as that which they exercised in Paraguay. » (2)

Even Robertson, though incapable of appreciating such men or their works, vindicates them from the

(1) *Buenos Ayres*, ch. XXII, p. 256.
(2) Mansfield, *ubi supra*.

calumnies of their implacable persecutors. « It is, » he observes, « in the new world that the Jesuits have exhibited the most wonderful display of their abilities, and have contributed most effectually to the benefit of the human species... The Jesuits alone made humanity the object of their settling there. »(1)

Sir James Mackintosh, a man who better deserved the title of philosopher, and who was able to admire « the heroic constancy with which they suffered martyrdom, » declares, in his turn, — that « the Jesuits alone, the great Missionaries of that age, either repaired or atoned for the evils caused by the misguided zeal of their countrymen ; » and after quoting the well-known eulogy of Lord Bacon, he adds, — « Such is the disinterested testimony of the wisest of men to the merits of the Jesuits. » (2)

A multitude of American writers of our own day have delivered the same verdict; let the testimony of one suffice. « Their missionary zeal among the Indians in the remotest provinces, » says a Secretary of Legation in Mexico, « was unequalled. The winning manners of the cultivated gentlemen who composed this powerful order in the Catholic Church gave them a proper and natural influence with the children of the forest, whom they had withdrawn from idolatry and partially civilised. » And then, denying « that there was just cause » for the affected « alarm » of the king of Spain, and hinting that « he and his council were willing to embrace any pretext to rid his colonial possessions of the Jesuits; » this

(1) *Charles V*, book VI, vol. VI, p. 203. (1817).
(2) *Works*, vol. II, pp. 250, 1.

gentleman notices, with just indignation, that « all expression of public sentiment, as well as amiable feeling, at this daring act against the worthiest and most benevolent clergymen of Mexico was effectually stifled. » (1) Sir Woodbine Parish, an English diplomatic agent, repeats the same reproach, when he quotes the touching protest addressed by the Christian Indians of San Luis to the Governor of Buenos Ayres, in 1768. « Our children, who are in the country and in the towns, when they return and find not the Sons of St. Ignatius, will flee away to the deserts and to the forests to do evil. » The only reply of the sycophant Bucarelli was to send troops against them, but, adds Sir Woodbine, « he found them not in arms, but in tears. » (2)

Lastly, another English writer of our own day, retracting with a noble candour earlier language, thus estimates the Society whose labours he had once misjudged. « I have formerly ranked its operations in Paraguay and Brazil amongst those of its worst ambition; but more extended inquiry has convinced me that, in this instance, I, in common with others, did them grievous wrong... Their conduct in these countries is one of the most illustrious examples of Christian devotion — Christian patience — Christian benevolence and disinterested virtue upon record ». And then he adds, in words which he seems to have adopted from another, and which may fitly conclude these impressive confessions ; « No men ever behaved

(1) *Mexico*, *Aztec*, *Spanish*, *and Republican*, by Brantz Mayer, vol. I, ch. XIII, p. 243. (1852).
(2) Ubi supra.

with greater equanimity, under undeserved disgrace, than the last of the Jesuits; and the extinction of the order was a heavy loss to literature, a great evil to the Catholic world, and an irreparable injury to the tribes of South America. » (1)

The evil was consummated, and, as Sir Woodbine Parish observes, « upwards of a million of Indians » were now deprived of the pastors and guides by whom they had been, as it were, created anew; and whose gentle rule they obeyed with such docile and loving confidence, that, as Ulloa relates, « even if they had been punished unjustly, they would have believed that they deserved it. » We have seen, by the unsuspicious testimony of Protestant writers, to what degree of civilization they had attained. No longer dwelling in huts composed of branches, or lying naked on the untilled earth, from which they gathered only the fruits which it spontaneously offered, the Fathers had taught them to build stone houses, and to roof them with tiles; agriculture, directed by science and aided by an effective system of irrigation, gave birth to new products of which they had not suspected the existence; their wide pastures nourished vast herds of cattle; public magazines afforded a safeguard against famine, and carefully organised hospitals a refuge against disease or accident; noble churches, decorated with no mean skill by their own art, displayed treasures of silk and jewels and gold which only their own intelligent industry, and the profits of a well regulated commerce, had enabled them to procure; they had troops and

(1) Howitt, *Colonization and Christianity*, ch. x, pp. 121, 141.

arsenals, ever at the service of the king, never employed against him; they had become, by the prudent cultivation of their own resources, almost independent of foreign productions; they grew their own sugar and their own tea, and distilled enough alcohol for the wise uses to which they applied it; they were artists and manufacturers, as well as soldiers and herdsmen; they made all kinds of musical instruments, even the organs whose tones filled their vast churches, and sung with a sweetness and precision which modern travellers still attest with admiration; and lastly, though the ecclesiastical Council of Lima, — mindful, perhaps, that they had but lately been hunters of men, and eaters of human flesh, — prescribed the most rigorous precautions in admitting the Indians to the Sacraments, even refusing Holy Communion till after seven years of blameless life, so great was their purity and devotion that these injunctions had become well nigh superfluous, and the Bishop of Buenos Ayres, who had minutely examined them by virtue of his office as « apostolic visitor, » could report to astonished Europe, « They form perhaps the most precious portion of the flock of Jesus Christ. »

And now the apostles, who out of such rude materials had built up so fair an edifice, were taken from them. « Here ended, » says M*r* Southey, whom we quote for the last time, « the prosperity of these celebrated communities. The ' administrators ' — who now supplanted the missionaries — « *hungry ruffians from the Plata*, or fresh from Spain, neither knew the native language, nor had patience to acquire it. »

Before these « rapacious and brutal » agents, emissaries of rapine, fraud, and obscenity, the Indian sunk down in despair, or fled away in dismay. The administrators were appointed, as the new authorities, — apt representatives of Pombal, Choiseul, and Aranda, — gravely announced, « to purify the Reductions from tyranny; » and the immediate result of their presence was, that « the arts which the Jesuits had introduced were neglected and forgotten; their gardens lay waste, their looms fell to pieces; and in these communities, where the inhabitants, for many generations, had enjoyed a greater exemption from physical and moral evil than any other inhabitants of the globe, the people were now made vicious and miserable. Their only alternative was, to remain to be treated like slaves, or fly to the woods, and take their chance as savages. »

Such is the last chapter of a history more full of sadness than any in the modern annals of our race. Out of « a population of one hundred thousand persons, inhabiting thirty towns under the control of the Jesuits, » by the borders of the Parana and the Uruguay, which were more exposed than remoter districts to the arts of the « hungry ruffians » who now devastated them, « not a thousand souls, » observes Sir Woodbine Parish, « remained in 1825! » « Upwards of *four hundred towns,* » says Dobrizhoffer, « which formerly stood around Guadalcazar, a city of Tucuman now destroyed, utterly perished. » Other tribes, it is true, suffered less, because the agents of European infidelity could not reach them; but these also were deprived of their fathers and teachers, and left to find their way in darkness. And yet they have kept the faith, by that special privilege which distinguishes every church founded in the sixteenth century, and have survived a trial hardly paralleled in ecclesiastical story; nay more, their number is again steadily increasing, and « many of the Missions at this day, » as M. d'Orbigny has told us, « push the Catholic religion even to fanaticism, » — which probably means no more, in the mouth of such a witness, than that they are fervent Christians. The same writer,— who seems to belong to that class of which France unhappily produces so many, who classify the phenomena of religious life with the same frigid composure with which they arrange the statistics of the animal or vegetable world, — furnishes in his elaborate work many deeply interesting proofs of that marvellous inflexibility of faith of which the history of Catholic Missions supplies examples in every land, and which, to a Christian reader, are the most valuable portion of his remarkable volumes. All the Chiquitos, he has already told us, « have persevered, and at this day nothing would induce them to return to the life of the woods. » Amongst other nations, he observes, the customs introduced by the Missionaries « are still maintained; » and he relates that whenever an old sermon of one of the Jesuit Fathers is read to them, they eagerly assemble, and listen with profound attention. « The old men still remember with sorrow the expulsion of the Fathers in 1767, and all repeat; ' By them we were made Christians, by them we were brought to the knowledge of God, and the possession of happiness. ' » (1)

(1) Tome II, p. 606.

Wherever he goes, and he went everywhere, M. d'Orbigny says; « I am never weary of admiring the unparalleled results which the Jesuits obtained in so short a time amongst men who had so lately quitted the savage state. » And then he contrasts their social and religious condition before and after the suppression of the Society. « Under the Jesuits a severe morality was observed, their present rulers are themselves examples to the Indians of misconduct. » « The epidemics which now afflict them were unknown, » he says, « in the time of the Jesuits, » being kept at a distance by rigorous sanitary arrangements. Besides, the Jesuits nursed them in all their sickness, and now they are left to die like the beasts of the field. Finally, contrasting the economical and agricultural statistics under the Religious and under the Civil Administration, he declares, in eloquent words, that « Nature herself seems to have resumed her original aspect. » (1)

Sir Woodbine Parish also, who speaks, like M. d'Orbigny, after personal experience, gives examples, which would be surprising if the fruits of such apostolic toils could excite astonishment, of the abiding power and influence of the Missionaries. Thus at Cordoba, which was a sort of metropolis of the Missions, « the effects of the preponderating influence of the monastic establishments *are still visible in the habits of the generality of the people.* » (2)

Lastly, for it is time to bring this sketch to a close,

(1) Tome I, p. 281.
(2) Part III, ch. XVIII, p. 281.

an official French writer, who was attached to the diplomatic mission to the Plata, confirms, in 1850, all the other witnesses. M. de Brossard is not wholly exempt from the vulgar prejudices of his day, and has not shaken off the superstition, which makes the Jesuits a bugbear and a scarecrow in the eyes of so many shallow and half-educated Frenchmen; but he was capable of expressing with energy the generous impressions which actual observation produced in his mind. « One thing is certain, and ought to be declared to the praise of the Fathers, that since their expulsion the material prosperity of Paraguay has diminished; that many lands formerly cultivated have ceased to be so; that many localities formerly inhabited present at this day only ruins. What ought to be confessed is this,— that they knew how to engrave with such power on their hearts reverence for authority, that *even to this very hour*, the tribes of Paraguay, beyond all those who inhabit this portion of America, are the most gentle, and the most submissive to the empire of duty. » (1)

(1) *Les Républiques de la Plata*, par M. Alfred de Brossard, ch. IV, p. 31.

PART II.

NORTH AMERICA.

It is time to quit South America, that we may search in the northern continent for the last and most notable example which the world offers of the contrast between the work of the Church and the work of the Sects. In tracing this final chapter of a history which we have now almost completed, we shall once more use, as we have done throughout these volumes, the testimony of Protestant authorities; and if we have had reason to feel surprise at the vigour with which they have denounced the operations of their co-religionists in all other lands, the astonishing candour and truthfulness which, with rare exceptions, are the honourable characteristic of American writers, — including the eminent names of Washington and Franklin, of Irving and Channing, — will be found to supply evidence at least as valuable as any hitherto produced, and perhaps still more remarkable than any for copiousness, precision, and emphasis. It is impossible not to be struck by the fact, that while, on the one hand, the inhabitants of the United States have pushed the right of religious division, and the sovereign independence of the individual, to results which have appalled even the boldest thinkers among them, and have generated at last that chaos of spiritual confusion which their own writers have partly described to us; on the other, a large portion of their literature, since they became a distinct nation, is a protest against the unappeasable jealousies, the eager malice, and fierce resentments, which breathe in every line of the polemical writings of British protestants. In refusing to transplant to her free shores the effete feudalism of England, America has declined also to become the heir of her arrogant and superstitious bigotry. Almost the only, certainly the most conspicuous, exceptions to this rule are found, as we might have anticipated, among the members of the American Episcopalian sect; as enamoured at this hour of their dull and frigid forms, as incapable of generous and expansive life, as when they first provoked the disgust of the Virginians by their petty tyranny, ignoble greed, and querulous self-love. Imitating the model which they had left behind, they have attempted to restore it in their new home, but without success; and while the majority of American sects, wisely allowing the echoes of sectarian fury to die away, and refusing the heritage of cruel traditions and implacable hatred which have given a special tone both to the literature and the legislation of England, have frankly acknowledged

that the Church wears as noble a front in a republic
as in an empire, and have even been willing to draw
their own ranks closer together, not to oppose, but
to make room for her; the Episcopalians, affecting
to be neither wholly Catholic nor frankly Protestant,
but doomed in all lands to restless jealousy and the
pangs of that unfruitful labour in which « there is
not strength to bring forth, » still repeat the fretful
maledictions which seem, with them as with others,
to be the sole positive element of their religion.

In the United States, whose religious phenomena,
as far as they relate to the history of Missions, we
shall presently review, there is hardly room, except
in one sect, for that peculiar form of the passion of
hate which is begotten by the memory of wrongs inflicted but not repented, and is the product of cruelty,
avarice, and misbelief, contemplating their own work
with such intense but still unsatisfied malice as to
generate a new progeny more hideous than themselves.
The Americans never decapitated, in the interests
of a new religion, a More 'or a Fisher, nor tortured
a Campion, nor tore out the bowels of a Lacy; and
being guiltless of the blood of the righteous, have
no motive for cherishing hatred against them. Hence
the marked contrast between their controversial writings and those of British protestants. What the English can say of the Church of God, and of her works,
we have seen; the Americans will tell us, in their
turn, how they have learned to estimate both.

The first province which we must traverse in our
way towards the North, after passing the Isthmus
of Panama, is Guatemala. If we stay here for a moment, we have at least a sufficient apology to offer

for what might otherwise be deemed a needless delay. The history of the early missions in this comparatively obscure province has been recently sketched, by an English Protestant writer, with such rare fidelity of research and humanity of temper, that it would be unpardonable to neglect altogether his interesting record. « It will be a pleasure, » he says, and his readers will confirm the declaration, « to recount the proceedings of the Dominican monks of Guatemala, instinct with the wisdom of the serpent, as well as the harmlessness of the dove. »

It was by Pedro de Alvarado, one of the most famous of the *conquistadores* of the New World, that this province had been annexed to the crown of Spain, in 1523. Animated, like all the warriors of his age and class, by a burning religious zeal which even their many faults never quenched, he had announced to the natives of Guatemala that he « came to show the Indians the way to immortality. » The promise was to be abundantly fulfilled, though not by himself. In 1529, the celebrated Dominican, Domingo de Betanzos, — of whose life and character Mr Helps gives an account almost as remarkable for elevation of sentiment as for purity of style, — set out from Mexico for the scene of Alvarado's conquest. It was a weary journey of four hundred leagues, but he went on foot, « eating little, and that only of wild fruits, and sleeping in the open air. » He had scarcely reached the new city of Santiago, when he was summoned back to Mexico to attend a Council of his Order. In the spirit of patient obedience he retraced his steps, though not till he had commenced the building of a humble monastery, which was to be governed a little later by a disciple of his own, who became, as often happens, more illustrious than his master.

It was in 1532 that Las Casas, also a Dominican, arrived in Nicaragua, on his return from Peru. Four years later he entered Guatemala, and " took up his abode in the convent which Domingo de Betanzos had built. " With him went Luis Cancér, Pedro de Angulo, and Rodrigo de Ladrada, " all of whom," observes the English historian, " afterwards became celebrated men." " These grave and reverend monks," he continues, " might any time in the year 1537 have been found sitting in a little class round the Bishop of Guatemala, (Francisco de Marroquin), an elegant scholar, but whose scholarship was now solely employed to express Christian doctrines in the Utlatecan language, commonly called Quiché. As the chronicler says, ' It was a delight to see the Bishop, as a master of declensions and conjugations in the Indian tongue, teaching the good fathers of St. Dominic.' This prelate afterwards published a work in Utlatecan, in the prologue of which he justly says, ' It may, perchance, appear to some people a contemptible thing that prelates should be thus engaged in trifling things solely fitted for the teaching of children; but, if the matter be well looked into, it is a baser thing not to abase one's self to these apparent trifles, for such teaching is the ' marrow ' of our Holy Faith. ' The Bishop was quite right. It will soon be seen what an important end this study of the language led to; and, I doubt not — indeed, it might almost be proved — that there are territories, neighbouring to Guatemala, which would have been desert and barren as the sands of the sea but for the knowledge of the Utlatecan language acquired by these good fathers, — an acquisition, too, it must be recollected, not easy or welcome to men of their age and their habits. » (1)

In the neighbourhood of Guatemala, on its northeastern frontier, was the province of Tuzulutlan, called by the Spaniards, « The Land of War, » because they had thrice invaded and been thrice repulsed from it. Las Casas, whose whole life was a struggle in favour of the Indian against his oppressors, engaged on behalf of the Dominican fathers to attempt the conversion of this formidable people, « whom no Spaniard dared to go near, » but only on a condition that the battle should be waged with spiritual weapons alone, and that no Spaniard should be suffered to enter the province for the space of five years. The Governor of Guatemala accepted the « compact, » and then they made their missionary preparations; « using, » says Mr Helps, « all the skill that the most accomplished statesmen, or men of the world, could have brought to bear upon it. » It is probable that the fathers themselves relied still more, as St. Paul was wont to do, upon « the most fervent prayers, severe fasts, and other mortifications, » which, as he relates, preceded their perilous attempt.

It would be pleasant to transcribe the whole narrative of Mr Helps, in which he traces, with rare refinement of language and feeling, the gradual progress of the fathers and the means by which it was effected. One of the points, he says, to which « the

(1) Helps, book XV, vol. III, ch. v, p. 331.

cautious Cacique » of the province directed the most careful attention, in order to test the real character of the new teachers, was « to observe whether they had gold and silver like the other Christians, and whether there were women in their houses. » The Dominicans, as we might have anticipated, endured with success an investigation which would have been fatal to certain « missionaries » of whom we have read in these pages; and so, when this point was sufficiently cleared, the prudent Cacique « was the first to pull down and burn his idols; and many of his chiefs, in imitation of their master, likewise became iconoclasts. »(1)

« The mission was supremely successful, » says Mr Helps, as such missions are apt to be; and Las Casas, who was always looking ahead, and providing with all his might against possible dangers, was gladdened by the arrival of a Brief from Paul III, pronouncing « a sentence of excommunication of the most absolute kind against all who should reduce the Indians to slavery, or deprive them of their goods. » And then « the great Protector of the Indians, » as Mr Helps justly styles Las Casas, passed through Tuzulutlan, and penetrated to Coban. Being well received, he hastened to inform the other fathers, « and they all commenced with great vigour studying the language of Coban. Each success was with these brave monks a step gained for continued exertion. »

After a while the converted Cacique of Tuzulutlan came on a visit to the monastery at Santiago, and was presented by the learned Bishop to the Governor

---

(1) Ch. vii, p. 350.

Alvarado. « Now Alvarado, » says our eloquent historian, « though a fierce and cruel personage, knew (which seems to have been a gift of former days) when he saw a man. When the bold Adelantado met the Cacique, the Indian Chieftain's air and manner, his repose, the gravity and modesty of his countenance, his severe look and weighty speech, won so instantaneously upon the Spaniard, that, having nothing else at hand, he took off his own plumed hat, and put it on the head of the Cacique. » The soldiers who stood round murmured when they saw the great captain pay honour to an Indian; but Alvarado was a better judge than they of the qualities of the new Christian, and continued to treat him with the same distinction during his stay in Guatemala. By this specimen also he understood what sort of converts the fathers had won in that « Land of War, » which his own troops once dared not enter, « but which now, » as Mr Helps observes, « deserved that name less than any part of the Indies. » (1)

Indeed, the once dreaded province had already received from Charles V the significant name which it bears to this day of *Vera Paz;* and Mr Helps remarks that it is a notable instance « of an aboriginal tribe being civilized and enlightened by their conquerors, and not being diminished in numbers nor restricted in territory. » Its prosperity has lasted during nearly three hundred years; and the English historian, alluding to the final success of the great undertaking of Las Casas, observes, in words worthy of

(1) P. 369.

himself and of the subject, « It seems something wondrous when any project by one man really does succeed in the way and at the time that he meant it to succeed. We feel as if the hostile Powers, always lurking in the rear of great and good designs, must have been asleep, or, in the multiplicity of their evil work, have, by some oversight, let pass a great occasion for the hindrance of the world. » (1)

Of the four great and good men who accomplished this noble work, and by their wisdom and fortitude added provinces to the Kingdom of Christ, two will meet us again in Mexico; let us add a word upon the other two, Luis Cancér, and Pedro de Angulo. The latter was appointed Bishop of Vera Paz in 1556, but « did not live to enter his diocese. » His memory long survived, says Mr Helps, who has carefully studied all the original records, and never begins to write till he has examined every thing relating to his subject, and « the Indians forty years afterwards were wont to quote things which they had heard him say in the pulpit. He gained their love, it is said, so much, that ' they did not know where they were without him. ' » One of them, « giving an account of the effect which his preaching produced, used an expressive metaphor — especially expressive in that country — comparing the excitement in the hearts of his Indian audience to that of ants in an ant-heap when some one comes to disturb it with a stick. »

Luis Cancér, the first of the four to enter the province of Vera Paz, was the only one honoured with

(1) Ch. IX, p. 398.

the crown of martyrdom. He was put to death by the Indians of Florida, who knew not how to distinguish him from the violent and unjust Spaniards whom they feared and hated. « How seldom, » says Mr Helps, in allusion to this martyrdom, « do men recognise their true friends ! »

It is time to pursue our journey. Three provinces more had been won to religion and civilization, and this time the work was done by Dominicans. But if they succeeded, and the fruits of their apostolic toils remain to this day, — for paganism is almost unknown in these regions, — it was not because they were Dominicans, not because they were learned patient and wise, but because they had received from God a special vocation to this work, and had been sent forth by the Church to accomplish a task which none but her chosen apostles have ever undertaken, and in which none but they may ever hope to triumph. This is the only reflection which we miss, and which we could hardly expect to find, in the graceful and learned pages of Mr Helps.

It would detain us too long to speak of the other provinces of Central America. If we refer to them for a moment, it is with the object of recording the experience of an English Protestant missionary, who was not indeed of the school of Angulo or Las Casas, but should not on that account be passed over in silence. It is our business to trace a contrast. This gentleman announces, then, in 1850, after a somewhat disastrous career in these regions, and in language which his English friends would perhaps applaud, that « Romanism is the putrescent heart of Central America. » The rest of his book is in the same style. He observes with displeasure that even « the Carif women, » who are not socially speaking a high class, « have been seen joining in the prostrate adoration of an image of the Virgin, » and that he and his companions tried in vain « to preserve them from these calamities. »

From his own account, the state of the Protestant mission was not consoling. All its members were fighting together, within hearing of « the Carif women, » and with the usual lavish expenditure of Scripture texts. One of them retired « for want of a congregation, » a trial which the rest endured with greater fortitude. The narrator himself got into jail, and seems to have staid there a good while. Finally, the « mission house » was sold, and converted into a lunatic asylum. But this is not the most important information which we derive from this gentleman, whose « violent extramission » from Guatemala was related in an earlier chapter, and may perhaps account for his lively resentment. The people of Brazil, Mr Ewbank has told us, despise a Protestant missionary « from a rooted belief in his ignorance and presumption; » in Guatemala, as Mr Crowe relates with indignation, « a Jew is something akin to a demon, and a Protestant is something lower and more dangerous than a Jew. » He adds, however, as if to excuse this misconception on the part of the Guatemalians, that « the general deportment of the Anglo-Saxon visitors, or residents, has not been such as to raise the respect of the inhabitants for the Protestantism which they profess, » and that his own attempts to apply a remedy « have signally failed. » And so he returned to England, and the people of Central

America still rank him and his co-religionists below the Jew. (1)

And now let us enter Mexico. The conquest of Mexico by Spain has been compared by Lord Macaulay with that of Hindostan by the English. Only one point of contrast between the two events was left unnoticed, perhaps because unheeded, by the great Essayist. He nowhere reminds either himself or his readers, that Mexico became a Christian nation, while India has only been confirmed in her worship of demons. Such is the familiar contrast which history records, for the admonition of mankind, between the fruits of a Catholic and a Protestant conquest.

Mexico is Christian. Count up all the misdeeds of the violent men who subdued the Aztec race, — exaggerate, if it be possible, all their faults, and add a darker shade to their crimes, — still, when all is told, the fact remains, which you will never be able to obliterate, that paganism is extinct in Mexico, and triumphant in India.

And how was this conversion of a whole people, hitherto abandoned to a dark and bloody superstition, brought to a prosperous issue? How was this mighty work of renovation accomplished, the contemplation of which forced an eminent American writer of our own day to exclaim, « How easily has the Indian element in Mexican nationality been developed into civilised and productive co operation! »(2)

---

(1) *The Gospel in Central America*, by Rev[d] F. Crowe; ch. xii, p. 242; ch. xiv, pp. 294, 306, 457.

(2) *Texas*, by F. Law Olmsted, p. 297.

CHAPTER IX.

By what mysterious and persuasive arts was this new triumph of Christianity effected, of which a French writer epitomises the whole history in a few emphatic words, when he says; « The progress of religion in America, by the preaching of a few poor religious, notably of the order of St. Francis, was so universal, that in the space of forty years, six thousand monasteries and six hundred bishoprics were founded in that land? » (1)

It is only a brief answer which we can give to this question. No doubt it was to the labours of apostolic men, — such as Betanzos and Motolinia; Martin de Valencia and Peter of Ghent; Francisco de Soto, Las Casas, and Zumarraga; such, in a word, as that great company of valiant and gifted men who at the same hour were toiling for God's glory in every land, from Lake Huron to the Gulf of Siam — that this magnificent conquest was chiefly due. But justice claims even for the mailed warriors of Spain, who fought, like Cortez, with the sword in one hand and the cross in the other, some share in the noble work to which it is their glory, and almost their justification, to have contributed. It has been the fashion, with all but a few cautious and patient students of history, to load with undiscriminating obloquy the men who overthrew, by a prodigy of valour and policy, the throne of Montezuma. Yet something may be said in their behalf. It is not, indeed, to such red-handed warriors, impetuous as Jehu and resolute as Joab, that we can point as types of the Christian

---

(1) Migne, *Dictionnaire des Conversions*, Introd., p. 18. (1852).

character. Yet even these imperious soldiers, who shouted from morning till night their war cry of « Santiago, » — Cortez and Alvarado, Sandoval and Pizarro, — will be monuments to the end of time of the power and majesty of that Faith, from which, in spite of their errors, they derived all their strength, and without whose inspirations they would neither have attempted nor accomplished the immortal enterprise with which their names are for ever associated.

A tardy justice has begun to recognise in our own day the truth of this allegation. Even Protestant writers will tell us, that it was not a thirst for gold which was, or could be, the sole spring of action with a man so truly great as Cortez. « There is much to blame, » says one of the most elegant and discerning historians of this memorable epoch, « in the conduct of the first discoverers in Africa and America; it is, however, but just to acknowledge that the love of gold was not by any means the only motive which urged them, or which *could* have urged them, to such endeavours as theirs. » (1) They were penetrated, he adds, with the most profound conviction of « the fatal consequences of not being within the communion of the Church. » He does not, of course, share their belief, but he is keen enough to see that it affords the only rational explanation of their conduct.

A French writer, equally devoid of partial sympathies, detects also the same motive in all their actions. « They redeemed, » says M. de Brossard, in

---

(1) Helps, vol. I, ch. I, p. 28.

words which we cannot accept without modification,
« the disorders of their private life by deeds of charity
and an ardent faith. » And this was especially true
of Cortez. « An object which Cortez never lost sight
of, » says Mr Helps, « was the conversion of the natives. » It was Cortez who first requested that religious might be sent from Spain. « I supplicate your
Imperial Majesty, » he says in one of his letters,
alluding to the possibility of converting the natives,
« that you would have the goodness to provide religious persons, of good life and example, for that end. »
And when the Franciscans arrived, it was in the
following words that he presented them to the people
of Mexico. « These are men sent from God, and
ardently desiring the salvation of your souls. They
ask neither your gold nor your lands, for despising
all the goods of this world, they aspire only after
those of the next. » (1)

It is an error to suppose that Cortez, a man filled
with tender and generous thoughts, was cruel by
nature, or that he was as careless of the blood of
others as he was of his own. He never slew for the
sake of slaying, and was as calm in victory as he was
terrible in battle. He deplored, with perfect sincerity, the very actions in which he took part, and
only inflicted death upon those who refused mercy.
It must be remembered too, that he had entered with
Montezuma that infernal shrine in which the hearts
of men smoked in golden platters before the idols of
the nation, and that he quitted it trembling with
religious horror and indignation, and became thence-

(1) Henrion, tome I, ch. xxxvi, p. 390.

forward as truly the minister of the Most High in chastising the demon-worship of this guilty race, as Joshua was when he led the armies of Israel across the Jordan. Nor let it be forgotten that to him is due, at least in part, the significant and atoning fact, that the noblest temple which has ever been reared in the New World stands on the very site of that foul and impious den, from which Cortez hurled with his own hand both the blood-stained priests who were lodged within it, and the idols which, but for him, might perchance have been worshipped at this hour.

Lastly, it is evident that Cortez was otherwise appreciated, both by the Mexicans themselves, and by the prelates and missionaries who were their most courageous and devoted protectors, than by the crowd of careless or half-informed critics who have neither done justice to the merits, nor rightly discriminated the faults, of this illustrious man. When he returned from his first visit to Spain, « he was received, » we are told, « with vivid demonstrations of delight by great numbers of the people in New Spain, both Spaniards *and Indians*. » (1) Zumarraga, the first Bishop of Mexico, and Domingo de Betanzos, men as valiant as himself though in another cause, and always strenuous protectors of the Indians, were not only his personal friends, but the chosen executors of his will; while another prelate of the same class, Sebastian de Fuenleal, who would have refused homage to any mortal potentate unless he could offer it with a good conscience, chose him

(1) Helps, vol. III, ch. VI, p. 198.

for his counsellor. « Far from looking upon Cortez as an enemy, » says Mr Helps, « the wise Bishop acted entirely in concert with the Captain-General. It was Don Sebastian's practice to take counsel with many persons as to what ought to be done, but with the Marquis alone, or, at least, with very few persons, as to the mode of executing what had been resolved upon. » (1)

Cortez was a warrior who had something of the temper of St. Louis, and more of Richard Cœur de Lion. Like the last, he turned aside neither to right nor left, but clove a straight path through all that barred his way; like the first, every blow he dealt was a defiance to the pagan, a victory for the cross. He was inconsistent, as men of war are wont to be; but he was no vulgar swordsman, battling only for wealth and honours. His great heart was filled to the brim with that faith which meaner men call « fanaticism, » but which alone made him what he was, which gave lustre to all his actions, and which he assisted to plant so deeply in the soil of Mexico, that, in after days, it overshadowed all the land.

Even Alvarado and Pizarro, men far inferior to Cortez, were no such graceless ruffians as modern critics, possessing neither their heroic valour nor their religious instincts, would have us believe. It is no small praise to the first, that, with all his faults, he was honoured with the friendship of the learned and saintly Bishop of Guatemala. His last will remains to prove that he knew at least how to deplore his injustice and violence, and desired to atone for

(1) Ch. VIII, p. 218.

them; and when he lay on his death-bed, mangled by that avenging rock which had crushed his stalwart limbs, and was asked where his pain was sorest, the spirit within him broke forth in the sorrowing cry, « My soul, my soul! »

Pizarro too, an adventurer and an outcast from his youth, whether he was starving in the Island of Gorgona, with his fourteen dauntless followers, or leading on his handful of comrades to battles in which they were one against a thousand, or plucking the Inca with his own hand from his litter in the great square of Cassamarca, was ever, after his kind, a soldier of the cross. « In the midst of all their misery, » says a Protestant historian, « they did not forget their piety. » In Gorgona, where they spent three heavy months of doubt and suffering, while « subsisting upon shell-fish, and whatever things, in any way eatable, they could collect upon the shore; » « every morning they gave thanks to God: at evening-time they said the *Salve* and other prayers appointed for different hours. They took heed of the feasts of the Church, and kept account of their Fridays and Sundays. » (1) And when the decisive hour arrived, and Pizarro stood face to face with Atahuallpa, it was Father Vicente de Valverde, who, at the conqueror's request, « advanced towards the Inca, bearing a cross in one hand, and holding a breviary in the other, » and explained to the Peruvian prince, still at the desire of Pizarro, the mysteries of « the true Catholic Faith, » and « the history of Jesus Christ. » Finally, when this intrepid war-

(1) Helps, vol. III, p. 447.

rier came to his end, and the violent man fell under the swords of assassins, he drew the sign of the cross on the floor with his own blood, kissed with his dying lips the emblem of salvation, and with that supreme act of love and contrition Pizarro passed to his account.

Compare these men, who in every case won kingdoms for their Divine Master, and who banished paganism from every land which they entered, with the English captains who scattered the hosts of the Mogul or the Mahratta. Little recked *they* of the glory of God, or of the progress of the Faith. Fanaticism, as they would have called the sublime enthusiasm of a St. Paul or a Las Casas, was not their line. No word did *their* tongues ever utter in honour of the Cross, no hymn did they chant in praise of the Crucified. « Not a temple has been thrown down *by the English,* » says a Protestant writer, « not a single deity removed by proclamation from the calendar. » (1) To live as the heathen blushed to live, and sometimes to die as even the heathen would have been ashamed to die; to smile complacently on the foul superstitions which they neither rebuked themselves, nor would suffer others to rebuke; to « *discountenance Christianity as a most dangerous innovation,* » while they attended banquets in honour of Ganesa, fired royal salutes to do homage to Sivah, or gathered wealth from the worship of Juggernaut; such, as their own historians have told us, were the tactics of the English conquerors of Hindostan. And they were the same from first to last. The hero of

(1) Mead, *The Sepoy Revolt,* ch. XIX, p. 245.

Plassey, almost as great a soldier as Cortez, found an exit from life through the shameful gate of suicide; the victor of Assaye and Seringapatam died as his own war-horse died, and with scarcely more thought of the Unseen. No province did they, or such as they, ever win to Christ. They found India pagan, and they left it pagan. One lesson only they imparted to Hindoo or Mahometan, which he learned but too well. They taught him, by their own example, to hate and despise the religion of which *they* were professors, and to deride a doctrine the very preachers of which, when at last they arrived in India, were so manifestly types of worldliness and self-indulgence, that far from producing any impression upon the mocking pagans who doubted « whether they believed their own Scriptures, » a conspicuous member of their order ingenuously confessed, « Your profession of religion is a proverbial jest throughout the world. »

There is no need, even if we had space, to recount the toils by which men of another faith, and other gifts, won Mexico to the cross of Christ. Here, as in every other land in which they encountered only such impediments as were common to St. Paul or St. James, they did the work for which God raised them up, and for which He endowed them with adequate gifts. They failed only, where St. Paul or St. James would perhaps have equally failed, in countries where the heathen have been fatally prejudiced against Christianity, by the divisions and contradictions, the irrational precepts, or the effeminate habits, of Protestant teachers. Against *such* obstacles even apostles contend in vain, or only at a fearful disadvantage.

CHAPTER IX.

In Mexico they had a fair field, and had to fight only against the corruptions of the human heart, and the devices of the evil one. They overcame both. All South America, from the Isthmus of Panama to the frontiers of Patagonia, and from the valleys of Peru to where the floods of the Amazon and the Orenoco mingle with those of the Atlantic, was converted by them; and then they spread their conquests in the North, through Guatemala, Nicaragua, Mexico, Texas, and California. They had done all that apostles could do. Canada and the United States, which would have shared the same privilege, were snatched from them; because *there*, as we shall see, a hundred spurious forms of Christianity, stripped of every divine element, and each battling against every other, had inspired only the disdain of the barbarian, who formed such an estimate of the doctrine and its teachers, that he not unfrequently went down to his untimely grave, imprecating with his latest breath a malediction upon both.

One special trial beset the Apostles of Mexico, and it should be noticed, because there is perhaps nothing in their career more admirable than the struggle by which they overcame it. It was not from such men as Cortez or Pizarro that they ever encountered opposition in their holy work, but from a later generation of ignoble adventurers, vulgar soldiers or greedy lawyers, who soon swarmed in the fair regions which the great Marquis had added to the crown of Spain. Against these men, whose crimes were often unredeemed by a single virtue, Las Casas and Zumarraga, and all their brethren, fought with a patient but unyielding courage which even the most prejudiced writers have celebrated with applause. « The Roman Catholic clergy in America, » says the unbelieving Robertson, « uniformly exerted their influence to protect the Indians, and to moderate the ferocity of their countrymen. » (1) « We must express our admiration, « says an English naturalist, » for the exalted piety of the Roman Catholic Missionaries, who, in these countries, inhabited by human beings in the lowest state of degradation, endured poverty and misery in all forms, to win the Indians to better habits and a purer faith. » (2) « The learned and thoughtful men, » says Mr Helps — « for such the monks and ecclesiastics must be held to be, looking before and after, knowing many of the issues of history, and often appealing to great and general principles, are steadily arrayed against the mere conquering soldier, — the good Bishop Zumarraga and his confraternity, against Nuno de Guzman and his followers. » (3)

Sometimes the civil authorities, who wished to employ the Indian only as a beast of burden, cunningly affected in their appeals to Spain to defend « the prerogatives of the State » against « the encroachments of the Church; » but Charles V was too sagacious a monarch to be much moved by arguments of which he appreciated the real character, but which the same class of statesmen use in our own day to frighten feebler potentates.

On the other hand, notable examples are found of

(1) *Charles V*, notes, vol. X, p. 400.
(2) *Narrative of the Voyage of H. M. S. Herald*, by Berthold Seeman, F. L. S., vol. II, ch. IX, p. 153. (1853).
(3) Book XIV, ch. V, p. 186.

active and generous co-operation with the clergy on the part of the lay Auditors of Mexico. In 1531, when there were only a hundred Dominicans and Franciscans in the whole country, the Auditors, « sent to the Emperor, beseeching him to send out more monks, being, doubtless, of the same mind with a subsequent Viceroy of Mexico, who, when there was much question about building forts throughout the country (a suggestion urged upon him by the authorities at home), replied, that towers with soldiers were dens of thieves, but that convents with monks were as good as walls and castles for keeping the Indians in subjection. » (1)

Again; when a new generation of Auditors « made the noble endeavours to provide homes and instruction for the numerous orphans who had lost their parents by reason of the cruel work imposed upon them in the mines, » Quiroga, one of their number, — « who it must be remembered, was a lawyer, and therefore less likely to be led away by a love for monastic institutions, » — urgently recommended the Council of the Indies « to make a settlement of the young Indians in each district, at a distance from other *pueblos*, and in each settlement to place a monastery with three or four *religiosos*, who may incessantly cultivate these young plants to the service of God. » And so perfectly did these shrewd men of the world of that age comprehend, what the same class affect to doubt in our own, that monasteries are both cheaper and more potential institutions than prisons or workhouses, that Quiroga, filled with admiration at

(1) Helps, book XIV, ch. VI, p. 200.

what the monks had already done, exclaims; « I offer myself, with the assistance of God, to undertake to plant a kind of Christians such as those were of the primitive Church; for God is as powerful now as then. I beseech that this thought may be favoured. » (1)

Nor was this the language of mere enthusiasm. What the religious could do had been already sufficiently proved in many a province of America, and Mexico was not destined to be an exception. Already the Indian, refusing to see in them the emissaries of a foreign power, had learned to regard the fathers first with astonishment, and then with veneration. « Their poverty, their temperance, their simplicity of life, » says a Protestant writer, « recommended them at once to the Indian. » (2) And as time went on, and fresh colonies of Dominicans and Franciscans arrived, all filled with the same charity, and displaying the Christian religion in its noblest and most attractive form, the Mexican understood that these men came to him with hands filled only with gifts and blessings. It was they who obtained from the Holy See the menace of excommunication against his selfish oppressors, and from the royal authority such decrees as the following; « that no Indian should carry any burdens against his will, whether he was paid for it or not; » that « when they were sent to the mines they were to be provided with clergy there; » that the « Protectors, » of whom the noble and generous Las Casas was one, should « cause that

(1) Helps, book XIV, ch. VI, p. 208.
(2) Id., ch. XV, p. 313.

the Indians be well treated, and taught in secular things, and instructed in the Articles of the Holy Catholic Faith. » (1)

What marvel if the Indian abandoned himself with love and confidence to such teachers as a bountiful Providence had now provided for him? How should men who are thus described even by Protestant writers fail to win his heart? Of the Bishop-President of Mexico, Don Sebastian Ramirez de Fuenleal, who arrived in 1531, Mr Helps gives the following portrait. « No single subject of government occupied his attention to the exclusion of others. He founded churches; he divided Mexico into parishes; he established a college, and was the first man to propose *that a learned education should be given to the Indians*. His efforts in this matter were successful; and it is curious that one of the best chroniclers of the Bishop's proceedings (Torquemada) was instructed in the Mexican language by a most accomplished Indian, who had been educated at this college. » (2)

« The clergy, » says the same careful and conscientious historian, « not only taught spiritual things, but temporal also. They converted, they civilized, they governed; they were priests, missionaries, schoolmasters, kings. A considerable share in the credit of this good work must be given to the unwearied labours of the Franciscan and Dominican monks. That the missionary spirit in that age was so potent and so successful as it was, must in some measure be attributed to the intense belief which the

(1) Helps, book XIV, ch. xiv, pp. 175-177.
(2) *Id.*, p. 219.

missionaries entertained of the advantage to be derived from outward communion of the most ordinary kind. »

St. Paul seems to have shared the same « intense belief, » if we may judge from his summary exhortation to Titus how to deal with « *a man that is a heretic*, » (1) or his equally emphatic warning to the Philippians, « *Beware of dogs*. » (2) « Earth has no privilege, » is in every age the confession of loving faith, « equal to that of being a member of His Church; and they dishonour both it and Him who extenuate the dismal horrors of that outer darkness in which souls lie that are aliens from the Church. » Only they who have received this « royal grace » can understand their unutterable calamity who possess it not, or the « appalling difficulties of salvation outside the Church. This is the reason why the saints have ever been so strong in the instincts of their sanctity, as to the wide, weltering, almost hopeless deluge which covers the ruined earth outside the ark. Harsh, to unintelligent uncharitable kindness intolerably harsh, as are the judgments of stern theology, the saints have even felt and spoken more strongly and more peremptorily than the theologians. The more dear to the soul the full light and sacramental life of Jesus, the more utter the darkness, the more dismal the death, of those who are without that light and life, in their fulness and their sacramentality. The eternal possession of Mary's Immaculate Heart, together with all the intelligences of the countless

(1) Tit. III, 10
(2) Philip. III, 2.

angels, would not suffice to make one act of thanksgiving for the single comprehensive mercy of being catholics, and of acknowledging St. Peter's paternal supremacy. » (1)

But this ardent conviction, of the « advantage to be derived from communion » with the Catholic Church, which alone has inspired all apostolic works, and which St. Peter and St. Paul, St. James and St. Jude, expressed in such startling words, « would not alone have caused the rapid progress of these missionaries, » Mr Helps truly observes, « had there not been to back it the utmost self-devotion, supreme self-negation, and also considerable skill in their modes of procedure. » Was not the « supreme self-negation » a result of the « intense belief, » and were not both the fruit of divine grace, which during some twenty centuries has always lavished these noblest gifts upon one class of men, and always refused them to every other?

Sometimes the same English historian whom we have so often quoted, and always with pleasure, gives individual examples of that great company of preachers by whom Mexico was evangelised. Of the Franciscan Martin de Valencia, head of the Order in Mexico, he speaks thus. « When he arrived in Mexico, he maintained the most rigid mode of life. He went barefoot, with a poor and torn robe, bearing his wallet and his cloak on his own shoulders, without permitting even an Indian to assist in carrying them. In this fashion he used to visit the convents

---

(1) Father Faber, *The Blessed Sacrament*, book IV, § 5, p. 502.

under his jurisdiction. Being already an old man when he arrived in Mexico, he could not learn the language with the same facility as his companions; so that what he most devoted himself to, was teaching the little Indian boys to read Spanish..... He sang hymns with the little children, and as we are told, did great good in the Indian villages where he resided. » Like Moses, he would sometimes go apart from the world to draw nearer to God, for whose sake he lived this life, and was accustomed to « retire to an oratory on a mountain, where he might enjoy the most profound contemplation. »

Francisco de Soto, « a man of singular piety, who afterwards refused the Bishopric of Mexico, » was a missionary of the same class; and Toribio Motolinia, who wore out his life in « teaching, catechising, and baptizing the Indians; » and of whom it is said, that « he baptized no less than four hundred thousand of them. »

But it was Peter of Ghent, Mr Helps assures us, « who perhaps did most service. » He was a Flemish lay brother, « who in his humility, never would be anything but a lay brother. » From him the Mexicans learned « to read, to write, to sing, and to play upon musical instruments. He contrived to get a large school built, » in which, besides more elementary matters, he taught them painting, carving, and other arts. « Many idols and temples owed their destruction to him, and many churches their building. He spent a long life — no less than fifty years — in such labours, and was greatly beloved by the Indians, amongst whom he must have had thousands of pupils. The successor of Zumarraga one day generously exclaimed, ' I am not the Archbishop of Mexico, but brother Peter of Ghent is. ' »

Of Domingo de Betanzos, who became « the principal Dominican in New Spain, » we have already heard in Guatemala. It was a sharp life which he and his brethren led, following the strictest rule of their ascetic Order, and « so versed in self-denial, » as our historian observes, that « the sternest duties of a missionary life were easy to them. » They were men throughly penetrated with the maxim of St. Paul, « No man being a soldier of God entangleth himself with secular business. » (1) They could be merciful to the poor, for none were so poor as they. They could rebuke the rich, for they had often resigned wealth and honours in order to have the right to do so. The very sight of them suggested thoughts of penance, hope, and manly effort. Of Betanzos, to whom « his brethren were attached beyond measure,» — for monks have more loving hearts than the egotistical votaries of pleasure, who are too feeble even to love in earnest — we read as follows. « The principal men in New Spain held him in high estimation; the Indians were delighted with his disinterestedness; and the whole country reverenced him, and looked up to him as a father. » (2) When he had done his work in Mexico, the brave old man, « moved by a desire for martyrdom, » wanted to go to China, and so kindled the heart of the noble Bishop Zumarraga, says Mr Helps — though he only considers it a proof of « high-souled fanaticism, » — that he

(1) II Tim. ii, 4.
(2) Helps, ix, 407.

was ready to resign his bishopric to go with him. The Pope, however, refused permission, and they both died in the land for which they had done so much.

Ortiz, afterwards Bishop of Santa Martha, was of the same school, and Julian Garces, « a very learned man and an elegant Latin writer, » who was the first Bishop of Los Angelos in Tlascala; and Antonio de Montesino, subsequently martyred in India, and Lorenzo de Bienvenida, who boldly admonished Philip II not to peril his own soul by tolerating the injustice of the Spaniards; (1) and a hundred more, who displayed in Mexico the same virtues, waged the same battles, and gained the same victories, as their fellow labourers in other lands.

And now if we enquire, without attempting to enter into impossible details, what was the final result of all this apostolic toil, the kindly and accomplished historian whom he have followed will tell us. « Two important letters, » he observes, — the one addressed by Bishop Zumarraga, in 1531, to a General Chapter of the Franciscan Order, held at Toulouse; the other by Bishop Garces a year or two later to Pope Paul the Third, — afford information from which « we are able to form something like a complete picture of the state of this early Church in relation to the Indians. »

The Bishop of Mexico relates, that already more than a million Indians had been baptized by the

---

(1) *Voyages*, etc., *pour servir à l'histoire de la Découverte de l'Amérique*, par H. Ternaux Compans, tome II, p. 307. See also the letter of Juan de Zumarraga in tome V.

Franciscans alone; « five hundred temples have been thrown down, *and twenty thousand idols broken in pieces, or burnt.* It place of these temples have arisen churches, oratories, and hermitages. But, as the good Bishop says, that which causes more admiration is, that whereas they were accustomed each year in this city of Mexico to sacrifice to idols more than twenty thousand hearts of young men and young women, now all those hearts are offered up, with innumerable sacrifices of praise, not to the Devil, but to the Most High God. » (1)

Both the venerable writers speak with enthusiasm of the piety and docility of the Indian children, and the Bishop of Tlascala says of those in his own diocese, « they not only imbibe but exhaust the Christian doctrines » — « now hauriunt modo, sed exhauriunt, ac veluti ebibunt. » Of their exactness in frequenting the divine office, and in the practice of confession, as well as of « the dove-like simplicity » with which they accused themselves of their faults, they speak with equal admiration; while « the Bishop of Mexico mentions that the children steal away the idols from their fathers, for which, he says, some of them have been inhumanly put to death by their fathers; but they live crowned in glory with Christ. »

Lastly, the English writer whom we have so often quoted, — referring to that final victory of the Faith which was accomplished in Mexico by « the untiring efforts of such men as Las Casas, Betanzos, Zumarraga,... and the various prelates and monks who

(1) Helps, III, 300.

laboured with or after these good men, » — not only declares with a noble frankness that « it is a result which Christians of all denominations may be proud of and rejoice in, » — an excessive statement, since only one « denomination » has ever had the smallest share in producing such results,—but is led to make the following weighty reflection upon the whole history. « We are told that in the sixteenth century there was a revival throughout Europe in favour of the Papacy, which set the limits to Protestantism — those limits which exist even in the present day; but we cannot say that any such revival appears to have been greatly needed, or to have taken place, in Spain. The fervent and holy men, whose deeds have been enumerated, were in the flower of their youth or their manhood before the Reformation had been much noised abroad; and it is evident, from the whole current of the story, that the spirit of these men *was not a thing developed by any revival*, but was in continuance of the spirit with which they had been imbued in their respective monasteries. All honour to their names! »

Let us conclude, according to our custom, with a few Protestant testimonies to the fact, which we have noticed in every other land, that neither suffering, nor neglect, nor lapse of years, have been able to shake the faith of the converted Mexican. Las Casas and Zumarraga, Betanzos and Peter of Ghent, are no longer among them; the disorders of Europe have reached, and sometimes convulsed, even their remote dwellings ; profligate rulers, whom their want of political education obliges them to accept, have involved their nation in shameful disorder; but the Mexican people, innocent of the crimes which scandalize without corrupting them, are still Catholic in their inmost heart, still preserved by the Mother of God, who always guards her own, from the taint of heresy.

Four witnesses will suffice, and that we may take extreme cases, they shall be an agent of the Bible Society, two American Protestants, and a Scotch Presbyterian. « Every man, » says the Rev. Mr Norris, — whose bibles and discourses the Mexicans seem to have rejected with amused contempt, — « professes himself a Catholic, and is very devout and religious in his way; in some respects they are worthy of imitation by enlightened Christians. » (1) It is true that elsewhere Mr Norris calls their religion « idolatry; » but men whose own « worship » hardly equals the decent courtesy which one civilised man offers to another, and who have still to learn in what the union of the creature with his Creator consists, may well deem that homage idolatrous which is so far deeper and more tender than their own, even when the objects of it are only the saints in Heaven. Of worship in its true sense, that which is due to God alone, such men would speak with more profit, if they had any personal experience of it.

Of one Mexican province, Mr Brantz Mayer speaks as follows, in 1852. « The aborigines of Jalisco, formerly warlike and devoted to a bloody religion, are most generally tillers of the ground, *adhering to the doctrine of the Catholic Church.* » (2)

(1) Strickland, *Hist. of American Bible Society*, ch. XX, p.175.
(2) *Mexico*, etc., vol. II, ch. VIII, p. 295.

Even the most frivolous writers suspend the jibe or the jest to notice the deep religious feeling of the Mexicans, in spite of neglect or scanty instruction. An American traveller of this class, who confesses that he drew his knife on a priest, and scoffs at the « ridiculous mummeries » of processions and prayers, notices with a sneer that « the Mexicans are jealous of their churches and do not, willingly, allow a heretic to enter alone ; » and then he sums up his impressions in these words. « The religious feeling which pervades all classes, young and old, is remarkable. Never do you see any of them pass a church without uncovering their heads, and turning their faces thitherwards ; while, at the sound of the bell, every hat is removed and all stand uncovered where they are, until the sound is over. » (1)

Finally, a well known writer, Madame Calderon de la Barca, speaks thus of modern Mexico. « There exists no country in the world where charities, both public and private, are practised on so noble a scale ; generally speaking charity is a distinguishing attribute of a Catholic country. » And this is confirmed by an American protestant, who visited Mexico as a prisoner, and had some reason to speak of its rulers with resentment. » It is not in Mexico alone, » says Mr Kendall, — after describing « the institutions for relieving the distresses of the unfortunate, and the different orders of sisters of charity, those meeks handmaidens of benevolence, whose eyes are ever seeking the couch of sickness, » — « that this holy

---

(1) *A Campaign in New Mexico*, by Frank S. Edwards, ch. VI, p. 92.

feeling of charity exists; but wherever the religion of Rome is known, there do we find the same active benevolence exerted, the same attention to the wants of the suffering. » (1)

Of the existing race of monks, usually the butt at which every witless traveller aims his shafts, Madame de la Barca, in spite of the prejudices of her Scotch training, candidly observes; « I firmly believe that by far the greater number lead a life of privation and virtue. » Throughout the whole country, this lady adds, « at every step you see a white cross gleaming among the trees.... *here every thing reminds us of the triumph of Catholicism.* » Of the Indians themselves, their « superstitions, » and perpetual « religious processions, » she gives much the same account, though with less bitterness of language, as we received from Mr Scarlett, Mr Mansfield, and others, with respect to their brethren in the south; she adds, however, while vehemently disapproving such external manifestations, which are usually dramatic representations of facts in the life of our Lord or of the Saints : « It is singular, that after all there is nothing ridiculous in these exhibitions; on the contrary, something rather terrible. » (2)

If it be true that « out of the abundance of the heart the mouth speaketh, » and that national customs represent national feelings, we may perhaps conclude, that a people who spend a large part of their lives in devout processions and religious exhibitions, can

(1) *Narrative of the Texan Santa Fé Expedition*, by George Wilkins Kendall, vol. II, ch. XVII, p. 340.
(2) *Life in Mexico*, by Madame C. de la B.; Letter XXIII, pp. 177, 288.

hardly be indifferent to religion. Such spectacles are not indeed witnessed in England or Holland, and no man expects to see them. The Mexicans may fitly represent the scenes of the Nativity, the Passion, or the Resurrection, for these events are to them realities. Such sights are familiar to the eye and heart, and kindle the sad or joyous sympathies, of every inhabitant of the land. If any one should attempt to introduce them in any village of England, the incongruous spectacle would be speedily suppressed, and perhaps with reason; for every one would feel that it awakened only uneasiness and repugnance, by forcing them out of their habitual train of thought, and rudely disturbing the ordinary current of their life.

If now we once more pursue our journey northwards, we shall find two provinces, one on the eastern, the other on the western frontier of Mexico, which deserve a moment's attention. Texas and California, both lately absorbed by that energetic and all-devouring race which is perhaps destined one day to over-run the whole continent, will introduce us, not only to that order of missionaries with whose labours and successes we are now sufficiently familiar, but also, for the first time in America, to the agents of another religion, who have already nearly completed the work of ruin, violence, and demoralisation, which has marked their presence in every other land. A few words must suffice for each province.

A well known American writer, who published in 1857 an account of the present state of Texas, will give us, in two or three pregnant sentences, all the information we need in illustration of the contrast which we have so often traced. Speaking of the work of the Catholic misssionaries, he says, « The missions bear solid testimony to the strangely patient courage and zeal of the old Spanish fathers. » (1) Yet one hundred and thirty years have passed away since the *latest* mission of San Antonio was founded by the Franciscans, in which, after so long an interval, such evident traces of their wisdom and goodness are still apparent even to Protestant eyes.

Of the Indians themselves, M*r* Olmsted says, « We were invariably received with the most gracious and beaming politeness and dignity. Their manner towards one another is engaging, and that of children and parents most affectionate. » And then follows the usual account of the woful results of their unwilling contact with a Protestant people. « Since 1855, the diminution has been rapid... *at all points of contact with the white race they melt gradually away.* » (2) There is, then, no exception to the universal law. Wherever the Anglo-Saxon sets his foot, bringing in his train selfishness, arrogance, and insatiable cupidity, the aboriginal races disappear; and if he is accompanied, as sometimes happens, by the ministers of his religion, they disappear so much the quicker. A little later we shall find the Indians themselves noticing this invariable fact.

Nor can this doom surprise us, as respects Texas, when we learn from protestant evidence how the natives are treated by their new masters. It is, says

---

(1) Olmsted, *Texas*, p. 154.
(2) P. 296.

Mr Olmsted in expressive language, « the mingled puritanism and brigandism » of his fervid countrymen which make it impossible for them « to associate harmoniously » with the mild and courteous Mexican. « Inevitably they are dealt with insolently and unjustly. They fear and hate the ascendant race. » Mr Froebel also notices « the injustice and over-bearing with which the Anglo-Americans everywhere treat the Hispano-American and Indian population. »

Yet the Mexicans, of all ranks, could teach their rude guests a lesson of charity and courtesy, if the latter were capable of profiting by it. When the Americans who invaded Mexico from Texas, many of whom were brigands of the vilest class, were captured, and marched as prisoners through the whole country to the capital; M^rKendall, who shared their fate without deserving it, gives this account of « the Mexican population generally, » through whom the lawless adventurers were conducted. « They seldom manifested any feelings of exultation in our presence. On the contrary, the mild and subdued eyes of the poor Indians were turned upon us invariably in pity, while the crowds through which we passed, in all the large cities, appeared rather to be actuated by commiseration than triumph or hatred, Jews and heretics though they thought and termed us. » (1)

The lesson appears to have been unfruitful. At Bexar, Mr Olmsted relates how the Mexican householders, using a right which American institutions are supposed to guarantee, voted at a certain election against « the American ticket, » and apparently

(1) *Narrative*, etc., ch. vi, p. 131.

against the introduction of slavery, which Catholic Mexico has suppressed. For this act of citizenship they were publicly assailed, in terms which may suffice to warn us that we are once more coming into the presence of Protestantism, as « political lepers, voting at the bidding of a rotten priesthood. » (1) We may easily anticipate the fate of the Mexican in Texas.

But he will not perish without an effort to save him. There are missionaries at this hour in Texas whom the best and bravest of other days would have welcomed as brothers. Even Zumarraga and Las Casas might have rejoiced to claim for a colleague Bishop Odin, the Vicar Apostolic of Texas; even Betanzos and Peter of Ghent would have recognised as fellow-labourers such men as Timon and Domenech, Dubuis and Chazelle, Calvo and Estany, Clark and Chanrion, Fitzgerald and Hennessy; who now toil, or have recently finished their course, in that arduous field. The Abbé Domenech has lately described their labours, their sufferings, and their patience. If we refer for a moment to his well known pages, it is for the sake of adding one more proof that the Church still produces the same class of missionaries — Spanish, French, English, or Irish — as have borne her message to all lands from the time of St. Paul to our own.

When Bishop Odin visited Europe in 1845, and appealed in the city of Lyons to the Levites of France to follow him, for the love of Christ, to the banks of the Brazos, the Nuèces, and the Rio Grande, these

---

(1) P. 499.

were the attractions which he offered to their zeal. « You will not always find any thing to eat or drink ; you will be without ceasing in travels through unknown regions, where the distances are immense, the plains boundless, and the forests of vast extent. You will pass your nights on the moist earth, your days under a burning sun. You will encounter perils of every kind, and will have need of all your courage and all your energy. » (1)

The invitation was accepted as frankly as it was given. Amongst those who embraced the proposed career was the Abbé Emanuel Domenech, who arrived in Texas in 1846. From the window of his humble dwelling in Castroville he looked out upon the tomb of his predecessor the Abbé Chazelle. Excessive labour, and the want of all nourishing food, had reduced the latter, as well as his companion the Abbé Dubuis, to that mortal languor and exhaustion for which in their utter poverty they could find no remedy. The one lay on the ground, the other on a table, both stricken with typhus fever. They had none to succour them, and water, of which a neighbour placed every morning a pail full at their door, was their only medecine. On the tenth day of their illness,—it was the great Feast of the Assumption,—the Abbé Dubuis resolved to make an attempt to offer once more the Holy Sacrifice. « Let us confess for the last time, » he said to his dying companion, « the strongest of the two shall then say Mass, and give Holy Communion to the other. » With diffi-

(1) *Journal d'un Missionaire au Texas et au Mexique*, par l'abbé E. Domenech, ch. I, p. 2.

culty Dubuis accomplished the pious design, and then Chazelle fell to rise no more. He was in his last agony, when his companion staggered to his side, and in a feeble whisper pronounced over him the final blessing of the Church. A little later, he bore him with tottering steps to a grave in the garden, and there « the dying interred the dead. »(1)

The abbé Dubuis recovered. You think perhaps that he now abandoned a scene so full of sorrowful memories in the past, of formidable anticipations in the future? But men who have received the apostolic vocation accept all that it imposes. At the close of the year 1847, we find the Abbé Dubuis writing from Castroville to his friend the Curé of Fontaines, near Lyons, a letter which concludes with these words : — « To this hour I have never known one moment of disgust or regret; and if I were still in France, I would quit it immediately for the mission of Texas, which I shall only abandon when strength and life are taken from me. » (2)

Yet it was a hard life which these brave missionaries led in Texas. Salary they had none, not even the traditional twenty pounds a year which their brethren receive in India and China. They lived on alms, when alms were offered, and dispensed with them when they were not. Sometimes they dined on a rattle snake, sometimes on a cat, and oftener still they did not dine at all. Once the Abbé Dubuis failed to say Mass, though the congregation were assembled; he could not speak, not having tasted food for

(1) Ch. ii, p. 50.
(2) App. p. 471.

forty-eight hours. He and the Abbé Domenech were joint proprietors of a single cassock, — for as they sometimes galloped eighty miles to administer a sick person, their vestments were subject to dilapidation, — so that while one said Mass, the other staid at home in his shirt-sleeves.

Nor does their Bishop seem to have fared much better than his clergy. The Abbé Hennessy relates to a friend in Paris the manner of living in the Episcopal Palace. « To give you an idea of the comfort and luxury of our life, let it suffice to say, that here, in Galveston, the whole amount of our weekly expenditure, for the Vicar Apostolic and the three priests who live with him, is four dollars, or about sixteen shillings. Monseigneur Odin, choosing poverty and straitness for himself, is only rich and lavish towards the poor. » (1) In a letter which this apostolic bishop addressed to his parents, he says; « Sometimes discouragement almost seizes me, when I know not what means to adopt to procure even the most indispensable provisions; but God is so good a Father that He always comes to our help. » (2)

We are not surprised to learn from the Abbé Domenech that the Protestant clergy in Texas had no sympathy with such a mode of existence. Each of them, he says, had 500 l. a year, besides what he could earn by the ingenious operations in which such men are skilled. One of them, who had three marriageable daughters, announced to his flock — he had chosen for his text the appropriate words, « In-

(1) P. 465.
(2) *Annales de la Propagation de la Foi*, tome III, p. 533.

crease and multiply » — that he would give 3,000 piastres with each of the young ladies to any eligible suitor. « Put me down for two of them, » exclaimed an Irish catholic, who had strolled into the Protestant temple. (1)

But if the Protestant ministers lived in Texas as they are wont to live everywhere else, carefully limiting their prudent operations to the principal cities, and diligently avoiding even the remote possibility of unwelcome perils; the Catholic missionaries would have taught them, if they could have comprehended the lesson, what men can do who have forsaken all for Christ's sake. The Abbé Domenech, amongst others, was familiar with startling scenes. He is on one of his ordinary errands of mercy, journeying from Dhanis to La Leona, and comes suddenly upon the bodies of seven Mexicans, pierced with arrows, scalped and mutilated. The still smouldering embers of their camp fire showed how recent the massacre had been. A few miles beyond La Leona, — for he had boldly continued his way where charity called him, he finds a woman suspended to a tree, still living, though her scalp had been torn off; and at her feet three Mexicans, just slaughtered by a party of marauding Indians. The missionary pursued his course unhurt.

At another time the house of the Abbé Estany is attacked by the *Comanches*. He makes his way through a storm of arrows, and receives no wound; but all that he possesses, clothes, books, and Church vessels, are carried off or destroyed.

(1) Domenech. ch. III, p. 281, 2d voyage.

The Abbé Dubuis, who had braved a hundred deaths, is surprised in his turn by a party of savages. There is no escape, and he quietly advances to meet them. « Do me no harm, » he says, with a calm voice; « I am a captain of the Great Spirit, and a chief of prayer. » They leave him in peace.

But death had no terrors for such men as these; it was but the passage to eternal life. Once the Abbé Domenech received an express, bidding him hasten to the assistance of Father Fitzgerald, dying at Victoria. He sets out at a gallop, almost leaps over a panther lying in his path, and at length stands by the bedside of his friend. « I spoke to him, » he says, « but he did not answer. I wished to embrace him; his lips were rigid. He was just dead. At twenty-six years of age, far from his family, his country, and his friends, without even the succours of religion at his departure out of the world, he had breathed his last. In beholding this youthful victim of Christian charity, my heart was oppressed; I fell on my knees, and being unable to pray, I wept.... But in spite of the sad end of my poor friend, I envied his lot; for him no doubt any longer existed about the future; he had died in the midst of his work. » (1)

But it is time to leave Texas, where missionaries of the same class continue at this hour the same valiant and patient apostolate, calmly expecting, amid all their toils sufferings and dangers, the hour when they shall be joined to their brethren who have gone before, and receive the recompense to which St. Paul

(1) Ch. vi, p. 176.

looked forward during all the vicissitudes of his ministry, — the bonds and scourging, the hunger and thirst, the perils and contradictions, — and which such as they have earned a right to share with him.

The history of California, a land which effectively illustrates the peculiar civilisation of the nineteenth century, has been written by Venegas and others. Here the same facts meet us which we have noticed in every other region of the earth. Not one of the usual phenomena is wanting. The zeal and devotion of the Catholic missionaries; their unbounded success; the love and veneration which the converted natives displayed towards them; the commercial and agricultural prosperity which existed, as Humboldt observes, under « the strict though peaceful rule of the monks; » and finally, the swift havoc and ruin introduced by men of the Saxon race; all recur in their accustomed order, and all are eagerly attested, as usual, by Protestant writers.

« The name of California, » says Mr Berthold Seeman, in 1853, « is for ever united with the unselfish devotion of the Franciscan friars. » (1) Yet the children of St. Francis had been preceded by men of whom another Protestant traveller thus speaks. « The Jesuits, before they were supplanted by the Franciscans, » observes Sir George Simpson, « had covered the sterile rocks of Lower California with the monuments, agricultural, architectural, and economical, of their patience and aptitude; not only leaving to their successors apposite models and tolerable workmen, but also bequeathing to them the invalu-

---

(1) *Voyage of H. M. S. Herald*, vol. II, ch. IX, p. 153.

able lesson, that nothing was impossible to energy and perseverance. » (1) We shall presently hear what the same impartial writer says of the Protestant missionaries in the same regions, and the results of their apparition.

Mr Forbes, — who celebrates with frank admiration « the pure and disinterested motives of the Jesuits, » whom he generously lauds as « true soldiers of the Cross, » and contrasts in energetic terms with the « illiterate fanatics » whom the Sects have sent to take their place, — records also, like Sir George Simpson, « the minute but not uninteresting warfare which they maintained for so many years against the rude natives of California and its still ruder soil, until at length they triumphed over the former, and as much over the latter as was possible. » (2)

He describes too the work of their successors, after careful observation of it. « The best and most unequivocal proof of the good conduct of the Franciscan Fathers is to be found in the unbounded affection and devotion invariably shown towards them by their Indian subjects. They venerate them not merely as friends and fathers, but with a degree of devotedness approaching to adoration. » And then he exclaims, as if he found it impossible to restrain the unwelcome confession; « experience has shown how infinitely more successful the Catholic Missionaries have been than the Protestant. » He even becomes enthusiastic in tracing the contrast, and adds; « Nor can there be agents more fitting than the persevering

(1) *Journey round de World*, vol. I, ch. VII, p. 334.
(2) *California*, ch. I, p. 17.

and well-disciplined Friar, whose whole life and studies have been directed to this end; whose angry passions no injury can rouse, whose humility and patience no insult or obstacle can overcome. With him our Missionaries can bear no comparison. » (1)

Sir George Simpson is more cautious, for he was a British official, yet he also relates how the Protestant missionaries abandoned in despair their attempts on the natives of Columbia, because « they soon ascertained that they could gain converts only by buying them; » and he adds, almost resentfully, « the Church of Rome is peculiarly successful with ignorant savages. » Yet so intelligent a person can hardly suppose that *these* were the easiest class of disciples to win — much less, that they were the easiest to retain.

Let us hear other witnesses, but all Protestants. « We visited the missions, » says Dr Coulter, in 1847, « making a few days' stay at each, enjoying the lively, humane, and agreeable conversation of the Padres, who were, without an exception, a pleasant set of men.... The Padres now have perfect control over the Indians of the Missions. » (2)

Captain Beechey had made exactly the same observation a few years earlier. « The converts are so much attached to the Padres, that I have heard them declare, they would go with them if they were obliged to leave the country. » (3)

Mr Walpole, writing two years after Dr Coulter,

(1) Ch. v, pp. 230, 242,
(2) *Western Coast of South America*, vol. I, ch. xv, p. 154; ch. xvi, p. 170.
(3) *Voyage to the Pacific*, vol. II, ch. I, p. 21.

and with scant sympathy for Catholics, says; « To me the Catholic Missionaries of America always appeared far superior to all other Catholics: under their fostering rule the rude savage ceased his wars, settled down and tilled the land in peace, — witness Paraguay and California ! » (1)

These witnesses are all English Protestants; let us hear at least one American. Captain Benjamin Morrell visits the Mission of St. Antony of Padua, near Monterey, and this is his report. « The Indians are very industrious in their labours, and obedient to their teachers and directors, to whom they look up as to a father and protector, and who in return discharge their duty towards these poor Indians with a great deal of feeling and humanity. They are generally well clothed and fed, have houses of their own, and are made as comfortable as they wish to be. The greatest care is taken of all who are affected with any disease, and every attention is paid to their wants. » (2) Such testimonies are instructive, yet every one must feel that they deal only with the surface of things, and do not lay bare the hidden sources from which all these blessings spring.

Captain Morrell finds 1200 Christian Indians in the Mission of St. Clara. « No person of unprejudiced mind, » he exclaims, « could witness the labours of these Catholic Missionaries, and contemplate the happy results of their philanthropic exertions, without confessing that they are unwearied in well doing.» And then he adds, that although « the Mexicans and

(1) *Four Years in the Pacific*, vol. II, ch. I, p. 25.
(2) *A Narrative of Four Voyages*, ch. VI, p. 208. (1832).

Spaniards are very indolent and consequently very filthy, » « the converted Indians are generally a very industrious, ingenious, and cleanly people. » (1)

One exception there is to these candid testimonies, and it is found, as might be anticipated, in the writings of a Protestant minister. The Rev. Joseph Tracy gravely informs his readers, that the Jesuits and Franciscans in California taught only the « forms of religion, » « without improving their intellects, their morals, or their habits of life! » (2) Perhaps there are no two works, in the whole range of Protestant literature, at once so trivial and so profane, — so full of idle words, childish vaunts, and $\pi\alpha\nu\tau o\lambda\mu o\varsigma$ $\text{'}\alpha\mu\alpha\theta\iota\alpha$, — as Mr Tracy's history of American Missions, and the « Reports of the American Board for Foreign Missions. »

Once more we have noticed one of those peaceful triumphs, rich in blessings to suffering humanity, and which have extorted the admiration even of men whose unhappy prejudices they fail to correct, and whose conscience they leave unawakened. The poor Indians were wiser. *They* could discern Whose ministers such workmen were, and that it was only by the communication of His Spirit that they found strength to lead such lives, or accomplish such victories.

But the history of California does not end here. The Catholic missionaries had done, in this land as in every other, all that men having the gifts and the calling of apostles could do. They had forced the rugged soil to yield ample harvests, they had fertilized the yet more barren heart of the savage with the dew

(1) P. 212.
(2) *History of American Missions*, p. 197.

of heavenly graces. Two other classes were now to enter these regions, — Mexicans who had forfeited their birthright as Catholics, and Protestants who had never possessed it. Both have inflicted irreparable injury upon the tribes of the North-West.

Let us speak of the Mexicans first. Affecting to follow the precedents of modern European policy, of which the chief maxim seems to be the exclusion of all ecclesiastical influence in the government of human society, the civil authorities resolved to secularise all the Missions. The result has been, as in every land where the same experiment has been tried, a swift relapse into the barbarism from which the Church alone has saved the world, the immediate decay of material prosperity, and a vast augmentation of human suffering. History might have taught the Mexicans to anticipate these inevitable fruits. When England laid her hand on the possessions of the Church, which had been for centuries the patrimony of the poor, she took her first step towards her present social condition. Prisons and workhouses became the dismal substitutes for monasteries, and jailors supplanted monks. England has not profited much by the change. The new institutions are at least ten times more costly than the old, and the benefits derived from them have been in inverse proportion. They now receive only prisoners, and disgorge only criminals; while a whole nation of heathen poor, a burden on the present resources of the country and a menace for her future destiny, have sunk down, as even English writers will tell us, to the level of the most degraded tribes of Africa or America, and are as utterly void of religion or of the knowledge of God, as the Sioux, the Carib, or the Dahoman.

Here is the history of the same proceedings in California. « In 1833, » says Möllhausen, « the government of Mexico, jealous of the great influence of the clergy, secularised the missions, and confiscated their property to the state. » It was Gomez Farias who devised the felony, and, as Mr Brantz Mayer relates, ruined in a single province twenty-four missions, inhabited by 23,025 Christian Indians. We will quote immediately the exact statistics of the operation and of its results.

It was not long before the spoilers were ejected in their turn by the Americans, a more energetic race, who, not content with destroying the missions, have proceeded to destroy the Indians also. They would have been ashamed not to surpass so pusillanimous a criminal as Gomez Farias, who contented himself, like a mean robber, with appropriating the property of others. « When California became attached to the United States, » says Möllhausen, « the former property of the missions of course passed into the hands of the American government, and their dwellings are now lonely and desolate and falling rapidly to decay; the roofs have fallen in, the stables are empty; the once blooming gardens and orchards are choked by a wild growth of weeds, and it will probably not be long before the waves of commercial activity will sweep over them, and obliterate the last traces of their existence. » (1)

---

(1) *Journey from the Mississipi to the Coasts of the Pacific*, ch. xv, p. 334.

A few merchants may perhaps improve their fortunes by the change, but it will be at the expense of the whole Indian population, whom they are now busy in exterminating, and who, at no remote day, will have ceased to exist. Already, except in a few of the missions, where the Franciscans still linger, starving amid ruins, but protecting the Indian to the last, they begin to be « brandy drinking, wretched creatures, » says Möllhausen; and then he adds, « it is impossible not to wish that the Missions were flourishing once more, or to see without regret the fallen roofs and crumbling walls of their abode, a mere corner of which now serves as a shelter for a few Catholic priests... The energetic and heroic sacrifices of such missionaries as the Padres Kino, Salvatierra, and Ugarte, obtained their reward; and, up to 1833, when three new missions had been founded, they enjoyed the fruits of their labours. »

« The spoliation of the missions, » says Sir George Simpson, « excepting that it opened the province to general enterprise, *has directly tended to nip civilization in the bud.* » And even the new « enterprise » to which it has furnished a field is so unfruitful, as he admits, except in unprincipled speculations which enrich a few and ruin many, that whereas in the time of the Missions the province exported wool, leather, soap, wheat, beef, and wine, the policy of its actual possessors has annihilated almost all these branches of commerce.

Before we notice, in conclusion, the effect of the American conquest upon the Indians, and the characteristic operations of American missionaries, let us show what have been the admitted results, up to the present date, of the suppression of the Missions. In 1844 M. Duflot de Mofras published his work on Oregon and the north-western provinces of Mexico. Here is the evidence of this intelligent and impartial writer.

It was not till 1842 that Santa Anna robbed the Bishop of California of all the religious funds which still remained from former spoliations, and committed their administration to a coarse and greedy soldier of his own class. « You see, » said an Indian Alcalde to M. de Mofras, « to what misery we are brought : the Fathers can no longer protect us, and the authorities themselves despoil us. » (1) The Indians have learned once more to regard the white man as their natural enemy, and, as M. de Mofras observes, « since the destruction of the missions, » it has become dangerous to travel from Sonora to California. A few fathers still linger in the scene of their once happy labours; the rest have been driven from the country, carrying with them for all their wealth the humble robe of their Order. In 1838, Father Sarria died of exhaustion at the foot of the altar, at the mission of St. Soledad, when about to say Mass, after an apostolate of thirty years. Father Guttierrez received a daily, but insufficient, ration, dispensed by a man who had formerly been a domestic servant, but who was now civil administrator of the Mission! The Father President Sanchez died of grief, when he beheld the havoc and ruin to which he could apply no remedy.

(1) *Exploration du Territoire de l'Oregon*, tome I, ch. VII, p. 345.

The Mission of San Francisco Solano was only founded in 1823 by Father Amorós. It increased so rapidly, that at the time of the suppression it contained 1300 Christian Indians, and possessed 8000 oxen, 700 horses, and other property in proportion. Don Mariano Vallejo, the new civil administrator, seized every thing which it was possible to carry away or sell, and pulled down the mission house to build himself a dwelling out of the materials. (1)

Yet some of the missions still remain, perhaps because neither Mexicans nor Americans have yet found time to destroy them, and still present something of their former aspect. « We cannot express the surprise, » says M. de Mofras, « with which the traveller is struck, on seeing in the neighbourhood of Indian villages, where the land is cultivated with extreme care, and there exists a perfect system of irrigation, the *pueblos* of the whites in a state of profound misery, under the *free* government of most of the so-called republics ! » The common salutation, he says, of a Dominican or a Franciscan to an Indian is still, « Amar a Dios, hijo! » and the answer, « Amar a Dios, padré ! » The Americans will probably introduce another language.

Perhaps it would be impossible to indicate more briefly or more impressively the historical results of the secularization of the Missions, after their long career of peace and prosperity, than M. de Mofras has done in his interesting pages. Even men who are careful only about financial success can appreciate

(1) P. 445.

such statistics as are exhibited in the following table. It has sometimes been said, in jest, that there is nothing so eloquent as figures; let the reader consider, in sober earnest, what lesson he may derive from these.

UPPER CALIFORNIA.

UNDER THE ADMINISTRATION OF THE RELIGIOUS, IN 1834.

Christian Indians	30,650
Horned Cattle	424,000
Horses and Mules.	62,000
Sheep	321,500
Cereal Crops	70,000 hectares.

UNDER THE CIVIL ADMINISTRATION, IN 1842.

Christian Indians	4,450
Horned Cattle.	28,220
Horses and Mules.	3,800
Sheep	31,600
Cereal Crops (1).	4,000 hectares.

It appears, then, that in the brief space of eight years, the secular administration, which affected to be a protest against the inefficiency of the ecclesiastical, had not only destroyed innumerable lives, replunged a whole province into barbarism, and almost annihilated religion and civilization, but had so utterly failed even in that special aim which it professed to have most at heart, — the development of material prosperity, — that it had already reduced the wealth of a single district in the following notable proportions. Of horned cattle there remained

---

(1) P. 321.

about *one fifteenth* of the number possessed under the religious administration; of horses and mules less than *one sixteenth;* of sheep about *one tenth;* and of cultivated land producing cereal crops less than *one seventeenth.* It is not to the Christian, who will mourn rather over the moral ruin which accompanied the change, that such facts chiefly appeal; but the merchant and the civil magistrate, however indifferent to the interests of religion and morality, will keenly appreciate the cruel and blundering policy of which these are the admitted results, and will perhaps be inclined to exclaim with Mr Möllhausen, « It is impossible not to wish that the Missions were flourishing once more! »

And these facts, which even worldly craft may teach men to deplore, are every where the same. Far away to the South, in the plain where the Lake of Encinillas lies, on the borders of Chihuahua, is « one of the richest and most valuable localities in the world for cattle-grazing, in times past supporting innumerable herds. Now it is almost a desert! » (1) It is the history of Paraguay on a smaller scale.

Yet there are American writers, whom no official rebuke has ever disavowed, who appear almost to exult in this universal ruin. Lieutenant Whipple, a highly respectable officer of the United States, from whom Mr Schoolcraft derived some of the materials for his great work on the Indian nations, after noticing, in 1849, that the Lligunos, converted by the Franciscans, still number eight thousand, continues as follows. « They profess the greatest reverence for

(1) Froebel, ch. IX, p. 340.

the Church of Rome, and, glorying in a Christian name, look with disdain upon their Indian neighbours of the desert and the Rio Colorado, calling them miserable Gentiles. » He confesses, too, speaking of the single mission of San Diego, that « for many miles around, the valleys and plains were covered with cattle and horses belonging to this mission; » yet the only reflection which the Christian zeal of the Indians and the skilful administration of their pastors suggested to him is expressed in the silly taunt, that they were « slaves of the priests, » and the worse than silly boast, that « now they are freed from bondage to the Franciscans, » his countrymen will teach them « their duties as Christians and men! » (1) We shall see immediately what they have really taught them.

The Americans, whom Mr Whipple dishonours by such indiscreet advocacy, are in fact completing the work of destruction with characteristic energy; and here is an account of their proceedings. After emptying every other province of the United States, they are now rapidly effecting the same process in California. On the 15th of March, 1860, the *Times* newspaper contained the following extract from the *San Francisco Overland and Ocean Mail Letter*. « Never, as journalists, have we been called upon to comment on so flagrant and inexcusable an act of brutality as is involved in General Kibbe's last Indian war — a scheme of murder conceived in spe-

---

(1) *Historical and Statistical Information respecting the Indian tribes of the U. S.*, by H. R. Schoolcraft, L. L. D., part. II, p. 100. (1851).

culation and executed in most inhuman and cowardly atrocity. If the account of M*r* George Lount, a resident of Pitt river, be true, General Kibbe and all the cowardly band of cutthroats who accompanied him should be hung by the law for murder; for murder it is, most foul and inexcusable. Sixty defenceless Indian women and children killed in their own *rancheria* at night, by an armed band of white ruffians! The massacre of Glencoe does not afford its parallel for atrocity. *This band of Indians were friendly,* had committed no outrage, were on their own lands, in their own homes. » But this was only a beginning; later operations are thus narrated by the same witness.

« The Indians have been driven from their hunting ground by the white man's stock. Their fishing racks have been destroyed by the caprice or for the convenience of the white man. Their acorns are exhausted by the white man's hog, and, *driven to desperation* by actual want and starvation, they have stolen the white man's ox. » This was the pretext for another onslaught. « When Governor Wellar, authorised W. J. Jarboe to organize a company to make war on the Indians... in 70 days they had 15 battles (?) with the Indians; killed more than 400 of them; took 600 of them prisoners, and had only three of their own number wounded, and one killed... Under the license of the law; under the cover of night; in the security of your arms; in the safety of your ambush; you have murdered in cold blood more than 400 sleeping, unarmed, unoffending Indians, men, women, and children. Mothers and infants shared the common fate. Little children in baskets, and even babes, had their heads smashed to pieces or cut open. It will scarcely be credited that this horrible scene occured in Christian California, within a few days' travel from the State capital. » And not only were the actors, or promoters, of this enormous crime a General of the United States Army, and a Governor of a province, but « a bill of nearly § 70,000 is now *before the Legislature* awaiting payment, to be distributed, in part, among these crimsoned murderers! »

More than forty years ago, an American Protestant clergyman, alluding to the early atrocities of his Protestant countrymen against the Indian race exclaimed; « Alas! what has not our nation to answer for at the bar of retributive justice! » (1) If this writer had lived to hear of the scenes just described, he would perhaps have felt that his nation has done little as yet to propitiate the justice of God, and that it would have been well for California to have been left, as of old, to the Jesuits, the Franciscans, and the Dominicans.

We have been told that, at least in one case, the victims were « friendly and unoffending. » In the early history of North America, as we shall see when we come to speak of the Atlantic States, this was almost invariably the case. The Catholic colonists on both banks of the St. Lawrence, as well as those in Maryland under Lord Baltimore, were always on the best terms with the natives. Even Penn, who was admonished by the religious maxims of his

---

(1) *A Star in the West*, by Elias Boudinot, L. L. D., ch. VIII, p. 255. (1816).

society to eschew rapine and war, had no difficulty
in making amicable treaties with the Indians in his
neighbourhood, though he appears to have always
made them to his own advantage. It was not till Protestants had robbed and murdered them, and had
repaid their good offices, as the Indians afterwards
reminded them, with horrible outrage and ingratitude, that the latter swore eternal enmity against
them. They became cruel and vindictive, because
the white man had set them the example. If North
America had been colonised by Catholics alone, there
would have been at this day, as in the Southern continent, whole nations of native Christians.

But it was the doom of the red man to perish before the face of the Anglo-Saxon. He might be friendly
and unoffending, but this could not save him. « I never found, » says Mr Gerstaecker, speaking of the
Wynoot Indians of California, « a more quiet and
peaceable people in any country than they were. »
While of the tribes of this region generally he adds;
« They are really the most harmless nations on the
American continent, let white people, who have
driven them to desperation, say what they please
against them. » And then he quotes Mr Wozencraft,
U. S. Indian Agent, who made this official report.
« A population perfectly strange to them has taken
possession of their former homes, destroyed their
hunting grounds and fisheries, and cut them off from
all those means of subsistence a kind Providence had
created for their maintenance, and taken away from
them the *possibility* of existing. But not satisfied
with that, these men deny them even the right we
have granted to paupers and convicts — the right of

working and existing. » (1) « Goaded by hunger, » says a Wesleyan writer, « and stimulated by revenge, they have begun to trespass on the lands of the colonists. » (2) — because they can no longer find subsistence on their own. Yet Mr Kirkpatrick reported, in 1848, of the Oregon Indians, — « Long before a missionary went into that country, these people were as honest, kind, and inoffensive as any I have ever met with, either civilised or savage. »

And now a word, in conclusion, on the Protestant missionaries. There are not many of them here, because, as Mr Gerstaecker has told us, « there is no profit in view; » but there are a few, and of the usual class. The same writer tells us that he encountered two of them, of rival sects, « but as we find in the present age only very few men who really teach the Gospel for Christ's sake » — he means amongst his co-religionists — « the two pious brethren had long given up preaching to the heathen. *With the natives they would have nothing at all to do* — should they live upon acorns and young wasps, and sleep in the wet woods all for nothing? They did not find sufficient encouragement. » (3) Yet some of them appear to have remained there, for Mr Chandless observes, in 1857 « religious freedom, I suppose, exists; there seemed to be a sort of Protestant Church there (in South California), with a bishop, self-ordained, and pretending to some direct revelation from heaven. » (4)

(1) *Journey round the World*, vol. I, ch. VI, pp. 343-7.
(2) *Colonization*, by Revd John Beecham, p. 7.
(3) Vol. II, p. 10.
(4) *A Visit to Salt Lake*, by William Chandless, ch. X, p. 316.

MISSIONS IN AMERICA.   217

Few men, we may believe, are so undiscerning as to need any assistance in reflecting upon the contrast between the Catholic and Protestant history of California. Let us pass on without needless comment, and enter the territory of Oregon. (1)

We will speak of the Protestant missionaries first, and all our information will be derived, as in other cases, from themselves or their friends. When Oregon was annexed to the United States, the various sects endeavoured, according to their wonted policy, to get the start of each other in appropriating the promising field. The very first missionaries, however, who arrived, and whose instructions were to labour amongst the Flatheads, positively declined, after a brief trial, to execute their mission. The motive of their retreat was characteristic. « The means of subsistence, » we are told by two of their number, — for as they see no dishonour in the confession, they are not ashamed to make it, — « in a region so remote, and so difficult of access, were, to say the least, very doubtful. » (2) The doubt was enough to put them to flight. Yet these gentlemen were probably familiar with certain words of St. Paul, in which he thus describes the life of a true missionary. « Even unto this hour we both hunger and thirst,

---

(1) It is an instructive fact, that when the Fathers of the Society of Jesus were banished from Piedmont, the exiles immediately resumed their apostolic labours in California! In 1857, they had already 151 students in their College at San Francisco, under the direction of thirteen Fathers, and five lay professors. *Prospectus of Santa Clara College*, San Francisco, 1858.

(2) *Ten Years in Oregon*, by D. Lee and J. H. Frost, Missionaries, ch. XII, p. 127.

and are naked, and are buffeted, and have no fixed abode. » (1) We shall presently meet with missionaries of the school of St. Paul who *did* stay with the Flatheads, in spite of « the doubtful means of subsistence, » and who will tell us what was the result of their residence among them.

One of the most influential of the American sects is the Methodist Episcopal body. Here is an account, by an eminent Methodist preacher, of their proceedings in Oregon.

« No missionary undertaking has been prosecuted by the Methodist Episcopal Church with higher hopes and a more ardent zeal. That the results have fallen greatly below the usual average of missionary successes, and inflicted painful disappointment upon the Society and its supporters, none, we presume, any longer hesitate to confess. » This particular mission, he adds, « involved an expenditure of 42,000 dollars in a single year; » nor can we be surprised even at such enormous prodigality, when we learn how it was composed. « At the end of six years there were *sixty-eight* persons connected with this mission, men, women, and children, all supported by this Society. How such a number of missionaries found employment in such a field, it is not easy to conjecture, especially as the great body of the Indians never came under the influence of their labour. » And then follows this curious narrative. « They were, in fact, mostly engaged in secular affairs — concerned in claims to large tracts of land, claims to city lots, farming, merchandizing, blacksmithing,

(1) 1, Cor. iv, 11.

grazing, horse-keeping, lumbering, and flouring. We do not believe that the history of Christian Missions exhibits another such spectacle. » We have seen that it exhibits a good many such, and in every land. « The Mission » he continues, « *became odious to the growing population*... irreconcileable differences arose among the Missionaries, which led to the return of several individuals to the United States, and to a disclosure of the real state of the Mission. » Finally, he adds, that of all the Indians who had ever held relations of any kind with these men, « *none now remain.* » (1)

Another American writer gives the same account of the Wesleyan operations, especially at the *Great Dalles* of Columbia. After describing a murder of a very atrocious kind, committed in the very presence of the preacher while surrounded by his nominal flock, and by one of his own congregation, he adds, « the occurrence is but a type of a thousand atrocities daily occurring among these supposed converts to the merciful precepts of Christianity... Yet these men had been, and still are, represented as evangelized in an eminent degree! » (2)

The Rev. C. J. Nicolay, apparently an English episcopalian minister, gives exactly the same account of the other sects in Oregon. « It has ever, » he says, « been thought a just ground of complaint against men whose lives are devoted to the service of God, » if they try to make « a gain of godliness. » But this reproach, he remarks, « will appear, by

(1) *The Works of Stephen Olin*, L. L. D., vol. II, pp. 427-8.
(2) *Traits of American Indian Life*, ch. x, p. 174. 1853.

their own showing, to lie at the door of the American missionaries who have established themselves in Oregon. In their settlements at Okanagan, etc., etc., this charge is so far true, that their principal attention is devoted to agriculture, but in the Wallamette they sink into political agents and would-be legislators. » Presently he adds, — after quoting the statement of the American navigator Wilkes, that « their missionary intentions have merged in a great measure in others more closely connected with ease and comfort, » — that « the missionaries had made individual selections of lands to the amount of a thousand acres each. » Finally, this gentleman cautiously observes; « It appears that the Roman Catholic missionaries were placed in advantageous contrast to their Protestant brethren. » (1) We shall hear more of this familiar contrast presently.

But if the candid narratives of Messrs Lee and Frost, Olin and Nicolay, reveal the true character and results of all the Protestant missions in this region, we must not suppose that the missionaries themselves admitted, as long as they had any hope of concealing them. Their commercial and agricultural pursuits; their dealings in « city lots; » their « horsekeeping, lumbering, and flouring; » were too importantly aided by their ample salaries to permit them to indulge in such imprudent candour. They sent home, therefore, exactly the same periodical reports which missionaries of the same class were constantly forwarding from every other land, and which the So-

---

(1) *The Oregon Territory*, by Revd C. J. Nicolay, ch. VII, pp. 155, 177, 183, 184. (1846).

cieties at home expected and *required,* as the only means of obtaining a fresh stream of subscriptions. Their employers were willing to forgive them anything, even the cupidity which had made them « odious to the growing population, » so long as they abstained from the additional and unpardonable crime of confessing their failure. And so, in 1844, these well instructed agents wrote home thus; « A gradual advance in Christian knowledge is perceptible! » (1) They knew it was untrue, and when they had nothing more to gain, they crudely confessed it. « It is acknowledged on all hands, » we are told, in this very year, by two of their number, who were candid because they were abandoning the hopeless work, « that the present prospects in respect to civilizing and christianising these natives are exceedingly gloomy. » They confess too, that while their own costly efforts only ended in failure, « the Catholic worship is established at Vancouver. » (2) But this did not prevent the missionary societies from publishing reports which they *knew* to be false, in order to raise fresh means for perpetuating the same lamentable schemes, in which the agents, as they had already ascertained, were only sordid speculators, merchants and horse-dealers, who had adopted for a season the title of missionaries. Let us notice a few examples of their inexhaustible ingenuity.

In 1843, only a few months before their own agents confessed the whole truth,— it is by a careful

(1) *U. S. American Board for Foreign Missions,* Reports, p. 212. (1844).
(2) Lee and Frost, ch. XXIII, pp. 215, 311.

collation of dates that we learn to appreciate the fidelity of Protestant missionary reports, — the bait held out to languid subscribers at home was contained in the published statement, that « Mr Spalding, » one of the Oregon missionaries, « believes a considerable number have experienced the renewing grace of God. » (1) Mr Spalding believed nothing of the kind, as they very well knew, and had such excellent reasons, as we learn from American writers, for repudiating the opinion imputed to him, that he was himself only saved by the influence of a Catholic missionary, at the risk of his own life, from being slaughtered by the homicidal fury of these « renewed » savages. « For this, » we are told, « he was indebted to the timely aid and advice of the Rev. Mr Brouillet, of the Roman Catholic Mission... his Catholic friend assisting him from his own small stock of provisions. » (2) For two days the Indians appear to have pursued him, but without success, Father Brouillet having nobly exposed his own life by putting them on a wrong scent, a trick which only their respect for him induced them to pardon. But he was too late to prevent the massacre of Dr Whitman and his wife, by the Cayoux Indians, and « the entire destruction of Wai-let-pu mission, » consisting of fourteen members, over which that unfortunate gentleman presided. All he could effect was to rescue their bodies from further dishonour; and Mr Paul Kane, who had been the guest of Dr Whitman just before this lamentable event, relates that « the Catholic

(1) *Reports*, p. 171. (1843).
(2) *Traits of American Indian Life*, ch. VI, p. 121.

priest requested permission to bury the mangled corpses, which he did » — here Mr Kane is certainly mistaken — « with the rites of his own church. The permission was granted the more readily, as these Indians are friendly towards the *Catholic* missionaries. »(1) « This terminated the mission, » says the Rev. Dr Brown, » among the Indians West of the Rocky Mountains. (2) « Such is the instructive history from which we may appreciate, not only the relative influence of Catholic and Protestant missionaries, but the immoral fictions by which the revenues of Protestant « societies » are annually recruited.

But there were other missions in these distant regions, conducted by men who were not anxious about « means of subsistence, » knew nothing of « lumbering » or « city lots, » and who have succeeded, after long and patient toil, in converting multitudes of the very tribes with whom the Protestant agents, as their own friends have told us, « would have nothing at all to do. » We have seen, by their own confession, how speedily the latter abandoned the *Flatheads;* let us enquire how the Catholic missionaries fared amongst them.

The Fathers of the Society of Jesus entered twenty years ago the territories which lie to the west of the Rocky Mountains. Here such men as de Smet and Hoecken, Dufour and Verhaegen, have emulated the courage and fortitude which for more than three centuries have been a tradition in their Society.

---

(1) *Wanderings of an Artist among the Indians of North America*, ch. XXI, p. 320.
(2) *Hist. Prop. Christianity*, vol. III, p. 155.

When Father de Smet, a name honoured throughout Christendom, presented himself to the *Flatheads*, they had already acquired some knowledge of Christian truth from a band of Catholic *Cherokees*, who had been driven from their own hunting grounds, and found a refuge with the *Flatheads*. The hospitality of the latter was to be nobly recompensed. « During twenty years, » says Father de Smet, « according to the counsel of the poor *Cherokees*, who had established themselves amongst them, they had approached, as much as possible, towards our articles of belief, our morals, and even our religious practices. In the course of ten years, three deputations had the courage to travel as far as St. Louis, that is to say, to cross more than three thousand miles of valleys and mountains, infested with *Black-Feet* and other enemies. At length their prayers were heard and beyond their hopes. »(1)

The Christian *Cherokees* had done what they could, and their work was now to be completed. In October, 1841, Father de Smet could already give the following report. « All that is passing before our eyes in the Rocky Mountains strengthens us in the hope, which we have long since conceived, of seeing once more a new Paraguay, flourishing under the shadow of the Cross, with all its marvels and affecting recollections... What proves to me that this pleasing imagination is not merely a dream, is, that at the moment while I write these lines, the noisy voices of our carpenters, and the smith whose hammer is ringing on the anvil, announce to me that we

(1) *Annals*, vol. IV, p. 231.

are no longer projecting the foundations, but fixing the roof, of the house of prayer. This very day, the representatives of *twenty-four different tribes* assisted at our instructions; while three savages, of the tribe of the *Cœurs-d'Alène,* who had heard of the happiness of the *Flatheads,* came to entreat us to have compassion upon them also. » In spite of these successes, and of still greater ones to be noticed presently, there will be no new Paraguay in Oregon, for a reason which the course of this narrative will sufficiently indicate.

Of the converted *Flatheads,* the same missionary gives an account, full of interest and importance, but which we are compelled to abbreviate, and which shall be confirmed immediately by Protestant evidence. « They never attack any one, » he says, « but woe to him who unjustly provokes them. » In other words, in becoming good Catholics they have not ceased to be valiant warriors. On one occasion they were assaulted by a band of a thousand *Black-Feet.* « Already the enemy poured down upon them, while they were on their knees, offering to the Great Spirit all the prayers they knew, for the chief had said, ' Let us not rise until we have well prayed. ' » The fight lasted five successive days, when the *Black-Feet* retired, leaving the ground strewed with their dead and wounded.

And these brave *Flatheads,* whose chief, says Father de Smet, « considered as a warrior and a christian, might be compared with the noblest characters of ancient chivalry, » are as remarkable, in his judgment, for their virtues as for their valour. « I have spoken of the simplicity and courage of the

Flatheads; what more shall I say? that their disinterestedness, generosity, and rare devotedness towards their brethren and friends, their probity and morality, are irreproachable and exemplary ; that quarrels, injuries, divisions, enmities, are unknown amongst them. I will add, that all these qualities are already naturalized in them through motives of faith. What exactness do they show in frequenting the offices of religion! What recollection in the house of prayer! What attention to the catechism ! What fervour in prayer! What humility, especially when they relate actions which may do them honour. »(1) The Protestant governor of the State will presently give us his testimony on the same subject.

Elsewhere he says, — « Often we remark old men, even chiefs, seated beside a child ten or twelve years old, paying for hours the attention of a docile scholar to these precocious instructors, who teach them the prayers, and explain to them the principal events of the Old and New Testament. » And once more. On Christmas Eve, 1843, « Fathers Mengarini and Zertinati had the happiness of seeing, at the midnight Mass, almost *the whole nation* of the *Flatheads* approach the Holy Table. Twelve little musicians, trained by Father Mengarini, performed with admirable precision several pieces of the best German and Italian composers. The history of this tribe is known to you; its conversion is certainly well calculated to show forth the inexhaustible riches of the Divine Mercy. » (2)

(1) IV, 353.
(2) VII, 360.

It is not uninteresting to learn how the missionaries, who had once more accomplished such a work as this, were content to live, in the earlier years of the mission, among their wild flock. The « means of subsistence, » about which our Lord enjoined His disciples, and principally such as were to teach others, to « take no thought, » were meagre and precarious. The Protestant ministers, who loved not this distasteful precept, had promptly made the discovery, and fled away to more genial regions. Father de Smet, who might have been taking his ease in his own fair land, gaily describes what he calls « a supper, » which he ate with his disciples, and which « consisted of a little flour, a few roots of *camash*, » — a species of wild onion, — « and a bit of buffalo grease. The whole was flung together into the cauldron, to form a single *ragout*. A long pole, for the heat kept us at a respectful distance, was transformed into a ladle, which it was necessary to turn continually, until the contents of the kettle had acquired the proper thickness. We considered the dish delicious! We had but one porringer for six guests. But necessity makes man industrious. In the twinkling of an eye my Indians were ready for the attack on the cauldron. Two of them provided with bits of bark, two others with bits of leather, the fifth armed with a tortoise shell, plunged again and again into the cauldron with the skill and regularity of a smith beating on his anvil. It was soon drained. »

At another time, by way of varying their delicacies, it was « wild roots and moss-cakes, as hard as dried glue, » which furnished their table, and of which a broth was composed « which has the appearance and taste of soap. » But enough of these trivial hardships, to which the missionaries rarely refer, and then only by way of jest.

The *Flatheads* were not the only tribe won to Christianity by the Jesuits in Oregon. When *they* had been gathered into the fold, Father de Smet started for Columbia; where, as Sir George Simpson has told us, the Protestant missionaries « soon ascertained that they could gain converts only by *buying* them. » The Jesuits, like St. Peter, had « neither silver nor gold; » but they worked, as he did, « in the name of Jesus of Nazareth, » and with similar fruits. « During the journey, » says Father de Smet, « which lasted forty-two days, I baptized one hundred and ninety persons, twenty-six of whom had arrived at extreme old age. I announced the word of God to more than two thousand Indians, who will not delay, I hope, to place themselves under the standard of Jesus Christ. » And then he relates an anecdote of a certain Protestant, a Mr Parkers, one of that class who have inflicted so much injury upon the heathen in every land. This gentleman had wilfully broken a cross, erected over the grave of an Indian child, and had announced that he did it « because he did not wish to leave in this country a monument of *idolatry*, set up in passing *by some Catholic Cherokees.* » « Poor man! » says Father de Smet, « if he now returned to these mountains, he would hear the praises of the Holy Name of Jesus resounding on the banks of the rivers and lakes; in the prairies as well as in the bosom of the forests; he would see the Cross planted from shore to shore, over a space of three hundred leagues, commanding the loftiest-summits of the *Cœurs-d'Alène*, and the principal chain which separates the waters of the Missouri from those of the Colombia; and saluted with respect in the valleys of Wallamette, of Cowlitz, and of the Bitter-Root. At the moment that I write, Father Demers has gone to carry it to the different nations of Caledonia; everywhere the word of Him who has said that this glorious sign would attract men to Him begins to be verified in favour of the poor sheep so long wandering over the vast American continent. Would that this cross-breaker might pass again through these same places. He would see the image of Jesus suspended from the necks of more than four thousand Indians; and the youngest child, who is but learning the catechism, would tell him — ' M' Parkers, it is God alone whom we adore, and not the cross; do not break it, for it reminds us that a God has died to save us. ' » (1)

Father de Smet, whom we must now quit, has been joined since that date by many fellow-labourers of his own school. In 1852, he could already report, speaking only of his personal toils, amongst the Indians *West* of the Rocky Mountains, « The total number of baptisms administered by me in the different tribes amounts to 1586. » And he was then contemplating a still more perilous ministry. « The account which I receive of the dispositions of the *Black-Feet*, » he says in one of his letters, « is frightful... I place all my confidence in the Lord, who can change, at His good pleasure, and soften

(1) IV, 367.

these implacable hearts. My business is to carry the Gospel to the very places where the excursions of these marauders are most frequent. No consideration can turn me aside from this project. » (1) It appears to have been at least partially executed, as we learn incidentally from the following statement in an English journal. « An interesting marriage ceremony has been recently performed at Illinois. The parties were Major Culbertson, the well known Indian trader and agent of the American Fur Company, and Natowista, *daughter of the Chief of the Blackfoot Indians...* They were married a few days since by Father Scanden, of St. Joseph's, Missouri, according to the ritual of the Catholic Church. Mrs Culbertson is said to be a person of fine native talent, and has been at times a very successful mediator between the American Government and the nation to which she belongs. » (2)

The Potawattomies are another tribe who have accepted in great numbers the teaching of the Catholic missionaries. At the request of their chiefs, Father Verhaegen did not hesitate to present in person to the government at Washington the petition which they had entrusted to him. Fortified by the generous co-operation of General Clark, agent for Indian affairs in the district west of the Mississippi, this missionary commenced his labours among them, accompanied by Father Hoecken. They had peremptorily rejected, like the Omahas, and many other tribes, the Protestant teachers offered to them by the

(1) *An.* VII, 382; XIII, 319.
(2) *Weekly Register*, October 15, 1859.

government. They had detected, as Father de Smet observes, that « the chief solicitude of the ministers is reserved for their commercial speculations, and when they have amassed large profits, they return to their native country, under pretence that there is nothing to be done among the savages. »

Twelve months after Father Hoecken had entered the territory of the *Potawattomies*, he could give this description of them. « They are sincerely attached to the practices of religion, respectful towards the missionaries, assiduous in approaching, at least every three weeks, the sacred tribunal (of penance) and the Holy Table. Scarcely a day passes that some one of them is not seen approaching one of those sacraments. On festivals, the number of those who receive Holy Communion varies from twenty to thirty. » Already more than a thousand Potawattomies professed the Catholic faith; and the same missionary adds, that they manifest « an entire obedience, not only to the commands of the priest, but to the slightest intimation of his wishes. »

Yet these missionaries were, if possible, poorer than the savages themselves, willingly accepted their humble food and lodging, and abased themselves to share their daily life. « For myself, » says Father Hoecken, in one of his letters to a member of the same Society, « I have no other wish than to live among the Indians, and to find on the other side of the Rocky Mountains the spot from which I am to rise at the last day. »

The same apostolic missionary, though he would

(1) *Annals*, II, 38.

have displayed only charity and courtesy towards the men who had abandoned in disgust the work to which he had devoted his life, gives this account of the reception which they experience from the Indians. « The Protestant ministers have endeavoured to obtain followers among these savages, but their efforts have not been attended with success. Instead of listening to them, they are questioned, and put to a severe examination. ' Where is your wife? ' said an Indian to one of them; a gesture was the only answer of the minister, who pointed with a finger to his residence, where his wife was. — ' Your dress, no doubt ', continued the savage, ' is a black robe? ' ' No, ' replied the minister, ' I do not wear one. '—' Do you say Mass? ' ' Oh, never, ' answered the minister eagerly.—' Do you wear the tonsure? ' ' No. '—' Then, ' they all exclaimed together, ' You may go back from whence you came. ' » (1)

The *Winnebagoes* display the same dispositions. Father Cretin relates that they have repeatedly petitioned the government authorities to send them Catholic Priests, but that their prayer was always answered by an embassy of Protestant ministers. When a treaty was negotiated in 1845 between this tribe and the United States, a solemn assembly was convened, and the Governor of Wisconsin unfolded the terms which he was commissioned to offer them. Their territory consisted of two million three hundred thousand acres of excellent land, watered by six considerable rivers. This magnificent tract they were asked to abandon, the invitation

(1) II, 40.

being equivalent to a command, for a recompense which they neither wished to accept nor dared to refuse. After a day's deliberation, the Indians again met the Governor, prepared to give a reply to his proposals. *Wakoo*, an aged chief, the most celebrated orator of the tribe, rose to speak in the name of his nation, « a large crucifix glistening on his breast. » From his noble address we extract the following words.

« If I alone speak to day, far be it from you to suppose that I am the only one able to express the feelings of my tribe. All the chiefs here present know how to make known their thoughts, but being accustomed from my youth to speak in the councils of my nation, I have been chosen as the eldest to defend, in the name of all, our common interests. Thou comest on the part of our great father (the President) to demand the cession of our territory. But can he have forgotten the magnificent promises which, on two different occasions, he gave me at Washington? I remember them, for my part, as if they had been spoken only to day..... ' Depend upon me, ' said our great father, ' I will always defend you. You shall be my children. If any wrong be done to you, address yourselves always to me. Your causes of complaint shall cease so soon as they shall be known to me, and I will defend you. ' And I, a child of nature, who have but one tongue, believed in the sincerity of these promises. Yet, in spite of our remonstrance, all our affairs have been arranged without our being even consulted. They have sent away agents whom we loved, to give us others, without asking our opinion. We have forwarded petitions, to which no attention has been paid. They promised us that they would leave us always the lands which we occupy, and already they wish to send us I know not where. My brother, thou art our friend. Tell our great father, that his children require a longer halt here, before they enter on the path of a new exile. *The tree which is continually transplanted must quickly perish.* »

Here the orator interrupted himself, to notice the charges brought against his tribe, as a pretext for « dispensing with justice towards them, » and for palliating the tyranny of which they were to be victims. « Why, » said he, « reproach us with vices which you have yourselves encouraged? Why come to the very door of our tents to tempt us with your fire-water? » And then he went on thus. « Our great father has said to us, I will send to you men who will teach you how to live well. These men have come, but though they are tolerably good, *our young men do not listen to them any better than to ourselves; we wish for Catholic Priests.* They will make themselves heard, be assured of it. I take God to witness that what I say expresses the wishes of my nation. » And then he sat down amid the applause of the assembled chiefs. (1)

We have seen, in every chapter of this work, the triumphs of Catholic missionaries attested by the unsuspicious evidence of Protestant witnesses. Here is their testimony to the same order of facts in the valleys of the Rocky Mountains. In 1855, Governor Stephens forwarded to the President of the United

---

(1) VI, 364.

States an official report on the territory committed to his charge. Of the *Flatheads* he speaks as follows. « They are the best Indians in the territory, honest, brave, and docile, They profess the Christian religion, and I am assured that they live according to the precepts of the Gospel. » After describing their manner of life, the same authority adds, that they are « sincere and faithful, » and « strongly attached to their religious convictions. » (1)

Of the tribe called *Pend-d'Oreilles*, Mr Stephens observes, that the mission established among them has been in existence nine years, and that for a long time the missionaries lived in huts, and fed on roots. They have now a church, he says, « of which all the ornaments are so well executed, that one is tempted to suppose they must have been imported » : yet they are entirely the work of the missionaries and their neophytes. « When the missionaries arrived, » he adds, « these Indians were impoverished, wretched, and almost destitute of clothes. They were in the habit of burying alive both the aged and infant children. At this day almost the entire tribe belongs to the Saviour's fold. I have seen them assembled at prayer, and it appears to me that these savages are, in every respect, in the way of true progress. These Indians have a great veneration for their Fathers, the Black Robes. They say if the missionaries were to leave them, it would certainly cause their death. » He then praises their habits of industry, and adds, that while the Fathers have brought 160 acres under cultiva-

(1) Quoted in the work entitled, *Cinquante Nouvelles Lettres du R. P. De Smet*, pp. 292, et seqq. (Paris 1858).

tion, « the produce of the harvest belongs to the Indians, because very little suffices for the wants of the missionaries.» Finally, after noticing their « pious fervour, » the Governor remarks, that « religion has destroyed the state of slavery in which woman groans in all the unbelieving tribes. »

Of the *Cœurs-d'Alène*, of whom 500 are Christians, the same official reports thus. « Thanks to the labours of these good fathers, they have made great progress in agriculture. Instructed in the christian religion, they have abandoned polygamy; their morals have become pure, and their conduct edifying. *The work effected by the missionaries is really prodigious.* There is a magnificent church, almost finished, entirely built by the Fathers, the Brothers, and the Indians. »

Lastly, he declares of the *Potawatomies*, « they are hardly Indians now! » — while their daughters are educated by those Sisters of the Sacred Heart from whom the noblest of other races receive instruction in the capitals of Europe, but who have not feared to traverse an ocean and a continent, to carry religion and civilisation to the most hidden recesses of the Rocky Mountains.

It is not expedient to pursue with further detail the history of missionary labours in these remote western regions, nor to multiply the illustrations which it affords both of the character of the missionaries and the results of their toil. We have sufficiently traced, here as elsewhere, the contrast which it is the main object of these volumes to exhibit. One remark, however, may be added, before we enter those more famous provinces of the East, which lie between the frozen wastes of Hudson's Bay and the sun-lit waters of the Gulf of Mexico.

We have read the words in which Father de Smet avows the noble ambition, worthy of himself and his order, of reviving on the other side of the Rocky Mountains the glories of Paraguay. Would that it were possible for us to share his generous hopes. If such a triumph could indeed be accomplished in Oregon or Columbia, Father de Smet and his colleagues sufficiently resemble their illustrious predecessors of the Society of Jesus both to attempt and to effect it. Even Protestant writers have recognised this fact. « There is an unseen element at work, » says one of those candid witnesses of whom we have quoted so many, « in the remote wilderness of the Oregon, whose success is guaranteed by all the precedents of history; it is the agency of the Catholic Church. »(1) But the conditions of her warfare are no longer the same. In Paraguay, the enemy whom the missionaries of the Cross fought and vanquished, rescuing more than a million victims from his grasp, had no such army of auxiliaries as are now doing his fatal work on the shores of the Pacific. The apostles who converted, one after another, the ferocious hordes of South America, and built up whole nations of peaceful, civilized, and christian men, where before their coming only bloodthirsty savages dwelt, owed their astonishing success, not only to their own patient valour and invincible charity, but to the oneness of the faith and the unalterable harmony of

(1) *The Statesmen of America in* 1846, by S. Mytton Maury, p. 309.

the doctrine which they carried with them. Never during two centuries, was the half-awakened pagan of the Southern continent embarassed by the divisions, the contradictions, or the worldly lives of another order of teachers, who have made Christianity hateful to his brethren in so many other lands, both in the east and west. And thus it came to pass, as we have seen, that even the brutal Omagua or the cannibal Chiriguana confessed, at first with reluctant admiration, a little later with loving reverence, that men who were always pure, meek, and just, came forth from God, and that the message which they brought, since it never varied, must have come from Him also. This is an advantage which the less fortunate tribes on the other side of the Rocky Mountains are now losing for ever. Already twenty sects are fighting together before their eyes. The Anglicans have recently entered Columbia, carrying with them the two weapons which they have used in other lands,—unlimited pecuniary resources, and undying hatred of the Church. They cannot convert the heathen themselves, but they can prevent others doing so. This is their mission. And therefore there will be no new Paraguay to the west of the Rocky Mountains. « I am fully impressed with the belief, » is the official report of Mr Nathaniel Wyeth, « that these Indians *must* become extinct under the operation of existing causes. » (1) There are indeed labourers in that distant field who, if they had fair play, could convert, as their fathers did, the inhabitants of a whole continent; but even hope hides her

---

(1) Schoolcraft, part. I, p. 226.

face in presence of the deadly evils which Protestantism generates in every pagan land. The inevitable fate of the Indian, when once he comes in contact with its emissaries, is to perish from the face of the earth. We are about to consider the last and most afflicting proof of this fact in the sorrowful history of Canada and the United States.

The first European settlements in Canada, as in India, were made by a company of merchants; in the former country by French Catholics, in the latter by English Protestants. The usual significant contrast marked the proceedings of the two classes. « The stockholders and directors of the East India Company, » says an English writer, « never gave education or religion a thought in their earliest enterprises; and when they had attained to sovereign power in the East, the use they made of it was to *prohibit* both the one and the other for a long period.... The French Company for trading to Canada were, on the contrary, so impressed with the duty of providing instruction and religion for the Indians among whom they were going to place settlers, that they undertook » — and then he describes at length the noble efforts which they made, and of which we are going to examine the results. (1)

The Canadian Company established under the auspices of Cardinal Richelieu, who wisely prohibited the admission of Protestant colonists as sure to be fatal to the welfare of the heathen, bound themselves by a solemn compact « to maintain mission-

(1) J. S. Buckingham, *Canada*, ch. xv, p. 203.

aries for the conversion of the savages. » (1) The pledge was faithfully observed, in the same religious spirit which made Champlain exclaim, « The salvation of one soul is of more value than the conquest of an empire. » « The principal design of the French settlements in Canada, » says M⟨r⟩ Alfred Hawkins, — we shall quote, as usual, only Protestant authorities, — « was evidently to propagate the Christian religion. » With this object, they sent the agents whom the Catholic Church always provides for such labours, and it is in the following words that M⟨r⟩ Hawkins attempts to describe them.

« The early history of Canada teems with instances of the purest religious fortitude, zeal, and heroism; of young and delicate females relinquishing the comforts of civilisation to perform the most menial offices towards the sick, to dispense at once the blessings of medical aid to the body, and of religious instruction to the soul, of the benighted and wondering savage. » He alludes, no doubt, though he does not name them, to such ministers of consolation as Marguerite Bourgeoys, Marie Barbier, Marguerite Le Moine, Marie Louise Dorval, and a hundred more, « renowned for their piety, » as the Swedish traveller Kalm observed in the last century (2), and of whose labours M⟨r⟩ Hawkins thus speaks. « They must have been upheld by a strong sense of duty. But for such impressions, it would have been beyond human nature to make such sacrifices as the *Hospitalières*

---

(1) *Histoire du Canada et de ses Missions*, par M. l'Abbé Brasseur de Bourbourg, tome I, ch. II, p. 33. (1852).

(2) *Travels in North America*, Pinkerton, vol. XIII, p. 658.

made, in taking up their residence in New France. Without detracting from the calm philosophic demeanour of religion at the present day, » — it is a Protestant who speaks, — « it is doubtful whether any pious persons could be found willing to undergo the fatigues, uncertainty, and personal danger, experienced by the first missionaries of both sexes in New France. Regardless of a climate to whose horrors they were entirely unaccustomed, of penury and famine, of danger, of death, of martyrdom itself; sustained by something more than human fortitude, by divine patience, they succeeded at length in establishing, on a firm foundation, the altars and the faith of their country and their God. » (1)

We shall see them presently at their work, but a preliminary consideration claims a moment's attention. Before we examine their labours, it is necessary to show, by a few examples, what kind of reception the new teachers met with from the Indians, before the latter were finally estranged by actions which would have embittered a more forgiving temper than theirs.

« The untutored Indians, » says Mr Hawkins, « treated the first Europeans with true Christian charity. The efforts of the Jesuits for the conversion and instruction of the savages, the universal kindness and benevolence of the Missionaries wherever they succeeded in establishing themselves, perpetuated this friendly spirit *towards the French*. » (2)

---

(1) *Picture of Quebec, with Historical Recollections*, ch. x, p. 177.
(2) *Ibid.*, ch. 1, p. 5.

When the Ursulines arrived at Quebec in 1639, « as the youthful heroines stepped on shore, » observes Mr Bancroft, « they stooped to kiss the earth which they adopted as their country, and were ready, in case of need, to tinge with their blood. The governor, with the little garrison, received them at the water's edge. Hurons and Algonquins, joining in the shouts, filled the air with yells of joy. Is it wonderful that the natives were touched by a benevolence which their poverty and squalid misery could not appal? » (1)

A little later Mr Bancroft will tell us that the sympathy of the Indians *towards the French* never waned, and that as the latter « made their last journey » down the valley of the Mississippi, after the English conquest, « they received on every side *the expressions of passionate attachment* from the many tribes of red men. » Familiarity, therefore, had only confirmed the love which they had inspired on their first arrival, and which had been deepened by an intercourse of more than a century. It is not easy to exaggerate the importance of this fact, from which impartial writers have justly concluded, that if the French alone had colonised America, conversion, and not extermination, would have been the lot of its native tribes.

But a welcome as sincere, though less enthusiastic, had greeted the Protestant emissaries from England and Holland. They confessed it themselves. « To us, » said the Rev. Mr Cushman, one of the early Protest-

(1) *History of the United States*, by George Bancroft; vol. II, p. 787. (Ed. Routledge).

ant missionaries, « the Indians have been like lambs; so kind, so submissive and trusty, as a man may truly say, many Christians are not so kind or sincere. » (1)

From every part of the Eastern States came the same reports. « The Virginia tribes, » destined to be repaid with merciless cruelty and ingratitude, « literally sustained the colony planted at Jamestown with supplies of Indian corn from their own fields. » (2) Of those in New England an Anglican minister gave this account. « The Indians doe generally professe to like well of our comming and planting here. » (3) When the English first arrived at Pokanoket, where they afterwards massacred men women and helpless children, leaving not a soul alive, « the native inhabitants received them with joy, and entertained them in their best manner. » (4) In the South the same facts occurred; though we learn from a public petition presented to « the Lords Proprietors of Carolina, » that « the Indian nations in the neighbourhood of the said Province had been so inhumanly treated, that they were in great danger of revolting to the French. » (5) Lastly, in that region which was more than any other exclusively English in its character, laws, and traditions, but of which the

(1) Schoolcraft, part. I, p. 25.
(2) *Id.*, part. II, p. 29.
(3) *New England's Plantations*, by a reverend Divine now there resident; p. 13. (1630).
(4) *History of the Town of Plymouth*, by James Thacher, M D., p. 39. (1835).
(5) *An Historical Account of the Protestant Episcopal Church in South Carolina*, by Frederick Dalcho, M. D.; p. 83.

injured natives learned to cherish a more deadly hostility towards their guests than in any other part of America, Mr Howison relates, that on their first arrival, « a friendly interchange of courtesies took place. » In the isle of Roanoke, where the English landed, « the wife of the Chief ran, brought them into her dwelling, caused their clothes to be dried, and their feet to be bathed in warm water; and provided all that her humble store could afford of venison, fish, fruits, and hominy for their comfort. » And when « the English, in unworthy distrust, seized their arms, this noble Indian woman obliged her followers to break their arrows, in proof of their harmless designs » — so that the colonists themselves described them, in letters to England, as « gentle and confiding beings. » (1)

We shall see hereafter more ample and affecting illustrations of the same truth, and these may suffice for the present. Enough had been said to indicate the contrast which we shall presently exhibit in all its details, and to prepare us for the future consideration of these two impressive facts, — that while in the *South*, where the preachers of the Gospel were everywhere received with clubs and arrows, and everywhere dyed the soil with their blood, they converted the whole continent; in the *North*, where a simple and confiding hospitality greeted the emissaries of Protestantism, they have only created a desert. This is the lesson which we shall learn from the history upon which we are about to enter.

It was not at the same date, nor in the same spot,

---

(1) *History of Virginia*, by Robert R. Howison; ch. I, p. 53.

that the English and Dutch began to arrive in America, but they brought with them the same religious ideas, as well as the same motives and aims; and as their sole object was to acquire territory and amass wealth, they began by deliberately bribing the *unconverted* tribes, after stimulating them with strong liquors, to make war on the *Christian* Indians in alliance with France. Even Gookin, a fierce adversary of the Catholic religion, who vehemently deplored the rapid success of the early missionaries among the natives, confessed, that « this besetting sin of drunkenness could not be charged upon the Indians before the English and other Christian nations came to dwell in America. » (1) He had reason to say it. When Hendrick Hudson was received by the Indian tribe with whom he came in contact on landing, his first act was to intoxicate them all with whiskey, which they drank with repugnance, and only to show, by an admirable courtesy, their confidence in their new visitors. (2) Monseigneur de Laval, Bishop of Quebec, who anticipated the terrible effects which intemperance would produce among the inhabitants of North America, denounced the penalties of mortal sin upon all who should give spirits to the Indians; (3) and Mr Bancroft will tell us hereafter that the admonition was entirely successful; but the English and Dutch were not subject to his authority, and would have laughed at his censures. And the natives quickly distinguished the different

---

(1) Gookin's *Historical Collections*, § 3, p. 7. (1772).
(2) Schoolcraft, part. II, p. 24.
(3) Brasseur de Bourbourg, tome I, ch. vii, p. 140.

policy of their Catholic and Protestant guests. « You yourselves, » they said to the Dutch, « are the cause of this evil; you ought not to craze the young Indians with brandy. Your own people, when drunk, fight with knives, and do foolish things; you cannot prevent mischief, till you cease to sell strong drink to the Indian. » (1) To the English they addressed, again and again, still more earnest reproaches. « It is the English, » they were accustomed to say, « who corrupt us. » (2) When the English governor of Boston, striving to alienate the natives from the French, made them enticing offers, on condition that they should consent to admit « an English minister, » the answer which he received from their representatives is perhaps as worthy of record as any which the Indian annalists have preserved.

« Your speech astonishes me, » said the orator whom they deputed to speak on their behalf. « I am amazed at your proposal. You saw me long before the French did; yet neither you, nor your ministers ever spoke to me of prayer or of the Great Spirit. They saw my furs, and my beaver skins, and they thought of them only. These were what they sought. When I brought them many, I was their great friend. That was all.

On the contrary, one day I lost my way in my canoe, and arrived at last at an Algonquin village near Quebec, where the Black Robes taught. I had hardly arrived when a Black Robe came to see me. I was loaded with peltries. The French Black Robe

(1) Bancroft, vol. II, p. 563.
(2) Henrion, tome II, 2de partie, p. 609.

disdained even to look at them. He spoke to me at once of the Great Spirit, of Paradise, of Hell, and of the Prayer which is the only path to heaven. I heard him with pleasure. I staid long in the village to listen to him. At length Prayer was pleasing to me. I begged him to instruct me. I asked for Baptism, and I received it. Then I returned to my own country, and told what had happened to me. They envied my happiness, and wished to share it. They set out to find the Black Robe, and ask him to baptize them. This is how the French behaved to us. If when you first saw me, you had spoken to me of prayer, I should have had the misfortune to learn to pray like you, for I was not then able to find out if your prayer was good. But I have learned the prayer of the French. I love it, and will follow it till the earth is consumed and comes to an end. Keep, then, your money and your minister. I speak to you no more. » (1)

The Swedish traveller Kalm appears to allude to this, or to some similar oration, when he says, to the great displeasure of his editor, Pinkerton, « the English do not pay so much attention to a work of so much consequence as the French do, and do not send such able men to instruct the Indians as they ought to do. » (2) Mr Talvi, also, an American author, but contrasting unpleasantly with the candid and generous writers of that country, — his solitary allusion to the Catholic missionaries being a vulgar and heartless jest, — confesses, that « the Indians them-

(1) *Lettres Édifiantes et Curieuses*, tome VI, p. 211.
(2) Pinkerton, vol. XIII, p. 588.

selves, now that the Christianity was to be enforced upon them which the Whites, » he means the English, « had not taught them to love, asked, why the latter had been silent about it twenty-six years, when the matter was so weighty that their salvation depended upon it? » (1) And lastly Mr Halkett forcibly observes, « It cannot be doubted that the Indians, for successive generations, have looked upon the Whites as a fraudulent, unjust, and immoral race; preaching what they did not practise. We need not, therefore, be surprised to find that the Indians do not scruple, even at the present day, to express, through their chiefs, their decided reluctance to receive the instructions of the missionaries. » (2)

We shall see presently further examples, both of the contrast and of the native comments upon it; meanwhile, let us endeavour, by the aid of Protestant writers, to sketch the outlines of the history of missions in Canada, and of the fortunes of its aboriginal tribes.

The first mission to the Hurons was commenced in 1615 by one whom Mr Bancroft calls « the unambitious Franciscan, Le Caron, » who « years before the Pilgrims anchored within Cape Cod, had penetrated the land of the Mohawks, had passed to the north into the hunting grounds of the Wyandots, and, bound by his vows to the life of a beggar, had, on foot, or paddling a bark canoe, gone onward and still onward, taking alms of the savages, till he reach-

---

(1) Talvi's *History of America*, vol. II, ch. XIX, p. 78.
(2) *Notes on North American Indians*, by John Halkett Esq.; ch. XIII, p. 305.

ed the rivers of Lake Huron. » « It was neither commercial enterprise » says the same distinguished writer, « nor royal ambition which carried the power of France into the heart of our continent : the motive was religion; » and he adds, the only « policy » which inspired the French conquests in America « was congenial to a church which cherishes every member of the human race without regard to lineage or skin. » (1)

By the year 1636, fifteen Fathers of the Society of Jesus had entered Canada, and commenced that astonishing warfare, celebrated with honest enthusiasm by American writers, of which the fruits were long ago described by Father Bressany, who had himself no mean share in producing them. « Whereas at the date of our arrival, » he says, — writing with the hand which the savages had cruelly mutilated, after tormenting him for a whole month, — « we found not a single soul possessing a knowledge of the true God; at the present day, in spite of persecution, want, famine, war, and pestilence, there is not a single family which does not count some Christians, even where all the members have not yet professed the faith. Such has been the work of twenty years. » (2) A little later, as is well known, the whole Huron nation was Christian.

It was in June, 1611, that Fathers Biart and Massé arrived in Canada ; and it is a notable fact that the first Jesuit slain in America, in 1613, fell by

---

(1) Vol. II, p. 783.
(2) *Missions dans la Nouvelle France*, par le R. P. F. G. Bressany. S. J.; p. 109. (Ed. Martin, 1852).

the hands, not of the savages, but of the English. (1) American Protestants have described the labours of these first missionaries and of their successors. A few examples of the language which they employ will fitly introduce the history which we are briefly to trace.

« Within thirteen years, » says professor Walters, « the wilderness of the Hurons was visited by sixty missionaries, chiefly Jesuits. » One of them, Claude Allouez, discovered Lake Superior. Marquette, of whom Mr Bancroft says, « the people of the West will yet build his monument, » « embarks with his beloved companion and fellow missionary, Joliet, upon the Mississippi, and discovers the mouth of that king of rivers, the Missouri. A third member of this devoted band, » continues Mr Walters, « the fearless Ménan, settles in the very heart of the dreaded Mohawk country, on the banks of the river which still bears that name. The Onondagas welcome the missionaries of the same illustrious society. The Oneidas and Senecas likewise lend an attentive ear to the sweet tidings of the gospel of peace. When we consider that these missionaries were established in the midst of continual dangers and life-wasting hardships, that many of of the Jesuits sealed with their blood the truth of the doctrines they preached, and the sincerity of their love for these indomitable sons of the American forest; we are not surprised at the eloquent encomiums which have been passed upon their dauntless courage and their more than

---

(1) Charlevoix, *Histoire de la Nouvelle France*, tome 1, liv. 3, p. 211. (1744).

human charity and zeal. » And then he adds, with that singular freedom from peevish bigotry and irrational prejudice which is the characteristic of so many American Protestants; « we have sufficient data to prove, that there is not a State of our Union wherein Catholicity has obtained a footing, whose history does not exhibit many interesting traits of heroic self-denial, of dangers overcome, of opposition meekly borne, of adversaries won to our faith by the Catholic Missionaries. » (1)

Mr Washington Irving is not less emphatic in his generous admiration of the same great company of apostles. « All persons, » he observes, « who are in the least familiar with the early history of the West, know with what pure and untiring zeal the Catholic missionaries pursued the work of conversion among the savages. Before a Virginian had crossed the Blue Ridge, and while the Connecticut was still the extreme frontier of New England, more than one man whose youth had been passed among the warm valleys of Languedoc, had explored the wilds of Wisconsin, and caused the hymn of Catholic praise to rise from the prairies of Illinois. The Catholic priest went even before the soldier and the trader; from lake to lake, from river to river, the Jesuits pressed on unresting, and, with a power which no other Christians have exhibited, won to their faith the warlike Miamis and the luxurious Illinois. » (2)

Even Protestant ministers, forgetting in presence of so much heroism and virtue their conventional

(1) Rupp, *Hist. of Rel. Denominations of U. S.*, pp. 119-20.
(2) *Ibid.*, *Knickerbocker*, June, 1838.

phraseology, which they seem to have agreed to suspend over the graves of martyrs, have caught up the strain. « How few of their number, » exclaims the Rev. Mr Kip, « died the common death of all men! » And then, after enumerating the various kinds of death by which they finished their course, he continues thus. « But did these things stop the progress of the Jesuits? The sons of Loyola never retreated. The mission they founded in a tribe ended only with the extinction of the tribe itself. Their lives were made up of fearless devotedness and heroic self-sacrifice. Though sorrowing for the dead, they pressed forward at once to occupy their places, and, if needs be, share their fate. ' Nothing, ' — wrote Father le Petit, after describing the martyrdom of two of his brethren, — ' nothing has happened to those two excellent missionaries for which they were not prepared when they devoted themselves to the Indian Missions. ' If the flesh trembled, the spirit seemed never to falter. Each one indeed felt that he was ' baptized for the dead, ' and that his own blood, poured out in the mighty forests of the West, would bring down perhaps greater blessings on those for whom he died, then he would win for them by the labours of a life. He realised that he was ' appointed unto death. ' ' *Ibo, et non redibo,* ' were the prophetic words of Father Jogues, when for the last time he departed to the Mohawks. When Lallemand was bound to the stake, and for seventeen hours his excruciating agonies were prolonged, his words of encouragement to his brother were, ' Brother! we are made a spectacle unto the world, and to angels, and to men. ' When Marquette was setting out for the sources of the Mississippi, and the friendly Indians who had known him wished to turn him from his purpose, by declaring, ' Those distant nations never spare the stranger; ' the calm reply of the missionary was, ' I shall gladly lay down my life for the salvation of souls. ' » (1)

Yet these candid men, who could thus applaud in all sincerity the gifts and graces which they recognised in the missionaries of the Cross, and sometimes confess in glowing words the supernatural « constancy and patience which, » as Mr Hawkins observes, « must always command the wonder of the historian, and the admiration of posterity, » were content to utter barren applause! Less impressed by actions which they often attribute only to enthusiasm or peculiarity of temperament than the more discerning Huron or Oneida, who knew how to trace them to their true source, and who quickly comprehended that only the « Master of Life » could form such men, or inspire such actions; these Protestant historians derive no lessons from deeds which they record without comprehending, and of which their own annals contain not even a solitary example, and deem their task fully accomplished when they have elaborated the unprofitable panegyric which they would apply, with hardly the variation of a phrase, to the prowess of a Hannibal, or the constancy of a Regulus.

One advantage, however, we derive from their unsuspicious testimony, that it renders all Catholic

(1) *The Early Jesuit Missions in North America*, by the Revd Wm Ingraham Kip, M. A.; preface, p. VIII.

evidence superfluous; one inference we draw from the facts which they proclaim, that the missionaries would have done in the northern what they did in the southern continent, if they had not been hindered in the former by a fatal impediment, from which they were delivered in the latter. If Canada and the United States had belonged to France or Spain, instead of to England or Holland, no one can doubt, with the history of Brazil and Paraguay in his hands, that the inhabitants of both would have remained to this day; and that the triumphs of Anchieta and Vieyra, of Solano and Baraza, would have been renewed by the banks of the St. Lawrence and the Ohio, in the forests of Michigan, the prairies of Illinois, and the savannahs of Florida and Alabama.

In both fields of apostolic warfare the agents were exactly the same. « Every tradition, » says the most laborious historian of the United States, « bears testimony to their worth. They had the faults of ascetic superstition, » — they shared them with St. Paul and St. Francis Xavier, — « but the horrors of a Canadian life in the wilderness were resisted by an invincible passive courage, and a deep internal tranquillity. Away from the amenities of life, away from the opportunities of vain glory, they became dead to the world, and possessed their souls in unalterable peace. The history of their labours is connected with the origin of every celebrated town in the annals of French America: not a cape was turned, not a river entered, but a Jesuit led the way. » (1) Let us see through what perils and sufferings it conducted them.

(1) Bancroft, II, 783.

In 1641, a bark canoe left the Bay of Penetangushene for the Sault Ste. Marie, at the invitation of the Chippewas, who had heard of the messengers of the Great Spirit. « There, at the falls, after a navigation of seventeen days, they found an assembly of two thousand souls.... Thus did the religious zeal of the French bear the cross to the banks of the St. Mary and the confines of Lake Superior, and look wistfully towards the homes of the Sioux in the valley of the Mississippi, five years before the New England Eliot had addressed the tribe of Indians that dwelt within six miles of Boston harbour! » Raymbault and Jogues travelled in that canoe. The former perished by the rigour of the climate, the latter was destined to a more tragical fate. Returning by the Ottawa and the St. Lawrence to Quebec, with « the great warrior Ahasistari » and a party of Christian Hurons, he was attacked by a band of Mohawks. The Hurons leaped ashore, to hide in the thick forest. « Jogues might have escaped also; but there were with him converts who had not yet been baptized, and when did a Jesuit missionary seek to save his own life, at what he believed the risk of a soul? Ahasistari had gained a hiding place; observing Jogues to be a captive, he returned to him, saying, ' My brother, I made oath to thee that I would share thy fortune, whether death or life. I am here to keep my vow.' » (1)

Ahasistari was burned alive. He had been baptized, after due trial of his sincerity, Mr Bancroft relates, « and enlisting a troop of converts, savages

(1) Bancroft, II, 791.

like himself, ' Let us strive,' he exclaimed, ' to make
the whole world embrace the faith in Jesus.'» The
noble barbarian accepted martyrdom with exultation, and sang at the stake, not his own warlike
deeds, but the praises of Jesus and Mary. Réné
Goupil, a novice, in the act of reciting the rosary
with Father Jogues, was killed by the blow of a
tomahawk, « lest he should destroy the village by
his charms. » Jogues was not yet to die. They allowed him, because of his infirmities, to wander about,
and often « he wrote the name of Jesus on the bark
of trees, as if taking possession of these countries in
the name of God. » His torments were long and horrible, but his martyrdom was to be postponed for
four years. They tore out his hair and nails by the
roots, cut off his fingers by one joint at a time, and
only suspended his tortures when they seemed likely
to deprive him of life. Yet he never wavered. Ransomed at length by the Dutch, he was released, and
having visited Rome to obtain a dispensation to say
Mass in spite of his mutilated hands, the sovereign
pontiff replied, « *Indignum esset Christi martyrem
Christi non bibere sanguinem.* » Having obtained the
permission which he solicited, instead of seeking the
repose which his sufferings seemed to have earned,
he returned immediately to America, and being re-
captured by the Iroquois in 1646, was again cruelly
tortured, and finally obtained, on the 18th of October,
the crown of martyrdom. (1) His actual murderer

(1) Charlevoix, tome I, liv. 6, p. 390. « Verissimum patientiæ
et in proximum charitatis portentum. » Tanner, *Vita et Mon.
Martyr. Soc. Jesu*, p. 510.

was burned to death in the following year by the Algonquins, « but the holy martyr seems not to have abandoned him in his last hour, » says Charlevoix, « for he died a Christian. »

On the 4th of July, 1648, Father Antoine Daniel, while labouring in a Huron village, was surprised in his turn by the Mohawks. His flock was cut down on every side, while he moved amongst them, calm and fearless, baptizing the catechumens and absolving the christians, and when his task was done, quietly advanced to meet his murderers. « Astonishment seized the barbarians, » says Mr Bancroft, who thus describes the closing scene. « At length, drawing near, they discharge at him a flight of arrows. All gashed and rent by wounds, he still continued to speak with surprising energy, — now inspiring fear of the divine anger, and again, in gentle tones, yet of more piercing power than the whoops of the savages, breathing the affectionate messages of mercy and grace. » At last they slew him, « the name of Jesus on his lips. » The whole Huron nation mourned him, and some of them related, as Mr Bancroft notices, « that he appeared twice after his death, youthfully radiant in the sweetest form of celestial glory. » (1)

On the 16th and 17th of March, 1649, Fathers Jean de Brebeuf and Gabriel Lallemand, both apostles of the Hurons, passed to their eternal reward through one of the most appalling trials which man ever inflicted or endured. The first had been twenty years in the mission, and had converted more than

---

(1) Bancroft, II, 796.

seven thousand Indians; the last was weak and delicate, and had only just commenced the apostolic career. Among his private papers was found, after his death, a writing in which he devoted himself to martyrdom. « Oh, my Jesus, sole object of my love, » he had written, « it is necessary that Thy blood, shed for the savages as well as for us, should be efficaciously applied to their salvation. It is on this account that I desire to co-operate with Thy grace, and to immolate myself for Thee. » (1)

They were both captured by the Iroquois, allies of the English, and implacable enemies of the Hurons, after a battle in which every combatant of the latter tribe was either killed or taken. Occupied during the conflict in baptizing the dying, and in exhorting all « to have God alone in view, » they only ceased to teach and console when there was no longer a Huron left to need their ministry. De Brebeuf was first led to the stake, and as he continued to proclaim with a loud voice the faith for which he was about to die, « the savages, unable to silence him, cut off his lower lip and his nose, applied burning torches to all parts of his body, burned his gums, and at length, » for he still continued to admonish them, « plunged a red hot iron into his throat. » And then they brought forth his young companion, stripped him naked, and covered him with sheets of bark that he might be slowly roasted. It was at this moment, when he saw the horrible condition of his venerable friend, that he cried out, « We are made a spectacle to the world, to angels, and to men! » De Brebeuf

(1) Bressany, p. 258.

replied to him by a gentle inclination of the head, when Lallemand, whose fetters had been consumed by the fire, ran to him, cast himself at his feet, and respectfully kissed his wounds. Shortly after de Brebeuf was scalped, while still living, and then Lallemand's agony began. They poured boiling water on his head, in mockery of baptism; they plucked out one of his eyes, and placed a burning coal in the empty socket; the smoke from the burning sheets of bark filled his mouth so that he could no longer speak, but as the flame had again burst his bonds, he lifted up his hands to heaven. Finally, after an agony which was skilfully protracted during *seventeen hours*, the victim was immolated, and the sacrifice complete. « The lives of both, » says Mr Bancroft, « had been a continual heroism; their deaths were the astonishment of their executioners. » The Protestant historian omits to add the impressive fact, that many of their murderers were afterwards converted, and that it was from *their* voluntary account that the details of their martyrdom were collected. (1)

« It may be asked, » adds Mr Bancroft, « if these massacres quenched enthusiasm? I answer, that the Jesuits never receded one foot. » Father Bressany, who wrote his own history with his mutilated hand, has described, as if speaking of another, the tortures which made him say, « I did not think it possible for man to survive such an ordeal. » Yet he lived to return to Europe, where he had professed literature, philosophy, and mathematics, before he devoted

---

(1) Charlevoix, tome II, liv. 7, p. 18; Bressany, ch. v, p. 251.

himself to the conversion of the heathen; and it was a common remark of those who heard him preach in the churches of Italy, « *He* has no need to say, ' I bear in my body the marks of the Lord Jesus. ' » Even the Indians used to say to him, « Show us your wounds, they speak to us of Him for whom you received them. »

In the same year which saw the death of De Brebeuf and Lallemand, Father Garnier was also martyred. He had already been pierced through the breast and stomach, and was dragging himself along the ground in order to give absolution to a dying Huron, when he was cut in two by a hatchet. On the 18th of December, still in the same year, Father Noël Chabanel met a similar fate. Léonard Garreau, Nicolas Viel, and « and the fearless René Mesnard;» Buteux and Poncet; Le Maistre and Vignal; Souel and Constantine; Du Poisson and Doutreleau; all gave their lives for the faith, after toils which only divine charity could inspire or support. Besides these, the historian of the United States, as if a moment of transient enthusiasm made him almost a partaker in their faith, celebrates Pinet, « who became the founder of Cahokia, preaching with such success that his chapel could not contain the multitude that thronged to him; » and Binneteau, « who left his mission among the Abenakis to die on the upland plains of the Mississippi; » and Gabriel Marest, « who, after chanting an ave to the cross among the icebergs of Hudson's Bay, » was captured by the English, but found his way back to America; and Mermet, « whose gentle virtues and fervid eloquence made him the soul of the mission at Kaskaskia, » far away in the valley of the Mississippi; and Marquette, « still honoured in the West; » and Guignes, who had travelled six hundred leagues from Quebec to the territory of the Sioux, and when on the point of being burned alive by the Kickapoos, was saved by an aged chief who adopted him as his son; (1) and Étienne de Carheil, « revered for his genius as well as for his zeal, » and « who spoke the dialects of the Huron-Iroquois tribes with as much facility and elegance as though they had been his mother tongue; » and Picquet, who for more than thirty years laboured amongst the savages, and in three years gathered round him three hundred and ninety-six heads of families, — of whom the Marquis du Quesne used to say, « The Abbé Picquet is worth more than ten regiments, »— whom de Bougainville eulogised as « theologian, orator, and poet, » — and whom Amherst tried to conciliate, after the conquest of Quebec, though the English had often set a price on his head. (2)

To these let us add one whom Mr Bancroft calls « the faithful Senat, » who, « when D'Artaguette lay weltering in his blood, might have fled, » but « remained to receive the last sigh of the wounded, regardless of danger, mindful only of duty; » and Lamberville, who, as an English writer observes, captivated even the hereditary enemies of the Christian Hurons, and « so won the confidence of the Iroquois by his unaffected piety, his constant kindness,

---

(1) *Lettres Édifiantes*, tome VII, p. 67.
(2) Bancroft, II, 838, 916, 964; *Lettres Édifiantes*, tome XXVI, pp. 18-63.

and his skill in healing their differences and their bodily ailments, » that even these irreclaimable savages, hired by the English to fight against their Christian brothers, « looked upon him as a father and a friend; » (1) and Marest, who, after travelling many weeks to the distant home of the Potawattomies, « carrying with him only a crucifix and a breviary, » found himself clasped in the arms of a brother whom he had not seen for fifteen years, but who, in the interval, had become a Jesuit like himself, and whom he was destined to meet for the first time in an Indian cabin more than two thousand miles from the sea.

Lastly, let us allude to, though we cannot name them, that multitude of generous apostles, who, like Anne de Noué, tasted the *martyrium sine sanguine*, drowned, starved, or frozen to death, and « whose fate, » as Mr Halkett observes, « was not ascertained, and who were never afterwards heard of. » (2)

Yet their labour was not in vain, and its fruits survive even to this hour, in spite of the multiplied disasters of every kind which have concurred to blight them. « If any Indians still remain in Canada, » says M. Brasseur de Bourbourg, « it is to the Catholic Church alone that their preservation is due. » We shall see presently how much reason he had to say it. The whole Huron nation was converted, and Protestant writers will tell us that its survivors still do honour to their apostolic teachers. Abenakis and

---

(1) Howitt, *Colonization and Christianity*, ch. xx, p. 321.
(2) *Notes on N. American Indians*, ch. II, p. 43.

Algonquins, Ottàwas and Onondagas, received the
message of peace, « and in the heart of the State of
New York, the solemn services of the Roman Church
were chanted as securely as in any part of Christendom. » (1) The Cayugas and Oneidas, the Senecas and Miamis, welcomed the preachers of the
Gospel; and a single missionary, Claude Allouez,
« lighted the torch of faith for more than twenty different nations. » (2) « To what inclemencies, from
nature and from man, » says the Protestant historian, « was each missionary among the barbarians
exposed! He defies the severity of climate, wading
through water, or through snows, without the comfort of fire; having no bread but pounded maize, and
often no food but the unwholesome moss from the
rocks; labouring incessantly; exposed to live, as it
were, without nourishment, to sleep without a resting place, — to carry his life in his hand, or rather
daily, and oftener than every day, to hold it up as a
target, expecting captivity, death from the tomahawk, tortures, fire. » And yet, as he judiciously
adds, these heroes had abundant consolation. « How
often was the pillow of stones like that where Jacob
felt the presence of God! How often did the ancient
oak seem like the tree of Mamre, beneath which
Abraham broke bread with angels! » (3) One reflection only he fails to make, — that the doctrine which
such men delivered in every land was the same which
St. Paul or St. Philip preached, by the same method,

(1) Bancroft, II, 799.
(2) Id., 804.
(3) Id., 806.

and which *they* also illustrated by the same actions, and sealed by the same death.

The men who preached the faith in Canada continued to the end such as its first apostles had been. One after another they displayed the same supernatural character, and even their enemies acknowledged in them the marks of the same apostolic vocation. But they were now to encounter that peculiar obstacle, unknown, as we have several times observed, in the age of St. Peter and St. Paul, and which has proved fatal in so many lands to the salvation of the heathen. They were rapidly converting one tribe after another, as their brethren had done in the South, and would not have rested from their labour till they had converted them all; but a price was now to be set on their heads, by men calling themselves Christians, and representing the government and the religion of England! « *In* 1700, *the legislature of New York made a law for hanging every Popish priest that should come voluntarily into the province;* » (1) and Lord Bellamont, the English governor, declared his intention to execute the law immediately upon every Jesuit whom he could seize. (2) They had tried every other plan; they had surpassed even the Mohawk, whom they made their ally in hunting down the missionaries of the Cross; and now they announced to the world, by a solemn legislative enactment, that they were prepared to murder every Catholic priest upon whom they could lay hands. Their success, it must be admitted, was complete ; but in

---

(1) Bancroft, II, 835.
(2) Brasseur de Bourbourg, tome I, ch. XII, p. 216.

accomplishing it, they not only destroyed Christianity and those who alone could propagate it, but extirpated by the same fatal policy the nations whom they could neither convert themselves, nor would suffer others to convert.

The conduct of Lord Bellamont, who only executed faithfully the instructions of his masters, was thus noticed by Mr Talbot, an Anglican missionary in America, in 1702. After expressing generally his reluctant admiration of the « zealous and diligent papists, » the protestant preacher continued as follows. « 'Tis wonderfully acted, ventured, and suffered upon that design; they have indeed become all things, and even turned Indians, as it were, to gain them. One of their priests lived half a year in their wigwams without a shirt; and when he petitioned my Lord Bellamont for a couple, *he was not only denied, but banished;* whereas one of ours, in discourse with my Lord of London, said, who did his Lordship think would come hither that had a dozen shirts?» (1)

The Dutch, though they twice humanely ransomed a Catholic missionary, were not in other respects superior to their co-religionists of England. As early as 1657, they were established at Orange, now the city of Albany, where they lived after a fashion which provoked such comments as the following. Of one preacher, who was sent out by the « Lutheran Consistory at Amsterdam, » his Dutch Calvinist colleagues gave the following graphic account. « This Lutheran parson is a man of a godless and scanda-

(1) *Missions of the Church of England in the N. American Colonies*, by Ernest Hawkins, B. D., ch. II, p. 33. (1845).

lous life, a rolling rollicking unseemly carl, who is more inclined to look into the wine-can than to pore over the bible, and would rather drink a kan of brandy for two hours than preach one. » He and his flock were accustomed, « when full of brandy, to beat each other's heads black and blue, » their pastor being « excessively inclined to fight whomsoever he meets. » (1) The disciples of the Dutch clergy generally are thus described, in 1710, by the Rev. Thomas Barclay, an Episcopalian minister, in an official report on the « State of the Church in Albany. » « There are about thirty communicants of the Dutch Church, but so ignorant and scandalous, that they can scarce be reputed Christians. » (2) It is fair, however, to add, that we shall hear exactly the same account, by their own friends, of the Episcopalian clergy and *their* flocks. It was probably their experience of such teachers and such congregations which made the neighbouring Indian tribes reason as follows. « What a difference between the Christians and the Dutch! They say that they all acknowledge the same God, but how unlike are they in their conduct! When we go to visit the French, we always come back with a desire to pray. At Albany they never say any thing to us about prayer. We do not even know whether they pray there at all. » (3)

Yet at this very date, the Indians collected in the island of Montreal had been so effectually converted to God,—and in many of the fixed missions, notably

(1) *Documentary History of New York*, vol. III, p. 105.
(2) *Ibid.*, p. 898.
(3) Charlevoix, tome II, liv. 8, p. 80.

at the Sault S¹ᵉ Marie, the same thing was true, — that European visitors could report, « the whole island of Montreal resembles a religious community; » (1) or, as the Bishop of Quebec observed in 1688, « You would take this village for a monastery, so extraordinary is their daily life. » (2) As Kaskaskia, far away in the valley of the Mississippi, Mʳ Bancroft says, « the success of the mission was such, that marriages of the French emigrants were sometimes solemnized with the daughters of the Illinois according to the rites of the Catholic church ; » while the Indians, he allows, were so thoroughly converted, that not only did they all assemble « at early dawn » to assist at Mass, and again « at evening for instruction, for prayer, and to chant the hymns of the church, » but, as the Protestant historian adds, « every convert confessed once in a fortnight, » and « at the close of the day, parties would meet in the cabins to recite the rosary, in alternate choirs, and sing psalms into the night. » (3) By the end of the seventeenth century, as Mʳ Owen observes, « the total of the Confederacy (Six Nations) who professed the Roman Catholic religion was computed to exceed eight thousand. » (4) And this was only one example of their success. « The whole Abenakis nation, » the martyr Rasles could say in 1722, « is Christian, and full of zeal for their religion. » « Among the Five Nations, » as a bitter Puritan lamented, « there is a great number of French Jesuits, and the chief of the

(1) Charlevoix, tome II, liv. 9, p. 163.
(2) *Lettres Édifiantes*, tome VI, p. 126.
(3) Bancroft, II, 839.
(4) *History of the Bible Society*, vol. I, p. 128.

poor silly Indians do entirely confide in them. » (1) As early as 1670, Roger Williams, a famous Protestant preacher, confessed to Mason, in the frightful language of his class, that « the French and Romish Jesuits, the firebrands of the world for their godbelly sake, are kindling at our back in this country their hellish fiers, *with all the natives of this country.* » (2) So that Judge Hall could truly observe, « the French Catholics, at a very early period, were remarkably successful in gaining converts, and conciliating the confidence and affection of the tribes; » while, as he adds, with singular candour, « Protestants, similarly situated, were bloodthirsty and rapacious. » (3)

In truth, as respects the fruits of their labours, it was the history of Brazil and Peru in another clime. In many a mission, from the Mohawk to the Genesee, and from the Hudson to the Mississippi, were gathered Christian Indians, who, as one whom Mr Bancroft styles « the honest Charlevoix » has recorded, « would have done honour to the first ages of Christianity. » « I give my life willingly, » said Teganaokoa, a native martyr, « for a God who shed all His blood for me. » When his fingers had been cut off by the heathen, because he lifted them up in prayer, and he was scoffingly bidden to continue his supplications; « Yes, » he replied, « I will pray, » and then made the sign of the cross with his muti-

(1) *Discoveries of the English in America*, Pinkerton, vol. XII, p. 410.
(2) *Massachusetts Historical Collections*, 1st series, vol. I, p. 283.
(3) Rupp, *Hist. Rel. Denom.*, p. 163.

lated hand. But men who could defy all the arts of the pagan, and who were once more converting a continent, were vanquished by the more subtle wickedness of so-called Christians. The Iroquois, a nation remarkable for their natural gifts, appear to have become perfectly demoniacal after intercourse with their white allies, by whom they were paid to fight against the French. « I have often, » says Charlevoix, « asked some of our Fathers, with many of whom who laboured longest in this part of the Lord's vineyard I had the happiness of living, what had hindered the seed of the word from taking root amongst a people whose intelligence, good sense, and noble feelings, they so much praised. All gave me the same reply, — that the chief cause of this evil was the neighbourhood of the English and Dutch, whose want of piety, though professing to be Christians, had induced these savages to regard Christianity as a mere religion of caprice — *comme une religion arbitraire.* »

But we have not been accustomed in these volumes to rely upon Catholic evidence, however weighty, and the testimony of Charlevoix, as we shall see immediately, is amply confirmed from other sources. On the 10th of August, 1684, at a general council of all the Iroquois nations, as we read in the Documentary History of New York, they solemnly invited the Catholic missionaries, in a moment of freedom from English influence, to take up their abode amongst them. « It is *you*, » they said, « who ought to possess our hearts. » And it was from *Christian Huron captives*, the very race whom they had most hated and injured, that they had learned « the great value of the Faith, and to prize without being acquainted with it. » They had seen the Catholic Indian suffer, and they had seen him die, and the lesson had not been lost upon them. Nor can it be reasonably doubted that, but for the counsels and example of the English, these noble tribes would *all* have been won to Christianity and civilisation. It was not till they had learned to despise the religion of their Saxon allies, and to imitate their vices, that they closed their hearts for ever against the message of peace. It has been the mission of the English, in all lands, to make the conversion of the heathen impossible. Here are fresh examples, recorded by themselves, of their mode of proceeding in the Atlantic provinces of America.

In 1687, Governor Dongan of New York, after reporting officially to the Lords of the Committee of Trade, that the Iroquois were « a bulwark between us and the French, » added these characteristic words; « *I suffer no Christians to converse with them* any where but at Albany, and that not without my license. » It was more advantageous to English interests that they should continue pagans, because if they embraced Christianity they were sure to be Catholics. He even avowed, with crude brutality, the odious treachery which he knew the English government would approve and reward. « The French Fathers have converted many of them — Mohawks, Senecas, Cayugas, Oneidas, and Onondagas, — to the Christian Faith, and doe their utmost to draw them to Canada, to which place there are already six or seven hundred retired, and more like to doe, *to the great prejudice of this Govern-*

ment, if not prevented; » and then he tells his masters how he had induced some to return by fraud, promising « to furnish them with priests, » — a promise kept, thirteen years later, by enacting a law « to hang every Popish priest that should come into the province! » (1) It was against such deadly influences that the apostles of North America contended, till both they and their flocks were annihilated.

Yet not a few even of the Iroquois had proved how powerfully grace could work in them, when they were suffered to come within its reach. All the early Canadian records speak, amongst others, of the Iroquoise saint, Catherine Teguhkouita. Born in 1656, and converted in early youth by the missionaries from Montreal, she led until her death, in 1680, a hidden life of prayer, seeking by her austerities to make atonement for the errors of her tribe. « She had placed a cross in the trunk of a tree, by the side of a stream, and this solitary spot served her for an oratory. There in spirit she placed herself at the foot of the altar, united her intention to that of the priest, and implored her angel guardian to assist at the sacrifice of the Mass in her place, and to apply to her the fruit of it. » Accustomed to practise in secret the most painful mortifications, and making her bed of rough thorns, a Christian companion suggested to her that this was an error in the sight of God, who does not approve austerities performed without the sanction of authority, and not consecrated by obedience. « Catherine, who

(1) *Documentary History of New York*, vol. I, pp. 41, 154.

dreaded even the appearance of sin, » says Father Cholenec, « came immediately to search for me, to acknowledge her fault, and ask pardon of God. I blamed her indiscretion, and directed her to throw the thorns into the fire. This she instantly did. » When she died, at the age of twenty-four, the same missionary relates that the very sight of her corpse filled the spectators with surprise and edification : « It might be said that a ray of glory illuminated even her body. » (1)

Margaret, another of these Indian virgins, was martyred by the pagan members of her own tribe, and amidst the greatest tortures which savage cruelty could inflict, « continued to invoke the holy names of Jesus, Mary, and Joseph. » The agony of thirst made her crave for water, yet when they offered it to her, she refused, saying, « My Saviour thirsted for me on the cross, it is just that I should suffer the same torment. » She survived so long under her tortures, that her murderers exclaimed with surprise, « Is this dog of a Christian unable to die? »

The apostles who had raised up to God, in many an Indian tribe, such worshippers as these, would not have failed in due time to renew the triumphs which their brethren had effected in Brazil, Peru, and Paraguay. They had begun, and would have completed, the same work. The Indian of the North, until brutalised by drink and maddened by cruelty, was at least as capable of appreciating Christian heroism and sanctity as his fellow barbarian of the South; and when he saw both displayed before his

(1) *Lettres Édifiantes*, tome VI, pp. 67, 97.

eyes, did homage after his kind. When the tribes of Kentucky had declared implacable war against the seed of the oppressor, they still respected, even in the paroxysm of their rage, one class, and one alone. The French Trappists, far from all human succour, dwelt without fear in the midst of them; and « the Monks themselves, » though blood was flowing all around them, « were never molested in their own establishment. The savages seemed even to be awed into reverence for their sanctity; and often did they pause in the vicinity of the rude Trappist chapel, to listen to the praises of God chanted amidst the bones of their own fathers. » (1)

Such is the spell, as we have seen in many lands, which Catholic holiness exerts even over the rudest natures. « So wide, » says Mr Bancroft with his usual candour, « was the influence of the missionaries in the West, » that when Du Buisson, defending Fort Detroit with only twenty Frenchmen against the forces of the English, « summoned his Indian allies from the chase; Ottawas, and Hurons, and Potawatomies, with one branch of the Sacs, Illinois, Menomonies, and even Osages and Missouris, each nation with its own ensign, came to his relief. ' Father, ' said they, ' behold! thy children compass thee round. We will, if need be, gladly die for our father. ' » (2) Multitudes, no doubt, would have shared the fate of Jogues and Lallemand and De Brebeuf, before the victory was finally accomplish-

(1) *Sketches of the early Catholic Missions of Kentucky*, by M. J. Spalding, D. D., ch. x, p. 173.
(2) II, 858.

ed; but others would immediately have taken their place, until Mohawk and Sioux, Shawnee and Delaware, subdued by their invincible courage, and won by their surpassing charity, would have imitated the Moxos and Chiquitos of the southern continent, and, like them, would have survived to this day, dwelling in the land of their fathers, and praising the God of Christians. But an enemy had now entered the field, before whom both the missionary and his flock disappeared, and whose operations it is time to notice. Two or three examples, out of many, will sufficiently indicate their scope and character.

« On the banks of the Kennebec, » says the historian whom we have so often quoted, « the venerable Sebastian Rasles, for more than a quarter of a century the companion and instructor of savages, had gathered a flourishing village round a church which, rising in the desert, made some pretentions to magnificence. Severely ascetic, — using no wine, and little food except pounded maize, — he built his own cabin, tilled his own garden, drew for himself wood and water, prepared his own hominy, and, distributing all that he received, gave an example of religious poverty... Following his pupils to their wigwam, he tempered the spirit of devotion with familiar conversation and innocent gaiety, winning the mastery of their souls by his powers of persuasion. He had trained a little band of forty young savages, arrayed in cassock and surplice, to assist in the service and chant the hymns of the church, and their public processions attracted a great concourse of red men. » (1)

---

(1) Bancroft, II, 938.

The apostolic labours of Father Rasles, and their success, made him odious to the English. They tried two plans for his destruction, of which Mr Bancroft mentions only one. « The government of Massachusetts, » he says, « attempted, in turn, to establish a mission; and its minister made a mocking of purgatory and the invocation of saints, of the cross and the rosary... Thus Calvin and Loyola met in the woods of Maine. But the Protestant minister, unable to compete with the Jesuit for the affections of the Indians, returned to Boston. » (1)

Their first project having failed, they adopted a second; and the English authorities now offered by proclamation 1000 l. sterling for the head of the too successful missionary! « The English regard me, » said the venerable man who was soon to be their victim, « as an invincible obstacle to the design which they have formed of acquiring all the lands of the Abenakis. » (2) His crime was unpardonable, but it will be well to learn by Protestant testimony how it was avenged. « After vainly soliciting the savages, » says Mr Bancroft, « to surrender Rasles, in midwinter, Westbrooke led a strong force to Norridgewock, to take him by surprise. » They had often hunted him before, but this time they were to be successful. In vain his flock had implored him to fly betimes. « The aged man, foreseeing the impending ruin of Norridgewock, replied, ' I count not my life dear unto myself, so I may finish with joy the ministry which I have received.' » When the English arrived, « Rasles

---

(1) Bancroft, II, p. 939.
(2) *Lettres Édifiantes*, tome VI, p. 148.

went forward to save his flock, by drawing down upon himself the attention of the assailants; and his hope was not vain. » Many of them escaped, « while the English pillaged the cabins and the church, and then, heedless of sacrilege, set them on fire. » (1) Mr Bancroft omits to add, what we learn from another source, that they « horribly profaned the sacred vessels, and the adorable Body of Jesus Christ. » (2)

And what was the fate of one who for thirty-seven years had devoted himself, in poverty and suffering, to the welfare of the natives? Mr Bancroft has recorded it. « After the retreat of the invaders, the Abenakis, » to whom the generosity of the missionary had given time to save their women and children, « returned to nurse their wounded and bury their dead. They found Rasles mangled by many blows, *scalped*, his skull broken in several places, *his mouth and eyes filled with dirt;* and they buried him beneath the spot where he used to stand before the altar. » Such was the work of a British military force, conducted by three British officers.

The vengeance of England was complete, and from that hour the fate of the red man in all the Eastern States was sealed. It is Mr Bancroft who draws the conclusion. « Thus died Sebastian Rasles, » he says, « the last of the Catholic missionaries in New England; *thus perished the Jesuit missions and their fruits,*— the villages of the semi-civilized Abenakis and their priests. » (3) Is it wonderful that there

(1) II, 859.
(2) Charlevoix, tome IV, p. 12.
(3) II, 941.

has been no new Paraguay in Canada or the United States?

One hundred and eight years after the martyrdom of Sebastian Rasles, D' Fenwick, Bishop of Boston, purchased the land which had been dyed with his blood, to build a church on the spot consecrated by his death. (1) In the following year, 1833, the same Bishop met the grandson of one of the English who had slain him, by whom the prelate was informed, that to the hour of his death, his grandfather ceased not to shed tears at the thought of that sorrowful day; and often called to mind that, having been wounded, he had been charitably nursed by one of Father Rasle's disciples, though her own husband had been killed by his English companions. It is worthy of notice, too, that a century after his death, a deputation of the Abenakis brought to D' Carroll, Archbishop of Baltimore, the crucifix of the martyr, a relic which they only agreed to transfer to his custody, on condition that he would send them a priest. » (2) So well had they kept the faith, during that long interval, that when Sir Guy Carleton sent to them Protestant ministers in 1785, « they drove them out of their village; » and the governor, generously appreciating their constancy, not only despatched to them a Catholic priest, but offered him a stipend of 50 l. a year. (3)

The action of the Indian woman noticed above, whose charity would perhaps be rarely imitated by

(1) *Annales de la Propagation de la Foi*, tome VI, p. 274.
(2) Brasseur de Bourbourg, *Histoire du Canada*, etc., tome I, ch. XXI, p. 85.
(3) *Id.*, ch. XXII, p. 88.

European Christians, affords an interesting example of the influence of religion among the disciples of the martyred missionary : a still more striking case, in which the hand of the Indian warrior was restrained, in the very heat of battle, by the power of Catholic sympathy, deserves notice. Nearly a century after the death of Father Rasles, in the war of 1812-13, an Irish Catholic, fighting with a body of American troops against a native tribe, was about to be overtaken by a chief. Falling on his knees, « he made the sign of the cross, and endeavoured as well as he could, to prepare himself for death. The warrior suddenly stopped, dropped his tomahawk, and falling likewise on his knees, embraced the white man, exclaiming; ' You are my brother ! ' » It is Bishop Fenwick who records this touching anecdote, which he received from the very man who owed his life to the forbearance suggested to a savage by a religious sentiment, which taught him to recognise a brother even in an enemy, whose hand had just been raised against him. (1)

The fate of the venerable Sebastian Rasles overtook many an apostle in the midst of his toils, and would have been shared by all if the English could have laid hands on them. The celebrated Abbé Picquet, who united rare energy and ability to the higher virtues of his calling, was also tracked by the English as a wild beast, and a price set on his head. Yet he was one who could have converted half the tribes of the North. In 1749, he commenced his mission at Ogdensburgh with six heads of families; in 1750, he

---

(1) Spalding, ch. II, p. 30.

had eighty seven round him; in 1751, three hundred and ninety-six. « People saw with astonishment several villages start up almost at once; a convenient, habitable, and pleasantly situated fort; vast clearances covered almost at the same time with the finest maize. » This was the system by which the Jesuits and Franciscans had conquered South America, but it was only a small part of his work. At the mission of *la Présentation*, « the most distinguished of the Iroquois families were distributed in three villages. » The Bishop of Quebec, « wishing to witness and assure himself personally of the wonders related to him, » visited *la Présentation*, « and spent ten days examining and causing the catechumens to be examined. He himself baptized one hundred and thirty-two, and did not cease during his sojourn blessing heaven for the progress of religion among these infidels. » Yet Picquet was hunted by the English, after gaining the illustrious title of « apostle of the Iroquois, » and finally, in 1760, was obliged to quit Canada for ever, in consequence of the death of Montcalm and the capture of Quebec. (1)

We have now perhaps sufficient knowledge of the men who announced the Gospel in Canada, and of the policy by which their work was frustrated. The English became masters of all the lands which lie between Cape Gaspé and the western shores of Lake Superior, and the same fate awaited the doomed native which has crushed, under the same masters, the aborigines of South Africa, of Australia, of Tahiti, and New Zealand. It only remains to show, by

(1) *Documentary History of New York*, vol. I, p. 432.

a few characteristic examples, how complete the ruin has been.

It may be allowed, however, in noticing the condition to which Protestantism has reduced the natives of British America, to indicate, as usual by the aid of Protestant witnesses, the traces which still exist of the Catholic missions, and the character of those who conduct them. In spite of murder, fraud, and oppression, English writers will assure us, both that the Catholic Indians of Canada are the *only* Christians who deserve the name, and that their teachers at this hour exactly resemble those who died to save their fathers.

The evidence is copious, but shall be confined within narrow limits. Exactly a century ago, the Rev. John Ogilvie, an Anglican missionary agent in America, thus addressed his employers. « Of *every* nation I find some who have been instructed by the priests of Canada, and appear zealous Roman Catholics, extremely tenacious of the ceremonies and peculiarities of that Church..... How ought we to blush at *our* coldness and shameful indifference in the propagation of our most excellent religion. The Indians themselves are not wanting in making very pertinent reflections upon our inattention to these points. » (1)

Other witnesses notice the same invariable facts at the present day. The *Chippeways*, Sir George Simpson relates, met him at Fort William, and represented to him that, « *being all Catholics*, they should like to have a priest among them. » (2) Like

---

(1) Ernest Hawkins, *Missions*, etc., ch. XII, p. 289.
(2) *Journey round the World*, vol. I, ch. I, p. 35.

the Christian natives of Hindostan, of China, and of Paraguay, they had preserved their faith, though separated, for more than *half a century*, from those who had declared it to them.

It is related of Cardinal Cheverus, — whose character excited so much admiration in America, to whom the State of Massachusetts voted a subsidy, and the first subscriber to whose church at Boston was John Adams, President of the United States, — that when he visited the Penobscot, he found an Indian tribe, who had not even seen a priest for half a century, but were still zealous Catholics, carefully observed the Sunday, and « had not forgotten the catechism! » (1)

In 1831, Bishop Fenwick found a whole tribe of *Passamaquoddies*, constant in the faith, and, as he observed « a living monument of the apostolic labours of the Jesuits. » (2)

Of the *Hurons*, the beloved disciples of the early missionaries, Mr Buckingham, an English traveller, speaks as follows. « They are faithful Catholics, and are said to fulfil their religious duties in the most exemplary manner, being much more improved by their commerce with the whites than the Indian tribes who have first come into contact with Protestants usually are. » Of the Indians in the neighbourhood of Montreal, the same Protestant writer says, « They are *always* sober, a rare occurrence with Indians of either sex. » « This difference, » he candidly observes, « is occasioned by the influence

---

(1) *Vie du Cardinal de Cheverus*, liv. 2, p. 68. (4me édition).
(2) *Annales*, tome V, p. 449.

of Christianity, as the *Caghnawaga* Indians *are Catholics.* » (1)

Of the *Abenakis*, whose fathers listened one hundred and fifty years ago to the voice of Sebastian Rasles, Protestant missionaries angrily relate, in 1841, after vainly attempting to subvert them, that they could do nothing against the « controlling influence of the Romish priesthood. » (2)

Of the Indians at *l'Arbre Croche*, on the east shore of Lake Michigan, « for sixty years or more the seat of a Jesuit Mission, » Dr Morse, a Protestant minister, reported thus to the United States government. « These Indians are much in advance, in point of improvement, in appearance, and in manners, of all the Indians whom I visited. » (3) Do we not say with reason that in Catholic missions, we see everywhere the power of God rather than of man?

Of the *Wyandots*, the same official witness reported, « nearly all the aged people still wear crucifixes. »

Of the *Onondagas*, Mr Schoolcraft observes, « They were ever strongly opposed to all missionaries *after* the expulsion of the Jesuits. » (4)

Of the *Micmas*, in Prince Edward's Island, Colonel Bouchette says, « They are *all* still Catholics »; of the tribes in New Brunswick, « the greater part of

---

(1) *Canada*, etc., ch. XI, p. 151; ch. XVII, p. 251.

(2) *History of American Missions*, by Revd Joseph Tracy, ch. XXXIII, p. 331.

(3) *A Report to the Secretary of* War *of the United States on Indian Affairs*, by the Revd Jedidiah Morse, D. D.; app. pp. 24, 91, 327.

(4) *Notes on the Iroquois*, ch. XII, p. 443.

the Indians profess the Romish religion; » of those at Cape Breton, « *All* the Acadians are Roman Catholics »; and of the Indians *generally*, who are in communion with the Church, « they are *a quiet temperate race.* » (1)

Of the great Mission in the Manitouline islands, the gentleman who is Protestant bishop of Toronto cautiously says, in 1842; « A considerable portion consists of half breeds, of French and Indian extraction, and these being *all* Romanists, possess a good deal of influence among the natives. » (2)

More ingenuous witnesses give a less meagre account of them. « There are upwards of *two thousand* natives in the island, » says Mr Kingston, in 1856, « the greater proportion of whom profess the Romish faith. At a settlement on the other side, a considerable number reside under four Jesuit Fathers, » — the Jesuits re-entered Canada in 1842, — « and they are said to be a very obedient, industrious, and intelligent set, and superior to the Protestants; but of the truth of the assertion I have no means of judging. » (3) Yet in a later portion of his work, when he had perhaps acquired ampler experience, Mr Kingston frankly describes the so-called Protestant Indians as « a very inferior race, » and observes that the only effect of their pretended conversion is, « that now they wear blanket coats, weave

(1) *British Dominions in North America*, vol. II, ch. VII, p. 85; ch. x, p. 148; ch. XI, p. 178.

(2) *The Church in Canada;* journal of a visitation by the Lord Bishop of Toronto in 1842, p. 10.

(3) *Western Wanderings*, by W. H. G. Kingston; vol. I, ch. VIII, p. 180.

mats, receive alms from the white man, and get drunk whenever they can. » (1)

Let these details be pardoned, for the sake of the lesson which they teach, and which is certainly of sufficient importance to merit ample illustration. We have seen in every other land the same contrast between the work of God and the work of man, and it is our business to trace it here also. For this reason, at the risk of repetition, we will continue the subject.

Sometimes we are told, not of tribes or nations, but of selected individuals, who had enjoyed every advantage, including a liberal education, which Protestantism could offer them — but the result was always the same. Mr Kingston tells us of one Indian, brought up « in the house of a clergyman, » married to an American woman, and finally employed as an assistant missionary. « He saved a good deal of money, built himself a house, and furnished it nicely,... but he was not content. He was ambitious of becoming a chief, and of forming a settlement of his own. » The spiritual influence of Protestantism never seems to go beyond this point.

Mr Buckingham also notices the case of « Peter Jones, » another Indian Protestant, who has been exhibited in England as a preacher, and married an Englishwoman. In spite of much acuteness, and a superior education, he not only « met with no success, » but even flatly denied « that any who had passed the middle period of life would ever be prevailed upon to change their religion. » (2)

(1) *Western Wanderings*, vol. I, ch. XVII. p. 314.
(2) *Canada*, ch. IV, p. 46.

And these are exceptional cases, representing, not the average results of Protestant teaching, but its choicest examples. The *mass* of the fallen and degraded Indians who have come, rather as pensioners than as « converts, » under its fatal influence, are described by travellers of all classes in the same terms. The Catholic Indians invariably refuse to associate with them, and consider them the most abject of mankind. And Protestant witnesses freely confess that their estimate is perfectly just. Thus Mr Kane, one of the latest writers on the western continent, while he lauds « the agricultural skill and industry » of the *Catholic* Indians near Manitouline, candidly describes the *Protestant* mission at Norway House in these words. « It is supported by the Hudson's Bay Company with the hope of improving the Indians, but to judge from appearances, with but small success, as they are decidedly the dirtiest Indians I have met with, and the less that is said about their morality the better. » (1)

Other writers go further, and do not hesitate to avow that, like all other barbarians under Protestant masters, they are doomed to inevitable destruction. Where divine charity is absent, mere human benevolence only reveals its own impotence. « Our system of trade and intercourse with the Indian tribes, » says Governor Chambers in an official report, « is in this region of country rapidly destroying them. » (2) « They hardly dare cultivate the soil, » observes

(1) *Wanderings of an Artist*, ch. VIII, p. 105.
(2) *Notes on the North West*, by Wm J. A. Bradford, part. II, p. 195. (1846).

Mr Beecham, even on the nominally « reserved » lands,
« lest some reason should be found for dispossessing
them! » (1) Dr Shaw declares, in 1856, that « *the
authorities* frequently swindled the poor Indians.» (2)
« I am satisfied, » adds Mr Bradford, « that at least
one quarter of the annuity paid to the Menominis is
collected by traders, at the annuity payment, for
whiskey. » (3) « Many an Indian, » says Mr Kane,
from actual observation, « returns to his wigwam
poorer than he left it; » and he relates that, at a distribution of the government bounty which he personally witnessed, « there was scarcely a man, woman,
or child, old enough to lift the vessel to its mouth,
that was not wallowing in beastly drunkenness. » (4)
Yet the Protestant clergy, incapable of dealing with
evils which can only be alleviated by another ministry
than theirs, do nothing whatever, either here or in
the United States, to mitigate these disasters; so that
Mr Bradford, with a candour not unusual in Americans, contrasts them with « the pious, peaceful, and
zealous disciples of the cross, » as he styles the Catholic missionaries, surmounting « with comparative
case » the complicated evils to which their rivals,
with all the aid of opulence and of government support, despair of applying a remedy. « The French-
man, » says this American writer, « forgets not that
the uncivilised, as well as civilised man, is his brother, and he deports himself as man to man. The

(1) *Colonization*, p. 9.
(2) *A Ramble through the United States*, etc., by John Shaw,
M. D., F. G. S., F. L. S., ch. III. p. 67. (1856).
(3) *Ubi supra*.
(4) Ch. II, p. 41.

sturdy Saxon treats the Indian like a dog. The American thinks everything is to be accommodated to him. » (1)

It would be idle to attempt to exhaust the Protestant witnesses, who record, from actual observation, the contrast which these passages illustrate between the influence of Catholic and Protestant agency upon the life and fortunes of the Indian. Let us close the series with these statements by two venerable prelates, whose testimony we may well accept, after what we have already heard, as conclusive. « These Indians, » says Monseigneur Gaulein, Bishop of Kingston, in 1838, « are all excellent Catholics, and seem to me industrious and fond of labour : a large number of savages have been recently baptized. » « I had often been told, » observes Monseigneur Loras, Bishop of Dubuque, in 1839, « that the savages when converted make excellent Catholics, and having become acquainted with them, have had occasion to admire their fervour. » (2)

Such are the disciples, by the testimony both of friends and enemies, and such the inflexible constancy of their faith, even where every influence has combined to destroy it. And now a word on the Missionaries. « *They* are not inferior, » says M_r Buckingham, « in zeal and devotion to the first founders and propagators of the faith on this continent; » while of their efforts to convert the pagan savages, in spite of the cruel disadvantages which attend them in a country under Protestant domination, he observes, « Of late

---

(1) *Notes on the North West*, part. 2, p. 89.
(2) *Annals*, vol. I, pp. 470, 79. (English edition).

years they are *more than usually* successful. » And then he contrasts the dignity of these apostolic teachers with the « inferiority » of the Episcopalian ministers, and laments to notice in that opulent body « more than the usual portion of formality in the ministers, and coldness in the congregations. » (1)

Mr Sullivan, another British traveller, of no mean capacity, frankly declares of the Catholic missionaries, « They exercise extraordinary influence amongst their proselytes, and also amongst several tribes of Indians. » (2)

Mr Halkett, also an eye-witness, observes as follows. « There is one point which cannot be disputed, that the Indians of British North America are treated by their present Roman Catholic instructors with great kindness and consideration. So far as benevolence, charity, and paternal care can afford comfort to the Indian, he receives it at their hands. » (3) In other words, they still display the same patient unwearied charity by which, two centuries ago, their predecessors first subdued the frowardness and captivated the affections of their wild flock; when, as Nicolini allows, « they visited daily every house in which lay a sick person, whom they served as the kindest nurse, and to whom they seemed to be ministering genii. By such conduct they brought this primitive population to idolise them. » (4)

The Honourable Charles Murray, after noticing, in

(1) Ch. xv, p. 220.
(2) *Rambles in North and South America*, ch. III. p. 60.
(3) *Notes on North American Indians*, ch. x, p. 232.
(4) *History of the Jesuits*, by G. B. Nicolini, ch. XIII, p. 302. (Bohn).

the generous language which might be expected from him, « the zeal and enterprise with which the Roman Catholic religion inspires its priests to toil, travel, and endure every kind of hardship, » continues thus. « In this labour, especially among the Negroes and Indians, they put to shame the zeal and exertions of all other Christian sects; nor do they labour without effect. During my stay in Missouri, I observed that the Romish faith was gaining ground with a rapidity that outstripped all competition. »(1)

It would be easy to multiply these confessions of Protestant travellers, but surely we have heard enough. One witness only shall be cited in addition, because a peculiar interest attaches to his evidence, with which we may fitly terminate this series.

In 1860, M' Kohl published his journal of travels on the shores of Lake Superior. « I may take it on myself, » says this gentleman, in eulogising « those excellent men, the learned pastors of the Canadian mission, » « to speak on this subject, for I have read all the old journies of the early messengers of the Church, and followed them with sympathising zeal. In our day, when religious martyrdom no longer flourishes, it is especially refreshing to travel in a country where this epoch has not entirely died out, and to associate with men who endure the greatest privations for lofty purposes, and who would be well inclined even to lay down their lives for their Church. In fact every thing I heard here daily of the pious courage, patience, and self-devoting zeal of these

---

(1) *Travels in North America*, by the Hon. C. A. Murray; vol. II, ch. XIII, p. 309.

missionaries on Lake Superior, caused me to feel intense admiration. They are well-educated and learned men, — many better educated, indeed, than the majority, — and yet they resign not only all enjoyments and comforts, but also all the mental inspiration and excitement of polished society. They live isolated and scattered in little log huts round the lake, often no better off than the natives. They must draw their inspirations entirely from their own breast and prayer. Only the thought of the great universal Church to which they belong keeps them connected with society and the world. It is true, however, that they find in this an incitement to exertion which our Protestant missionaries lack. The latter, broken up into sects, labour only for this or that congregation, while the former are animated by a feeling that, as soldiers of the Church, they are taking part in a mighty work, which includes all humanity, and encircles the entire globe. » (1)

Mr Kohl lived much, during his wanderings, with the men whom he thus describes, and whose labours appear to have excited his astonishment. Even a baptism, a wedding, or a funeral, he observes, involves in such a climate almost the privations and sufferings « of an Arctic expedition. » He is lodging on one occasion in the hut of a Jesuit Father, who had retired after the toils of the day. It was « the blessed cold Christmas season, » and the missionary was sitting over the evening fire with his guest. « All at once there was a knock at the door, and a breath-

(1) *Wanderings round Lake Superior*, by J. G. Kohl; ch. xix, p. 306.

less stranger, covered with snow and icicles, walked in. » His message was soon told. Forty miles away, through swamps and forests, his mother lay ill, and implored the succours of religion. On the instant the Father rose, and left the hut, « the missionary and the Indian walking side by side in their snow shoes.» They cross a frozen river, the ice parts asunder, and they fall through « up to their waists. » « At the end of the *third* day, » adds Mr Kohl, « the missionary was enabled to give the poor dying Indian woman extreme unction, and to see her eyes gently close in death. Would an Oxford gentleman rejoice at being presented to such a living? »

And these missionaries, he says, are all of the same class. Of one, whom he calls his « honoured friend, » and who was the author of an Ojibbeway Lexicon, Mr Kohl remarks; « There is hardly a locality on Lake Superior which is not connected with the history of his life, either because he built a chapel there, or wrote a pious book, or founded an Indian parish, or else underwent dangers and adventures there, in which he felt that Heaven was protecting him. » And then he relates a tale, which he received from a Canadian *voyageur*, and which he did well to communicate to his readers. A message had been brought from the other side of Lake Superior to one of these martyrs of charity with whom Mr Kohl dwelt. It was night, a tempest was raging, and seventy miles of water must be crossed, for to go round the lake would occupy many days; but the case was urgent, and the missionary did not hesitate. In an open canoe, paddled by a Canadian who only consented to the perilous voyage on the

Father's reiterated assurance that God would protect them, the darkness of night resting on the waters which the storm had lashed into fury, the missionary encouraged his faithful companion to strain every nerve. The weary hours of the night were passed in prayer and toil, and when the Canadian approached the long line of foaming breakers which beat against the opposite shore, with a cry of anguish he exclaimed, « Your Reverence, we are lost ! » « Paddle on, dear Dubois, » said the calm voice of the missionary, « straight on. We *must* get through, and a way will offer itself. » « My cousin shrugged his shoulders, » said the narrator to Mr Kohl, « made his last prayers, and paddled straight on, he hardly knew how... All at once a dark spot opened out in the white edge of the surf, which soon widened » — and they were saved. « Did I not say, Dubois, » was the only remark of the missionary, « that I was called, that I must go, and that thou wouldst be saved with me? Let us pray. » And then they knelt down by the shore of the Lake, and gave thanks to God.

On the very spot where they landed, Mr Kohl adds, a large cross has since been erected by a rich merchant, « which can be seen a long distance on the Lake, » and is known throughout the region as « the Cross of ....'s Traverse. » When Mr Kohl had heard the tale, he says, « I laid myself down on the knotted flooring, by the side of this excellent, gently slumbering man. » (1)

Such are the missionaries who still labour, as Lallemand and De Brebeuf once laboured, among the North

---

(1) Pages 182, 183. 307, 309.

American Indians. Two centuries have passed away since the first martyrs of this land entered into their reward, and not a single grace has been withdrawn, not a single gift diminished, which divine bounty once lavished upon *them,* and still confers upon their successors. It is no grateful task to compare them with their Protestant rivals, but we are tracing a contrast, and must needs go on with it. An amiable Anglican minister, very superior to many of his colleagues, has published to the world in what manner *he* set out upon his mission in Canada, and with what appliances. « Our own carriage, » he says, « a sort of double Dennet, drawn by my own horses, brought up the rear » — the van being formed by waggons of furniture and provisions. « This contained myself, my wife, and our eldest son, every corner being filled up with trunks, band-boxes, and endless etceteras. » After this description of his going forth, the writer, who had evidently good feelings and intentions, gravely observes, « I may not presume to class myself with those heroic and warlike churchmen of old..., » but the disclaimer appears to betray a lurking hope that, in spite of his equipage and his band-boxes, his readers might be of a different opinion. (1)

The same clergyman informs us that his missionary colleagues in Canada « absolutely ridiculed the idea » of Baptism conferring grace; while from higher authorities of the same sect we learn, that all the other religious phenomena which characterise

(1) *Memoirs of a Church of England Missionary in the North American Colonies,* ch. XII, p. 73; ch. XXII, p. 141.

the present state of England are being successfully reproduced in Canada. « We remark, far and wide, » says the gentleman who is Protestant bishop at Toronto, « the prevalence of religious division, and its attendant is too frequently in this diocese a feeling of hostility to the Church of England. » (1) On the other hand, the episcopal officer of the same community at Montreal sorrowfully recognises, amongst the *Catholics* of Canada, « the order, unity, discipline, habitual and unquestioning conformity to rule, common and fraternal feeling of identity with the religious institutions of the whole race, » which, as he had detected, « attaches to the system of the Roman Catholic Church, » and which, he considers, « carries with it a great lesson to the Protestant world. » (2) And these statements are more than confirmed by Lord Durham, when he says, « In the general absence of any permanent institutions of civil government, the Catholic Church has presented almost the only semblance of stability and organization, and furnished the only effectual support for civilization and order. » (3)

On the whole, when we combine the facts which have now been hastily reviewed, — when we compare the admissions of M* Buckingham and others, that the *Catholic* Indians « fulfil their religious duties in the most exemplary manner, » and « are always sober, » with the confessions of M* Kingston and M* Kane, that the *Protestant* natives are « a very

(1) *The Church in Canada*, p. 37.
(2) *Church in the Colonies*, n° 9, p. 12.
(3) *Report and Despatches of the Earl of Durham in Canada*, p. 97. (1839).

inferior race, » and « get drunk whenever they can; » when we find English writers admitting that the Catholic missionaries are, even at this day, « more than usually successful » in converting the heathen, while the most competent Protestant agents freely confess, that adult Indians « can never be prevailed upon to change their religion; » when we note, on the one hand, the peaceful and industrious progress of the natives under their Catholic guides, in spite of the coldness of the civil authorities, and on the other, the squalid misery of the pensioners under an official patronage which, as Mr Bradford laments, « is rapidly destroying them ; » lastly, when we compare « the order, unity, and fraternal feeling » which cements the one, with « the prevalence of religious division » which dissolves and scatters the other, and contrast, by the aid of Protestant witnesses, the character and mode of life of the two orders of missionaries, of whom the one are destitute strangers, scowled upon by the rulers of the land, the others opulent representatives of British power and influence; we may surely accept without surprise the conclusion announced by an English traveller, whose scrutiny of all these facts compelled the reluctant avowal, — « It appears to me that Roman Catholicism is best adapted for civilising the Indians. » (1)

We might now quit Canada, to examine in the wide territories of the American Union the final example of the contrast which we have traced in

(1) *Letters from the United States, Cuba, and Canada*, by the Hon. Amelia M. Murray; Letter IX, p. 127.

every other region, but a special motive compels us to linger for a moment among the people who have found a home by the banks of the St. Lawrence. The religious history of the French Canadians is perhaps only indirectly connected with the immediate subject of this work, yet there are sufficient reasons for a brief allusion to it. Like some other races of whom we have read in these volumes, — like the Maronites in Syria, the Chinese in Corea and Annam, and the Indians in Paraguay, — the Canadians are what they are solely by the power of the Catholic religion. By it they have been created and sustained. To its penetrating influence their whole social and individual life bears witness. Take away the faith which has been the light of their homes and hearts, and the Canadians would have no place on earth. They would be absorbed in the dull inert mass of semi-pagan life by which they are surrounded.

The resistance which the Catholics of British America, and especially the Canadians, have opposed to the deadly influences which threatened for more than a century to destroy their peaceful communities, and to dry up the fountains of their life, forms one of those chapters of modern history at which the statesman glances with indifference or disgust, but in which the Christian loves to trace the providence of God. Subject to masters of an alien race and creed, who could neither appreciate their virtues nor respect their independence, every thing has been tried which eager malice could invent, or unscrupulous fraud devise, or shameless violence execute, to exhaust their constancy. In a single year, as Haliburton relates, nearly fifteen thousand Catholics were forcibly deported from the province of Nova Scotia, and their goods confiscated, by the authority of the British government. (1) And the policy which suggested this crime prevailed in Canada, as Burke indignantly reminded his nation, until the fear of rebellion provoked a tardy and calculating justice. « All the laws, customs, and forms of judicature, » says Mr Bancroft, « of a populous and long established colony were in one hour overturned, by the ordinance of the 17th of September, 1764; and English laws, even the penal statutes against Catholics, all unknown to the Canadians, and unpublished, were introduced in their stead... In the 110 rural parishes there were but nineteen Protestant families! The meek and un-resisting province was given over to hopeless oppression. The history of the world furnishes no instance of so rash injustice. » (2) Mr Bancroft appears to have forgotten Ireland.

The same facts occurred throughout all the regions then acquired by England on the American continent. « The council at Halifax voted all the poor Red Men that dwelt in the peninsula to be ' so many banditti, ruffians, or rebels; ' and by its authority, Cornwallis, ' to bring the rascals to reason, ' offered for every one of them ' taken or killed, ' ten guineas, to be paid on producing the savage *or his scalp.* » The Catholic inhabitants of Acadia were treated even worse than those of Canada. Under the French, says the Protestant historian, « they formed, as it were,

---

(1) *History of Nova Scotia*, quoted by Brasseur de Bourbourg, tome I, ch. XVI, p. 290.
(2) IV, 151.

one great family. Their morals were of unaffected purity. » But this did not save them. The possession of virtue and innocence was a slender title to the esteem of the English; and so, continues our authority, « the Acadians were despised because they were helpless, Their papers and records, the titles to their estates and inheritances, were taken away from them.... When they delayed in fetching fire-wood for their oppressors, it was told them from the Governor, ' if they do not do it in proper time, the soldiers shall take their houses for fuel. ' »

Finally, as these too lenient measures failed to destroy their faith, or to exhaust their patience, all their remaining property was seized by the crown officers, and they were banished *en masse*. « Some were charitably sheltered from the English, » says Mr Bancroft, « in the wigwams of the savages! » But even this did not satisfy their new masters. « To prevent their return, their villages, from Annapolis to the isthmus, were laid waste. The live stock was seized as spoils, and disposed of *by the English officials*.... The Lords of Trade, more merciless than the savages, wished that every one of the Acadians should be driven out; and when it seemed that the work was done, congratulated the king that ' the zealous endeavours of Governor Lawrence had been crowned with an entire success. ' I know not if the annals of the human race keep the record of sorrows so wantonly inflicted, so bitter and so perennial, as fell upon the French inhabitants of Acadia. » (1)

(1) III, 138, 146.

Long years after, the successors of Cornwallis, and Lawrence, and the Earl of Loudoun, still resembled their predecessors, still imitated their example as closely as they dared; and Lord Durham, whose fretful but honest temper was soothed by the simple virtues of a people whom he learned to love, and strove to defend, could tell his government, with a warmth which he did not care to subdue, that « *they* had done nothing to promote education, though they had applied the revenues of the Jesuits, destined for educational purposes, » and whose college the English converted into a barrack, to the miserable schemes of official patronage; and reminded them, that with cynical contempt of truth and honour, they gave a large annual stipend, out of these very revenues, to an Anglican preacher, as « chaplain of the Jesuits! »

The fate of the once famous college of the Jesuits at Quebec, now tenanted by the military police of the province, will be regretted by all who appreciate the objects which it was destined to promote. « From this seat of piety and learning, » says a Protestant writer, issued those dauntless Missionaries who made the Gospel known *over a space of six hundred leagues*, and preached the Christian Faith from the St. Lawrence to the Mississippi. » (1)

Yet the Canadians, who received from England, until the time of Lord Durham, only coarse insult or heartless oppression, have stedfastly maintained, by the counsels of their spiritual guides, a sincere and manly loyalty to their foreign rulers. In 1755, Ca-

(1) Hawkins, *Quebec*, etc., ch. x, p. 193.

nada would have been lost to England, but for the vigilant action of the Catholic clergy. « England holds the Canadas, » observes a Protestant writer, « by the influence of the Roman Catholic Hierarchy a𝐥. The Sulpicians of Montreal are her Vice-gerents.» (1) « A large part of the Catholic clergy, » said Lord Durham, « support the government against revolutionary violence. » (2) But if the Catholic people of Canada have hitherto refused, though often urged by agents from the United States, to rebel against their hard and unsympathising rulers, they have rejected with inexpressible repugnance both their religion and their habits, while they have jealously preserved their own distinctive life, their language, their faith, and their traditions. Let us see what Protestants say, in spite of religious and national prejudices, of a people whom they have so deeply wronged, but whom they are constrained to praise, even when they wish to revile.

« The French Canadians, » says Sir Francis Head. « retain all the social virtues of the French, without their propensity to war. » (3) « They are mild and kindly, » observes Lord Durham, « frugal, industrious and honest, very sociable, cheerful and hospitable, and distinguished for a courtesy and real politeness which pervades every class of society. » (4) « They vastly surpass, » observes Dr Shaw, in 1856, « the people of England in the same rank of life; » and then, alluding to the religion which has made

(1) *The Statesmen of America*, p. 305.
(2) *Despatches*, p. 11.
(3) Sir Francis Head's *Narrative*, p. 194.
(4) *Despatches*, p. 17.

them what they are, he adds, « I have seen them flocking in great numbers as early as 5 o'clock in the morning, and have been informed that they frequently assemble as early as 4 a. m.; proving one thing at least, that they are not indolently religious. » (1) « I confess, » says Mr Godley, an Anglican Protestant, « I have a strong sympathy for the French Canadians; they are ' si bons enfants ' — contentment, *gaieté de cœur*, politeness springing from benevolence of heart, respect to their superiors, confidence in their friends, attachment to their religion » — these are amongst the qualities which he detected in them. (2) « Every thing we saw of the French Canadians, » writes Mr Buckingham, « induced us to believe that they are amongst the happiest peasantry in the world... I think the Canadian more sober, more virtuous, and more happy than the American. » (3)

Such are the Canadians, in the judgment of upright Protestants, willing to acknowledge, even when slow to imitate, the virtues of the simple and winning race whom they describe. But these frank and cordial eulogies of amiable and discerning witnesses have not been allowed to pass, and the fact is worthy of notice, without the protests of that uneasy rancour which heresy inspires, and which could awaken even in a woman's heart the thoughts expressed in the following words. « The enslaving, enervating, and

(1) *Ramble through the United States*, etc., ch. III, p. 90.
(2) Godley's *Letters from America*, vol. I, letter 5, p. 89.
(3) *Canada*, etc., pp. 211, 18, 20, 264, 270. Cf. Lieut. Col. Cunynghame's *Glimpse at the Great Western Republic*, ch. XX, p. 252.

retarding effects of Roman Catholicism are nowhere better seen than in Lower Canada, where the priests exercise despotic authoritiy. » And as if this were too weak to do justice to her feelings, this English lady presently adds, that all the evils of that country, whatever they may be, are due to the « *ignorance and terrorism* caused by the successful efforts of the priests. » (1) Her book was intended for English readers, and she appears to have anticipated that they would welcome such statements. Yet in the next page she confesses, that « there are in Lower Canada *upwards of eleven hundred schools*, » of which, it may be added, nearly one hundred are at this moment under the direction of Christian Brothers; (2) and Mr Buckingham informs us, speaking of the religious schools in Quebec, « so highly is the tuition given here prized by *all* classes, that Protestant families send their daughters quite as freely to the Ursuline Convent for education as Catholics. »

Elsewhere, the lady whom we quote, forgetting her own gloomy picture of the « enslaved » Canadians, gives the following account of these victims of a « despotic priesthood. » « The peasants of Lower Canada are among the most harmless people under the sun; they are moral, sober, and contented, and zealous in the observance of their erroneous creed. They strive after happiness rather than advancement, and who shall say that they are unsuccessful

---

(1) *The Englishwoman in America*, ch. xiv, p. 312.
(2) *The Metropolitan Catholic Almanac*, Baltimore, 1860; p. 278.

in their aim? On Sundays and Saint's days they assemble in crowds in their churches. Their wants and wishes are few, their manners are courteous and unsuspicious, they hold their faith with a blind and implicit credulity, » — she neither knows what their faith is, nor how they hold it, — « and on summer evenings sing the songs of France as their fathers sang them in bygone days on the smiling banks of the rushing Rhone. » (1) Yet after this description of a charming people, — whom she calls, in various places, « moral, sober, contented, amiable, courteous, not ambitious, sincere, and devout, » — she scoffs complacently at the divine religion which has generated these very virtues as « the great antidote to social progress. » All her own ideas of an unexceptionable religion appear to be connected with railroads, steamboats, much commerce, and a diligent police. Unfortunate Canadians, who refuse to say to such objects of worship, « These are thy gods! » «With *them*, » says an English Protestant of a higher class, « churches come first, railroads afterwards, which appears to *us* a very paradoxical arrangement. They make the church the *first* object, and we the *last*. » (2) And for this reason it is, — because their souls are penetrated with the divine admonition, « *unum necessarium*, » and Christian faith counsels them not to be « *troubled about many things*, » (3) that the Canadians have found grace to remain what they are; for this reason their life

(1) Ch. XIII, p. 284.
(2) Godley, letter 4, p. 71.
(3) S. Luke, X, 42.

contrasts so visibly, in purity and dignity, in true
wisdom and enlightenment, in familiar knowledge of
God and of holy religion, with the feverish « progress » and restless greed of the American, or the
dismal sottishness of the English boor.

Colonel Bouchette, who knows more of the Canadians than the tourist whom we have quoted, and
who forcibly observes that neither the crimes nor the
social misery of England exist among them, declares
with energy, that « the Catholic religion is in Canada
no more the instrument of the people's degradation,
than is the Quaker religion in Pensylvania; » and he
not only confesses that English destitution is as little
known in Canada as English unbelief, but that « *a bold
spirit of independence* reigns throughout the conduct
of the whole population, » and that « its priesthood use
only the influence of the understanding, are merely
the advisers, and not the rulers of their flocks. » (1)

As Canada is often referred to by English writers
as an example of the social stagnation of a Catholic
people, it may be permitted to add a few words on
this familiar theme. Catholic States, we are told, rarely emulate the material progress of their Protestant
rivals. Yet nothing is more incontestable than this,
that in Canada, as in every other Catholic land,
neither social misery nor social crime have ever attained the proportions which distinguish England,
Prussia, and other non-catholic nations. As respects
Great Britain, a Protestant authority affirms the notorious fact, that « in no country is so large a proportion of the inhabitants sunk in pauperism and

---

(1) *British Dominions*, etc., ch. XVII, p. 414.

wretchedness. » (1) In Prussia, the same experienced writer, honestly comparing the Catholic and Protestant districts together, affirms as follows with respect to the Rhine provinces. « The people are Roman Catholic; and in manufactures, trade, capital, and industry, *are very far in advance*, of any other portion or people of the Prussian dominions. » (2) Belgium, the most Catholic province of northern Europe, is also the most prosperous. In France, where the products of the so-called Reformation are held in lower esteem than in almost any country of the world, successive revolutions, which would have utterly destroyed the financial equilibrium of England or Holland, have scarcely inflicted a shock either on the national credit or the public welfare, so solid is the basis of her prosperity. And lastly, whereas it is usual to point to Spain and Portugal as notable instances of the decay of Catholic states, they are, in fact, pregnant examples of exactly the opposite truth. It is history which teaches us, that both those kingdoms attained the summit of their opulence and might precisely at the moment when Catholic principles and traditions most powerfully influenced their rulers and people, and that they *began to decay* only when their degenerate statesmen first adopted the political maxims which Protestantism introduced into the world, and broke that intimate alliance with the Catholic Church to which they owed all their glory and renown. If Portugal, once so illustrious in arms and in commerce, has become contemptible in

(1) Laing, *Residence in Norway*, ch. IV, p. 156.
(2) Laing, *Observations on Europe*, ch. XIII, p. 316. (1850).

CHAPTER IX.

Europe, it is because she has suffered her religious life to ebb away, and though of old she filled the world with her apostles, has now hardly vigour enough to produce even a domestic clergy; while the great Spanish nation, after a temporary eclipse, is resuming at the same moment, amid the applause of Christendom, both the Catholic instincts which made her in other days the mightiest empire in the universe, and the material prosperity which she knew how to create under Ferdinand and Isabella, to develope under Charles the Fifth, to preserve under Philip the Second, and to restore once again under the daughter of Ferdinand the Seventh. (1)

Let us return for a moment to Canada, and to the English lady, who, as a specimen of the singular pertinacity of British prejudice, deserves additional

---

(1) It is not, of course, denied that the influence of religion, in proportion to its energy, will generate indifference to the material progress which the world esteems so highly. It was the doctrine of S*t* Paul, and the world has always resented it, that Christians should use this world « *as if they used it not.* » « The world, » says an eminent writer, « is a counterfeit of the Church of God, and in the most implacable antagonism to it... The view which the Church takes of the world is distinct and clear, and far from flattering to its pride. It considers the friendship of the world as enmity with God. It puts all the world's affairs under its feet, either as of no consequence, or at least of very secondary importance... It provokes the world by looking on progress doubtingly, and with what appears a very inadequate interest, and there is a quiet faith in its contempt for the world extremely irritating to this latter power. » D*r* Faber, *The Creator and the Creature*, ch. III, p. 378. It is perhaps only an incidental and subordinate, but still a startling illustration of the mortal apathy of our countrymen, that this wonderful book should exist in their own language, and remain utterly unknown to them.

notice. The Canadian clergy, whose despotic influence, she informs us, creates « ignorance and terrorism, » — but who « only use the influence of the understanding, » as Colonel Bouchette observes, and number among them, as Mr Kohl has told us, the most learned men on the western continent, — are thus described by Lord Durham. « The Catholic priesthood of this Province have, to a very remarkable degree, conciliated the good will of persons of all creeds; and I know of no parochial clergy in the world whose practice of all the Christian virtues is more universally admitted, and has been productive of more beneficial consequences. » (1) And if this be not a sufficient rebuke to the lady whom we are quoting, perhaps her own words will supply whatever is wanting. She is noticing the ravages of the cholera at Toronto, and these are the reflections which she makes. « The priests of Rome then gained a double influence. Armed with what appeared in the eyes of the people supernatural powers, they knew no rest either by day or night; they held the cross before many a darkening eye, and spoke to the bereaved of a world where sorrow and separation are alike unknown. » (2) But no virtues could soothe her enmity, instruct her prejudice, nor inspire the thought of imitating, however feebly, the charity which these priests could have taught her; and so, after exhausting the vocabulary of disdain and reproof, she finishes, as she began, by a general defiance to all Catholic people and nations, and by the

(1) *Despatches*, p. 97.
(2) Ch. XII, p. 263.

peremptory declaration, addressed to humanity at large, that « America and Scotland are the two most religious countries in the world ! »

If we accept the imprudent challenge conveyed in these words, we shall hardly be led into a digression, for we shall still be illustrating one of the facts proper to our subject. « Scotland, » says Dr Shaw, contrasting her expressly with Canada, « claims the honour of standing pretty near *first* in the catalogue of crime. » (1) « Nearly every tenth Scotsman, » says another local witness, « is a bastard; » (2) and, « speaking of the country districts, it is the *exception* and not the rule if a master has not been chargeable, sometime or other, with corrupting those under him. » (3) The latest Report of the Scottish Registrar General, (1860,) reveals once more, with almost unofficial candour, « the excessive incontinence » of this Presbyterian nation, and deplores that « the immorality is not confined to the humbler classes. » (4) Lastly, a well known Presbyterian writer attests the enormous inebriety of the same people, and the characteristic fact, indicating, as he observes, « the moral and religious condition of Edinburgh, » that the sum of 2,170 l. is spent *every Sunday* in that metropolis of Calvinism, « in drinking whiskey or other spirits; » (5) while Dr Barclay registers the proverb, « as besotted and as pharisaical as Glasgow, » and another authority adds, « if Scotland is the most

(1) *The United States,* etc., ch. IV, p. 106.
(2) *Quoted in the Times,* July 17, 1858.
(3) *Banffshire Journal,* quoted in the *Times,* February 24, 1859.
(4) *The Times,* November 26, 1860.
(5) Laing, *Observations on Europe,* ch. II, p. 37.

Sabbatarian and Calvinistic country upon earth, its town populations at least are the most drunken of drunkards. » (1)

America is thus described by a competent witness, Dr Onderdonck, a Protestant bishop. « A spirit of misrule, of impiety, of infidelity, of licentiousness, is stalking through the length and breadth of our land, threatening ruin to every interest connected with individual, domestic, social, and civil welfare. It must be resisted, it must be kept at bay, it must be crushed, *or we are a ruined people.* » (2) This is not a cheerful description of « the most religious country in the world ; » in which, we are further informed, « nearly four fifths of the children, and two thirds of the male population, are unbaptized! »(3) « There is not a country, » adds Mr Francis Wyse, « where infidelity is more generally diffused amidst the bulk of the population; » (4) and this infidelity, an American writer will presently assure us, « is *the usual recoil* » of his countrymen « from the Puritanism of their childhood : » — another proof that atheism is the logical result of a religion which, in its best form, can only appeal to emotion and sentiment, and when these are exhausted, dies away in apathy and gloom. « A great portion of our country,» observes an Episcopalian minister, in 1858, « is witness to the most alarming theological progress towards the Rationalism of Germany. » (5) In other

(1) *Saturday Review*, April 20, 1861.
(2) *Sermon preached at the consecration of Christchurch.*
(3) Godley, *Letters from America*, vol. II, p. 102.
(4) America, *Its Realities and Resources*, vol. I, ch. IX, p. 270.
(5) Revd A. C. Coxe, *Statements and Documents concerning the*

words, the mass have no religion at all, and the few have a religion which is a denial of revelation.

Again. The total absence of any moral result from Protestant *education* in America, the universality of which has been so much vaunted, is so notorious, as to force from a candid and experienced observer the following avowal. « Many well judging persons, of different religious persuasions, have assured me, that the only really *useful* and *corrective* education is that of the Catholic schools and colleges. So far as I have known, these Seminaries are crowded, not only with pupils of their own creed, but with those of other sects. And I have high official authority for saying, that the Ministers and Missionaries of the Roman Catholic Church are at this moment doing more good for the cause of virtue and morality throughout the whole continent of America, than those of any other religious denomination whatever. » (1)

And if we ask, in conclusion, what have been the fruits of that peculiar system which America has borrowed from Scotland, for re-awakening religious emotion where it has ebbed away or become extinct, every witness, of whatever creed, except those who trade in that form of hysterical mania, will give us the same reply. « If a victorious army, » says a conspicuous American preacher, « should overflow and lay us waste, or if a fire should pass over and lay every dwelling in our land in ashes, it would be a blessing to be coveted with thanksgiving, in comparison to the moral desolation of *one* ungoverned ' re-

Board of Managers of the American Bible Society, p. 28. (New York, 1858).
(1) *The Statesmen of America in* 1846, p. 491.

vival ' of religion. »(1)« Had the inhabitants of Bedlam been let loose,» observes Mr Fearon, in describing one of these orgies, « they could not have exceeded it.»(2) Yet this is the mode by which Protestant ministers, of many sects, endeavour to acquire a transient influence over souls from which divine faith is absent, and which can therefore only be reached through the medium of disorderly sentiment and fluctuating emotion. This is their remedy for evils which their unblessed ministry can only aggravate. The physical excitement of an hour is followed by furious impiety or cold despair; and « neither revivals, nor cholera, nor anything, » (3) can again stimulate even the spasmodic life which the rude experiments of an unhallowed art have quenched for ever.

It does not appear, then, that Canada, to which we will now return, has much reason to envy the condition of Scotland or America. Even the writer whose idle words have suggested these remarks, and who does not seem to affect consistency, deplores « the obliquity of moral vision which is allowed to exist among a large class of Americans; » declares that « Mammon is the idol which the people worship; » and confesses that « the most nefarious trickery and bold dishonesty are invested with a spurious dignity if they act as aids to the attainment of that object. Children from their earliest years imbibe the idea, that sin is sin—only when found out.»(4) And

(1) *Quoted in Visit to the American Churches*, by Andrew Reed, D. D.; vol. II, pp. 41, 49.
(2) *Sketches of America*, by Henry Bradshaw Fearon, p. 164.
(3) Dr Reed, vol. II, p. 187.
(4) Ch. xv, pp. 326, 423.

this is « the most religious country in the world. » Perhaps we may conclude, either that this writer attaches no meaning whatever to her own words, and neither believes them herself nor wishes others to believe them; or that the energy of her religious tastes induces her to prefer the immoral and impure Scotchman, or the « nefarious and Mammon worshipping American, » to the « sober, moral, courteous, and devout Canadian, » so long as the former consents to revile what the latter reverently esteems — the Faith which was preached in America by Vieyra and Monroy, by Lallemand and de Brebeuf, and of whose influence the Canadian nation is one of the noblest monuments.

The events of which we have thus far attempted to trace the outlines, but which it would have been beside our purpose to review with the minute precision of historical detail, have conducted us over a wide field, and have demanded, even in so rapid a survey, a large and conspicuous place in this too meagre and crowded narrative. Yet we have suppressed at every page illustrations which our limits warned us to exclude, and have altogether omitted several provinces of which the religious history would have furnished exactly the same facts which we have gathered elsewhere. In the frozen regions which lie between the St. Lawrence and the Arctic Circle, we should have found, by the testimony of Protestant writers, missionaries of the same class as we have encountered in the Valley of the Amazon and the mountains of Peru, in the forests of Michigan and by the shores of the Canadian Lakes. We should have learned also, by the same evidence, what manner of

men the Sects have despatched to these gloomy
wastes, and what has been the fruit of their unwilling sojourn in the tents of Greenland and the huts of
Labrador.

In a recent work by D' Rink, Danish Superintendent of South Greenland, which is said to have excited much attention in Stockholm and throughout
the Scandinavian peninsula, the results of Protestant
teaching amongst Finns, Greenlanders, and other
northern races, appear to be revealed with unusual
candour. D' Morison had admitted, at an earlier
date, the futility of all the Lutheran projects in these
regions, and had confessed, in guarded phrase, that
« the moral and spiritual results of this mission
were not such as to warrant any glowing picture of
its successful issue. » The Danish Superintendent
seems to have spoken with less reserve. In a letter
from Stockholm, dated the 15th of September, 1858,
and published in English Protestant journals,
D' Rink's unwelcome revelations are thus noticed.

« During the last few years, religious movements
have taken place amongst the half-civilised Lappanian and Finnish tribes, which excited their minds
to so great a degree, and animated them to such
tumultuous excesses, that the Swedish-Norwegian
Government found it necessary to send troops to
that distant region in order to restore peace... The
excitement of the public mind is still so great that
measures have been taken to suppress any possible
new outbreak at its very birth. »

The source of these « tumultuous excesses, » it
appears, was a monstrous kind of religious fanaticism, generated by the rival schemes of Lutheran

missionaries. « There can be no doubt, » says the Swedish narrative, « that these commotions have arisen from a gross misunderstanding *between the Christian teachers*... So far has been proved from the most minute investigations, that Christianity, as yet, is by no means deeply rooted amongst these tribes » — although the missionaries, we are told, have been at work « more than a century! » « Remains of heathenism, gross superstition, credulity, as well as inclination to religious fanaticism and enthusiasm, have, on the contrary, shown themselves as fully developed. Here is ground, the working of which would yield a rich harvest to different religious sects. The Roman Catholic missionaries, who are settled at Quananberfjore, and amongst whom are several Jesuits, were doubtless aware of this state of affairs before their arrival, and will assuredly not fail to draw from it every possible advantage. »

The account then proceeds to furnish examples of the effects of Protestant religious instruction upon the Greenlanders, constantly exhibiting the same phenomena during the last seventy years. « Disturbances have in former times repeatedly broken out amongst the Greenlanders, the origin of which is alone to be found in their misconceived religious views. In 1790, and in 1803, several women gave themselves out as holy, and one who was called Mary Magdalene declared herself to be a prophetess, spoke of the visions and revelations she had had, and gained a considerable number of followers. She took advantage of the activity of her disciples to bring about a blind obedience to her commands, and had two of her enemies killed. Some bad deeds of her husband, to whom she had given the name of Jesus, brought her after a few months so glaringly into notice, that the missionaries endeavoured to bring the lost sheep back into the bosom of the church. » Whether they succeeded, does not appear; but these events induced them « to carry out the plan of training the most able and intelligent among the natives as Catechists » — a project which led to unpleasant results. « It is from one of these Greenland pupils that the last excitement has proceeded... In the summer of 1854 a young man of Frederikstal, who had been selected as Catechist, became unusually still, and sought retirement. Shortly afterwards, unusual meetings were held by the Greenlanders of this place and its neighbourhood, and soon the usual religious services were obliged to be discontinued for want of worshippers. » The next event was that « the Catechist declared himself to be a prophet, and that it was his intention to form a new company entirely distinct from the Europeans. He pretended to have had revelations and interviews with the Saviour; assumed, in consequence, the name of Gabriel, and gathered together many followers, all of whom promised him implicit obedience. The falling away was so universal, that but few Greenlanders remained true to the Missionaries. »

But this was not the end. « The new Gabriel performed religious ceremonies, married several couples amongst the new believers, and sent people to the next mission station in order to gather followers thence. Then other Greenlanders pretended to have had visions, and a feverish madness possessed the whole population. Some pricked their hands, and allowed others to suck out the flowing blood, in order to taste the sweetness of the Saviour's blood! Some were commanded to open their mouths, when Gabriel breathed into them the Holy Ghost. » The madness lasted a year, and then seems to have died out; « but who, » says the Scandinavian writer, « can answer for it that no mishap will arise in future from the same religious delusions? It is by no means impossible that the safety of the Europeans may be by such cases endangered » — this is what they seem to have felt most acutely in Sweden — « and the usefulness of the missionaries brought into question. »

The peculiarity in the Protestant missions of Greenland appears, then, to consist in this; that while in every other land they have encountered only apathy, indifference, or aversion, here they have engendered fierce religious mania. In the torrid climes of Asia, or of Central and Southern America, they hardly attract attention, or at most provoke a smile; in the icy wastes of the North they breed « religious delusions, » « feverish madness, » and « tumultuous excesses. » The Chinese may rob, or the Hindoo revile them; the wily Armenian may become their pensioner, and the red Indian sink under their patronage to a lower depth of shame; but the Greenlander, refusing to imitate such examples, takes a line of his own, and learns from them just enough of Christianity to burlesque its doctrines and profane its mysteries, to usurp the titles of the Saviour, and to parody the functions of His archangels. It is satisfactory to know that a better day has dawned for him, and that the Jesuits have arrived in Greenland.

And now we approach the final scene of that long series which we have contemplated in so many lands, from where the sun rises in the furthest East to where it sinks in the distant West, and in which we have recognised everywhere the same unvarying forms, and have read the same eternal truth — how great man becomes when upheld by the might of God, how little when abandoned to his own.

In that famous Republic, now as conspicuous for social as for religious schism, and whose almost unrivalled prosperity only a political and moral corruption still more unexampled could have so grievously menaced, we find the last and saddest example of the contrast which we have reviewed in other lands. Yet here dwells a people from whom we might have hoped better things. Capable, in the natural order, of the most arduous efforts which man can conceive or sustain, it is only in that which touches the life of the soul that they are feeble, uncertain, and perplexed. Vigorous beyond all other races in the pursuit of material goods, they are blind and impotent only in spiritual things. The gift of divine faith, without which man is only an intellectual animal, they have lost, or never possessed. Hence the weakness of the supernatural element in all classes of Americans; whose religion oscillates between a pretentious but shallow infidelity and a coarse and sensual fanaticism, — between the impiety of the mass, to whom religion is only a name, and the degrading *man-worship* of the few, who have put away Christian liberty to become the serfs of smooth-tongued preachers, or the captives of mercenary zealots. And thus they wander to and fro, or sit down upon the earth, without definite aim or serious purpose; labouring without fruit, and resting without repose; a proverb, like the nation from which they sprung, both for godlessness and fanaticism, for religious apathy and religious dissensions; great in their own eyes, which discern not what they really lack, but only a sign and a portent in the sight of the Angels, who behold in them that most piteous type of human infirmity, Samson with his head shorn, the giant robbed of his strength.

The story of Protestant missions in the United States is told in a single sentence by an American writer, from whom we have already learned, that Paganism is nearly extinct, because the Pagans are nearly annihilated. *That* is the history of religion in North America, as far as the natives are concerned. But the reproach of this unexampled catastrophe does not rest with Americans. The causes which produced it were already in operation a century before the Union existed. The destruction of the Red man, like the institution of slavery, was a legacy bequeathed by England. It was by British colonists, and British officials, that the Indian was first provoked to deeds of blood, and then hunted to death like a wild beast when he had yielded to the temptation. It would have been easy to make him a friend, as was proved by Lord Baltimore in Maryland, by Penn in Virginia, and by the French everywhere. But the friendship of the credulous savage would only have been importunate to men who coveted his lands and not his alliance. The Indian soon discovered that he was doomed, and resolved, since he was tracked as a beast of prey, to die like one. And therefore he fell, rending and tearing, with teeth and claws, the hunter who had brought him to bay. This was the explanation which he often gave, with an energy of language peculiar to himself, of the atrocities which the white man had taught him to commit. « When you first arrived on our shores, » said an Indian Sachem of Long Island to the masters of New York, « you were destitute of food; we gave you our beans and our corn; we fed you with oysters and fish; and now, for our recompense, you murder our people. The traders whom your first ships left on our shore to traffic till their return, were cherished by us as the apple of our eye; we gave them our daughters for their wives; among those whom you have murdered *were children of your own blood.* » (1) And the greatest historian of the United States justifies the argument of the Indian, when he shows that from all classes, — from Puritans, from Dutch Calvinists, and from English Episcopalians, — they received the same treatment. « New England, » he says, and we shall see presently how true it was, waged « a disastrous war of extermination; the Dutch were scarcely ever at peace with the Algonquins; the laws of Maryland refer to Indian hostilities and massacres, which extended as far as Richmond. Penn came without arms; he declared his purpose to abstain from violence; he had no message but peace; *and not a drop of Quaker blood was ever shed by an Indian.* » Elsewhere the same writer notices, in words already

(1) Bancroft, II, 564.

quoted, the impressive fact, that the *French* authorities, who had treated the native as a brother, « as they made their last journey through Canada, and down the valley of the Mississippi, on every side received the expressions of passionate attachment from the many tribes of red men. »

Such was the influence of Catholic colonists, here as in other lands. « The French, » M̃ Bancroft observes, « had won the affection of the savages,.... and retained it by religious influence, They seemed to be no more masters, but rather companions and friends. More formidable enemies now appeared, arrogant in their pretensions, scoffing insolently at those whom they superseded, *driving away their Catholic priests*, and introducing the traffic in rum, which till then had been effectually prohibited. » (1)

The present condition of the Indians of North America is, then, the direct and inevitable result of the proceedings inaugurated nearly two centuries ago, and constantly renewed, by the Protestants of England and Holland. They have perished because the English could make more profit by their death than by their life; and they have perished without leaving a trace behind. « All the Indian tribes, » says M. de Tocqueville, « which formerly inhabited the territory of New England, the Naragansets, the Mohicans, the Pequods, no longer exist but in memory; the Lenape, who received Penn one hundred and fifty years ago, on the banks of the Delaware, have at this day disappeared. I myself saw the last of the Iroquois; they were begging alms!... These savages

(1) IV, 79.

have not simply *retreated*, they have been *destroyed*. » (1) It was in allusion to such facts that a Protestant minister already quoted, and who had dwelt amongst the Delawares, was led to exclaim, « Alas! what has not our nation to answer for at the bar of retributive justice! »

The three classes, as we have said, who made war on the Indian, were the Dutch, the Puritans of New England, and the English Royalists. The operations of the first we need not stay to notice, but a few words may be allowed with respect to the other two.

The « Pilgrim Fathers » of New England have been the heroes of many a romance which has been accepted by the world as history. Even Mr Bancroft, though he reveals something of their real character, avows the customary sympathy with their supposed « love of freedom, » maintenance of « individual rights, » and defence of « intellectual liberty. » Yet the annals of mankind contain, perhaps, no such example of unrelenting tyranny on the one hand, of abject bondage to human traditions on the other, as that which is displayed in the acts, the laws, and the literature of the Puritans of New England. Professing to frame their daily life by the maxims of the New Testament, it may be affirmed without exaggeration, that no race of men, since the Gospel was first preached on earth, have ever violated its spirit with such remorseless consistency. They were not perhaps conscious hypocrites, for most of them had deceived themselves before they deceived others; but this, if we judge them by the narratives of their own histo-

(1) *De la Démocratie en Amérique*, tome III, ch. v, p. 115.

rians, is nearly the only crime of which these Arabs of the Reformation were guiltless. It would be difficult to find in them so much as one lineament of the true Christian character. Humility, modesty, meekness, patience, forbearance, obedience, charity — against these, and all the kindred graces of the disciples of the Cross, every word and deed of their life was an unvarying protest. Never were they so utterly unchristian, in every thought, feeling, and desire, as when they were preaching what they called « the Gospel; » never were they so full of cruel arrogance, haughty defiance, bitter menace, and incurable self-righteousness, as when they vehemently called God to witness that they were His peculiar people. They had fled from England to enjoy « liberty of conscience, » and they proved their love of liberty by refusing it to all who dared to interpret a text otherwise than themselves. « To say that men ought to have 'liberty of conscience,' » exclaimed one of their oracles, « *is impious ignorance.* » (1) And they proceeded forthwith to chastise what they called, in their singular jargon, « the profaneness of *polypiety.*» It would almost seem as if they had bound themselves by a vow to abhor and revile all creatures of God, save only themselves. At one moment they rejoiced to have placed an ocean between themselves and « the iron yoke of wolvish bishops; » at another to have broken asunder « the chains of Presbyterian tyrants; » Baptists were mulcted in heavy fines, and when they failed to pay, « were unmercifully whipped; » Quakers they branded with a hot iron,

(1) Bancroft, I, 336.

or lopped of their ears, or hung up by the neck; « Witches, » a title which included all their opponents for whom they could find no other, and especially rival ministers of religion, were executed in troops, « ' There hang eight firebrands of hell, ' said Noyes, the minister of Salem, pointing to the bodies swinging on the gallows. » (1) When Burroughs, an obnoxious preacher, was hanging from the gibbet, and the spectators showed symptoms of tardy regret, « Cotton Mather, on horseback among the crowd, addressed the people, cavilling at the *ordination* of Burroughs, as though he had been no true minister!.... and the hanging proceeded. » « By what law, » said Wenlock Christison, a Quaker, « will ye put me to death? — We have a law, it was answered, and by it you are to die. — So said the Jews to Christ. But who empowered you to make that law? — We have a patent, and may make our own laws. » « I appeal then, » said their victim « to the laws of England. » It was a luckless appeal, and only provoked the prompt reply, « The English banish Jesuits on pain of death, and with equal justice we may banish Quakers. The jury returned a verdict of guilty; the vote was put a second time, and there appeared a majority for the doom of death. » (2)

It is worthy of remark, that *seventy-seven* of the New England Puritans « were in orders in the Church of England,» (3) and that, as Burke notices, « several who had received Episcopal ordination » joined them; yet, as he adds, « The truth is, they had no idea at

(1) Bancroft, II, 762.
(2) *Id.*, I, 342.
(3) Rupp, *Hist, Rel. Denominations*, p. 271.

all of freedom. The very doctrine of any sort of toleration was so odious to the greater part, that one of the first persecutions set up, was against a small party which arose amongst themselves... The persecution which drove the Puritans out of England might be considered as great lenity and indulgence in the comparison. » Then describing some of their unrelenting atrocities, he adds, « things of this nature form the greater part of the history of New England for a long time. In short, this people, who in England could not bear being chastised with rods, had no sooner got free from their fetters than they scourged their fellow refugees with scorpions; though the absurdity, as well as the injustice of such a proceeding in them, might stare them in the face. » Lastly, referring to the charges of « witchcraft » which these ex-Anglican ministers brought against their rivals, Burke says; « An universal terror and consternation seized upon all. The prisons were crowded; people were executed daily; yet the rage of the accusers was as fresh as ever. » A magistrate, he adds, who has just committed forty persons for sorcery, and then refused to go on with his disgusting task, « was himself immediately accused of sorcery, and thought himself happy in leaving his family and fortune, and escaping with his life out of the province. » Finally, « several of the most popular ministers, after twenty executions had been made, addressed Sir William Phips, » the Anglican governor, « with thanks for what he had done, and with exhortations to proceed in so laudable a work. »(1) Yet even Mr Bancroft, beguiled by that

(1) *An Account of the European Settlements in America*, pp. 151, 159, 160. (1758).

bastard philosophy which puts words in the place of things, could commend in swelling phrase the attachment to freedom, to intellectual vigour, and to the great principles of human progress and enlightenment, displayed by the New England Puritans!

This is not the place to examine the whole history of the « Pilgrim Fathers, » with which indeed we are not immediately concerned; yet something we may learn from it incidentally, in considering the fortunes of the unhappy Indian tribes who dwelt within their reach. It was not likely that zealots who spared neither man nor woman in their cruel vanity, and who, as M\\r Bancroft observes, « would not bow at the name of Jesus, nor bend the knee to the King of kings, » would learn mercy in dealing with Indians — much less that they would sacrifice themselves in order to labour for their salvation. « No one, » says D\\r Wilberforce, « had so much as a thought of attempting to convey to the unhappy tribes around them the blessed message of salvation. » (1) So easily does fanaticism co-exist with utter godlessness; so wide is the gulf between sectarian zeal and christian charity. « It is requisite to recollect, » says a recent Protestant writer, « that the Puritans, although burning with religious zeal, did little for the conversion of the American Indians. » (2) Little in truth! — but, on the other hand, they did more than any of their contemporaries, perhaps more than all of them put together, to kindle the fires of that inextinguishable hate which made the Eastern States a field of

(1) *A History of the Protestant Episcopal Church in America*, by Samuel Wilberforce, ch. III, p. 82.
(2) D\\r Thomson, *New Zealand*, vol. I, part. 2, ch. III, p. 303.

blood, and which only the utter annihilation of their primitive inhabitants could appease. « The Puritans, » says M' Howitt, « gave at length as much as 1000 l. for every Indian scalp that could be brought to them! » (1)

« They seized without scruple, » says the Protestant bishop of Oxford, « the lands possessed of old times by the Indians, and it is calculated that *upwards of 180,000 of the aboriginal inhabitants were slaughtered by them* in Massachusetts Bay and Connecticut alone. »(2) This was their mode of effecting conversions; and these men were not Spanish soldiers, nor Portuguese slave dealers, but « ministers of the Gospel, » and champions of the « Reformation. » These were the Vieyras, the Clavers, and the Las Casas of Protestantism. « As long as slavery was *profitable*, » says a living American writer, » the Puritans not only enslaved *both the Indians and the Negroes*, making them ' taxable property,' but carried on a brisk traffic in their flesh, selling them in the best markets to the highest bidder. »(3)

Cotton Mather, who ruled amongst them as prophet and pontiff, and who was ready at any moment to prove or disprove anything which any other man could affirm or deny by a torrent of Scripture texts, not only hounded on his fierce sectaries to thirst for their blood, but publicly offered thanks to the God of heaven when it covered the land as with an inundation. In a book which he entitled *Prevalency of*

(1) *Colonization and Christianity*, ch. xx, p. 317.
(2) *Ubi supra*.
(3) *New York Herald*, January 20, 1861.

Prayer, exulting, like some Mexican hierophant, as he counted with gleaming eyes and dripping hands the reeking hearts which he had piled around him, the Puritan leader exclaims, without pity and without remorse, « God do so to all the implacable enemies of Christ, and of his people in New England! (1) « The efficacy of prayer for the destruction of the Indians, » we learn from Dr Thacher, was a favorite topic also with Dr Increase Mather, who told his hearers, not to « cease crying to the Lord against Philip, » the chief of the New England Indians, « until they had prayed the bullet into his heart. » Yet, as Thacher admits, « Philip possessed virtues which ought to have inspired his enemies with respect. » (2) But this could not save him. Apostles have shed their own blood, during eighteen centuries, that by dying they might purchase life for their enemies: but it was reserved for Protestant ministers to shed the blood of the heathen, and then claim the approval of heaven for doing it.

It would be only too easy to multiply illustrations of the demoniacal spirit of the New England ministers. Their only thought towards the heathen was to slay them. « Many heathens have been slain cries one of them; » and then he adds with exultation, « another expedition is about to set out! » The letter addressed to sympathising colleagues, which announces this view of the relations of Puritans to the Indian nations, concludes with these words : — « May we see

(1) *History of the Indians of North America*, by Samuel G. Drake; book II, ch. VII.
(2) Thacher, *Hist. of Plymouth*, p. 391.

each other hereafter in our Bridegroom's chamber, securely sheltered behind the blue curtains of the Heavens, in the third Heaven of Abraham's bosom. » (1)

There is no need to examine more minutely the dealings of the Puritans with the natives, nor to trace the history of the furious dissensions which raged amongst themselves. In spite of banishment, tortures, and death, — in spite of enactments only matched in the penal code of Great Britain, — new sects continually sprang into being, equally confident and imperious, by whom the peculiar and exclusive religious polity of the New England pulpit oligarchy was finally stifled and quenched. It was a marvel that it lasted so long. Every innocent joy, the fruit and blossom of true religion, was suppressed by the founders of Salem, « because their followers regarded gaiety as sinful. » (2) « All those that weare long locks, » was one of their judicious rules for their Indian victims, « shall pay five shillings. » (3) And this hideous burlesque of Christianity, which substituted for grace and virtue fierce animal excitement or hysterical delusions, and that blasphemous arrogance to which the Prussian monarch alluded when he said, « the Calvinists treat the Saviour as their inferior, » perished at last, devoured, like a putrid corpse, by the worms which it had bred. « If the

(1) *Documentary History of New York*, vol. III, p. 964.
(2) Chalmers, *History of the Revolt of the American Colonies*, vol. I, p. 40.
(3) *The Day-Breaking of the Gospell with the Indians in New England*, Mass. Hist. Coll., 3rd series, vol. IV, p. 20. Cf. *Hutchison Papers*, vol. I.

account given by Dʳ Mather of the colony of Rhode Island be correct, » says Mʳ Halkett, « its red aborigines must have been somewhat bewildered with the variety of Protestant sectaries who had planted themselves among them. » It was truly a singular exhibition of Christianity, by Mather's own account. « It has been, » he confessed, when his reign was over, « a *colluvies* of Antinomians, Familists, Anabaptists, Antisabbatarians, Arminians, Socinians, Quakers, Ranters,— every thing in the world except Roman Catholics and real Christians, » by which latter phrase he designated himself and his diminished flock, « so that if a man had lost his religion, he might find it at that general muster of Opinionists.» (1) Well might Ninigret, a celebrated Indian sachem, reject Mayhew's offer to preach to his tribe, with the scornful reply, « If my people should have a mind to turn Christians, *they could not tell what religion to be of.* » (2) And even Mather himself, after his long career of pride and cruelty, — « an example, » as Mʳ Bancroft admits, « how far selfishness, under the form of vanity and ambition, can stupify the judgment, and dupe consciousness itself, » — betrayed at last the hollowness of the earth-born creed which he had once imposed with such terrible penalties, fell headlong into the abyss prepared for those who mistake blind self-confidence for Christian faith, and « had temptations to atheism, and to the abandonment of all religion as a mere delusion. » (3)

(1) Halkett, ch. xii, p. 281.
(2) Drake, book II, ch. iv, p. 82.
(3) Bancroft, II, 766.

Such was the beginning and end of one of the most hateful sects to which the Church of England, the cradle of almost every modern heresy, ever gave birth. And its fruits were confessed, even by the cruel sectaries who had watched their growth. A general decay of all religious sentiment followed the fierce animal excitement which they had mistaken for the meek spirit of holiness, until Cotton Mather, repeating language which was then universal in New England, could say, in 1706; « It is confessed by all, who know any thing of the matter, that there is *a general and horrible decay of Christianity* among the professors of it. » (1) The monstrous delusion revealed itself at last. And at the present day, the condition of what is called « religion » in Massachusetts and Connecticut appears to be a proverb even in the United States. The first Anglican church in Boston became the first Socinian temple (2), and this was only a presage of what was to come. « Infidelity, » says an American Protestant, « has made rapid strides in New England; and at present, not one half of the adult population are in the habit of attending *any* religious worship, or even belong to any Christian sect. » (3) And even they who profess some corruption of Christianity, some human doctrine which has its roots deep in the earth, and shoots upwards with rank luxuriance only to shut out the pure light of heaven, are for the most part avowed or concealed Unitarians, blaspheming the

(1) Gillies, *Hist. Collections*, vol II, ch. II, p. 19.
(2) Wilberforce, ch. XII, p. 446.
(3) *New York Churchman*, vol. IX, n° 25.

Incarnate God, and enemies of the Cross of Christ. « They are introducing themselves, » we are told, « into every village; » (1) so that « of all the congregational ministers in New England, there are not probably, at this day, twenty-five who believe the doctrines of the Nicene Creed. » « Infidelity, » says a capable witness, in 1858, « has been cultivated Young America's *usual* poor recoil from the Puritanism of its childhood. » (2) Yet there are men who believe that New England theology was one of the most auspicious products of Anglicanism, and that the « Pilgrim Fathers » were benefactors of mankind.

That the Puritans should have exterminated, instead of converting, the Indian tribes of the northeastern states, can hardly surprise us. The savage had sufficient intelligence to comprehend, and sufficient wit to express his conviction, that the professors of a religion which formed such characters, and produced such fruits, must be as hateful in the eyes of the « Great Spirit » as they were mean and odious in his own. « It is very remarkable, » says Hubbard, speaking of Massasoit, the famous sachem of the Narraghansetts, who for forty-five years was the constant associate and firm ally of the English, « that how much soever he affected the English, he was

---

(1) *First Annual Report of the Executive Committee of the American Unitarian Association*, 1827. Cf. *Church Advocate*, vol. I, p. 90; Colton's *Church and State in America*, p. 39; *Remarks on the Moral and Religious Character of the U. S.*, p. 51.

(2) *The Life and Times of Aaron Burr*, by J. Parton; ch. IV, p. 63.

never in the least degree well affected to their religion. » (1) The unhappy barbarian, whose whole nation was afterwards to be destroyed by them, knew it too well by its fruits. He knew also, by a sorrowful experience, that in spite of their grim affectation of integrity and contempt for earthly goods, none were so greedy and insatiable as they. Winthrop was one of the most famous among them, and Gorton hardly of lower repute; yet both these preachers, to say nothing of others, had learned the profitable art which Anglican missionaries were to practise elsewhere, at a later date, with more success, and on a larger scale. « In the records of the United Colonies for the year 1647, » observes an American writer, « it is mentioned that ' M*r* John Winthrop *making claim to a great quantity of land* at Niantic by purchase from the Indians,' » — have we not reason to say that these men are always and every where the same? — « although he was a famous ' saint ' among his party, ' the commissioners set aside his claim with considerable appearance of independance.' » (2) Four years earlier, the Rev. Samuel Gorton obtained lands in the same manner from Miantunnomoh, « which was grievous to the Puritan fathers of Massachusetts, » not because they condemned a proceeding which they would gladly have imitated, but because Gorton had collected disciples of his own, and presumed to set *them* at nought. (3) And this acquisitiveness, which clung like a gar-

---

(1) *Indian Biography*, by B. B. Thatcher Esq., vol. I, ch. vi, p. 139.
(2) Drake, book II, ch. vi, p. 108.
(3) *Id.*, book III, ch. v, p. 73.

ment to their limbs, marked their proceedings to the end. As late as 1768, we still find Sir William Johnson indignantly complaining to General Gage of certain « New England Ministers » in these expressive words. « I was not ignorant that their old pretensions to the Susquehanna Lands was their *real*, though religion was their assumed object. » (1) And once more, in 1746, the Council of New York informed Governor Clinton that Whitfield, the celebrated preacher, « had purchased several thousand acres of land at the forks of the river Delaware, » and requested his attention to the transaction. « This scheme, » the Council added, « was carryed on by Whitfield till he had gull'd a sufficient sum out of the deluded people, under colour of charity for the orphan house at Georgia, and this Negro Academy, but, as most rational to suppose, with real design under both pretexts to fill his own pockets; and when he had carryed on the farce so far as he could well expect to profit by, *he sells this estate* at Delaware to Count Zinzendorf. » (2) But we have heard enough of the « Pilgrim Fathers, » and of their kindred, and it is time to speak of the operations of the Church of England in the same land, and of the agents by whom they were conducted.

The history of Anglican Missions in the American Colonies has been written by the Rev. Ernest Hawkins, a highly respectable minister of the Establishment. It does not take a wide range, is somewhat barren of incident, and will not detain us long. « The Church

(1) *Doc. Hist. N. York*, vol. IV, p 398.
(2) *Ibid* , vol. III, p. 1024.

of England is not rich in missionary annals, » says this gentleman, just three centuries after she had come into existence; and his own account does not permit us to believe that change of climate has removed her sterility, or that she has enjoyed a more fruitful career in the new world than in the old. There is indeed some reason for surprise that M*r* Hawkins should have thought it necessary to write a history which has neither a plot nor a hero, and which contains absolutely nothing, from the first page to the last, except the continual repetition of the same statement, that the Anglican missionaries had no success in America, and sincerely regretted the fact. Here is a list of some of them, whom we reasonably infer to have been the most conspicuous of their number, since they occupy the most prominent place in the pages of M*r* Hawkins.

The reader will observe how exactly they resemble one another in this particular, that they all visited America, and all ran away again. M*r* Urmston, he says, after « vainly demanding the payment of his dues, » returned to England. M*r* Rainsford « abandoned his mission, » « being unable, » says M*r* Hawkins, — whose *dramatis personæ* are constantly escaping from him, — « to undergo the fatigues of an itinerant mission. » M*r* Gordon only staid a year, being driven away « by the *distractions* of the people, and *the other* inconveniences in that colony. » M*r* Adams was just going to « set out for Europe, » but died before he could start. M*r* Wesley staid one year and nine months, and then « shook off the dust of his feet, and left Georgia. » M*r* Neil complained, as late as 1766, « few Englishmen that can live at home will undertake the mission. » Mr Moor, however, staid three years before he ran away. Mr Barton announced his opinion about the same time, that « in the conversion of Indians many difficulties and impediments will occur, which European missionaries, » — he meant to say English — « will never be able to remove; » and then he recounts the « hardships » which such a work entailed, and which always put his Anglican friends to flight. Mr Talbot wrote a little earlier to the « Society for the Propagation of the Gospel in Foreign parts, » this characteristic tale : — « *All* your Missioners hereabouts are going to Maryland, for the sake of themselves, their wives, and their children. » We shall see presently what they did in Maryland. Lastly, Mr Hawkins adds, « Nor must it be concealed that cases occurred of Clergymen dishonouring their holy calling by immorality, or neglect of their cures. » (1) And this is about the sum of the information which we derive from his book.

In reading such a narrative, two conclusions appear to suggest themselves; the first, that the Anglican clergy would hardly condemn their colleague who candidly observed to « my Lord of London, » « Who did his Lordship think would come hither that had a dozen shirts? » — and the second, that if Mr Hawkins has not succeeded in producing a « history, » it was only for want of materials.

Yet he might have indefinitely swelled the cata-

---

(1) *Missions of the Ch. of Eng. in the N. A. Colonies*, ch. IV, pp. 72, 86; ch. V, p. 97; ch. VI, pp. 125, 131; ch. VII, p. 146; ch. XI, p. 265.

logue of fugitive ministers, if he had not deemed his
own sufficiently ample. He might even have assisted
his readers to form a more exact estimate of their
real character, if that had been his object. Colonel
Heathcote, an ardent Protestant, informed the Society for the propagation of the Gospel, in 1705,
that Mr Talbot, whom Mr Hawkins would fain represent as a true missionary, ran away, « having not
thought it worth the while to stay at Albany. »
The Rev. Thomas Barclay deserved also a conspicuous place in the same series of missionary portraits. This gentleman informed the English society
in 1710, that his Dutch colleague at Albany was
« a hot man, and an enemy to our church, but a
friend to his purse, for he has large contributions
from this place. » And then he added, with that
admirable self-possession with which most English
people are familiar, « As for myself, *I take no money,
and have no kind of perquisite.* » Yet two years
later, this ascetical Anglican minister, to whom
money was an offence, was publicly tried before the
Commissioners at Albany, for employing a person
« to get 50 l. for him upon interest to pay his debts,
which his wife was to know nothing of, » and then
sorely libelling his agent because he failed to get
the loan. (1) Mr Hawkins might have filled his volume with equally dramatic incidents. He might
also, if that had been his design, have informed his
readers that the congregations of these Anglican ministers were worthy of such pastors. As late as the
18th century, Colonel Morris, another sympathising

(1) *Doc. Hist. N. York*, vol. III, pp. 125, 898, 904.

correspondent of what is called the Society for the propagation of the Gospel, gave this description of the English in America. « Whereas nine parts in ten of ours will add no credit to whatsoever Church they are of, nor can it be well expected otherwise ; for as New England, excepting some families, was the scum of the old, » — though the teaching class was mainly composed of ex-Anglican ministers, — « so the greatest part of the English in this province was the scum of the new, who brought as many opinions almost as persons, but neither religion nor virtue, and have acquired very little since. » (1)

Another Anglican writer, deservedly esteemed, like M*r* Hawkins, for character and ability, has applied himself to the production of a much larger work on the same subject. He also tells us of M*r* Morrell, who, after spending a year in New Enggland, « was compelled to retire, baffled and discomfited. » (2) M*r* Bancroft has described to us another class of missionaries, « who never receded one foot; » and M*r* Washington Irving has added, that « *they* pressed on unresting, with a power which no other Christians have exhibited. » M*r* Hawkins, having other matters to discuss, dismisses this class briefly as — « *French Romanists* » ! This is what an educated Anglican clergyman deems a suitable description of men whom St. Paul would have greeted with the kiss of charity, and whom the God of St. Paul endowed with gifts and graces which Amer-

(1) *Doc. Hist. N. York*, vol. III, p. 247.
(2) *History of the Colonial Church*, by the Rev*d* J. S. M. Anderson; vol. I, ch. XII, p. 457.

ican Protestants have celebrated with respectful enthusiasm, and of which even the American savage recognised the supernatural beauty. M˸ Hawkins, however, reserving his sympathy for the hirelings whose career he has described, appears to approve the verdict of D˸ Selwyn; who, as we have seen, is so little impressed by the ministry of apostles such as Lallemand and de Brebeuf, St. Francis and de Britto, Schall and Verbiest, that he cannot endure even the sound of their names, and deems their very existence « a blot on the mission system. »

M˸ Anderson concludes from *his* researches, that in the 17th century, « the vital energies of the whole body of the Church throughout the Colony were rapidly sinking beneath the baneful influences which oppressed her. » He relates also, from original records, that the worst influence of all was that of the Clergy, of whom he quotes this animated description. « Many came, such as wore black coats, and could babble in a pulpit, roar in a tavern, exact from their parishioners, and rather by their dissoluteness destroy than feed their flocks. » (1) If M˸ Anderson and M˸ Hawkins could have found more cheerful topics, we may assume that they would have selected them.

When so distinguished a person as M˸ Anderson undertakes to write a « History of the Colonial Church, » we may be sure that nothing will be omitted which industry could detect, or art embellish, to adorn and illustrate the theme. It is probable, however, that in spite of the attraction of his

---

(1) Vol. II, ch. xɪv, p. 132.

name, few persons would attempt, without a special motive, the continuous perusal of volumes of such dimensions, and that fewer still would succeed in the attempt. The impossibility of accomplishing such a task is due, not to the incapacity of the writer, but to the weariness and aridity of the subject. Never, perhaps, was so vast a collection of pages illumined by so slender an array of facts. In reading Mr Anderson's immense volumes, which profess to trace the fortunes of Anglicanism in the Colonies, we seem to be invited to examine a history in which there are neither scenes nor actors, neither agents nor events; wherein much is said, but nothing is done; and in which the solitary truth which struggles to the surface, but which might have found adequate expression in fewer words, consists in the patient iteration of one fact — that the Church of England was always *going* to do something worthy of record, and never did it. So absolutely void are these endless pages, not only of any semblance of incident or vestige of action, but even of any definite character by which one chapter may be distinguished from another; so full of words which reveal nothing and suggest nothing, of sentences which incessantly resolve themselves into mist; that the reader can only ascertain by diligent reference to notes and index where he is, whither he is going, and to what point of the narrative he is supposed to be giving his attention.

There are certain regions, described by American writers, — the interminable prairies which stretch many a league along the northern frontier of Mexico, — in which, as they relate, the eye discovers neither tree, nor shrub, nor hillock, to serve as guide or landmark, but only one dead level, which has everywhere the sky for its boundary, and in which any living form, though it were the meanest of God's creatures, would be welcomed with enthusiasm. Here the hapless traveller wanders, without aim and almost without hope, tracing again today the path which he vainly followed yesterday, and ever returning to the spot from which he set out; moving in a fatal circle, which grows less and less, as strength fails and courage ebbs away; till he falls in despair on the earth which refuses to aid his baffled sense, or to give him so much as a hint which way lies the road that leads to the haunts of men. In reading Mr Anderson's illimitable volumes we seem about to share the fate of this doomed traveller; but a movement breaks the spell, and closing his book, we find that we have already quitted the desert into which he had beguiled us, and which, by the prescriptive rights of prior discovery, he has chosen to call — « The history of the Colonial Church. »

What the Anglican Church really did in America, and what sort of agents she employed, there as elsewhere, we learn only imperfectly from Mr Anderson and Mr Hawkins; but other writers, of similar religious persuasions, will supply the information which they thought it prudent to withhold.

Berkeley, a Protestant bishop, filled with generous but unfruitful designs for the welfare of the American Colonies, detected, by actual observation, that the clergy who possessed « a dozen shirts, » and the position which such an estate implies, rarely crossed the Atlantic. « The Clergy sent over to

America,» says this celebrated person, « have proved, too many of them, very meanly qualified, both in learning and morals, for the discharge of their office. And indeed little can be expected from the example or instruction of those, who quit their country on no other motive, than that they are not able to procure a livelihood in it, which is known to be often the case. » (1) The Church of England, however, sent such representatives, in default of others, and continued to send them, during the seventeenth and eighteenth centuries. Berkeley, who seems to have understood that the character of the missionaries « hath hitherto given the Church of Rome great advantage over the reformed churches, » not only deplored the fact, but indicated its probable results. « In Europe, the protestant religion hath of late years considerably lost ground, » he says; and then, looking across the sea, he anticipates still more unwelcome events. « The Spanish missionaries in the South, and the French in the North, are making such a progress as may one day spread the religion of Rome throughout all the savage nations in America. » (2) We have seen that in the south the work which he dreaded is done; and if in the north they failed to convert all the savage tribes, it was only because England massacred both them and their flocks, till she left them none to convert.

The principal scene, as is well known, of the operations of Anglicanism in America lay between

(1) *A Proposal for the better supplying of churches in our Foreign Plantations*, works, vol. II, p. 422. (1784).
(2) P. 432.

CHAPTER IX.

Cape Cod and the Chesapeake Bay; though the great majority of its agents confined their wanderings to the still narrower tract between the mouth of the Hudson and the mouth of the Potomac. English soldiers and traders carried their arms and their strong liquors to the foot of the Alleghanies and the shores of Lake Erie and Lake Michigan; but English missionaries preferred to spend their stipends in the cities of the coast, and left the wilderness to the savage and the apostles of France. Massachusetts, Maryland, and Virginia were the chief fields of English enterprise; and with a few words upon each of them, — upon Boston, Baltimore, and Richmond, — we may sufficiently indicate both the method of their operations and their effect upon the aboriginal tribes.

There is not a State of the Union which has not found, and merited, at least one historian, and there is not a difference of opinion among them all as to the character of the English proceedings. But it would be a mere ostentation of research to affect to quote the original records, when all have been collected in one work, and all cited by the same author. Mr Bancroft's voluminous history, supplemented by English witnesses, will furnish all the facts which in such a sketch as this demand our attention, or which our limits will permit us to notice.

Beginning at the extreme northern point of the country which we are now to visit, and selecting the least dishonorable epoch of the English sway, — when Eliot, an exile from England and a fugitive from her national church, by whose officers he had been « deprived, » had gathered together a certain number of « praying Indians, » soon to be dispersed and annihilated — we find this account of the actual and final result of all which had been accomplished at that date among the Indians. « Christianity hardly spread beyond the Indians of Cape Cod, Martha's Vineyard, and Nantucket, and the seven feeble villages round Boston. The Naragansetts, a powerful tribe, counting at least a thousand warriors, retained their old belief; and Philip of Pokanoket, at the head of seven hundred warriors, professed with pride the faith of his fathers. » (1) While the few scattered villages, scanty in number and exhausted in strength and vigour, which nominally accepted the religion of their masters, are thus described by the same historian. « The clans within the limits of the denser settlements of the English, especially the Indian villages round Boston, were broken-spirited, from the overwhelming force of the English. In their rude blending of new instructions with their ancient superstitions — in their feeble imitations of the manners of civilization — in their appeals to the charities of Europeans, they had quenched the fierce spirit of savage independence. They loved the crumbs from the white man's table. »

So well was the character of these unwilling « converts, » sorrowful pensioners of a niggard bounty, understood even on this side of the Atlantic, that a distinguished English writer did not scruple thus to describe them and their pastors. « The missionaries always quarrelled with their flocks, and made but few converts; nor among them produced any real

---

(1) Bancroft, I, 421.

improvement. » And again; « The instruction of the Indians in schools, among the Europeans settled in great towns, was another method which was adopted, and with no better success.... these pupils returned to their naked and hunting brethren *the most profligate and the most idle members of the Indian community.* » (1)

But their end was at hand. A little later, Pokanoket, who asked only permission to live, and « who is reported to have wept when he heard that a white man's blood had been shed, » consented at length to a war which might relieve, but could hardly augment, the sufferings of the Indians, and the last remains of the New England tribes hurried to their doom. « The Indian cabins were soon set on fire. Thus were swept away the humble glories of the Naragansetts; the winter's stores of the tribe, their curiously wrought baskets, full of corn, their famous strings of wampum, their wigwams nicely lined with mats, — all the little comforts of savage life were consumed. And more — *their old men, their women, their babes, perished by hundreds in the fire.* Then, indeed, was the cup of misery full for these red men. » (2) « Sad to them, » adds the historian, « had been their acquaintance with civilisation. The first ship that came on their coast kidnapped men of their kindred, and now the harmless boy, » the only son of Philip, « that had been cherished as the future sachem of their tribes, the last of the family of Massasoit, was sold into bondage to toil as a slave under

(1) *Edinburgh Review*, vol. VIII, p. 444.
(2) Bancroft, I, 427.

the sun of Bermuda ! » (1) Such were the deeds of Englishmen in America. When the inevitable hour of England's reckoning arrives, the cry of the American native will surely mount up to heaven, and add a heavier burden to the maledictions already registered against her.

Let us come to Maryland. Here dwelt a Catholic Colony, under a Catholic lawgiver, and Protestants will tell us how the one governed and the other throve. « Within six months, » says Mr Bancroft, « the colony of Maryland had advanced more than Virginia had done in as many years... But far more memorable was the character of the Maryland institutions. Every other country in the world had persecuting laws; ' I will not, ' — such was the oath of the governor of Maryland, — ' I will not, by myself or any other, directly or indirectly, molest any person professing to believe in Jesus Christ, for or in respect of religion.' Under the mild institutions and munificence of Baltimore, the dreary wilderness soon bloomed with the swarming life and activity of prosperous settlements; the Roman Catholics, who were oppressed by the laws of England, were sure to find a peaceful asylum in the quiet harbours of the Chesapeake; and there, too, Protestants were sheltered against Protestant intolerance. Such were the beautiful auspices under which the province of Maryland started into being... Its history is the history of benevolence, gratitude, and toleration. » (2)

Fenimore Cooper, and a multitude of eminent American writers, have noticed the relations which

(1) P. 430.
(2) I, 188.

were quickly formed between the Catholics of Maryland and the Indian tribes. *They*, as an English Protestant observes, « fairly paid, » the natives for their land, and « their generosity won the hearts of their new Indian friends. » (1) But let us continue Mr Bancroft's account.

« The happiness of the Colony was enviable. The persecuted and the unhappy thronged to the domains of the benevolent prince. If Baltimore was, in one sense, a monarch, his monarchy was tolerable to the exile who sought for freedom and repose. Numerous ships found employment in his harbours... Emigrants arrived from every clime; and the colonial legislature extended its sympathies to many nations, as well as to many sects. From France came Huguenots; from Germany, from Holland, from Sweden, from Finland, the children of misfortune sought protection under the tolerant sceptre of the Roman Catholic. Bohemia itself, the country of Jerome and of Huss, sent forth its sons, who at once were made citizens of Maryland with equal franchises. » (2)

Such was Catholic Maryland, the solitary oasis of the northern desert, and the refuge for all who found elsewhere only cruelty and oppression. Lord Baltimore died, and « immediately on the death of the first feudal sovereign of Maryland, the powerful influence of the Archbishop of Canterbury had been solicited to secure an establishment of the Anglican church, which clamoured for favour in the province

---

(1) Buckingham, *America*, vol. I, ch. xx, p. 388.
(2) Bancroft, I, 523.

where it already enjoyed equality. The prelates demanded, not freedom but privilege; an establishment to be maintained at the common expense of the province... The English ministry soon issued an order, that offices of government in Maryland should be intrusted exclusively to Protestants. Roman Catholics were disfranchised in the province which they had planted! » (1)

« It is a striking and instructive spectacle to behold, at this period, » says Professor Walters, of Philadelphia, « the Puritans persecuting their Protestant brethren in New England, the Episcopalians retorting the same severity on the Puritans in Virginia, and the Catholics, against whom all others were combined, forming in Maryland a sanctuary where all might worship, and none might oppress, and where even Protestants might find refuge from Protestant intolerance. » Yet these very men, he adds, « with ingratitude still more odious than their injustice, projected the abrogation not only of the Catholic worship, but of every part of that system of toleration under whose shelter they were enabled to conspire its downfall! » (2)

If anything be wanting to complete the picture, it is supplied in the fact, noticed by Mr Baird, an American minister, that the character of many of the Anglican clergy who were now despatched to Maryland to supersede the Catholic missionaries, was notorious for « shocking delinquency and open sin. » (3) « A

(1) P. 528.
(2) Rupp, p. 115.
(3) Baird, *Religion in the U. S. of America*, book II, ch. xx, p. 210.

great part of them, » was the confession of the Protestant bishop of London to the celebrated Dr Doddridge, « can get no employment at home, and enter into the service more out of necessity than choice. Some others are willing to go abroad to retrieve either lost fortunes or lost character. » (1) « Ruffians, fugitives from justice, » adds Mr Bancroft; « men stained by intemperance and lust, (I write with caution, the distinct allegations being before me,) nestled themselves in the parishes of Maryland. » (2) And it was to procure an « establishment », on the Anglican model, for men who are thus described by those who knew them best, but who sent them in spite of this knowledge, that religious liberty was suppressed, and Catholics disfranchised, in the English colony of Maryland. « In the land which Catholics had opened to Protestants, » says Mr Bancroft, « the Catholic inhabitant was the sole victim to Anglican intolerance. » (3)

Not that this was an exceptional incident in the history of Anglicanism, for, as the historian observes, it displayed exactly the same character in Ireland. Here also, in the words of Edmund Spenser, the Anglican ministers who supplanted the pastors of the ancient faith were « generally bad, licentious, and most disordered; » « men of no parts or condition, » as Mr Bancroft adds, « and as immoral as they were illiterate. » (4)

Let us hear a single witness from our own coun-

(1) Baird, *Religion*, etc., book, II, ch. xx, p. 211.
(2) III, 98.
(3) II, 717.
(4) IV, 45.

try, and then pass on to Virginia. « While the Catholics of Maryland, » says Mr Buckingham, who visited America twenty years ago, « acted with so much liberality to their Protestant brethren, these last, who had many of them come to seek refuge from Protestant persecution in the north, returned this liberality with the basest ingratitude, and sought by every means to crush those by whom they had been so hospitably received. » And finally, when « the Church of England was declared, by law, to be the constitution of the State of Maryland, Catholics were prohibited under the severest penalties from all acts of public worship, and even from exercising the profession of teachers in education. » (1)

It is satisfactory to learn from the same witness the ultimate result of this conflict between cruel bigotry, working by profligate agents, and distrustful of its own power, and the unquenchable life of faith, surviving injustice and barbarism, and accomplishing in weakness what all its combined enemies could not effect in their pride of strength. We shall see that, in the words of Mr Bancroft, « persecution never crushed the faith of the colonists. » Of all the religious bodies who inhabit Baltimore at this day, « first come the Roman Catholics, » says Mr Buckingham, « who far outstrip any other separate sect, in numbers and in zeal... The Catholic Archbishop, and all the subordinate priesthood, » who now serve nineteen churches within the city itself, « are learned, pious, and clever men; the Sisters of Charity have among their number many intelligent and devoted

(1) *America*, ch. XX, p. 387.

women; and these, with the seminary for the education of Catholic youth » — there are now seven seminaries, and six colleges — « secure not merely the permanence of the present supremacy of Catholic numbers and Catholic influence, but its still further steady and progressive increase. » (1)

It only remains to speak of Virginia, the special domain of Anglicanism as long as Virginia was English, and whose history is, perhaps on that account, more full of reproach to its former masters than that of any other State in the Union.

The accounts of the Anglican clergy in Virginia, even as late as the second half of the eighteenth century, appear to surpass every thing in the annals of Church of England missions, and throw even New Zealand into the shade. Sir William Berkeley, Governor of Virginia, used to ask, with a not unreasonable curiosity, « why the worst are sent to us? » « In Virginia, » says Mr Bancroft, who had examined all the original records, « some of the missionaries, of feeble minds and uncertain morals, prodigious zealots from covetousness, sought, by appeals to England, to clutch at a monopoly of ecclesiastical gains... The crown incorporated and favoured the Society for Propagating the Gospel in Foreign Parts. » (2) Under the patronage of that Society, as the Protestant historian relates, « the benefices were filled by priests ordained in England, and for the most part of English birth, too often ill-educated and licentious men, whose crimes quickened Virginia to assume the ad-

---

(1) *America*, ch. xx, p. 387.
(2) II, 769.

vowson of its churches. »(1) Yet the people of Virginia could have endured a good deal in this way, if the crimes of their clergy had not exceeded what prescription permitted; but it was one effect of their enormity that the episcopalian sect finally sunk into contempt in Virginia. « The Episcopal Church in Virginia, » says Dr Reed, « became slothful and impure under its exclusive privileges, so as to have made itself despised by the people. » (2) « For want of able and conscionable Ministers, » was the joint confession of a multitude of Anglican witnesses, « they of the reformed religion themselves are becoming exceeding rude, more like to turne Heathen, than to turne others to the Christian faith. » (3) And it is admitted that this state of things, characteristic of Anglican missionary operations, continued for two centuries. Between 1722 and the beginning of the nineteenth century, observes Dr Samuel Wilberforce, « instead of any growth throughout an extent of country one hundred miles long and fifteen broad, *every church and chapel had been forsaken*... Such was the deadly trance which had fallen on the Church. » And then this English prelate, unwilling perhaps to avow the real causes of the decay, and the mingled avarice and sensuality which had made Episcopalian ministers hateful throughout the colony, refers it all to « the absence of endowment, »

(1) III, 95.
(2) *Visit to the American Churches*, by Reed and Matheson, vol. II, p. 100.
(3) *A Petition exhibited to the High Court of Parliament*, by William Castell, Parson of Courtenhall, which Petition is approved by 70 able English Divines; (1641, ed. Force).

of which he had learned to appreciate the importance in his own community, but the want of which in America, he adds, with a naïveté remarkable in so acute a person, « impairs its character, and moral weight. » (1) Yet it was at this very time, that men of another faith, already apostles and soon to be martyrs, were traversing in hunger and poverty, utterly unmindful of « the absence of endowment, » the shores of Lake Superior, the banks of the Mohawk, and the valley of the Mississippi, and showing the wondering savage what was the religion of St-Paul, and how men trained in *his* school could live and die.

The Anglican missionaries in America appear to have taught them a different lesson, and sometimes by a method which does not seem to have been ever adopted by any other class of religious teachers but themselves. On the 18th of May, 1725, as an American annalist relates, a British officer shot a poor unoffending Indian, who was actually scalped on the spot by the Rev. Jonathan Frye, a military chaplain, whose prowess is appropriately celebrated by another missionary, the Rev. Mr Symmes. We learn, without excessive regret, that he was killed the same day by the tribe of the murdered man, after a battle which was one of the great events of the epoch, and which was recorded in a popular song described by Mr Drake as « for several years afterwards the most beloved song in all New England. » The following verse, as an illustration of the character of English missionaries in America, deserves particular notice. We may

(1) Ch viii, p. 276; ch. xii, p. 436.

hope, for the honour of humanity, that no such action was ever celebrated in similar language. Here is the triumphal dirge.

« Our worthy Captain Lovewell among them there did die;
They killed Lieutenant Robins, and wounded good young Frye,
Who was our English Chaplain; he many Indians slew,
And some of them he scalped when bullets round him flew. » (1)

American Protestants have observed, and the fact is worthy of note, how strangely the history of the Anglican colony of Virginia contrasts, from its earliest origin, and in every particular, with that which was formed by Lord Baltimore. Even at the first moment of their arrival, « the emigrants themselves were weakened by divisions, and degraded by jealousy. » A large proportion of them perished by sickness or famine, and « disunion completed the scene of misery. » (2) Unlike the Catholics of Maryland, they soon made the Indians their enemies, and reaped during many years, till they had created a desert around them, the fruits of their own want of charity.

Towards the close of the seventeenth century, an English colonist, explaining how the « Virginians, Susquehanians, and Marylanders, of friends became engaged enimyes, » relates, that « the English had (contrarie to the law of arms) beate out the Braines of 6 grate men *sent out to treate a peace* : an action of ill consequence, as it proved after. » (3) Mr Howison, the historian of Virginia, who records touching

(1) Drake, book III, ch. ix, p. 130.
(2) Bancroft, I, 95.
(3) *An Account of our Late Troubles in Virginia*, by Mrs Ann Colton; (1676).

examples of the generous confidence and hospitality with which the Indians welcomed the English setlers, notices, that a poor native having stolen a silver cup, of which he probably did not know the value, « For this enormous offence the English burned the town, and barbarously destroyed the growing corn. Had the unhappy savage stolen the only child of the boldest settler, a more furious vengeance could not have followed! To such conduct does America owe the undying hatred of the aboriginal tenants of her land, and the burden of infamy that she must bear when weighed in the scales of immaculate justice. » (1) The whole history, he says, « is a dark record of injuries sustained, and of insult unavenged. » (2)

But no misfortunes could instruct either the insatiable avarice or the cruel bigotry of the Anglican colonists. In 1643, « it was specially ordered, that no minister should preach or teach, publicly or privately, except in conformity to the constitutions of the Church of England, and non-conformists were banished from the colony. » « The government of Virginia, » says M*r* Bancroft, « feared dissenters more than Spaniards; » (3) and yet, so incapable was the Anglican Church of performing the functions which she had violently usurped, and which she sent « illeducated and licentious men » to perform, that « there were so few ministers, that a bounty was offered for their importation! » St. Paul had said, « The charity of Christ constraineth me; » but the Anglican clergy

(1) *History of Virginia*, ch. 1, p. 57.
(2) Ch. v, p. 260.
(3) I, 1028.

could only be attracted by a « bounty. » And they never varied, either in their character or in their operations, till the day of their downfall. « The English Episcopal Church became the religion of the state; and though there were not ministers in above a fifth part of the parishes, yet the laws demanded strict conformity, and required of every one to contribute to the support of the established Church... no nonconformist might teach, even in private, under pain of banishment; no reader might expound the Catechism or the Scriptures. The obsolete severity of the laws of Queen Elizabeth was revived against the Quakers. Absence from church was for them an offence, punishable by a fine of twenty pounds sterling. » (1) « Virginia, » says Mr Howison, « is the proper field for those who wish to study one of the closing pages of American intolerance. » (2)

Yet England pursues exactly the same policy at the present day, wherever she can do so with safety. Thus in Prince Edward's Island, « the *established* religion is that of the Church of England, though it has perhaps fewer professors than any denomination known there! » (3) It need hardly be said what is the « established » religion in Ireland.

The same contrast which distinguished the clergy marked the conduct of the civil rulers in the Catholic and Protestant colony. Under Lord Baltimore, « the virtues of benevolence and gratitude ripened together, » and « the people held it a duty them-

(1) I, 497.
(2) Ch. VII, p. 431.
(3) Bouchette, *British Dominions*, etc., vol. II, ch. XI, p. 178.

selves to bear the charges of government, and they readily acknowledged the unwearied care of the proprietary for the welfare of his dominions... The colony which he had planted in youth, crowned his old age with its gratitude. » (1) Very different were the rulers of Virginia. « The illegal grants favoured by Sir John Harvey had provoked the natives into active hostility. » (2) His successors surpassed him. Berkeley was greedy, selfish, and cruel. When they had captured an Indian sachem, more than a hundred years old, and exposed him in Jamestown, mortally wounded, to die amidst the jeers of the English; « Had I taken Sir William Berkeley prisoner, » was the rebuke of the savage, « I would not have exposed him as a show to my people. » Culpepper, the confederate of Arlington, was still worse. « He valued his office and his patents only as property. Clothed by the regal clemency with power to bury past contests, he perverted the duty of humanity into a means of enriching himself, and increasing his authority. Nothing but Lord Culpepper's avarice gives him a place in American history... All accounts agree in describing the condition of Virginia, at this time, as one of extreme distress. Culpepper had no compassion for poverty — no sympathy for a province impoverished by perverse legislation — and the residence in Virginia was so irksome, that in a few months he returned to England. » He was succeeded, in his turn, by Lord Howard of Effingham, a man as shameless as himself. « It is said he did not scruple to share

(1) Bancroft, I, 525.
(2) Howison, ch. v, p. 285.

perquisites with his clerks. In Virginia, the avarice of Effingham was the public scorn; in England, it met with no severe reprobation. » (1) The governors of Virginia, then, were worthy of its clergy; and both continued to represent with equal dignity the crown and the church of England, till the colonists, weary of the cruelty of the one and the immorality of the other, gave the signal of that righteous revolution out of which sprang the great American Union. It was surely a fitting retribution, that Virginia, once a proverb for its royalism, should be the first to shake off the yoke which English bigotry, injustice, and cupidity had made intolerable; and the national historian might well relate, with honest exultation, that « *Virginia* rang the alarum bell — Virginia gave the signal for the continent! » (2)

It is a characteristic fact, which should not be omitted even in this hasty sketch, that the only remonstrants against the American revolution were a few of the Episcopalian clergy, dreading the loss of their incomes and privileges, and warring to the last against the liberties of their fellow creatures. « The present rebellion, » said Dr Inglis of New York, in 1776, — and the sentiment appears to have gained for him the Protestant bishopric of Nova Scotia, — « is certainly one of the most causeless, unprovoked, and unnatural that ever disgraced any country; » and then he ventured upon a prediction equally creditable to his discernment, and exclaimed, « I have not a doubt that, with the blessing of Providence,

(1) Bancroft, p. 533.
(2) *Id.*, IV, 196.

his majesty's arms will be successful, and finally crush this unnatural rebellion. » (1)

One or two names there are, in the dark religious annals of British America, which contrast favourably with those of the adventurers whose career we have traced, and whose misdeeds hindered the conversion of a hundred tribes, and lost half a continent to the crown of England. Eliot and Brainerd, both witnesses against British oppression, appear to have been animated by a real desire for the improvement of the heathen, and to have done their best to promote it. So far as they were sincere in their good intentions, they deserve our sympathy and respect. Eliot had collected at one time, apparently by the kindness of his deportment, and frequent relief of their necessities, a considerable number of « praying Indians. » « I never go unto them empty, » he says himself, « but carry somewhat to distribute among them. » (2) Naturally attracted by conduct which contrasted so strongly with the usual habits of his countrymen, they came to consider him as their friend, and had good reason to do so. Yet it may be doubted whether he ever produced even a superficial impression upon their conscience. Often they perplexed him with questions to which his barren theology could suggest no reply. An Indian sachem, as we are told, having embarassed him with such enquiries, « the good man seemed at a loss for an answer, and waived the subject by several scripture

---

(1) *Doc. Hist. of N. York.* vol. III, pp. 1052, 1064.
(2) Dr Morison, *Fathers of the London Missionary Society*, vol. I, p. 82.

quotations ! » (1) « The natives of our forests, » says his American biographer, « derived no permanent benefit from the exertions of Mr Eliot and others. (2) He confessed himself, just before his death, « There is a dark cloud upon the work of the Gospel among the poor Indians. » (3) Even of his nominal disciples, Mr Drake says, « there is not the least probability that even one fourth of them were ever sincere believers in Christianity. » (4) When « Philip's war » broke out, his whole work came to an end; and whereas the Catholic Indians, until they were slain by the English, would always prepare for battle by the reception of the sacraments, and fight in the name and the defence of their religion, « many that had been at the head of the ' praying ' towns, the Indian *ministers* themselves, were found in arms against their white Christian neighbours, » and flung off altogether the disguise of Christianity. Lastly, it is an unpleasant fact, which one would have gladly missed in the history of such a man as Eliot, who was at least superior to his contemporaries, that one of his grandchildren claimed « a tract of one thousand acres of land at a place called the Allom Ponds, given by the Indian proprietors *to the late Rev. John Eliot.* » (5)

Brainerd, who seems, like Henry Martyn, to have been devoured by melancholy, and who was never of

(1) Drake, book III, ch. VI, p. 85.
(2) *Life of John Eliot*, in *Library of American Biography*, by Jared Sparks; vol. V, ch. XV, p. 301,
(3) *Ibid.*, ch. XVII, p. 335.
(4) Ch. VIII, p. 115.
(5) Jared Sparks, Appendix, p. 354.

the same mind many hours together, confesses his own failure, and others account for it. « The prevailing defect of his character, » says Dr Morison, « was a tendency to deep brooding and melancholy depression. » But he seems to have had other infirmities quite as little suited to the office of a missionary. « Mr Brainerd acknowledges, » said Dr Boudinot half a century ago, « that he *dared not* go among them.» (1) And when he did, but always, like Eliot, in the immediate neighbourhood of the English, it was not with much profit. « His account of the Delawares, » observes Mr Bancroft, « is gloomy and desponding : ' they are unspeakably indolent and slothful, ' he says; ' they discover little gratitude; they seem to have no sentiments of generosity, benevolence, or goodness. ' » (2) Yet we have heard Catholic missionaries commending tribes less happily endowed than the Delawares as « industrious and fond of labour, » and Protestants confirming their report. Even the few whom Brainerd employed as assistants appear to have exactly resembled the same class in China, and one for whom he procured « ordination, » and who became his own successor « in the charge of his congregation, » is thus described by Dr Smith : — « whatever professions this man might have made, or whatever opinion might have been formed of him, it is too evident that he was a stranger to the vital influence of religion. » (3)

So uniform were these results of Protestant mis-

(1) *Star in the West*, ch. VI, p. 227.
(2) Bancroft, II, 916.
(3) *History of the Missionary Societies*, by Revd Thomas Smith; Introd. p, XVI.

sionary labour, here as elsewhere, even in cases where the agents employed were men of pure intentions, that an American writer confessed, as late as 1792, « *there never was an instance* of an Indian forsaking his habits and savage manners, » under the influence of Protestantism; and then he cited the case of the Rev. Samuel Kirkland, a well known missionary, « who has taken all the pains that man can take, but his whole flock are Indians still ! » (1) Mr Kirkland himself declared to Sir William Johnson, « in general they treat me with no more respect than they would show to a dog. » (2) Yet these same Indians clung to missionaries of another creed with so much love and reverence that they willingly exposed their own lives to save them, and even displayed such delicacy and refinement in their respect, as they continue to do at this hour, that, as one of the latter relates, when a Father knelt down in their tents to recite his office, they not only suspended every occupation, but « hardly moved or breathed lest they should interrupt him. » (3)

Lastly, the Quakers, in spite of their temperance and humanity, were as unsuccessful as the rest. « The Quakers, » Mr Bancroft observes, « came among the Delawares in the spirit of peace and brotherly love, and with sincerest wishes to benefit the Indian; but the Quakers succeeded no better than the Puritans — not nearly as well as the Jesuits. » In 1822, Dr Morse could still report of this tribe, who seemed

(1) *Documentary History of New York*, vol. II, p. 1,110.
(2) *Ibid.*, vol. IV, p. 358.
(3) *Annales*, tome III, p. 558.

worthy of a better lot, « they are *more* opposed to the Gospel and the whites than any other Indians with whom I am acquainted. » It is exactly the same history as in China, Ceylon, Africa, and everywhere else; the more familiar they become with Protestant missionaries, the deeper is their hatred of Christianity. And long after, for every chapter of this sad history resembles that which preceded it, when Mr Elisha Bates was examined by a Parliamentary Committee, and was asked what had been effected among the heathen by the well intentioned efforts of the Society of Friends, he candidly confessed; « I do not know that we could say that we have brought them to a habit of prayer : I know of *no instance* that would warrant me in saying so. » (1)

We have now perhaps reviewed with sufficient detail the history of Protestant missions in North America, fitly described by a partial annalist as « *the record of a series of failures.* » We have seen also, by sufficient testimony, why Jogues and Lallemand and De Brebeuf laboured in vain, and why the apostolic triumphs of their brethren in the South — in Brazil, Peru, and Paraguay, in Guatemala, Mexico, and California — were not renewed in Canada and the United States. It was not that the English massacred the apostles who were already rapidly effecting, among various tribes and nations, the same supernatural work which their brethren had accomplished in the South, for this was a trial which they had encountered and overcome in every other land, and which would only have contributed to their final

(1) *Parliamentary Papers*, vol. VII, p. 545. (British Museum).

success. They would have offered their heads to the
English, as they did to the Baures or the Chiquitos,
and the victims would, sooner or later, have worn
out their executioners. But in British America it was
not the pastors only who were slain. This was a loss
which could have been repaired. But what power
could gather together or summon back to new life the
flocks whom the persecutor had maddened by oppression, or driven far away from the graves of their
fathers, or exterminated by fire and sword? A new
race of apostles might indeed have entered the land,
but it would have been only to find a desert.

We have said that for this calamity, without
parallel in the history of pagan lands, and which
overwhelmed the inhabitants of a continent in hopeless ruin, Americans are not responsible. It must be
confessed, however, that if the crime was not theirs,
they have done little to repair it. It was an evil legacy
which the English bequeathed to them, but they have
made an evil use of it. Nearly forty years ago,
D'r Morse implored the government to « provide an
asylum for the remnant of this depressed and wretched people, who have long been insulated, corrupting,
and wasting away in the midst of us; » but the
Americans have shown more zeal to complete their
ruin, and to deprive them of their remaining lands,
than to grant them the « unmolested home » which
Morse foresaw they would never enjoy. (1) A few
testimonies will suffice to prove, that their present
masters have dealt almost as hardly with the scattered
fragments of the Indian nations, as the English did

(1) *Report on Indian Affairs*, pp. 24, 30.

with their yet unbroken masses, while they wandered in thousands, ignorant of their coming doom, by the rivers and lakes where God had given them a home. If the English left a curse behind them, the Americans have not substituted a blessing.

When that Union of many States was formed which now extends from the Atlantic to the Pacific, and which was created by the patient valour of a generation which nobly refused to accept the fate of Canada or Ireland, but whose unwilling fault it was that it left no heirs either of its virtue or its patriotism; two races of suffering men asked from the children of the new Republic the humblest lot which misery ever consented to implore or charity to concede — the right to labour and live. And they asked it in vain. Negroes and Indians, both victims of English cupidity and violence, were refused even the smallest measure of the rights which their vigorous masters had known how to win for themselves. Let us enquire what has been their fate in this paradise of freedom and independence, and what American christianity has attempted or achieved to improve their lot. We will speak of the Negro first.

Let it be permitted, however, in alluding briefly to this grave subject, which will afford a new test of the relative power of the Church and the Sects, to disclaim all sympathy with the professional advocates of Negro emancipation. Wherever the Church exercises her civilising influence, the Negro tends towards complete liberty, and while still in bondage is being wisely prepared for it; but though she utterly condemns the trafic in human flesh, in the words of Gregory XVI, « as injurious to salvation, and dis-

graceful to the Christian name, » she tolerates, like
St. Paul, while she everywhere strives to abolish,
the state of slavery. She knows that the Negro has
no worse enemy than the partisan of unconditional
emancipation. She knows also that, under the old
Law, slavery was so far from being condemned by
any divine prescription, that the conditions of its
existence were determined, again and again, in the
Hebrew code; and she is not ignorant that, although
during the human life of our Blessed Lord the Roman
Empire contained millions of slaves, neither He nor
any of His apostles, while denouncing every crime
which man could commit, so much as alluded to
the subject. It is, moreover, a well known fact, that
however little may have been done for his soul, the
American Negro has both more happiness and more
liberty in his bondage than he would have possessed
in his native land; that, with rare exceptions, he is
better fed, better clothed, more lightly tasked in his
strength, and more mercifully tended in his old age,
than any class of white labourers, in any country
whatever; and finally, that the coloured man is the
object of far more charity in the *slave* than he is in
the *free* states. In the former, he *generally* receives
only benevolence and consideration; in the latter, in
spite of the hollow professions of men who trade
even in philanthropy and religion, he *always* encounters contumely and neglect. « As a slave, » says an
American authority, with full knowledge of all the
facts, « he is happy and contented; as a freeman,
despised and contemned. » (1)

(1) *New York Herald*, January 25, 1861.

CHAPTER IX.

Half a century ago, a Protestant missionary, who had assured the Delawares that the religion which he taught would secure their happiness, received from them a reply which he records in these words. « They had determined, » they told him, with solemn irony, « to wait, in order to see whether all the *black* people among us were made thus happy and joyful, before they would put confidence in our promises;... that therefore they had sent back the two missionaries, with many thanks, promising that when they saw the black people among us restored to freedom and happiness, they would receive our missionaries. » Dr Boudinot adds, that this was « close reasoning, » and considers the incident « too mortifying a fact to make further observations upon. » (1)

It was England, as is well known, who introduced slavery into the United States. « English ships, » says Mr Bancroft, « fitted out in English cities, under the special favour of the royal family, of the ministry, and of parliament, stole from Africa, in the years from 1700 to 1750, probably *a million and a half souls*, of whom one eighth were buried in the Atlantic, victims of the passage; and yet in England no general indignation rebuked the enormity, for the public opinion of the age was obedient to materialism.... Protestantism itself had, in the political point of view, been the *triumph of materialism* over the spiritual authority of the Church. » (2)

But Protestantism, having substituted the material for the spiritual, was, at least in this case, consist-

---
(1) *Star in the West*, ch. VIII, p. 234.
(2) Bancroft, II, 997.

ent with itself, as the Negro found to his cost.
« From New England to Carolina, » we are told by
Mr Bancroft, « the notion prevailed, that ' *being
baptized is inconsistent with a state of slavery;* ' and
this early apprehension proved a main obstacle to
the culture and conversion of these poor people. » (1)
Apparently the obstacle has never been removed, or
only to give place to others equally fatal. Governor
Dongan, of New York, reported officially at the close
of the 17th century, that while the English colonists
generally wished « to bring up their children and
servants in that opinion which themselves profess,
I observe that they take no care of the conversion of
their slaves. » (2) Their American descendants have
not rebuked them by a display of greater charity.
The immense majority of the American Negroes,
amounting to four millions, confessedly remain, as
respects their spiritual development, in much the
same position as their kinsfolk in Dahomey or Ash-
antee. « They exist among us, » says Mr Howison,
the historian of Virginia, « a huge mass of mind,
almost entirely unenlightened. » And even in exceptional cases, in which, by the connivance of benevolent owners, and in spite of legal prohibitions, they
receive some sort of religious instruction, there is
too much reason to believe that it has only generated
that terrible malediction to which Holy Scripture
points, when it tells us of men, whose « last state
is worse than the first. » Two modes of dealing with
Negroes are recorded by Mr Law Olmsted, and other

(1) P. 994.
(2) *Doc. Hist. N, York*, vol. I, p. 187.

American writers, both of which deserve our attention.

One of them is described by Mʳ Olmsted, in quoting « Bishop Meade, of the Church of England in Virginia, » whose compositions the author of « Our Slave States, » judiciously selects, as affording the fairest specimen of « the most careful kind of preaching ordinarily addressed by the white clergy » to Negro audiences. When we have seen how Dʳ Meade appreciates the relations of that class to Christianity, we shall have no reason for surprise at the estimate furnished by Mʳ Howison of their actual condition in the State of Virginia. The extracts cited from this Protestant bishop by Mʳ Olmsted are taken, he tells us, « from a published volume of his sermons, recommended by him to masters and mistresses in his diocese, *for use in their households;* » and of which the contents, as Mʳ Olmsted appears to intimate, resemble rather the menaces of a turnkey than the exhortations of a Christian minister. « Your bodies, you know, » — it is thus that Dʳ Meade counsels masters and mistresses to address their slaves — « are not your own; they are at the disposal of those you belong to. » And the rest is in harmony with this beginning. « Poor creatures! you little consider when you are idle, when you are saucy and impudent,.... that what faults you are guilty of towards your masters and mistresses are faults done against God himself. » And so he goes droning on, page after page, without one tender word, one accent of divine charity; unmindful of the Apostle who sent back Onesimus to his master, « *not now as a servant, but a most dear brother,* » and entreating, « if he hath wronged thee in any thing, put that to my account; » unmindful, too, as Mr Olmsted happily observes, of the admonition of St. Gregory, that « slaves should be restored to that liberty in which they were born. » (1) But Dr Meade was content to take a lower model than St. Paul or St. Gregory, and to resemble a jailor rather than an apostle. If his language, as we are informed, be a specimen of « the most careful kind of preaching » to Negroes, we may easily understand what notions they form of the religion of the Gospel, as presented to them by Protestant teachers.

But the Episcopians, — the majority of whose clergy, we are told by one of their own members, « may be seen ministering at the altar of slavery, » (2) — are not the only monitors of the American Negro. Baptists, Methodists, and others, dispute their influence; and if the latter refuse to choose as their solitary text, « Your bodies are not your own, » it does not appear that the fruits of their instruction are more advantageous to the welfare of the slave. « It is evident, » says Mr Olmsted, « of the greater part even of those received into the fellowship of the churches, that their idea of religion, and of the standard of morality which they deem consistent with a profession of it, is very degraded; » — another proof of the impotence of Protestantism to deal with those fallen races whom it is the special glory of the Church, as we have seen in these pages, to raise to the dignity of men and christians.

(1) *Our Slave States*, by Frederick Law Olmsted: ch. II, p. 122.
(2) Quoted by Helper, *The Impending Crisis of the South*, ch. v, p. 262.

CHAPTER IX.

Of the use made by Negroes of the Bible, which a certain class of missionaries seem to spend their lives in exposing to derision, M\^r Olmsted gives such examples as the following. A baptized Negro, addicted to « certain immoral practices, » being admonished by a preacher, the following discussion ensued. « Dont de Scriptur say, rejoined the backslider, ' Dem as bleve and is baptize shall be saved? ' Want to know dat. »

« Yes, but » —

« Dat's all I want to know, Sar; now wat's de use o' talking to me? You aint a going to make me bleve wot de blessed Lord says aint so, not if you trie for ever. »

The minister attempted to remonstrate, but was finally silenced as follows. « De Scriptur say, if a man bleve and is baptize, he shall — he *shall* be saved. Now, massa minister, I *done* bleve, and I *done* baptize, and I *shall* be saved sure. Dere's no use talking, Sar. »

During his researches into the religion of Protestant Negroes, — who only faintly resemble the fancy type which M\^{rs} Beecher Stowe untruthfully drew, in order to promote the selfish designs of a political party, — M\^r Olmsted once asked a black clergyman if he was a preacher. « Yes, massa, he replied, ' Kordin to der grace. ' He commenced to reply in some scriptural phrase, soberly; but before he could say three words reeled off like a drunken man, entirely overcome with merriment. » (1)

The white teachers of the same unfortunate race

(1) *Our Slave States*, ch. II, p. 123; ch. VI, p. 377.

sometimes fall below even this specimen. Thus Mr Buckingham notices the case of a female slave, solicited to sin by her master's son, to whose earnest entreaty for succour in this emergency « her religious teacher, the minister of the church she had joined, » replied; « that her duty as a slave was clearly passive submission, and that resistance or refusal could not be countenanced by him. » (1)

On the whole, the coloured people of Protestant America may be ranged into three classes; the multitude, who have learned nothing, and whom Mr Howison describes as « a huge mass of mind almost entirely unenlightened; » the few, who, as a capable witness affirms in the *New York Times*, « join the church, perhaps in the great majority of cases, with *no idea* of religion, » and only display, as Mr Olmsted observes, « maniacal excitement, » and « a miserable superstition, the more painful that it employs some forms and words ordinarily connected with true Christianity ; » and lastly, the free Negroes of the North, whose lot is perhaps still more full of ignominy, whose liberty is a mockery and a delusion, and who display so little capacity of social progress that they have actually decreased in numbers, during the decennial period ending in 1860, even in the cities of Boston and New York.

In the island groups of the Atlantic, where perhaps a majority of the Negroes have been induced to accept various modifications of Christianity, the same facts recur. It may seem ungracious to find fault with an act upon which England prides herself

(1) *America*, vol. I, ch. xix, p. 361.

so much as the emancipation of her West Indian Negroes, yet it seems to be her fate, even when she strives to do a good work, to do it in the wrong way. « This English Negro-emancipation, » observes Dr Waitz, « will remain to all time as one of the most stupendous moral, economical, and political follies which the history of human culture has to point to. » (1) And then he proves, by arguments of which it is impossible to deny the force, the « utter irrationality » of the mode in which this act of sentimental but short-sighted and blundering benevolence was effected. The result of abandoning to the difficult task of self-government, without an hour's previous discipline, a population so absolutely void of foresight or self-control, has been in every way deplorable, and not a few of the Negroes, who have quitted the towns for the interior, are said to have already retrograded into utter barbarism. In the French colony of La Martinique, where emancipation was proclaimed with equal folly by the Provisional Government of 1848, ruin and chaos have ensued. M^r M^c. Leod has recently described the singular condition of the free blacks at Mauritius, and the virtual slavery of the *white* population. (2) The solitary exception is said to be found in the Danish island of Santa Cruz, where, although the Negroes were emancipated, they were left under the action of a special code, which *forces* them to labour, while it permits them to labour for their own advantage.

There is a remarkable concurrence of opinion as

(1) Quoted in *The Rambler*, vol. III, p. 323.
(2) *Travels in Eastern Africa*, vol. II, ch. v, pp. 162-5.

to the religious condition of the free blacks, in the islands as well as on the mainland. Dr Dalton has told us that the Protestant Negro considers « good works superfluous, » and Mr Trollope that « he never connects his religion with his life. » Like his white co-religionists in other climes, he bursts into violent religious excitement on Sunday, but is apt to relapse into something worse than forgetfulness during the rest of the week. Mr Coleridge adds the following information.

« The evil which the Methodists have done upon the long run is but scantily counterpoised by a certain sobriety of exterior which they have inflicted on their sect. » « The ministers, » he adds, always true to this ineradicable instinct, « *sell* to the poor negroes what are called ' tickets of membership, ' a sort of certificates of the purchaser's righteousness; » by which ingenious plan one of them confessed that he had amassed, in the course of twelve months, and from a single congregation, 624 l. (1) Of the Baptists, the most active rivals of the Wesleyans, Lord Metcalfe reported officially, as Sir Benjamin D'Urban reported from South Africa, « Instead of being ministers of peace, they are manifestly fomenters of discord. » (2) Of the native preachers, who are often represented in English missionary reports as models of zeal and piety, Mr Knibb, a protestant minister, informed the House of Commons that « the majority lead very unholy lives, and allow sins of

---

(1) *Six Months in the West Indies*, by Henry Nelson Coleridge; p. 172.
(2) *Papers of Lord Metcalfe*, edited by J. W. Kaye; p. 337.

various kinds in their different churches. » It is true that Mʳ Wildman gave much the same account, before the same Committee, of « the immorality among the ministers of the Established Church. » (1)

It is evident, then, that neither the past history nor the present condition of religion among the classes referred to are pleasant subjects of reflection. Protestantism has failed as completely with the Negro as with the Chinese, the Hindoo, and the Sioux. And with all it seems to have employed the same class of emissaries. A Protestant minister informs us, in a recent work, that in the island of St. Thomas, speaking of the middle of the 18th century, « concubinage at that period, and afterwards, was not looked upon as a sin, and in no way detracted from the standing and moral estimation even of clergymen. » We need not ask him, therefore, what was the character of their congregations. He even names some of the clergy whose irregularities were most notorious, and then adds, apparently as a melancholy illustration of the fact, that whereas « the Roman Catholics, in 1701, » were too few to be counted as an element in the population, « the congregation for many years has embraced at least a fourth of the inhabitants of the island, and is therefore very large. » (2)

Perhaps the Anglican operations in the West In-

(1) *Parliamentary Reports*, 16 July, 1832; vol. XX, pp. 278, 535.
(2) *Historical Account of Sᵗ Thomas*, by John P. Knox, Pastor of the Reformed Dutch Church; ch. x, pp. 139, 141. (1852).

dies may be thought to deserve special mention. It is true that the Negroes have very little share in the enormous expenditure which distinguishes, here as elsewhere, the barren labours of the parliamentary church. M. Victor Schœlcher notices with astonishment, that the annual cost of the « establishment » in Jamaica is 50,000 l. (1) » Of Barbadoes, Mr Coleridge frankly reports, that « the Codrington College is at present all but useless. » Though it offers the Principal « one of the most delectable houses in the Antilles, » he considers it « quite monstrous that the object of so magnificent a charity, and such large actual funds, should be the support of fourteen or fifteen boys, who might be educated much better elsewhere in the Island... What is done there is not done well, and yet done at an enormous expense. » It is just the history of the Protestant colleges at Malacca, Calcutta, Hong-Kong, and elsewhere : they consume, but never produce. Of Dominica Mr Coleridge gives the usual account, in speaking of his co-religionists, and then adds, in spite of violent prejudice, « I am bound to say that a general good report was given of the sobriety and temperate zeal of the Romish priests in the colony. » (2) Of Bermuda, another English writer records the characteristic fact, that when Dr Field, an Anglican bishop, visited the island to open a new church at Hamilton, and took the opportunity of mildly recommending «church principles; » « he had scarcely departed, before the Colonial Assembly voted — for the first time in the

(1) *Colonies Étrangères*, p. 59. (1843).
(2) *Six Months*, etc., p. 153.

history of Bermuda — a respectable stipend to the Presbyterian minister at Hamilton! » (1) This was their answer to his appeal.

But if the Anglican authorities in these islands can only spend money, without attracting the sympathy either of the coloured races of their own nominal disciples, other sects exert a more energetic if not a more beneficial influence. « Completely organised espionage, » Mr Coleridge says, » is a fundamental point in the system of the Methodists; the secrets of every family are at their command; parent and child are watches on each other; sister is set against sister, and brother against brother; each is on his guard against all, and all against each. » « The Baptist and Methodist clergy, » according to Mr Olmsted, « spend most of their force in arguing against each other's doctrines, » so that the amused Negroes acquire « a great taste for theological controversy. » The Methodists, however, are generally worsted by the Baptists, because « immersion strikes the fancy of the Negroes.» Mr Cartwright, a celebrated American preacher of the Methodist denomination, whose « Autobiography » appears to have found a larger number of readers than the Memoirs of Guizot or the History of Macaulay, is particularly severe on the Baptists. They were always opposing him, Mr Cartwright complains, « and would try to take our converts off into the water; indeed they made so much ado about baptism by immersion, that the uninformed world would suppose that heaven was an island, and that there was no way to get there but by *diving* or *swim-*

(1) *Bermuda*, by a Field Officer, ch. v, p. 93. (1857).

ming. » (1) But Mr Cartwright, who has probably had a larger number of hearers than any living man, and has been a celebrity in Boston and Philadelphia as well as in the wilds of Illinois, was a formidable opponent, and rarely mentions a conflict with the Baptists without adding cheerfully, that they were « annihilated, » or « finally evaporated and left for parts unknown. » His own preaching, on the other hand, was followed by results which, though not witnessed in the apostolic age, are certainly impressive. His hearers, he tells us, and it is perfectly true, sometimes « fell in every direction, right and left, front and rear. It was supposed that not less than three hundred (after one sermon) fell like dead men in a mighty battle; they were strewed all over the camp ground. » (2) « The power of God, » he says on one occasion, « fell upon the people gloriously. I kept my eye on William P..., and suddenly he fell at full length, and roared like a bull in a net, and cried aloud for mercy... Just about day-break, Monday morning, William P... raised the shout of victory, after struggling hard all night. » (3) William P... had « got religion. »

The Methodists in the West Indies have invented, perhaps to counterbalance the superior attractions of the Baptists, an entirely new sect, under a certain Mr Penwick; of which M. Schœlcher lightly observes, « If God grants life to this sect, which has already *fourteen* chapels, before half a century England will

(1) *The Backwoods Preacher; an Autobiography of Peter Cartwright;* ch. XI, p. 71. (31st edition, 1858).
(2) Ch. VIII, p. 46.
(3) Ch. XII, p. 77.

have its Penwickians, as it has already its Wesleyans, » He notices also that the Baptists, whom he calls « the radicals of Christianity, » « attack without mercy the established church, which revenges itself by discrediting them without pity. » And thus the Negro learns Christianity.

But there is a happier class of Negroes, who have Catholic masters, who have received the faith in its fulness, and whose condition has been thus described even by those Protestant witnesses whom alone we have determined to hear in this controversy. « In Spanish South America, » says Sir Woodbine Parish, « slavery was always more a name than a reality. The negroes were treated with even *more* consideration than the hired servants of the country. The laws protected them from ill usage, and religious feeling, in a state of society over which the priests had paramount influence, operated still more in their favour. » (1) And the same contrast is noticed, even by American writers, in every other region. In Brazil, where nearly half of the slave population have already acquired freedom, Dr Kidder, an American preacher who vainly recommended to them his own religious ideas, confesses, in 1857, that « some of the most intelligent and best educated men I met in Brazil *were of African descent;* » and that « *fuit* will be written against slavery in this empire before another century rolls round. » He even adds, « some of the closest students are Mulattoes. » (2) Mr Gardner, an English Protestant, declares that « the condition

(1) *Buenos Ayres*, part. 2, ch. IX, p. 115.
(2) *Brazil and the Brazilians*, ch. VIII, p. 133.

of the domestic slave in Brazil is perhaps even better than that of others;... on estates where there has been no medical attendant, I have often found the lady of the proprietor attending to the sick in the hospital herself. » (1) Their masters, says Mr Walpole, « with an eye to the everlasting welfare of their slaves, always have them baptized on their arrival in the Brazils. » (2)

« If what we see here, » says Mr Mansfield, « is any thing like a fair specimen of slavery, my opinion is that the cry against slavery, as raised in England, *is a vile sham, and lip-worship;* » while he observes of the Negroes themselves, « I only wish such cheerful faces were to be seen among our English poor. » (3)

At Bogota, we learn from Captain Cochrane, « the emancipation of slaves has been very great, and but few remain — the course of time will see them all set at liberty. » (4) In Central America, the negroes are all free, slavery having been declared « illegal. » In Peru, negroes imported as slaves at once acquire their freedom, without injury to themselves in a society which is profoundly Catholic.

« Avoiding on the one hand the precipitate measure of the English reform ministry, and on the other the ribald effrontery of the slave statesmen of North America, » says Mr Markham, « the Peruvians have steered a middle course between the extremes; » and

---

(1) *Travels in the Interior of Brazil*, ch. I, p. 19.
(2) *Four Years in the Pacific*, vol. I, ch. II, p. 47.
(3) *Paraguay, Brazil*, etc., by C. B. Mansfield Esq., M. A.; ch. II, p. 29.
(4) *Residence in Colombia*, vol. II, p. 38.

while the slave population is « becoming gradually accustomed to liberty, » they are treated with such charity and consideration that, as the same writer observes, « it is anticipated that few on receiving their liberty will leave their masters, to whom they are endeared by their almost paternal kindness, and the recollections of their earliest childhood. » (1)

In Chili, they « are treated with a degree of tenderness and humanity, » says Mr Hill, an ardent Protestant, « that greatly alleviates their servitude. A law has been passed declaring that no slave can henceforth be born in Chili, so that slavery may be regarded as virtually abolished in this fine country.» (2) In the province of La Plata, some of the Mulattoes have already become « professors and teachers of the liberal arts » — a wonderful example of the civilising influence of the Catholic religion. In Venezuela, slavery was abolished in 1854. « The Mexicans, » observes Mr Featherstonhaugh, for in every *Catholic* province the facts are uniform, « stand at a proud moral distance from the Americans in regard to slavery, which is abolished in their republic. (3) Even in Cuba, — where the culpable effeminacy of a wealthy and luxurious class diminished in some degree, in former years, the beneficial operation of the excellent code which regulates slavery, — Mr Olmsted notices that « every slave has the liberty of emancipating himself, by paying a price which does not depend upon the selfish exactions of masters...

(1) *Cuzco and Lima*, ch. II, p. 28.
(2) Quoted in *The Rambler*, vol. III, p. 330.
(3) *Excursion through the Slave States*, vol. II, ch. XXXIV, p. 188.

The consequence is, that emancipations are constantly going on, and the free people of colour *are becoming enlightened, cultivated, and wealthy;* » while « in no part of the United States do they occupy the high social position which they enjoy in Cuba. » (1) « There are circumstances of great superiority, » observes another American writer, with equal candour, « in the condition of the Cuban over that of the American slave. » (2)

Long ago Burke remarked, « as to the negroes (in the French Colonies), they are not left, as they are with us, wholly, body and soul, to the discretion of the planter. Their masters are *obliged* to have them instructed in the principles of religion. » (3) Lastly, Mr Sullivan dares to indicate distinctly the pregnant contrast which Mr Olmsted and others only venture to insinuate. In Catholic Cuba, he says, « the slaves are allowed to be instructed in their Bible, and are not kicked out of the cathedrals and churches, like so many dogs, as they are in America; » (4) — he means in the cities where Protestantism reigns, for in New Orleans, Mr Olmsted relates, apparently with admiration, that in the Catholic cathedral the negro and the white man knelt side by side — a spectacle with the writer of these pages has often witnessed in the Catholic churches of New York.

Such, in its outlines, is the contrast between the lot of the Negro under Catholic and Protestant masters respectively. A blessing and a curse represent,

(1) *Our Slaves States*, ch. vi, p. 445.
(2) *Gan-Eden, or Pictures of Cuba*, ch. xiii, p. 189. (1854).
(3) *European Settlements in America*, vol. II, ch. vi, p. 47.
(4) *Rambles in N. and S. America*, ch. iii, p. 60.

in this as in every other field, the relative action of the Church and the Sects. In Protestant America, we know what has been the history of the African; in every Catholic state, even on the same continent, he has found either prompt and complete liberty, or a constant and rapid approximation towards it, not by a violent and irrational emancipation following hard upon a debasing servitude, but by gradual culture and wise discipline; and even while still a bondsman, « religious feeling, » as Sir Woodbine Parish observes, secures for him such tender care and wakeful solicitude as is rarely conceded, in England or America, to free labourers. But if we have now sufficient evidence with respect to the fortunes of this section of American society, we have still to show, in conclusion, what Protestantism has done for the original tenants of the land, after slaughtering the pastors who were gathering them by thousands into the fold of Christ, and what has been its final influence upon races whom the missionaries of the Cross would have everywhere converted into a generous, a civilised, and a believing people.

« The Europeans, » says M. de Tocqueville, and Humboldt has used almost the same words, « after having banished the Indian tribes to remote deserts, have condemned them to a wandering and vagabond life full of inexpressible miseries. European tyranny has rendered them more disorderly *and less civilised* than they were before. » We have seen that in *South America*, hundreds of thousands of savages were raised to such a degree of virtue, civilisation, and prosperity, that « they enjoyed, for many generations, » even by the confession of a Southey, « a greater exemption from physical and moral evil than any other inhabitants of the globe. » « The moral and physical condition of *this* people, » continues M. de Tocqueville, « *has not ceased to degenerate in equal measure,* and their barbarism has increased in proportion to their sufferings. » And then, contrasting their woful decay with the unparalleled material progress of their Protestant lords, he adds this cry of righteous indignation. — « Never has there been witnessed in any nation either so prodigious a development, or so rapid a destruction ! » (1)

The story of that destruction is soon told. The Atlantic States had already been emptied of their inhabitants by the English; but many a tribe still remained, though in diminished numbers, by the banks of the Ohio and the Mississippi, as well as in the wide regions which lie between the confluence of the latter river with the Missouri and the far distant provinces of Oregon and California. In these remote tribes was vested the possession of lands of vast extent and incalculable value. As the flood of emigration rolled onwards, and bursting one barrier after another sought an issue in the wide plains of the West, the Indian found himself once more in the presence of men stronger and fiercer than himself, and able to wrest from him the lands which he was unable to guard.

We have learned, from American authorities, how his race has been exterminated — men, women, and helpless babes — That Anglo-Saxon lords might the sooner divide his inheritance; and Mr Julius Froebel

(1) *De la Démocratie,* etc., tome III, ch. v, p. 109.

assures us, in 1859, that they have found still more expeditious modes of removing tribes who could have taught them a lesson in humanity, if they had been willing to profit by it. « It is a fact, » he says, « that the whites have attempted to poison *whole tribes* of Indians, and I have myself often heard the question discussed how this could be effected in the best manner. A story of the designed introduction of the small pox amongst a remote Indian tribe is current in the west, and I have heard it related with every particular. » (1)

It was not, however, always by open violence, but more often by the fiction of a simulated purchase, that the Indian was deprived of his hunting grounds, and driven to wander again towards the setting sun. In vain he sometimes affected to adopt the nominal religion of his encroaching guests, in the hope of snatching from their sympathy the respite which their avarice denied. « I was struck with amazement, » said Dr Wolff, fifteen years ago, « to find, in the United States of North America, that many of the Indians, especially among the Cherokees, adopted outwardly the Protestant religion, in order, as they hoped, to prevent Congress from sending them further into the interior. » (2) Feeble device! which did not postpone even for an hour their inevitable doom. There was no Vicar of Christ here, as of old in Mexico and Brazil, to launch the sentence of excommunication against all who should wrong the Indian, nor would such a sentence have

(1) *Seven Years in Central America.* ch. v, p. 272.
(2) *Narrative of a Mission to Bokhara,* vol. I, ch. II, p. 54.

had any terrors for those who were now gathering round him. There was no Las Casas to defend, no Vieyra to instruct, no Baraza to die for him. The sons of St. Francis and St. Ignatius were far away, and the Indian was left to struggle alone. And so, in his own touching words, « the tree which was continually transplanted quickly perished. » « The Americans acquired, » says M. de Tocqueville, « almost for nothing — *à vil prix* — whole provinces which the richest sovereigns of Europe are too poor to purchase. » M. Everett reminded Congress, on the 19th of May, 1830, that they had already seized, by pretended treaty with the Indians, two hundred and thirty million acres, — an amount increased, when M. Schoolcraft compiled his statistical tables, to more than four hundred millions. The Osages alone gave up twenty-nine million acres for an annuity of a thousand dollars — which would hardly pay for the strong drinks by which the treaty was consecrated. (1) Many cases were still more flagrant in their mockery of justice. During the whole period of the Anglo-Saxon rule the same policy was pursued, and for nearly two hundred years men bearing the name of Christians have scandalized the pagan tribes of America by their unscrupulous fraud. « Your people, » said the orators of the Six Nations to Sir William Johnson in 1755, « when they buy a small piece of land from us, by stealing they make it large; » and Sir William confessed that it was true. The Delawares, he told the English authorities, « would never leave off killing the English, » for « they were

---

(1) De Tocqueville, tome III, ch. v, p. 123.

determined to drive all Englishmen off their lands which the English had cheated them out of. » (1)

The Americans have imitated the English, and defraud the Indian, now at their mercy, without even the affectation of justice. The second article of the « Treaty with the Winnibagos, » in 1846, imposes upon them the resignation « of all lands, wherever situated, now or heretofore occupied by said Indians, » and assigns « as their home » a tract West of the Mississippi, « *provided* such land can be obtained on just and reasonable terms! » (2) *Twelve* treaties, we learn, « have been made by the United States with the Muskogee nation (Creeks), and each of them has been a treaty of cession; » while the *remnant* of their lands « was in each case solemnly guaranteed to them by the United States. » At length, they were slain to the last man, not by hunters or pioneers, whose lawlessness might have found an apologist, but by an organized military force, under the command of General Jackson, afterwards President of the United States! (3)

And even this does not complete the contrast which marks the history of Catholic and Protestant colonization on this continent; for in the rare cases in which a tribe is permitted for a season to occupy some remote tract, insufficient for their wants unless they till the soil, and which their rulers are not yet prepared to utilise, the niggard concession, as even American writers complain, is only made a pretext

(1) *Doc. Hist, N. York*, vol. II, pp. 750-52.
(2) *The Statutes at large and Treaties of the U. S. of America*, 1846-7. (Ed. Minot).
(3) Featherstonhaugh, vol. II, ch. 41.

for new frauds. « The governmental philanthropy, » says Mr Olmsted, in 1857, « is in practice only a job, in which, as usual, the least possible is done, and the utmost possible is paid. » (1) The annuity system, which the most eminent authority calls « that delusive means of Indian subsistence », is in practice only profitable to the agents employed under it, while « few of the annuitants reach their home with a dime. Most of them have expended all, and lost their time in addition. » (2)

The Americans, then, by their own confession, have only pursued in their dealings with the Indians the cruel policy bequeathed to them by the English. Refusing to adopt from them other precedents, they have imitated them too well in this. And the inevitable result has been to add a deeper intensity to the scorn and disgust which the savage, not without cause, had already conceived for a religion which he was told was Christianity, and for the agents who were presented to him as its teachers. Such a religion, and such teachers, seemed to him so little divine, that he scarcely deemed them human. « By Christians, » observes Mr Möllhausen, « they have been cheated and betrayed—driven from the grounds of their fathers, and cut down like wild beasts — and for this reason they have repelled missionaries with displeasure and contempt. » They saw in such missionaries only traders and speculators, whose largest conception of purity, justice, and self-denial only consisted in constantly violating the two first in

(1) *Texas*, p. 298.
(2) Schoolcraft, *Notes on the Iroquois*, ch. I, pp. 12, 13.

their own practice, and never recommending the last save to their victims. In 1821, the Indians had seen a band of so-called missionaries appropriate « a tract of land, consisting of about fifteen thousand acres, from the Osage Indians. » (1) Ten years later, when a tribe in Indiana spontaneously offered land to the governor of the state for the maintenance of *Catholic* missionaries, their petition was answered by an embassy of Protestant ministers, attracted by the prospect of gain, and who contrived to filch from them by fraud 1820 acres. (2) « Genuine religion has suffered much, » says Professor R. Bishop, the historian of « the Sects in Kentucky, » from « the money making and speculating spirit » of these singular « missionaries. » (3)

There is something terrible in the disdain which, in our own as in other times, the Indian manifests towards the emissaries of Protestantism. « They treat me, » Mr Kirkland has candidly told us, « with no more respect than they would show to a dog. » Many years after, in 1821, a famous chief thus expressed to the Governor of New York his opinion of the same class. « I have observed that whenever they come among the Indians, they always excited enmities and quarrels amongst them,... and that the Indians *were sure to dwindle and decrease* in proportion to the number of preachers that came among them. » And then he noticed a recent case. « We have been threatened by Mr Hyde that unless we listen to his preaching

(1) *Fathers of the London Missionary Society*, vol. II, App. p. 604.
(2) *Annales*, tome VI, p. 158.
(3) Quoted by Spalding, ch. VI, p. 88.

and become christians, we shall be turned off our lands. We wish to know from the governor if this is to be so; and if he has no right to say so, we think *he* ought to be turned off our lands, and not allowed to plague us any more. We shall never be at peace while he is among us. » (1) Mr Hyde was removed.

Ten years later, the celebrated *Black Hawk* accepted a treaty with the United States at Prairie du Chien, and in the presence of the American officials the noble savage spoke as follows of the colleagues of Mr Hyde. « The white men are bad schoolmasters. They smile in the face of the poor Indians, to cheat them, to deceive them, and ruin their wives. They poisoned us by their touch. We were not safe. We were becoming like them — hypocrites and liars, adulterers, lazy drones, all talkers and no workers. » (2) Is it wonderful if the chiefs sometimes said, in words which have already been quoted, « Our young men do not listen to *them* any better than to ourselves — we wish for Catholic Priests. »

And they seem all to have formed the same judgment. « Brother, » said the most famous of all the Seneca chiefs, at a great meeting held at Buffalo by the request of the missionaries, « you say you have not come to get our land or our money, but to enlighten our minds. I will now tell you that I have been at your meetings, and saw you collecting money from the meeting. I cannot tell what this money was intended for, but suppose it was for your minister. » (3)

(1) Drake, book V, ch. vi, p. 103.
(2) *Id.*, ch. x, p. 161.
(3) *Id.*, ch. vi, p. 103.

« My friends, » replied an Ojibbeway chief not long ago to the invitation of some English ministers, « we believe that the white people have two tongues. » And then he gave the following reason for thinking so. « A black coat came amongst us in the town where I live, and told us the same words as you have spoken this morning. He said that the religion of the white men was the only good religion; and some began to believe him, and after a while a great many believed him, and then he wanted us to help him to build a house, and we did so. We lifted very hard at the logs, and when it was done many sent their children to him to learn to read, and some girls got so as to read the good book, and their fathers were very proud of it; and at last one of these girls had a baby, and not long after another had a baby, and then the black coat ran away, and we have never seen him since. My friends, we do not think this right. I believe there is another black coat now in the same house. Some of the Indians send their boys there to learn to read, but they dare not let their girls go. My friends, this is all I have to say. » (1)

The estimate which the Indians have formed, after an unvarying experience of two centuries, of the habits and character of the Protestant emissaries, has naturally created in them, as in the pagans of every other land, the invincible repugnance which their sullen attitude attests, and has aggravated tenfold their passionate aversion to Christianity. If preachers of another order, — men of austere virtue, admirable patience, and unwearied charity, — could

(1) Catlin, vol. I, p. 165. (2d edition).

only win them to the Cross at the price of prodigious labours and sufferings, and often at the cost of life itself; we may easily comprehend the failure of another class, who only excite, as we have seen, their contempt and abhorrence. « The American Indians,» says a late report of one of the most opulent missionary associations of the western continent, « are, for the most part, yet unblessed with the knowledge of Jesus Christ! » (1) What more effective proof can we desire of the monstrous contrast which we have traced in these volumes, and of which the history of missions in North and South America supplies the last, and perhaps the most impressive example?

There might still be hope of the effectual conversion of the few remaining tribes, though the task becomes more difficult every year, if Catholic missionaries were the sole representatives of Christianity. It is by the presence of the agents of Protestantism, and not by the indifference or obduracy of the Indian, that their labour is now frustrated. When Father Laverlochére visited the Sioux at Fort Albany, in 1849, amongst whom a Protestant missionary had dwelt for many years, and urged them to embrace the Faith, this was their reply : — « The prayer-man who has been with us is only a rogue and a pretender. *You, too, may be the same.* » And they refused to listen to him. (2) Such is the fatal result of the presence of Protestant missionaries. They make the conversion of the heathen *impossible.*

(1) Western Foreign Missionary Society; see *Foreign Missionary Chronicle*, p. 51. (Pittsburgh).
(2) *Annals*, XII, 163. (English edition).

Yet it is in this point alone that the American government, rarely unjust to Catholics, uses all its influence on the side of evil. When the Ottawas applied, in 1829, for Catholic missionaries, their petition was answered, as usual, by a prompt despatch of Protestant ministers. It is true that the Indians drove them away, with this emphatic admonition : — « Keep your errors for yourselves; our nation does not want missionaries with wives and children, but the *Black Robes*, like those who visited our grandfathers. » (1) And three years later, Father Rézé could say, writing from New York, « It is truly admirable to see these good Ottawas all converted in the space of three years, and become excellent Christians. » (2) But the executive authorities, — and this is perhaps the heaviest reproach which they have incurred, — though all these facts are known to them, and have been confessed without reserve, still neglect too often the prayer of the Indian, even while admitting that it is just. They know that Catholic missionaries alone can win him to christianity, and they continue to send him men who bind his neck with chains while they talk of liberty, who create a desert and call it civilisation. When the chief of the Kansas nation wrote to General Clark for a *Black Robe*, the agent, though a Protestant, reported officially in forwarding the application, that « only Catholic Priests can succeed in these missions. » When Monseigneur Dubourg, the venerated Bishop of New Orleans, visited the President and

(1) *Annales*, tome IV, p. 475.
(2) Tome VI, p. 180.

his ministers at Washington, « It was readily admitted that Catholic priests were fitter for the work than Protestant ministers; » and the minister for war, frankly confirming the admission, said to the Bishop, « Above all, try to procure Jesuits. » (1)

It is confessed, then, by all that is noble and high-minded in the United States,— though the confession comes many years too late, — that while the influence of Protestantism has only tended, during two hundred years, to propagate corruption, disorder, and death among the native tribes; the Catholic missionary, alone and unaided, as destitute of all material resources as his Indian disciple, but filled with the power of the Holy Ghost, has never failed to win him, by the force of his own example, and the divine gifts of which he is the steward and minister, to peace, contentment, industry, and virtue. What Protestantism has done for the Red Man is written in history. Even its professional advocates confess the truth which they dare not deny. « Alas! » exclaimed one of them fifty years ago, « what has not our nation to answer for at the bar of retributive justice! » And half a century later, in the year 1861, one of the most conspicuous religious teachers of Protestant America thus estimates, once more, in the presence of his congregation, the unrepented guilt of which the final reckoning is still to come. « Our nation has more sins than one. Its criminal treatment of the Indians is a fit subject for shame. *Every crime in the calendar has been committed against them :* slow persecution; the breaking of every treaty made with

---

(1) Henrion, tome II, 2ᵈᵉ partie, p. 664.

them when found convenient; and the robbery of their lands. » (1) He only omits the worst crime of all — the cruelty which deprived them of the very teachers who had proved a thousand times, that they, and they alone, could have done for them exactly what their fellow apostles had done for their more favoured brethren in the South.

Such is the contrast, immense and irreparable, which may be resumed in these two admitted results — that while in the *South*, nearly sixteen hundred thousand Indian Catholics are found at this day, though robbed for sixty years of their pastors, still inflexible in the faith, and proof against the assaults of heresy and unbelief, besides whole nations in Central America, Mexico, and California; in the vast territories of the *North*, from Oregon to Florida, and from Boston to Santa Fè, barely 300,000 Indians, remnant of a thousand tribes, now survive, of whom nearly all who are not Catholics are pagans. In 1851, the total number of Indians in the territory of the United States was 388,229. (2) In 1858, they had dwindled to 314,622, being a diminution of nearly *seventy four thousand* in seven years! While, « in Mexico and South America, » as the latest writer on the Western Continent observes, « *they still thrive, or increase*, and amalgamate and intermarry with the European races. » (3) Such, once more, is

(1) Rev[d] Henry Ward Beecher, quoted in *New York Evening Express*, January 5, 1861.
(2) Schoolcraft, *Historical and Statistical Information*, etc., part. 1.
(3) *Life and Liberty in America*, by Charles Mackay, L. L. D.; ch. xii, p. 145, 153.

that prodigious contrast between the work of the Church and the work of the Sects, which forced from a learned Protestant the reluctant confession — « It must be allowed to reflect honour on the Roman Catholic Church, and to cast a deep shade on the history of Protestantism. »

And now we may conclude this long but imperfect history, of which all the phases were sufficiently known to an English writer, familiar with men and their works in the United States, to elicit the most remarkable confession ever wrung from a Protestant conscience, and to constrain the unbought avowal — « *The Catholic Faith is the Shield of America.* » (1) It was not possible that enlightened men, capable of distinguishing between good and evil, should fail to mark the contrast between the Catholic and Protestant teachers in America. Hence the declaration of Mr Washington Irving, too strong and free to be caught in the meshes of sectarian bigotry, that the former laboured « with a power that no other Christians have exhibited. » Hence the homage of Dr Channing to the Catholic Church, when he said, without deriving instruction from his own words, — « Her Missionaries who have carried Christianity to the ends of the earth; her Sisters of Charity who have carried relief and solace to the most hopeless want and pain; do not these teach us, that in the Romish Church the Spirit of God has found a home? » (2) Hence also the sympathy of the just and upright

(1) *Englishwoman in America*, ch. III, p. 95.
(2) *Works of W. E. Channing*, p. 275. People's Edition. 1843.

Washington, when he exclaimed, in his « Address to the Catholics of the United States; » « May the members of your Society in America, animated alone by the pure spirit of Christianity, enjoy every temporal and spiritual felicity! » (1) Hence too those later confessions of American Protestants, disdaining the peevish malice of their English co-religionists, and frankly expressing the honest admiration which they cherished, not only for the martyred apostles who have long since finished their career, but even for some of their latest successors. « In seeing such men as Cheverus and Matignon, » said a Boston writer, when his city hardly knew the Catholic religion but by their labours, « who can doubt that it is possible for human nature to approach and to imitate the God-Man? » (2) Who can forget, says Professor Walters in our own day, with equally generous enthusiasm, « Father Farmer, still venerated by all who knew him; » or « John Carroll, the first Roman Catholic Bishop of Baltimore, the model of prelates, christians, and scholars », who was sent by Congress to Canada, in 1776, as joint commissioner with Franklin; (3) or « Bishop England, beloved and honoured by men of every religious denomination, and even now lamented in the South as one of her best and noblest sons? » Such are the testimonies of men convinced, by actual observation, of the truth of that judgment proclaimed by a Protestant writer, in words of almost astonishing candour — « The

(1) Quoted by Rupp, p. 165.
(2) *Boston Monthly Magazine*, June 1825; quoted in *Vie du Cardinal de Cheverus*, liv. II, p. 52.
(3) Franklin's *Works*, vol. VIII, p. 178, ed. Sparks.

Priesthood of the Catholic Church bear the griefs and carry the sorrows of their infirm and ignorant neighbours, and assuredly come nearer, in their walk through life, to the Saviour's model, than any Clergy of any Religion whatever. » (1)

It is not in vain, then, that men of God, filled with their Master's presence, and living only for His glory, have evangelised America. The harvest of which they planted the seed has been blighted as far as the natives are concerned, and has still to be reaped and garnered by the race which has cast them out; but already men predict its golden fulness. « If religion, with its immortal hopes, » says one of the leading organs of Protestantism in New York, « is to be preserved in the world, and cold infidelity is not to overrun all Europe and America, *there is nothing left but a return to the Catholic Church.* » (2)

It is after a journey which has led us through many climes, and carried us into the presence of many nations, that we arrive at length at the close of our long travel. But if we have left far behind, and well nigh forgotten, such men as Nobrega and Azevedo, Ortega and Baraza, Betanzos and Las Casas, the Blessed Peter Claver and St. Francis Solano, — the evangelists of Brazil and Peru, of Paraguay and Mexico, — it may be permitted to turn once more a parting glance of love and reverence towards the heroes and apostles whom other men

---

(1) *Englishwoman in America*, ch. 11, p. 78.
(2) *New York Herald*, quoted in *Morning Star*. August 23, 1859.

and other scenes have almost pushed from our memory. What words can express, what judgment measure, the immense and indelible contrast between the religious history of Brazil and New England, of Paraguay and Virginia, of Peru and Canada? Who but God shall judge between the two classes of men who lived to glorify Him in the one, to dishonour Him in the other? What less unerring and deep-searching eye can penetrate, in all their details, the secret motives, unpublished thoughts, and unrevealed desires, which *we* can only judge in part by their exterior signs? Who shall estimate, on the one hand, the martyr's love, the apostle's toil, the disciple's faith, victorious in suffering and triumphant in death; or take note, on the other, without partiality or excess, of the cowardice which trembled even in its safe retreats, the luxury which cried piteously for more delicate fare, the avarice which cheated the pagan of his lands, and the cruelty which robbed him of his life? Who shall recompense the labour which won a thousand tribes to the Cross, and converted the waste places of the earth into a smiling garden; or chastise the sloth, the meanness, and the treachery which could turn a paradise into a desert, uproot the fair plants which gentler hands had reared, and make the conversion of the heathen impossible even while pretending to secure it? Lastly, who but God who gave it shall assay the almost omnipotent charity which could knit together ten thousand savages in mutual love, and in the bonds of that indissoluble unity which two centuries of trial could not rend; who but He, the supremely Just, shall compare with his own gifts to His apostles, the vanity, fickleness, and caprice of another order of men, who were so little able to devise a definite and uniform doctrine, that they could only invent new forms of error in which there was nothing permanent but the pride which conceived and the malice which begot them, and which moved even the derision of the mocking savage, and forced from him at last the bitter taunt — « If I should have a mind to turn Christian, I could not tell what religion to be of! »

Such is the contrast which we have attempted to trace, in every state and province of this vast continent, and which may again be summed up in this one fact — that in America, the Church has created a hundred Christian nations; while the Sects have not only failed to build up one, but have destroyed without mercy even those which the missionaries of the Cross had begun to form, and have made a waste and a desert where *they* would have planted a paradise.

In reviewing such a history, — which has conducted us by a gradual progress from the glories of Brazil and Paraguay to the horrors of Virginia and New England, from the fruitful labours of the apostles of Jesus to the sordid arts of human sects, from the light of the sanctuary of God to the outer darkness of the world; we seem to resemble a man who has gone forth at the dawn of some summer's day, noting with glad heart how the bright sun called each leaf, and flower, and tree to live again in his joyous light, and to sing that new creation of which each revolution of the earth sees the beginning and the end. Then casting himself down by some glittering stream or fragrant bank, he has listened through the long hours of the day to « nature's mighty undersong, » thanking God who has made every thing so fair; till the golden light has become pale, and shadows of deeper and deeper hue have spread a veil over all the scene; and the wanderer, starting up in sadness, has slowly turned his steps homewards, marvelling how so bright a day had given place to so black a night.

CHAPTER X.

SUMMARY.

When our Lord would instruct His children how to distinguish, in every age, between true and false apostles, He gave them this precept—*By their fruits ye shall know them.* It is by this test that we have estimated the work of Catholic and Protestant missionaries in all parts of the world, and it is time to review the conclusions to which it has brought us. This shall be our present attempt.

Two classes of men have appeared before us in the history which we have now completed. Both claimed to be ambassadors from God to the lands of the heathen. Brothers in outward form, and kinsmen in the order of nature, in all else they have differed so widely, that we might almost deem them beings of a separate race. Every thing in them exists only in contrast, — faith and works, motive and action, life and death. The one, models of sanctity, of prudence, and heroism, have run through all lands like tongues of fire, kindling every dry branch, bidding the sleeper awake, subduing the fierce, and bowing down the strong; the others, often profoundly immoral, and in their highest mood only patterns of domestic propriety, have moved even the pagan to doubt whether they professed any religion whatever. Yet both were children of a common parent, subject to the same infirmities, and filled, at the outset of their career, with the same natural gifts. In spite of this common nature and origin, the one became apostles and martyrs, the others only tourists and merchants.

Whence this prodigious contrast between men otherwise equally endowed? What is that mysterious gift which has been imparted to the one, and refused to the others? What but the call and election of Him whom both profess to serve, but who has said to the first, « *Go, teach all nations;* » while He has declared of the last, « *I did not send them, yet they ran: I have not spoken to them, yet they prophesied.* » (1) Herein lies the interpretation of the mystery. Let us consider, then, what is the vocation to the apostolate, and what are its fruits.

There was one of old, in the very beginning of Christianity, whose claim to the title of apostle no man has ever doubted. In the broad light of day, in

(1) Jeremias, XXIII, 21.

the midst of his companions, the hand of God fell upon him. From that hour, blind and stunned, but soon to be filled with a heavenly light, the persecutor began to be an apostle. And what were the marks of his vocation? He, who best knew, has told us. Though « the least of the apostles, » in the order of election, he could offer, when provoked to compare himself with others, these proofs of his calling. « Are they ministers of Christ? I am more. In many more labours, *in prisons more frequently, in stripes above measure, in deaths often.* Of the Jews five times I received forty stripes save one. Thrice was I beaten with rods, once I was stoned;... » and then this man — already eight times scourged to blood; perpetually imprisoned; expelled by force from Antioch; cruelly assaulted at Iconium; let down in a basket by night from the walls of Damascus, because the Jews « watched the gates that they might kill him;» mangled with stones at Lystra, and dragged out of the city by a furious rabble, « thinking him to be dead; » brutally flogged at Philippi, where a jailor washed his bleeding back; hardly escaping with life from Thessalonica; almost torn to pieces in Jerusalem; bound again with fetters in Cæsarea; always in perils, in vigils, and labours; « in hunger and thirst, in fastings often, in cold and nakedness; » and at last, after long years of suffering, to be cut asunder by a pagan sword — could venture to say, « Let no man trouble me : I bear in my body *the marks of the Lord Jesus.* »

Such, in the judgment of St. Paul, are the signs of an apostle. To labour, to suffer, to die; to « fill up those things that are wanting of the sufferings of

Christ; » yet in suffering to rejoice, and in dying to overcome,—these are the fruits of his vocation. And for this reason it is that the history of the evangelisation of the heathen, in every land and in every age, is simply a martyrology. The path of the true apostle, like that of his Master, is a path of blood. Every where you may track his steps by that sign. At Jerusalem as at Rome, at Smyrna as at Antioch, at Lyons as at Corinth, by the rivers of Germany as in the plains of Poland, in the forests of Hindostan as in the cities of China, by the mountains of Brazil and Peru as by the frozen lakes of Canada —everywhere there is blood. Xavier and de Britto, Sanz and Dufresse, Ortega and Baraza, Brebeuf and Lallemand, and a thousand more, what are they but heirs of St. Paul, displaying the same vocation, accepting the same torments, and able to affirm with him, « Are they ministers of Christ? I am more. »

And it is by virtue of this vocation alone that they, and such as they, « wrought justice, » and « conquered kingdoms. » Yet who shall tell us all which that vocation includes? Evidently if we would attempt to describe, or even to comprehend, a state and calling so far above our own, — to know what it is to be summoned by God to the sublime dignity of the apostolate, — we must interrogate that illustrious company upon whom the lot has fallen. From *them* we learn how the apostle of Jesus Christ has received, often from his earliest youth, sometimes even in childhood, a vocation to the immediate service of the King of kings. And this first call, they tell us, is only the beginning of that supernatural career to which the chosen one is now destined. The gift of God is not barren, but a very fountain of power and life. With the vocation, therefore, He confers, in due season, all which it implies and presupposes; death to self and the world, boundless charity, and invincible fortitude. Then follow, in their harmonious order, the spirit of wisdom, of counsel, and of strength; until at length the elect messenger, docile to every inspiration of grace, and armed with the whole panoply of apostolic gifts, begins his appointed work. From that hour he no longer knows, except in God, father, or mother, or kinsfolk; for he can say with St. Paul, « Henceforth we know no man according to the flesh, » — and with the first apostle of China, « We have God for our father, all mankind for brothers, and the world for a home. » Charged to offer henceforth a sacrifice of expiation, suffering is not the object of his dread, but of his ardent desire; and death, no matter in what form so it be that of martyrdom, is now the prize which he covets, the destined crown of all his toil. « I have specially solicited this grace, » says one of whom we have read in these pages, « every time I elevated the Precious Blood in the holy sacrifice of the Mass. » To « die daily, » is henceforth the very condition of his life; and this he consents to do, by virtue of that mighty interior grace, without which the existence of the Catholic missionary would be simply impossible to human nature.

Such is the vocation to the apostolate, the highest to which mortal man can aspire, and compared with which regal or imperial state is paltry and obscure. To God alone it belongs to choose those who shall be admitted to this superhuman life, because He alone can give the wisdom and strength which make such a life possible to a fallen race. « Woe to the priest, » says one who evangelised India, « who comes to this land without being called of God. He would be the most unfortunate of men, and would provoke his own downfall and that of many others. » (1) But if he be called indeed, then the apostle may set forth on his journey, for the hand of God is upon him, and he must go whithersoever it shall lead him. Whether his path be over the burning sands of India, or along the ice-bound shores of northern climes, or in the far-off islands of the great sea, his mission is sure. He may succeed, or he may seem to fail; but if he triumph, the glory belongs to his Master, if he fall, as sooner or later he will do, his fall shall win an eternal crown for himself. Such is the vocation, such the destiny, of the apostle of Christ.

And now if we enquire, on the other hand, by whom the false apostles are commissioned, and under what auspices they set out, a monstrous contrast is revealed. If we would interrogate these men, or watch them at their work, we must quit the paradise of holy thoughts and pure desires, and descend to the dismal regions of vanity, covetousness, and caprice. Speak not to them of that dread apostolic vocation which to their apprehension is only a fiction, and which Protestant missionaries are so far from asserting, that they would be the first to disclaim it, some with fear, others with passionate contempt. « The very notion of a *call* to the ministry, » their advocates now admit, « *seems to have*

---

(1) *Annales*, IV, 155.

died out in English Society. » (1) « Our clergy, » says another, « as a sacred order or class, *have ceased to exist.* » (2) Ask them not, therefore, who called, or who sent them? If they bear in their body « the marks of the Lord Jesus? » If they have « made themselves eunuchs for the kingdom of heaven's sake? » With fluent jest, or angry taunt, they will mock you; perhaps even defame the gifts and graces which such as they neither possess nor understand. In accepting the wages of some « missionary society,» they have only chosen a craft or calling, like any other; they have secured a livelihood, and usually a more luxurious one than they could have obtained at home. It is their own employers who declare it. Many of them, we have been told by Berkeley, « quit their country on no other motive. » « It is only a certain kind of business with most of them, » says a living writer who had watched their proceedings in many lands, « a calling, by which, as in commerce and trade, to make a living. » (3) Accordingly, before they set out, bound and fettered in every limb with worldly ties, they have carefully arranged, with minutest detail, the salary which they are to receive, and the mode of payment; perhaps even, like the Anglican clergy in India, the exact allowance upon which they are to retire— for they have learned from the « bishop of Calcutta » that « asceticism is no part of the Gospel system. » Plague and pestilence are excluded by the terms of their contract;

---

(1) *Saturday Review*, January 21, 1860.
(2) Laing, *Notes of a Traveller*, ch. xxi, p. 433.
(3) Gerstaecker, vol. II, ch. vii, p. 234.

and if, in spite of every precaution, the unwelcome visitor appears, they flee before it. The sickness of a wife or a child terminates their mission at once. They are only men, fathers of a family, or solicitous to become so, and do not profess to be apostles. To be pensioners of God, — to hunger and thirst, — to be scourged or imprisoned, — this is an enthusiasm which only excites their disdain. To be « in fastings often, » to « endure hardness, » to have « no fixed abode, » not even « where to lay the head, » — this is an « asceticism » which they condemn, a « fanaticism » which they despise, though it be the asceticism of St. Paul, the fanaticism of the Son of God. It would evidently be irrational to talk of a « *vocation* » here. God does not take counsel in heaven about the going forth of such men as these. They have, like the birds of the air and the beasts of the field, the protection of His ordinary providence; more they do not desire or expect.

This, then, is the first point of contrast which the facts reviewed in these pages have disclosed to us between Catholic and Protestant missionaries to the heathen. The one have a vocation from God, the others have not. And both the tenor of their life, and the fruits of their labour, reveal the influence of this original disparity. They are Protestant witnesses who have told us, in every land, what is the character of either; how the servants of the Church show the marks of *vocation*, how the agents of the Sects display the absence of it. They are Protestants who have unconsciously described to us the phases of that conflict, in which, though all human means were on one side and none on the other, the issue was always the same; and in which we seem to witness in our own day, but on a larger scale and with more impressive results, the application of that terrible test which Elias dared to propose, long ages ago, to the servants of Baal, when he said, « Call ye on the names of your gods, and I will call on the name of my Lord : and *the God that shall answer by fire, let him be God.* » (1) Once more we have heard the false prophets calling, « from morn even till noon, » for the fire from heaven which will not descend at their cry. Once more we have listened to the prayer of the true apostle, sure of his own vocation, and venturing to deluge the sacrifice, the altar, and the trench round about it, with floods of water; but at whose word « the fire of the Lord fell, and consumed the holocaust, and the wood, and the stones, and the dust, and licked up the water that was in the trench.» They are enemies, more implacable than the ministers of Baal, who have unwittingly recounted for us this memorable scene, not, as of old, in the solitudes of Mount Carmel, but in every continent of the earth, and every island of the sea. Let us review again, for the last time, a few of the testimonies which we have heard, and visit once more, but only for a moment, the lands which we have already traversed.

1. During half a century, Protestant writers, filled with the same involuntary admiration which the pagans had often manifested with greater energy, have not ceased to celebrate the courage, devotion, and charity of the Catholic missionaries in China. From Ricci to the latest martyr who gained his crown

---

(1) III Kings, xviii, 24.

only yesterday, they have recognised, without understanding, the same tokens of a supernatural calling. Even Morrison was constantly comparing them with himself, though apparently without deriving instruction from the contrast. « He is willing to sacrifice himself — he offers himself up to God, » is his account of one whom he could agree to admire, at a safe distance. « They will be equalled by few, and rarely exceeded by any, » is the joint confession of Mr Milne and Mr Medhurst, « for they spared not their lives unto the death, but overcame by the blood of the Lamb. » « That they were holy and devoted men, » says Mr Malcolm, « is proved by their pure lives and serene martyrdom. » « They appeared to me, » observes Mr Power, « to surpass any men I ever met with, they were so forgetful of self, so full of pity and compassion for others. » « Their self-denying hard labour is truly wonderful, » says M^r D'Ewes. « It is a pity that all missionaries are not equally self-sacrificing, » adds Mr Scarth. « We cannot refuse them our respect, » says Colonel Mountain. « *They* regard neither difficulties nor discouragements, » writes Mr Sirr. « I cannot refrain, » exclaims Mr Robertson, « from admiring the heroism, the devotedness, and the superiority of the Catholic missionaries. » And the pagans repeat, but with deeper emphasis and more exact discrimination, the reluctant eulogies of Protestants, humbly begging forgiveness of the apostles whom they torment, or asking a blessing from those whom they murder.

On the other hand, the same impartial witnesses, who had seen them at their work, speak only with sorrow or disgust of the Protestant missionaries in

China, in spite of active sympathy with their religious opinions. Morrison, they tell us, « never ventured out of his house, » preached only « with the doors securely locked, » gave books with such precautions that « it could not be traced to him, » and only ventured on operations which were « not of a dazzling or heroic order. » Milne « found preaching the Gospel difficult in China, » and ran away. Gutzlaff made his fortune, and then « ceased to call himself a missionary. » Medhurst could only repeat, « Why are we not successful in conversions? » Tomlin abandoned the work to « the Pope, Mahomed, and Brahma. » Smith was content to revile the men whom he dared not imitate, to fling bibles on « dry banks, » and to provoke the scornful rebukes of his own flock. The rest « listened to far-off tidings of what was happening in the interior, » or « drank wine and played at cards on sunday, » or « refused to visit the sick in the hospitals, » or accepted « a skulking and precarious sojourn in obscurity and disguise. » Such is the Protestant account of them. « They surround themselves with comforts, » says Mr Power, « squabble for the best houses, higgle for wares, and provoke contempt by a lazy life. » « We are grieved to the heart's core, » writes Mr Sirr, « to see too many of the Protestant missionaries occupy their time in secular pursuits, trading and trafficking. » « They are mere stipendiary agents of a company, » says one Protestant writer. « They will not encounter risks or hazard dangers like the Catholics, » reports a second. « They adopt a low tone of morality and bring humiliation on their order, » writes a third. And the pagan Chinese, quite as discerning as these English and American Protestants, and much more exacting in their estimate of religious teachers, speak of them in their houses, and greet them in the streets, with the title of « *Lie-Preaching Devils.* »

The contrast exhibited in these testimonies need not surprise us. How should even Protestants consent to employ milder terms in describing the two classes, of whom the one consists of such men as Ricci and Schaal, Verbiest and Parennin, de Rhodes and de Fontaney, Borie and Imbert, Jaccard and Gagelin, de Maistre and Chapdelaine, Marette and Perboyre, Sanz and Dufresse, Melchior and Diaz, and hundreds like them; and the other of such as Morrison and Gutzlaff, Tomlin and Kidd, Gillespie and Williams, Edkins and Smith! (1)

(1) The *latest* appreciation by a Protestant authority of the true character of Protestant missions in China, and of those who conduct them, arrived in England after the second chapter of this work was printed. It is sufficiently remarkable to claim our attention, even at the inconvenience of a long note. The *Hong Kong Daily Press*, a journal devoted to British and Protestant interests, thus estimates, in 1861, both the missionaries and their work.

Of Dr Smith, the Anglican bishop, this authority speaks as follows. « The conduct of the bishop is most reprehensible... For the last three years we feel sure he has not done two months work in his diocese. He draws his stipend in consideration of the performance of specified duties — those duties he neglects for other vocations which are more lucrative or agreeable, and we will defy him to reconcile his conduct to common honesty, to say nothing about his duties as a bishop. »

Of the missionaries *generally*, this is the account of the same unsuspicious witness. After recounting the total failure of their costly but barren efforts, he adds; « Instead of attempting to remedy the defect, they are too conceited to admit it. *There is as*

SUMMARY.   413

The converts, as we have seen, — of whom a million belong to the Church, and « five, » by a sanguine estimate, to the Sects, — display the same difference of character as their teachers. What the *Catholic* Chinese were, from the sixteenth to the nineteenth century, we know; what they have been since 1805, hostile witnesses have told us. In spite of torments never exceeded in duration and intensity, more than

much devotion in all the Protestant Missionaries we know of in the South of China as there is in a bootjack. Their shameless indifference to their unscrupulous *laches* is really incredible to those who have not witnessed it. We have tried time and again to arouse them to a sense of their duties, but it seems to us that they are dead to the voice of truth, and are content to eat the bread of idleness, so long as they possess the power to deceive the patrons who maintain them. »

Of Protestant *Education* in China, and its results, contrasting them expressly with Catholic efforts in the same field, we have this equally candid account. « *All* the schemes which have hitherto been attempted, have resulted in utter failures. English education has been given to Chinese youths with no other object that we could see *but to qualify them for hypocrites or for sharpers.* »

Finally, here is the testimony of the same witness, given on the spot, and in the very midst of the scenes and the men whom he describes, to the admitted results of *all* the Protestant Missions in China. « The fact is, *that Protestant Missionary labour in the South of China is a grand swindle*, and the sooner it is exposed and denounced the better. In this part of the Empire, Christianity among the natives has turned into ashes, while further North it has generated into blasphemy. And there are Missionaries who come forward and actually advocate both the ashes and the blasphemy as the true types of our religion, and make their deluded patrons believe it too. »

And this is the *latest* account of Protestantism in China! The whole article of the Chinese journal will be found in the *Weekly Register*, November 16, 1861.

half a million have been added to the Church since Timkowski visited Pekin, and found that, « many thousand persons had embraced Christianity, even among the members of the imperial family, » and that the President of the Criminal Tribunal in that city was obliged to relax his severity, because « nearly all his relations and servants were Christians. » And so exactly have these Chinese neophytes, in every province of the empire, resembled the primitive disciples, that even the Mandarins have been forced to confess from their judgment seats, in presence of so much virtue and heroism, « Truly this Christian religion is a good religion! »

The rare Protestant converts, on the other hand, the scum of a Chinese sea-port, dishonest pensioners of an immoral bounty, — who at one time run off with « the communion plate, » at another with « cases of type, » or whatsoever else they can lay their hands upon, — have been everywhere of such a class, that, in the words of a candid witness, « anxiety to obtain them has been converted into anxiety about those who were obtained. » And even the teachers and catechists employed by English or American missionaries, brutalised by opium, and quite as willing, as Dr Berncastle observes, to teach Buddhism as Anglicanism or Methodism for the same wages, only accept Protestant baptism as a condition of their employment, and appreciate it so warmly, that their whole care thenceforth is to prevent others from sharing the baptism with them, lest they should share their wages also.

2. The contrast revealed to us in the Trans-Gangetic provinces is not less complete in those

which lie to the west of the Himalays. To compare
St. Francis-Xavier with Dr Thomas Middleton, —
de 'Nobili with « the rich and fashionable » Kiernander, — the martyr de Britto, who won tens of
thousands to Christ, with Schwartz, whose salaried
converts « were proverbial for their profligacy, » —
Laynez, majestic as the patriarchs of old, with
the love-sick and tearful Martyn, — Borghese, who
smiled at torture, with the ex-minstrel Buchanan, —
Martin, « the martyr of charity, » with the vain and
flippant Rhenius, — Bouchet, whom men compared
to St. Gregory Thaumaturgus, with the refined but
semi-pagan Heber, — Belmonte, the martyr; and
Bouttari, the « penitent without spot; » and Carvalho, beaten to death; and Beschi, at whose feet
the wisest Hindoo was content to sit as a scholar;
and hundreds more, who lived like St. Paul or
St. John the Baptist, — with Corrie, or Wilson, or
Cotton, respectable fathers of families, who consider
that « asceticism is no part of the Gospel system, »
and live in harmony with their creed, — this would
be both irksome and unprofitable. By the first the
Gospel was preached in India with such irresistible
power, in spite of the absence of all human aids,
that but for the events in Europe which tore away the
apostles from their unfinished work, even Protestants have frankly confessed, « the whole land would
probably have been converted. » As late as the middle
of the eighteenth century, they were still labouring
with such astonishing success, still fascinated the
Hindoo with such persuasive holiness, that « no
missionary converted less than a thousand pagans
annually, » while some gained almost as many every

month. And if the work of these sublime preachers of the Cross, which survived the combined neglect and oppression of sixty years, has been suspended, or only imperfectly resumed; it is not that the race of heroes and martyrs is extinct, but because the Hindoo has learned, from the example of his English teachers, to regard Christianity with such ever deepening contempt and abhorrence, that, as he has often declared, he « would rather go down into hell « than accept such a religion, or consort with its professors. When the English are driven out of India, an event which we may anticipate from the justice of God, the apostles of the Church will contend a second time, on more equal terms, with the evil spirits who rule her. Then the Hindoo will have before him once more only teachers whose lives illustrate their doctrines, and manifest, even to his dull gaze, the presence of God; then he will have seen the last both of the so-called missionaries whose luxury shocks and whose contradictions revolt him, and of their wretched disciples, atheists and outcasts, who only « become worse and worse, » as one witness has told us, whom the Anglo-Indians themselves refuse to admit into their houses, and « whose lax morality, » as English writers have honestly proclaimed, « shocks the feelings of even their *heathen* countrymen. »

3. The island of Ceylon fills but a small place on the earth's surface, yet if we seek a demonstration that God works by the Church, and not by the Sects, we may find it here. There is no need to compare again the two classes of missionaries, but who can be insensible to the contrast in their disciples? How uniformly they display their respective characteristics!

What history is more noble, more suggestive of divine gifts and influences, than that of the Catholic Cingalese, as narrated by Protestant writers? « Neither corruption nor coercion, » says Sir Emerson Tennent, — and we know how freely both were used, — « could induce them to abjure their faith. » For three hundred years these feeble Asiatics, by nature effeminate and pusillanimous, have endured every imaginable trial; first the fierce opposition of their pagan countrymen, which they soon wore out by joyful martyrdom; then the merciless cruelty, or more demoralising bribery, of the Dutch; and finally, during the present century, the patient artifices of the English and Americans, lavishing gold on every side, setting traps for them at one time in the shape of a school at another of a hospital, and always beginning again to day, with fresh resources, the project which they tried in vain yesterday. Yet the Cingalese, even peasants and fishermen, only smile at the policy which costs so much and effects so little. Filled, like their fathers, with that supernatural faith which outlives all assaults, they compel their most cruel adversaries to confess their inflexible stability, religious zeal, and unbroken unity; while even their pagan neighbours openly compare their loving obedience, generosity, and devotion, with the dissensions, incredulity, and indifference of their English rulers.

And what has Protestantism effected, with its gold and its tracts, its government patronage and missionary pensions, among the natives of Ceylon? It has gathered, as its own advocates tell us, at enormous cost, and after the incessant efforts of half a century, a handful of degraded followers, whose allegiance is never secure for twenty-four hours, who worship devils in secret, hurry from the Protestant temple to *purify* themselves in their own, and when sickness or sorrow comes upon them abandon in all haste the impotent religion which they had affected to adopt, but which has made no impression on their heart, has left their conscience untouched, their intellect uninformed, and their will unsubdued.

4. In the Antipodes, England and Protestantism found three nations expecting their rule : two they have already destroyed, and the third is making haste to disappear. Nothing, we learn from official authorities in 1860, can now save « a population which has once reached such a state of decrepitude. » And their moral corresponds with their physical condition. « Uncleanness, » says one of their Protestant teachers, « outwardly and inwardly, in body and mind, in all their thoughts, words, and actions, » is as rottenness in the bones of this doomed people. After the efforts of fifty years, and an expenditure which baffles computation, this is their condition, by the confession of the missionaries themselves; while the *religion* of their ill-fated disciples, though often educated by them from infancy, is frankly described by the most competent witnesses as « a mere name, » or at best, « a rude mixture of paganism and the cross. » When sick or afflicted, « they appeal, » says Dr Thomson, like the Protestant Cingalese, « to their old gods for health; » while in the hour of prosperity, they still secretly honour them with prudent foresight, « lest they should punish them with sickness. » Yet New Zealand, to which Protestantism has proved so deadly a malediction, enjoys the presence of five

Anglican bishops, besides a multitude of preachers of various sects; whose combined labours have been so utterly barren of all but woe to this once noble and vigorous race, that a Protestant writer could unwittingly publish in 1859 this bitter satire, « The work of Christianity in New Zealand is only begun ! » It will be finished, we may anticipate, when the last New Zealander has sunk into the grave which is already yawning for him.

Such, by Protestant testimony, has been the conclusion of all missionary labours in these islands, as far as the natives are concerned; while the British colonists themselves, we are told by those who know them best, « have no religious character, » except what Mr Cholmondeley considers peculiar to his Anglican co-religionists, and which he briefly describes as « the pretence and hypocrisy of the whole thing. » These offshoots of the English Establishment are destined, he fears, to become « either Roman Catholics, or atheists and materialists; » while other writers deplore that they are so incurably apathetic or perfidiously insubordinate, that not only « no interest was taken by the public » in any of the projects by which Dr Selwyn vainly essayed to stimulate their languid zeal, but the iteration of fervent appeals to their « church principles » only led to their ostentatiously sharing their funds with « the ministers of different religious bodies. » Such is the appropriate conclusion of a history which began, as Dr Lang has informed us, by adultery, drunkenness, and fraud in the « heads of the mission; » and which has exhibited to us Protestant missionaries, during thirty successive years, stumbling over one another in their hot haste to amass gold, and to rob the unsuspecting native both of his land and its produce; while it displayed the same class to the astonished New Zealander as chiefly occupied « in neutralising each other's labours, » or, in the words of Dr Selwyn, « in inflicting upon them the curses of disunion, » and introducing « a counterpart of our own divided and contentious church. » Is it wonderful that the sagacious Maori, more impressed by these phenomena — the only results of Protestantism which are absolutely uniform — than Dr Selwyn, perhaps because less familiar with them, should decide at last, that « Heathenism with love is better than Christianity without it? »

What Bishop Pompallier and his colleagues would have done for these noble savages, now corrupted almost beyond cure, we may easily infer from the triumphs of missionaries of the same order, in many a land, among aboriginal tribes immeasurably more ferocious and degraded. The Omagua was more brutal, the Guarani more bloodthirsty, the Huron less intelligent, than the savage of New Zealand; yet these and a hundred other tribes accepted Christianity and civilization when offered to them by Monroy or Cavallero, by Rasles or Mesnard, and with such fruit, that in vast communities of men so lately sunk in barbarism « not a single mortal sin was committed in twelve months, » and that at the present hour their piety and docility are still scoffingly attested by Protestant travellers. But the Catholic missionary in these less favoured islands, encountered by weapons more fatal than the knife or the axe, has struggled with only partial success against the more terrible martyrdom of universal corruption which he came too late to heal, of sordid avarice which even his example failed to admonish, and of the incessant religious dissensions which had already reared the pinnacles of the City of Confusion, before he had time to lay the foundations of the City of God.

5. There is no need to trace again the contrast noticed by De la Gravière and La Place between the natives of the Philippines and of Tahiti, of Wallis and Rarotonga, of Futuna and Hawaii, — between Christians exulting in the faith, and willing to die in its defence; and savages, robbed even of their natural virtues, abhorring the human religion which they were paid to profess, and flinging it away with disgust when the power to control them was lost. Why should we compare again such men as Medina and Sanvitores, Chevron and Bataillon, Chanel and Epaille, Grange and Bachelot, *all martyrs* in fact or desire; with such as Cheever and Bingham, Henry and Williams, Lawry and Bicknell, — traders and adventurers, with hardly an exception, hateful to the barbarians whom they oppressed, as well as to the English and American merchants, who found in them their keenest rivals? What is there in common between missionaries who are described by the *same* Protestant witnesses, on the one hand, as « men of learning and agreeable manners, » « exemplary in all their actions, » who « astonished the natives by their enthusiasm in the cause of Christ; » and, on the other, according to Sir Edward Belcher and Mr Forbes, Sir George Simpson and Mr Melville, Dr Ruschenberger and Mr Wheeler, Dr Meyen and Captain Erskine, and twenty more, as « tyrannical fanatics, »

or « madly intolerant, « or defiled by « monetary dirtinesses, « or blind with « greedy cupidity, » or fornicators like Lewis and his companions, or apostates like Veeson and Broomhall, or, at best, as intent only upon « enjoying their rich farms » — so that, as Mr Walpole unwillingly confessed, « between the men themselves no comparison could be dared? »

6. And what, again, is the history of African missions but a contrast from the first page to the last? Who is so blind as not to behold God on one side, with all His gifts, and on the other, only man, naked and feeble, busy in a work which always fails, and sowing the seeds of a harvest which he never reaps? See in North Africa the sons of St. Francis and St. Dominic, gladly dying by hundreds that so, by this sacrifice of propitiation, the wrath of God may one day be appeased, a Christian nation rule from the sea to the foot of the Atlas, and light dawn again over the land where once St. Augustine preached. In the East, see the same apostolic workmen braving all dangers and enduring all afflictions, — in Egypt and in Nubia, in the mountains of Abyssinia and by the shores of the White Nile, — passing through Gondar and Sennar, Enarea and Kaffa, and daring to penetrate even to Darfour and the distant Soudan, — patient in all temptations, returning to day to the spot from which they were driven yesterday, doing battle with Pagan, Moslem, or Monophysite, and deeming the toils of a life too richly recompensed if they can gather together a few hundreds here, a few thousands there, first fruits of a richer harvest, and presage of greater victories to come. And in this warfare of heroes, too often « vic-

tims, » as an English writer has told us, « to the excessive austerity of their lives, » but « leaving a memory venerated even by the pagans; » let us note once more what men can become whom God has raised to the dignity of apostles, « and whose funeral chant is sung, » as Mʳ Hamilton relates, by the Negro and the Nubian, kindled to love and admiration by virtues which they justly deemed more than human, and by sacrifices which are precious enough to win a blessing even for the race of Cham. Who among modern missionaries comes nearer to the old heroic type than Jacobis, anointed on the rock of Dhalac by a prelate a fugitive like himself, yet winning homage from German *savans* and English tourists as well as from the kings of Tigrè and Shoa, and enthroned at last in Gondar as high priest of God, and delegate of the Vicar of Christ; or Massaia, for fifteen years a wanderer between the Arabian Gulf and the mountains of Ethiopia, insensible to pain and want, « sorrowful yet always rejoicing, needy yet enriching many, having nothing yet possessing all things, » and willing to live thus to the end, that so, in his own words, he may « plant the Cross and kindle the evangelical fire » in that rude Gallas nation, whose fierce tribes have already yielded to the service of God five priests, and twice as many aspirants to the ecclesiastical state.

Compare this history, which begins with St. Francis of Assisi and ends with Massaia and Jacobis, with those records of weakness and shame, of strife and impurity, which make up the tale of Protestant missions in Africa, as related by Protestant historians. It is from *them* that we have learned, for we have used no other testimony, what their co-religionists are, and what they have done, in Africa. In Morocco you will hear, not of martyrs or confessors, but of the solitary Protestant minister, who scattered bibles which were thrown into the fire, and then ran away amid the hisses of the people; in Algeria, of Mʳ Ewald, whose operations were of the same nature, and led to the same result; in Tunis, of the Scotch mission, « since abandoned, » and of certain pretended converts whom the British Consul briefly described as « those wretches. » In Egypt you will find the English engaged in their usual work, and avenging their own religious misadventures by intriguing to prevent the reconciliation of the Coptic nation with the Catholic Church, content to mar in all lands what they imitate in none; or educating a few Egyptians and Arabs at Cairo, who, as Dʳ Durbin has told us, « resume, » when they quit the school, — like the Protestant students in China, India, Ceylon, and everywhere else, — the habits and principles which their unfruitful education was designed to correct. In Abyssinia you will meet Dʳ Gobat and Dʳ Krapf, both now reposing amid other scenes, of whom the first failed to attract the sympathy of the Abyssinians, who refused to believe that he was not a « Mussulman, » and the last has left nothing more notable on record than the prodigious statement, which would have surprised the disciples of St. Paul, that « an unmarried missionary cannot eventually prosper; » while each gained a solitary convert, of whom one « turned Muhammedan at Cairo, » and the other was « the unrenewed and unregenerate Wolda Gabriel. » In the West,

where the sons of St. Ignatius, before they were
banished, won whole nations, who still strive, after
the lapse of three quarters of a century, to repeat
their half-forgotten lessons, — Mr Murray tells us of
« the flagrant misconduct » of the first Protestant
emissaries, and of Mr Horneman who developed into
« a highly respectable marabout, or mussulman
saint; » and Mr Moister celebrates the Anglican
chaplain who never made a convert in fifty years,
and, unmindful of Oxford theology, worshipped the
fetish on his death bed; and Mr Walker commemo-
rates the Anglican « communicants, » who « obstinately adhered to their superstious usages ; » and
Mr Cruickshank the « converts, » who « exhibited a
a uniformity of weakness truly humiliating and deplorable; » and Mr Duncan the « scholars, » whose
knowledge only made them « more perfect in villainy. » Lastly, Dr Armstrong and Mr Calderwood
lament that « the Caffres have refused the Gospel, »
with the exception of a very small number of nominal
disciples, who, as a multitude of eye witnesses declare, « are the worst behaved of the whole tribe ; »
while the Protestant Hottentots, in whom Mr Moffat
detected « the unction of the Spirit, » are described
by the same authorities as « notoriously the most
idle and worthless of their nation : » and even their
teachers are said to be so incurably addicted to agricultural and trading pursuits, in preference to missionary toils, that Mr Merriman reproachfully observes, « I meet with examples of this wherever I
go. » They are Protestants, once more, from whom
we learn these facts, and without whose testimony
it would have been impossible to prove them.

7. In the Levant, where « British protection is fully enjoyed, » we have seen the usual enormous and perfectly useless expenditure, by agents whose « utter unprofitableness, » as Admiral Slade relates, « cannot be sufficiently pointed out. » We have witnessed the customary distribution of thousands of books, during more than a quarter of a century, which nobody read, and which it was discovered too late, when half a million volumes had been printed, that nobody was allowed to read. We have seen American missionaries courting their Athenian hosts with flattering speech, till the latter cast them out as « heresiarchs from the caverns of hell, » and then repaying the unexpected affront by reviling the contemptuous Greeks as « worse than Romanists. » We have visited the Malta College, with its ardent professors and ingenious lodgers, speculating with unfailing success upon the well known qualities of their English benefactors, and always repeating with quiet assurance the artifices which experience had taught them would never be practised in vain. We have seen too its choicest guests, — Achilli, who fascinated the too credulous Anglican with dexterous hints « that he would join himself to our church, » but who chose at last, when English benevolence decayed, the church of Mr Swedenborg; and Naudi, instructing an imaginary congregation of ideal converts, and repaying the bounty of the Church Missionary Society with « annual reports, » till Dr Wolf discovered, many years too late, that Levantine Protestantism was a pleasant fable, and Naudi a prosperous cheat.

In Turkey, we have found the missionaries from

beyond the Atlantic attracted in crowds by « the comforts and pleasant things about this life in the East, » and celebrating the « moral sublimity » of missionary nuptials; but not even attempting, as M**r** Walpole remarks, « any conversion except of the Christians. » We have been introduced also to their « converts, » a few score of shrewd Armenians, « infidels and radicals, » as one of their own preachers has assured us, « who deserve no sympathy from the Christian public, » but who never ask it in vain from men who are too much in want of disciples not to judge their frailties with indulgence. In Syria, as D**r** Durbin deplores, « they have come into collision with each other, » disputing before the Turk and the Greek about « the validity of their respective ministries. » In Jerusalem, where they inhabit palaces with « marble floors, » and bid against one another for Hebrew catechumens, who have learned to consider Christian Baptism « the only good business they have, » they run away, as D**r** Robinson notices, at the first rumour of pestilence, and leave the missionaries of the Cross to die amidst the sick whom *they* have abandoned. Lastly, in Armenia, where M**r** Perkins and his opulent colleagues disposed of about twice the revenue which the great Republic allots to its President, and rode forth on « horses of every breed » of which a monarch might have envied the possession, though half the hierarchy of Armenia accepted their pensions, « their expensive establishments, » as their friend D**r** Wagner detected, « have made no converts. » Such, as their own witnesses relate, is the history of Protestant missions in the Levant, Syria, and Armenia, — of

what even their warmest advocates call in derision
« their useless missions in the East. »

On the other hand, we have seen missionaries
of a different class, more solicitous to abide in
poverty than their rivals to secure luxury and ease,
toiling during three centuries in the same lands, —
dying in the galleys of Constantinople, or in the
plague-stricken cities of Syria, — spreading far and
wide the blessings of education, from the shores of
the Bosphorus to the mouth of the Euphrates, and
from the coasts of Palestine to the borders of the
Caspian Sea, — attracting scholars « from Beyrout
and Damascus, from Persia and Egypt, and even
from Nubia and Abyssinia, » — « saving millions of
souls, » as a generous English writer has told us,
and « spreading a sea of benefits, silently and unos-
tentatiously, » wherever Mussulmans rule and Christians suffer; till at length they have won to the faith,
and are daily winning out of every eastern nation,
that multitude of disciples whose « liberality and intelligence, » « decided superiority, » and « elevation
in the scale of civilisation, » even the most hostile
witnesses reluctantly attribute to their reconciliation
with the Catholic Church. Already, as we have seen,
« nearly all Syria, » the whole of Chaldea, and the
greater part of Armenia, have accepted their message, or announced their willingness to do so; while
every oriental tribe, easily discriminating between
the lowly ambassadors of the Church and the
worldly and contentious prophets of the Sects,
'draws nearer to them year by year; and even the
Turk, moved by the exceeding charity of those ministering angels who labour with them, and rebu-

king by a purer instinct the insatiable malice which can revile even such as these, asks in astonishment, « Whether they came down thus from Heaven? »

8. Lastly, in America, — but why should we resume a history so lately reviewed, and in which there is *all* on one side, and *nothing* on the other? Why should we compare again the divine ministry which has added millions of Indians to the fold of Christ, with the unblest efforts of men who have outraged many, but converted none, — have depopulated regions wider than the empires of the old world, — and have left at last, as a record and monument of their work, only a miserable remnant alive, till they have time to destroy *them* also, throughout the whole vast continent where the Anglo-Saxon reigns? Why should we recapitulate the details of that unmatched contrast, which even the savage was able to discern, and which forced from the thoughtful historian of man and his fortunes the sorrowful avowal — « It must be allowed to reflect honour on the Roman Catholic Church, and to cast a deep shade on the history of Protestantism? »

Such, in a few words, and in its general outlines, is the Contrast, of which every feature is attested by Protestant evidence, between the work of the Church and the work of the Sects; between the fruitful ministry of apostles, lifted by omnipotent love above human infirmity, and the sterile craft of « mere stipendiaries, » who have only succeeded in convincing the heathen in all lands, by their own confession, how little claim the religion of which such as they were exponents had to his respect. Yet that religion, so boastful at home so impotent abroad, is declared by its professors to be something higher and holier than even primitive Christianity; for it is nothing less, they everywhere proclaim, than a *second revelation*, designed to correct the failures of the first, — a *reformation* of that marred and tainted gospel which, according to the Anglican or Lutheran hypothesis, its unsuccessful author vainly strove to preserve from corruption and decay, — a *new Ark*, constructed to replace that which foundered long ages ago, — a *more perfect redemption*, to remedy one which Jesus wrought and Peter announced, but which had miserably lost, « by the space of nine hundred years and odd » (1) its power and efficacy.

It is true that this second revelation, unlike the first, was promulgated neither from Mount Sinai nor from Jerusalem, but from London, Geneva, and Glasgow; and that its most conspicuous prophets were neither saints nor martyrs, but polygamist princes, lascivious priests, and apostate monks. And if this original defect be deemed insufficient to determine the real nature of the new religion, inaugurated under such unusual auspices, and introduced by such questionable agents, the facts reviewed in these pages may perhaps assist our judgment. If the Author of Christianity co-operated, as some suppose, in its first promulgation, the care of its subsequent fortunes has certainly escaped His attention; and if we accept the theory of its advocates, we shall be obliged to admit, that the God of Moses and St. Paul has utterly failed, in a second attempt as feeble and fruitless as the first, to found a stable religion, or to build up a

(1) Anglican Homily, *On Peril of Idolatry.*

permanent church, by whose ministry the pagan world should be brought to a knowledge of its Creator. For they are Protestant witnesses who have convinced us of these facts, — that, in spite of the new revelation of the sixteenth century, He can neither hinder the old and « corrupt » faith, which He was supposed to have abolished, from gaining victories which all His efforts cannot secure for the partisans of the new, — nor take from the ministers of the ancient Church the supernatural virtues which He unaccountably forgets to bestow upon their rivals, — nor refuse, however reluctant, to place on their heads the crowns of glory destined for other objects of His predilection, but which *they*, incurably earthly and incorrigibly human, decline to earn, and are unable to merit. If the Anglican or Lutheran hypothesis were true, and it was really the divine purpose in these latter days to supersede the Church by the Sects, and henceforth to dispense blessings and to ransom heathens by the agency of the latter, the advocates of that hypothesis will be unable to avoid this intolerable conclusion; that there is nothing more infirm and impotent than the imaginary potentate from whom they profess to derive their religion, but whom they represent as always stumbling from one failure to another; who can create, by their own account, but cannot sustain, can resolve but never accomplish; and who, if the Reformation theory be true, though he has a throne in the midst of ruins, is equally unable to teach and to govern; can make instruments, but never use them; and continues in all ages as deplorably incapable of communicating his own will as of securing its execution.

If, however, on the other hand, we confess with St. Francis and St. Bernard, with Bossuet and Fenelon, with Anchieta and Baraza, with Peter Claver and Las Casas, with Brebeuf and Lallemand, with the doctors and apostles, the saints and martyrs of every land, that it is by the Church and not by the Sects that the God of Christians works, then every contradiction disappears and every difficulty is removed; then He has accomplished every purpose and fulfilled every promise; and Catholics, remembering the miracles which He has wrought by the Church, and by her alone, during the three last centuries as in the fifteen which preceded them, may still repeat with grateful adoration the joyous canticle of their fathers, — « Who is so great a God as our God? And what nation is there so great, who hath God so nigh unto them, as the Lord our God is in all things that we call upon Him for? »

It has been our attempt in these volumes, neglecting the familiar controversies of other days, to display the Church and the Sects *in action*, in every land where there were Gentiles to be converted; nor can that be deemed a partial or inadequate test of both, which has had three centuries for its period, and the world for its sphere. The general results of its application are now sufficiently manifest, but there are still certain points of detail which claim a moment's attention, even in this rapid summary.

That the agents of the Sects, having neither the gifts nor the calling of apostles, should have failed to convert the heathen, will surprise none who believe that such a work can be accomplished only by the co-operation of God. But the results of their intrusion into the apostolic office have not been simply negative. This would be an imperfect estimate of their failure. It is to their presence in every pagan land that their own disciples attribute, in moments of candour, what even they call the « growing hatred » of the pagan world towards Christianity and its professors. Protestantism, we have said, is the last scourge of Heathenism; and this is true in many ways, but especially in this, — that it has everywhere set up, not only a spurious type of Christian life, indolent effeminate and luxurious, which even the barbarian has ridiculed as scarcely less earthly than his own; but a miserable caricature of the Christian Church, in which he has detected only weakness and confusion, ceaseless strife and unappeasable disorder. Every where, therefore, he has confounded in a common disdain the few whose natural gifts might have merited his respect, with the crowd of adventurers who accompanied them. Martyn and Schwartz, like Tomlin and Gutzlaff, were equally in his eyes the salaried agents of some impure sect; Heber and Selwyn, no less than Morrison or Edkins, only amused him by the incoherence of their doctrine and the inconsistency of their practice, or revolted him by the incontinence of their domestic life. They were too like himself to suggest the belief that they had a mission from heaven, and too eagerly solicitous about common joys to encourage the idea that they had divorced themselves from earth. He perceived also that even these few, in spite of their higher qualities, came to him, like all the rest, with a « Protest » written on their foreheads against the only Church which he could have venerated; and when he saw these men, the chiefs of their sect, tearing the Seamless Robe into a thousand fragments, and running to him with the pieces in their hands to show him what they had done, — can we marvel if he turned his back upon them, or answered with scorn, like the Jews of old, *Quid ad nos? What is that to us?* Let us see, then, once more how the heathen have judged the Sects, and the incessant mutual conflicts which even they can trace to their true source, and in what language they have expressed their judgment. There is nothing in the whole history of Protestant missions more worthy of our attention.

1. « The existence of profound divisions among *ourselves*, » Lord Elgin observed during his residence in China, is « one of the first truths which we Christians reveal to the heathen ». « There is no greater barrier, » says an intelligent British official in that country, « to the spread of the Gospel than the division and splitting which have taken place among the various orders of Christians themselves. » « The great and fatal error, » adds a third witness, « is the rivalry of religious sects, and the attempt to gain followers at the expense of each other's tenets. » The Chinese, who contemplates this singular spectacle with a sentiment of compassion for the « outer barbarian » who cannot even agree about his religion, judiciously remarks, as Mr Colledge relates, « that Europe and America, » which have already sent him more than twenty different sects, « must have as many Christs as China has gods. » Yet the *Catholic* Chinese, united in every province of the empire in the same unvarying faith, have displayed during three centuries such inflexible unity, and

such ardent charity, that one of the most cruel of
their emperors declared in a public proclamation,—
« All who become Christians, whether rich or
poor, directly they embrace this religion have such
an affection for one another, that they seem to be of
one bone and one flesh. » Never, since the primitive
ages, was that word of our Lord more impressively
fulfilled ; « By this shall all men *know* that you are
My disciples, if you have love one for another. »

2. « The discordant tenets of the missionaries » in
India was deplored long ago by Dr Middleton with
unavailing regret; and in our own day, Mr Russell
still notes « the astonishment of the Asiatics » at
the implacable divisions of the various sects, « all
claiming to be of one religion. » « Their observation
uniformly is, » says M^r Le Bas, « that they should
think much better of Christianity, if there were not
quite so many different kinds of it. » It is a well
know jest among the Brahmins, who have contemplated the various English, German, and American
religions in the cities of Bengal and Madras, and
have watched with amusement their fretful jealousies and eager rivalry, that « their professors would
do far better to agree among themselves what Christianity *is*, before they pretend to teach it to others. »

3. In Ceylon, we have learned from Sir Emerson
Tennent, « the choice of sects leads to utter bewil-
derment. » « The native, » says another, « is perfectly aghast at the variety of choice. » Can we blame
him if he concludes that Christianity is a mere imposture, unworthy of his serious attention; until he
comes in contact with that ancient form of it which,
like God, « is the same yesterday, to day, and for

ever, » and which has already captivated the allegiance of so many of his countrymen? « The Protestant Church, » says an Anglo-Cingalese writer, who had heard the pagan comments upon « her multitudinous sects and schisms, » « has no chance in competition with the Roman Catholic; » but he does not appear to have asked himself, like the more discerning pagan, why the one is a very symbol of confusion and disorder, while the other remains eternally unchanged?

4. The bitter fruits of Protestantism in New Zealand have been described to us by Dr Selwyn. « The spirit of controversy, » he says, « is everywhere found to prevail, in many cases to the entire exclusion of all simplicity of faith. » We have seen what was his own mode of dealing with the evil. « The spirit of Christianity, » observes the Rev. Elijah Hoole, « is lost in the form, and the very form itself has become the subject of incessant and angry dispute. » « We have the awful sight, » adds the Rev. Mr Turton, « of father and son, mother and daughter, hating each other with a mortal hatred. » Such is, in all the earth, the deadly influence of Protestantism, — the observation of which forced one New Zealand chief to say, in reply to the overtures of a missionary, « When you have agreed amongst yourselves which is the right road, I may perhaps be induced to take it; » and suggested to another, whose experience of Protestant christianity had only occasioned a speedy relapse into heathenism, the ingenious taunt, « One beehive is good, but many are troublesome. »

5. In the islands of the Pacific, where, as Mr Wal-

pole observes, « every variety of dissenters exists among the teachers, » who, as Dr Ruschenberger adds, « deal damnation in a peculiar slang to all whose opinions differ from their own, » the poor savage makes the usual reflections, « as one sect succeeds another; » but as he is perfectly indifferent to all of them, and only estimates them according to their relative wealth, the varieties of their chameleon creed add nothing whatever to the contempt which he feels for the worldliness, cupidity, and injustice which is common to them all.

6. In Africa, — which abounds, as Dr Armstrong and his companions lamented, in « church troubles, » and where Mr Merriman deplores the ineffectiveness of English operations, « in consequence of their religious divisions, » — Dr Livingstone has told us, that « the mission stations are mere pauper establishments, » unlike « the self-supporting primitive monasteries, pioneers of civilization and agriculture from which we even now reap benefits; » and that one result of « such a variety of Christian sects, « each maintaining a pauper-establishment for the disciples whom they would never attract without it, is this — « that converts of one denomination are eagerly adopted by another, » to the great detriment, as he intimates, of their spiritual progress. The Presbyterian Hottentot, whatever his frailties, knows that the rival Wesleyan « establishment » is always open to him; the disorderly Baptist is sure of a hearty welcome among the Anglicans; the refractory Anglican is embraced with joy by the American Congregationalists ; the United Brethren dispute the honour of entertaining him with the Rhenish Mis-

sionary Society; and the Hottentot himself, solicitous only about his next meal, rejoices in the multiplicity of institutions where a new profession of faith will at least allay the pangs of hunger, perhaps even secure the luxury of a change of diet. Yet he uses these advantages without an emotion of gratitude, and « the moment the food and lodging are discontinued, he does not scruple, » says Mʳ Andersson, « to treat his benefactor with ingratitude, and to load him with abuse. » So that even the savage of South Africa, gross and irrational as he is, takes exactly the same view of his relation to the various Protestant sects as the more subtle Chinese or Hindoo; while his rival hosts, unable to heal what even they call their « accursed divisions, » make ineffectual attempts to hide them, — like the Anglican Archdeacon who humbly suggested a *joint-service* to the Wesleyan preacher, lest the barbarians should detect the discord which he devised this characteristic mode of concealing.

7. In Syria, as Dʳ Durbin has informed us, the Protestant missionaries, doomed to eternal warfare, « have come into collision with each other in the midst of these ancient churches, » — for it is the will of the imperious master whom they unwittingly serve, that they should display his banner in all lands. In Turkey, as Dʳ Southgate angrily records, they are only busy in promoting « horrid schism, » though he has no rebukes for the schism which he vainly struggled to establish himself, till his expensive failure led to his recall. In Armenia, as Mʳ Badger relates, the Americans proposed to veil the unwelcome fact « that there are *rival* Protestant sects

and interests, » by warning the Anglicans off the field — a suggestion which was perfectly unnecessary as they never thought of entering it, but which M`r` Badger warmly resented, and which he considered « as presumptuous as it is ludicrous. »

8. Lastly, America exhibits, on a still larger scale, and with the same fatal results which we have witnessed in every other land, the phenomena which mark the presence of Protestantism, and which make Christianity a laughing stock among all the races of the earth; so that one Indian Sachem observed, « If there is but *one* religion, why do white men differ so much about it? » — and another exclaimed, with a feeling of superiority which he did not attempt to conceal, « If I should have a mind to turn Christian, I could not tell what religion to be of. » A third displayed a still keener irony, when he retorted upon a Protestant missionary the lesson which he had taught him too well, and positively declined to become a Protestant on the Protestant ground, that « every man should paddle his canoe his own way. » Finally, a fourth, the chief of the Cree nation, after noticing the varieties of doctrine proposed to his tribe, lately assured M`r` Kane, that « as he did not know which was right, he thought they ought to call a council amongst themselves, and that then he would go with them all; but that *until they agreed* he would wait. » (1) Yet we have seen *Catholic* Indians, of many nations and climes, stedfastly adhering generation after generation, under all difficulties and temptations, to one unvarying doctrine, and

(1) *Wanderings*, etc., by Paul Kane; ch. XXIII, p. 393.

rejecting with vehement repugnance all the bribes and seductions of error; we have found Catholic Cherokees converting the Pagan Flatheads without the assistance of a missionary, and Christian Huron captives performing the same office for their Mohawk masters; nay more, we have seen the Indian warrior, in the fierce excitement of battle, embrace as a brother the fallen foe who had just aimed at his own life, because the sign of the cross had revealed to him that his enemy was a Catholic like himself.

Yet Protestant controversialists assure us, that this marvellous unity — which links in one brotherhood the savages of a hundred tribes, which suffering cannot rend nor corruption dissolve, and which *looks* so like the mysterious unity of the disciples of St. John and St. Paul — is only a trick of priestcraft, the result of some subtle organisation, some deep device of human policy! If it were so, we might be permitted to ask, why *they*, who boast of reason as if it were a gift peculiar to themselves, have never been able to imitate it? — why a purely human art, as they deem it, should baffle their most skilful analysis? — Why the Church can so easily unite all hearts, whether of bond or free, savage or civilised, in China and Peru as easily as in France or Ireland, in one immense harmony of faith, love, and adoration; while the Sects, a portent to themselves and a jest among the heathen, cannot so much as persuade the members of the same household to be « of one mind? »

It is true that Protestants have anticipated this enquiry, which does not occasion them a moment's embarrassment. Unity, they reply, is a chimera, and truth itself mutable and progressive. « Emulations, quarrels, dissensions, and sects, » which St. Paul classed as « works of the flesh, » they commend as both good and expedient — though they admit that they somewhat impede the diffusion of the Gospel among the heathen. « The diversity of our sects, » says M. Coquerel, a conspicuous French minister, « is our most honourable distinction. » (1) « Far from blushing, » exclaims another, « at these variations of creed, Protestants expect to derive glory from them. » (2) The Germans, we are told, « boast of it as their very highest privilege, and the very essence of a Protestant Church, that its opinions should constantly change. » (3) « The Protestant Church, » says M. de Sismondi, « admits that she herself may be mistaken; she claims only that liberty of thought which the Catholic Church renounces. » (4) « Scotland and England, » observes a British Protestant, deeply impressed with the advantages of disunion, « without their seceders and dissenters, would have been countries in which the human mind slumbered. » (5) Lastly, the Swiss, speaking by the mouth of their supreme ecclesiastical organ, frankly proclaim, that « the right of examination is the only element of fixedness which belongs to the Protestant

---

(1) *L'Ami de la Religion*, tome XXII, p. 208.
(2) *Mélanges de la Religion*, tome I, p. 84.
(3) See *The State of Protestantism in Germany*, by Revd H. J. Rose.
(4) *Progress of Religious Opinion during the Nineteenth Century*, p. 79; English Edition.
(5) Laing, *Residence in Norway*. ch. XI, p. 447.

religion. » (1) Is it possible to admit more candidly that Protestantism is the negation of the work of Christ, and that the pagan world has reason to ask its representatives, « whether they profess any religion whatever? »

We have seen now, by sufficient evidence, that the Church can both win souls in every land, and unite them all, of whatever race or clime, in one family and household; while the Sects, by their own confession, can neither convert the heathen, nor hide from them the shameful spectacle of their own strife and disorder; that the first can attract the pagan by the majestic unity which even he perceives to be divine, while the last only excite his contempt by the divisions and contradictions which even he can trace to their true source. There are yet other points in the contrast between the two which require to be noticed, before we conclude this summary of their respective operations.

There is nothing to which the Sects have professed to attribute so much value, among all the means by which they seek to extend their influence, as the diffusion of knowledge. One might suppose, in listening to their orators, that the history of those long ages during which the Church alone cultivated human science, and was the sole sanctuary both of learning and holiness, found no place in their ungrateful memory. Yet even enemies have confessed, that « law, learning, education, science, *all* that we term civilisation in the present social condition of the European

---

(1) *Défense de la Vénérable Compagnie des Pasteurs de Genève, à l'occasion d'un écrit intitulé* « Véritable Histoire des Momiers. »

people, spring from the supremacy of the Roman pontiffs and the Catholic priesthood over the kings and nobles of the middle ages. » (1) Guizot, Haxthausen, and other writers of their class, men of vigorous intellect and inexorable candour, have declared, that, but for the humanising influence of the Church, mind must have been everywhere beaten down by brute force, and have freely confessed, that when we thank God for all the treasures of knowledge and art which we now possess, we should thank Him also for the wakeful and generous providence of the Church to which we owe them. It is true that the Protestant revivers of pagan literature in the sixteenth century affected, for the first time in the history of the world, to regard Catholics as obscurantists, though the revival was chiefly due to the ceaseless activity of the latter, and the classical court of Leo X welcomed with almost as much enthusiasm the discovery of a new manuscript as that of Pius IX does the triumph of a new martyr. Yet even the most eminent of their own teachers have avouched, that, in spite of their eager self-laudation, the Church beat them out of the field with their own weapons; and that not only, in the words of Ranke, « Rome *continued to be a metropolis of civilisation, unrivalled* in *minute and various erudition,* » but that the Jesuit schools throughout Europe, as Bacon easily discovered, were so immeasurably superior to those of their complacent rivals, that « it was found that their scholars learned more in one year than those of other masters in two, and even Protestants *recalled*

---

(1) Laing, *Observations on Europe*, ch. xv, p. 394.

their children from distant gymnasia and committed them to their care. » (1)

But it is not only in the higher spheres of intellectual culture that men who received their noblest inspirations from that illuminating faith which, while marking the limits, has indefinitely extended the domain of reason,— orators and theologians, statesmen and philosophers, poets and artists, — have served as models to the ungrateful rivals who affected, often with powers ludicrously disproportioned to their claims, a universal supremacy. Even in lower fields of mental toil, the vain clamour of her boastful accusers has been perpetually rebuked by the calm but sleepless energy of the Church, as their costly but sterile efforts have been surpassed by her silent and peaceful triumphs. « In Catholic Germany, » says a well known Presbyterian writer, « in France, in Italy, and even in Spain, the education of the common people... is *at least* as generally diffused, and as faithfully promoted by the clerical body, as in Scotland... Education is in reality not only not repressed, but is encouraged, by the popish church, and is a mighty instrument in its hands, and ably used. » At this hour, he adds, « Rome has above a hundred schools *more* than Berlin, for a population little more than *half* of that of Berlin; » and « if it is asked what is taught to the people of Rome by all these schools — precisely what is taught at Berlin! » (2)

Such facts, which we cannot pursue further in this

(1) Ranke, book 5, vol. I, p. 379; book 8, vol. II, p. 208.
(2) *Notes of a Traveller*, ch. vi, p. 167; ch. xxi, pp. 439-41,

place, « put to flight a world of humbug, » as this ardent Protestant observes; and would acquire tenfold gravity, if we were to investigate them in relation to the moral results of education, as dispensed by the Church and the Sects respectively, in England, Prussia, or any other land. But it is with their education of the *heathen* that we have been concerned in these volumes, and which, that we may include this point also in our summary, appears to have accomplished such results as the following.

1. In China, where Mr Oliphant, M^r D'Ewes, Mr Minturn, and other Protestant travellers, could not but admire « the able and distinguished masters » who taught, not only the highest Chinese classics, but European languages, and the arts of music, painting, and sculpture, with a success which was « truly wonderful; » where even women, like the French Sisters of Charity, had no need of native aid; and where the compositions of native pupils, « who evidently regarded their spiritual masters with feelings of affection and gratitude, » won the applause of the pagan professors in the Imperial Academy of Pekin : the educational efforts of two hundred Protestant missionaries, almost all of whom were obliged, from lack of knowledge, to teach only by the aid of salaried Chinese, are thus estimated by the same friendly witnesses. « The children are taught only the most rudimentary works in their own classics. Their education seems likely, therefore, to be of little service to them, either amongst their own countrymen or foreigners. » They only learn English, says Dr Ball, the solitary accomplishment which their masters can dispense, « to turn it afterwards to

their own advantage for trading purposes. » « In too many instances, » adds the candid M*r* Oliphant, « the knowledge they have acquired only serves to increase their evil influence. » The sole effect of their « English education, » says another, is « to qualify them for hypocrites or sharpers. » Finally, the fruits of Protestant education in China, upon a large scale, and in their latest development — the ultimate results of half a century of « bible-teaching, essentially Protestant in its principles and tendency, » — have been the mental cultivation and christian virtues of the Tae-ping rebels!

2. In India, the effects of Protestant education, conducted by a thousand agents, during successive generations, and at prodigious cost, have been simply appalling. The scholars, we are told by one English authority, « reject heathenism without embracing Christianity, and become conceited infidels, worse to deal with than pagans. » They may have « a thorough knowledge of Holy Scripture, » and « explain in the clearest manner the cardinal point of justification; » they may even rebuke « popish idolatry, » by a suitable array of texts; but in spite of these accomplishments, derived from missionary preceptors, « they have no more faith in Jesus Christ, » we are told; « than in their own religion. They believe the Jesus of the English, and the Krishna of the Hindus, to be alike impostors. » Lastly, — for it would be idle to recapitulate testimonies which we have found to be absolutely uniform, — « the *educated* native is either a hypocrite or a latitudinarian, with the heart of an atheist under the robe of an idolater. The greater body are but too

surely tending a state morally *lower* than that from which education rescued them. »

3. In Ceylon, we have been told by Sir Emerson Tennent, « the moral results of education have been limited and unsatisfactory. » The Americans alone are said to have had more than one hundred thousand pupils in their schools; and though they, like the other sects, have had supreme control over this vast mass of scholars from infancy to manhood, they cannot touch their hearts! « The schools have done little good, » says Dr Brown ; « even the children educated in them, when they grow up frequented the idol temples, and scarcely a youth was to be seen at chapel, unless he was still a scholar. » We have been informed, on the other hand, by Protestant witnesses, how uniformly the *Catholic* pupils illustrate their belief by their practice, and that « neither corruption nor coercion could induce them to abjure their religion. »

4. In Australia, we have heard of natives who had been « *educated* at the mission, » not only living naked in the woods, but « murdering their children in after years. » In New Zealand, where multitudes have been the apt and intelligent pupils of Protestant missionaries, an official report affirms, in 1859, that simultaneously with « a remarkable activity of mind directed to the development of political ideas, » their education has only made them worse, morally, socially, and physically, than they were fifty years ago; while it has rather stimulated than repressed the universal impurity and corruption which they now display, « in body and mind, in all their thoughts, words, and actions. »

5. In the islands of the Pacific,— where Catholic missionaries have educated even the barbarous tribes of the Philippines with such success, that a Protestant traveller notices with admiration, « that there are very few Indians who are unable to read, » — the emissaries of another faith print, in a single group, and in every successive year more than twenty thousand volumes; yet we know, by their own confession, what their scholars have become, « from the hut of the menial to the royal palace; » and a native authority assures us that, in spite, or as he seems to think because of this educational process, « every thing that concerns the native race is both physically and morally *retrograde*. »

6. In Africa, we have seen the Protestant scholars at Cairo resuming their original habits as soon as their education was finished; in the West, it only « enables them to become more perfect in villainy; » and in the South — but we have heard enough of the Protestant Hottentot, who, as an English writer has told us, « can sing all day long about ' the sufferings of the Lamb, ' but knows no more about the Lamb, or His sufferings, than one of the lower animals; » so utterly unprofitable is the instruction of missionaries who can only succeed as a crowd of impartial witnesses attest, in making their disciples « the most idle and worthless of their nation. »

7. In Greece, Protestant education appears to have collapsed, as soon as the schoolmasters began to be missionaries. In Syria, as Dr Valentine Mott reports, « even the Armenians, though professing Christianity, joined with the deluded Turks in suppressing Protestant schools; » but he does not seem

to have understood that it was their profession of Christianity which inspired the act, and that even Armenians might reasonably combine to reject what even Dr Wolf calls « the vague and uncertain creed » proposed for their acceptance. In Armenia, in spite of the attractive bribes distributed by missionaries of the school of Mr Justin Perkins, not only was every effort to protestantise the natives perfectly fruitless, but they admit, by the mouth of their friend Dr Wagner, that if they ceased to pay the scholars their weekly tribute, « the schools would become directly empty. »

8. Lastly, a great English authority has recorded the same uniform result of Protestant education in the case of the American Indians, who, when their pupillage was over, « returned to their naked brethren the most profligate and the most idle members of the Indian community. » It was the observation of these invariable facts which provoked a famous Seneca chief to remind certain missionaries, who urged him to adopt their religious opinions, that « such of the Senecas as they nominally converted from heathenism to Christianity, only disgraced themselves by attempts to cover the profligacy of the one with the hypocrisy of the other; » (1) and of which the universality was candidly admitted by the Rev. Dr Wheelock, even with respect to his own Indian pupils, who so far surpassed all others, that they « had made considerable progress in Latin and Greek. » « Some who on account of their parts and

(1) *Indian Biography*, by B. B. Thatcher Esq.; vol. II, ch. XVI. p. 290.

learning, » says this missionary, « bid the fairest for usefulness, are sunk down into as low, brutish, and savage a manner of living as they were in before. » (1) Two Dutch ministers also relate, for all the sects record the same unwelcome facts, that after carefully educating an Indian so that, besides other accomplishments, « he could read and write good Dutch, » and manifested his piety by « answering publicly in the church, » they « presented him with a bible in order to work through him some good among the Indians; but it all resulted in nothing. He has taken to drinking of brandy; he pawned the bible, and became a real beast, who is doing more harm than good among the Indians. » (2)

There is a strange uniformity in these disastrous results of Protestant teaching, attested by Protestant writers, upon all classes of scholars, and in every region of the world, which might almost provoke mirth, if such an emotion were possible in the presence of evils so enormous. When we consider that millions of money are being expended by the various Sects, with ostentatious disdain of the Church, and expressly to impede her work in the world; and that after all their clamorous boasts and anticipations of triumph, after all their complacent eulogies of their own skill and enlightenment, they have succeeded at last in educating a few Chinese, whose knowledge « only increases their evil influence; » or Hindoos, only to render them « conceited infidels, worse than pagans; » or Cingalese, that when they quit school,

(1) *Documentary History of New York*, vol. IV, p. 506.
(2) *Ibid.*, vol. III, p. 108.

they may with greater zest « frequent their idol temples; » or Maoris, that they may become utterly defiled, « in mind and body, in all their thoughts, words, and actions; » or Hawaiians, that they may « plunge voluntarily into every species of wickedness and excess; » or Africans, that they may « become more perfect in villainy; » or Americans, that they may surpass in vileness « the most profligate and the most idle » of their uneducated brethren; — we should be more blind and undiscerning than even these unfortunate pupils, if we failed to derive instruction from such facts. That Protestant missionaries have neither vocation nor mission, though it may explain many points of the contrast which we have been tracing, hardly accounts for such phenomena as these. A certain number of them are at least very superior, both in morals and intellectual power, to their scholars. Some of them are even sincere and zealous men, honestly purposing to improve those whom they instruct. Yet every humane effort is baffled, every benevolent aim intercepted; and they educate whole generations, with every appliance which experience can suggest or wealth accumulate, but always with these results. They can only turn pagans into atheists, and it is from themselves that we receive the confession. Whence this frightful uniformity of disaster? If they are without apostolic gifts, and do not even claim them, yet by purely natural means alone they might have been expected to accomplish something better than this! Whence then, let us ask once more, this immense and universal blight, which pursues them everywhere like the cloud of darkness which hung over the Egyptians, and withers every flower and plant which their hands have touched? Is it not that in denying them all *supernatural* gifts, God has resolved to suspend and neutralise even those *natural* powers, which, as they confess with dismay, they everywhere employ only to inflict upon the heathen world a deeper curse, a more irreparable woe?

The special advantage of the investigation which we have pursued in these pages, and which, as we have said, it would have been impossible, for want of materials, to conduct with success at an earlier date, consists in this, — that it has led us out of the region of speculative controversy into that of historical facts. We have not debated claims or doctrines which a text may prove or disprove, but we have contemplated the Church and the Sects *in action*. This is the test, complete and decisive, which was indicated by our Lord Himself, and we have seen what it has revealed. Everywhere He has manifested, by manifold and persuasive tokens, His unceasing presence with the Church; everywhere He has refused so much as to recognise, except in anger, the barren ministry of the Sects. In presence of such facts, uniform in their character and universal in their range, we may not unreasonably ask our Protestant adversaries, whether they expect us any longer to treat seriously pretentions which history has disposed of, and which God has judged before our eyes? Even they can hardly feel surprise, if henceforth we decline an unprofitable and monotonous discussion which has lost all meaning, because a Divine sentence has closed it for ever; even they can no longer complain, if when they affect to teach

us, we are now content to smile; when they provoke,
to keep silence; when they revile, to pardon; when
they blaspheme, to pray for them.

It would be tedious to notice, one by one, all the
points of contrast between Catholic and Protestant
missionaries, and having sufficiently illustrated
throughout these volumes those of greatest moment,
it may seem superfluous to speak of some which
have less gravity. Yet there are still two which claim
a few words.

When St. Paul, the great exemplar of Christian
missionaries, exhorted all men to whom effectual
grace was given to abstain from marriage, the Church,
though proclaiming it one of the Sacraments of the
New Law, naturally proposed the higher state of
celibacy to all who should aspire to the dignity of
the Christian priesthood. If Protestants were content
to plead that this is no divine command, but only an
ecclesiastical precept, we might regret their inability
to comply with it, but could not justly reproach
them with preferring the lower calling which they
instinctively appropriate as most suitable to themselves. That Almighty God should always refuse them
the special grace which He always grants to His own
ministers, would still be a significant fact; but a
married clergy, though utterly unable to do the work
of God in the world, would only be a humiliating
spectacle, not a denial of any revealed truth. But if
the « counsel » of St. Paul concerning « virgins »
refers to all who would « attend upon the Lord
without impediment, » and in a special manner to
ministers of religion; much more to those who, like
himself, are set apart for the perilous toils of the

apostolate, and charged to display before the eyes of the heathen the loftiest type of Christian perfection. The disciples of St. Paul knew nothing of Protestant missions, and could not anticipate facts which have been disclosed to ourselves in the « memoirs » of missionaries, and the « reports » of their employers. They knew, however, that soldiers were not accustomed to take their wives and children into the battle field; and the proposal to send apostles to the heathen attended by such companions, would have seemed to *them* an unseemly jest on a grave subject.

It would not perhaps be impossible to fill a considerable volume with impressive examples, recorded by Protestant writers, of the inconveniences which even they have detected in the employment of married missionaries. The enormous and perfectly useless *cost* which such a system involves will occur to every one, but this is not the chief objection to it. The married missionary, as St. Paul intimates, is simply incapable, even with the best intentions, of performing duties which always demand the sacrifice of ease and comfort, and often of life itself. « He is divided,» as the Apostle says, and is too « solicitous for the things of the world, » to have much leisure for other thoughts, or to preach Christian virtue and heroism, upon which his own life affords such an ambiguous commentary, without the risk of exciting laughter even in a pagan auditory. Indeed he is very apt to give up preaching altogether for less toilsome recreations. Even Dr Krapf, of whom we heard in Abyssinia, tells us, that « the wish to settle down as comfortably as possible, and to marry, entangles a missionary in many external engagements which may lead him away from his Master and his duty; » and then he enumerates not only « house-building, » but other « irrelevant and subordinate matters. » Dr Colenso, with more energy of expression, deplores the fact that « wives often ruin a mission by their tempers and animosities. » Sometimes they produce the same unpleasant effect without displaying such moral infirmities. « For nearly three months, » says an amiable missionary, « I was confined, almost exclusively, to the sick chamber of Mrs S., » — a duty which he did well to perform, but which can hardly be said to have promoted his efficiency as a preacher of religion; indeed he adds that he abandoned the work, because, for the lady's sake, « medical advisers interdicted any future exposure to the privations of a missionary life. » (1) We need not multiply such examples; they occur at almost every page of Protestant missionary annals.

Yet the disciples of the so-called Reformation, though they admit and deplore such results, have adopted other maxims than those of St. Paul, and not satisfied with choosing the least excellent calling, always proceed to defame that which they have not grace to adopt. Celibacy, mortification, and confession are repugnant to mere human nature, and therefore the most convenient process is to condemn them at once. The Bible, which Protestantism has skilfully converted into a huge code of self-indulgence, will easily furnish a pretext. Like the pagans of old, who deified their own vices, and consecrated

(1) *Journal of a Residence in the Sandwich Islands*, by Revd C. S. Stewart, p. 394; 2^d edition. *Visit to the South Seas in the U. S. Ship Vincennes*, by the same author; Introd.

their favorite crimes by dedicating each to a particular demon, Protestants first reject some evangelical truth, and then worship the opposite error in its place. If they cast away the healing Sacrament of Penance, one of the most precious fruits of the ineffable tenderness of Jesus, they do so in a lofty spirit of morality, for « the practice of confession is immoral and degrading. » If they shrink from mortification, and even their missionaries occupy sumptuous dwellings, battle for augmented salary, and fare delicately every day, it is only by way of manly and intelligent protest, for, as their bishops considerately remind them, « asceticism is no part of the Gospel system. » If they refuse all filial love and honour to the most Blessed Mother of God, they are not content without adding, — if we may without defilement repeat words actually employed by a well known Anglican dignitary, — that « She », who once « covered with kisses the lips which shall pronounce the doom of all men, » « is expecting her judgment like any other woman ! » If they take away the Daily Sacrifice, and surpassing all human ingratitude, scoff even at that Sacramental Presence which constitutes the most amazing excess of Divine love, they presently cry out with the Church of England, that the Adorable Mystery « is a blasphemous fable. » They do not do things by halves. *Abyssus abyssum invocat* — « *one deep calls to another* » — and they are bent on sounding them all. If St. Paul says, without limitation or reserve, « It is good for a man not to touch a woman; » (1) *they* answer with one voice,

---

(1) Cor. VII, 1. Cf. Apoc. XIV, 4.

« It is evil! » Nay more, fulfilling the sacred proverb, and resolved to justify the mode of life which they choose for their portion, they assert with an air of calm superiority, that a married is a *more* acceptable servant of God than an unmarried minister. Who can estimate, they say, the advantage of teaching the heathen the sober joys of domestic life? — even at the risk of teaching them at the same time, as Ricci observes, that « conjugal fidelity » is the summit of Christian perfection. « The wives of missionaries, » one Protestant clergyman has assured us, « exalt the dignity of the pastoral character! » « An unmarried missionary, » says another, as if he thought Christianity began with such men as Cranmer and Beza, « *cannot* eventually prosper. » We almost seem to hear the old Greek exalting inebriety in honour of Bacchus, or the Roman compounding for lasciviousness by building a temple to Priapus. And though all Protestant missionaries are not so enamoured of human infirmity, and would not so openly deify it, yet almost all have shown, by actions more impressive than words, how extravagant they deem the injunction of St. Paul, how fastidious his example.

It is true, as we have seen, that they sometimes bear witness against themselves. All the non-catholic communities which have lost the grace of celibacy, and especially the Greek and Russian, still render homage to it after their manner. The latter, despairing of the continence of her ministers, yet abhorring the incongruity of priestly nuptials, compels all her secular clergy to marry *before* they enter the ecclesiastical state. « Is not this, » asks Mr Ivan

Goloviue, himself a Russian priest, « an explicit recognition of celibacy as the more perfect calling? » (1) Is it not also, we may ask in our turn, an equally explicit confession of inability to attain it? The Russian Church has no missionary organisation, or she would have learned, by actual experience, that even the instincts of the pagan world reject with scorn a married priesthood. « Directly the savage hears, » says an apostolic missionary in America, « that a teacher of religion has a wife, he regards him as on a level with himself. » Even the heathen witnesses against the uxorious effeminacy of the Sects, and has a deeper sympathy with the ethics of St. Paul than the most refined and educated Anglican, who *now* confesses that the grace of celibacy, without which missionary success is a pure chimera, is so wholly beyond his reach, that the very pretence of it ought to be discouraged. « The mere declaration » of an Anglican minister, says a conspicuous organ of the Establishment, « that he intends to lead a celibate life is worth nothing. » (2) Yet the ablest advocate of Protestantism in its most intellectual form, of that school which regards a mystery as a fable, and a sacrament as an empty sign, has lately announced, not as a religious truth, but as a postulate of common sense, that « one of the very first requisites for the ministry is a capacity for celibacy. » (3) How, then, shall we be indifferent to the fact, that our Lord has always conferred this necessary grace upon the Catholic missionary, and

---

(1) *Mémoires d'un Prêtre Russe*, ch. x, p. 167.
(2) *Christian Remembrancer*, vol. XXXVII, p. 241.
(3) *Saturday Review*, January 21, 1860.

always refused it to the Protestant; or how shall we doubt, with the history of Christianity before us, that where His gifts are always found, there He is Himself? (1)

If it were still possible to doubt, in presence of the facts which have now been reviewed, whether God works by the Church or the Sects, there is yet a final consideration which will perhaps be accepted as conclusive. When we have stated it, we shall have completed our task.

In the first ages of Christianity, while that battle was raging which deluged Western Asia and the southern provinces of Europe with blood, the victims were always and everywhere of one class. Not a pagan fell during three centuries by the hand of a Christian. The new Faith produced martyrs, but not a single assassin. And even when its preachers were able to remind Consuls and Senates that their disciples had become a mighty multitude, and a Roman army saw with astonishment in its ranks a Legion composed of Christians, not a hand was lifted in anger against the persecutor, even in self-defence. Such is the history of the first three centuries. Every where blood was shed, but it was the blood of apostles and martyrs.

In later ages, when the Church and the world

---

(1) « It is a vulgar prejudice, » observes a Presbyterian traveller, «.to suppose that the Catholic clergy of the present times are not as pure and chaste in their lives as the unmarried of the female sex among ourselves. Instances may occur of a different character, but quite as rarely as among an equal number of our unmarried females in Britain of the higher educated classes. » Laing, *Notes of a Traveller*, ch. XXI, p. 432.

were no longer two distinct camps, except in the sight of the Angels, and the corruptions of the last had overflowed, like a sea of mire, and left their stain even on the steps of the temple; the preachers and confessors were still the same, but the heathen saw them accompanied by men, also calling themselves Christians, who brought reproach on the name of Christ. « Take away your Spanish soldiers, » said Las Casas, « or we will not go among this people, for we should fail to persuade them. » In spite of this new difficulty, the heathen world was converted; and if blood was shed, it was still, as of old, the blood of preachers and confessors. Everywhere, as we have seen, the native races grew and multiplied, as they continue to do at this hour, under the shadow of the Cross. It was not spiritual blessings only which the messengers of the Church bore to them, but temporal also; and as the soul of the savage was renewed by grace, so the very land in which he dwelt seemed to blush at its former barrenness, and « the wilderness blossomed as the rose. »

They are enemies who have attested these facts. There were even cases, when the apostolic labourers had been removed by violence, in which, as they relate, « Nature herself resumed her original aspect. » The very earth seems to have mourned their absence, and once more hid her face from the sun under a robe of briars and thorns. In every pagan land, we have been assured by Protestants, the presence of the Catholic missionary has been fruitful only in benefits to its native tribes. Everywhere they increase under their Christian pastors, in numbers, in intelligence, and in prosperity. Everywhere also they mingle harmoniously with their Catholic rulers, and are amalgamated with them, not only by the bonds of a common faith, but even by the ties of marriage, and by community of social habits and interests.

On the other hand, the same witnesses avouch, that there is not so much as a solitary example of a Protestant conquest, leading to the introduction of Protestant ministers, which has not been *fatal* to the aboriginal tenants of the land. If there be an exception, let it be named. In China and India they could not indeed wholly destroy the natives, because they were themselves only a handful in the midst of millions; but even here they have succeeded in inspiring them with that mingled hatred and contempt to which the lapse of every successive year only adds new intensity. The Chinese, shocked by their worldliness and cupidity, still calls them, after an acquaintance of fifty years, « Lie-preaching Devils. » In Hindostan, « a century and more of intercourse, » we have been told by a native writer, « have not made the Hindu and the Englishman friends, nor even peaceful fellow-subjects. Day by day the estrangement is becoming more and more complete. That is your fault. » « It is not religion, » says a second, « but the want of it, which has brought so many evils to this land. » « Great God, » exclaims another pagan, also familiar with English Christians, « I never saw such Kafirs as the white men! »

And the same contrast is exhibited in every land. In the Islands of the Pacific we have seen the following facts. Wherever Catholic influence has prevailed, — as in the Philippines, where « an immense social improvement » has attended the conversion of millions of savages; in the Gambier Archipelago and the Marquesas, where « the control they have acquired must be seen to be believed; » in the Lobos Islands, where Mr Bennett found them « contented and happy, courteous and hospitable, notable and modest; » in Wallis, Futuna, and New Caledonia, where a few years ago their ferocity was a proverb;— the heathen, after slaying their first apostles, have accepted both Christianity and civilisation, and are at this hour increasing in numbers, in virtue, and in material prosperity.

In every group, on the contrary, which has found Protestant masters, demoralisation and ruin have accompanied them. The fact is patent and undeniable. In Australia, the natives are almost extinct. In New Zealand, once tenanted by the most vigorous race of barbarians in the world, Mr Fenton has told us that « their social condition is inferior *to what it was five years ago*, their houses worse, their cultivation more neglected, » — after an uninterrupted intercourse of fifty years with Anglican missionaries; and that nothing can now save « a population which has once reached such a state of decrepitude. » From other Protestant authorities we have learned, that the depopulation in the various groups of eastern and western Oceanica « is as ominous as it is unaccountable. » In the Society Islands, two thirds of the whole population disappeared in thirty years,— while their English teachers were occupied in depriving them both of their land and their commerce, « to possess themselves of it. » In the Sandwich Islands, they diminish by six thousand annually; so that, in the words of Mr Olmsted, « the total extinction of the nation is inevitable. » In the new English colony of Victoria, nine-tenths of the whole population perished, as M' Westgarth notices, in twenty years. In Van Dieman's Land, a nation went down into the grave within the same period. Everywhere the natives, once models of athletic beauty, melt away by thousands, as if smitten by some destroying angel, before the face of « missionaries » who seem able only to teach them new crimes, and when they have plundered them of all they possess, inform them in their sermons, that « offended Heaven is about to cut them utterly off from the land. » Robbed first of their scanty goods, and then of their natural virtues, — corrupted to the very heart's core by hypocrisy, and the stupefying influence of a religion which they despise even while affecting to adopt it, — the inhabitants of these doomed islands have been struck with a kind of leprosy, which has destroyed both soul and body. A few years hence, as a multitude of Protestant travellers proclaim, the natives of every island under English or American rule will be extinct. Protestantism will have created a desert.

In America, — where D' Mac Kay has informed us that the natives « *still thrive or increase* » in all the Catholic provinces, while in the territory of the United States they have diminished by *seventy-four thousand* in seven years, and are constantly descending to a lower depth of misery and degradation, — the frightful contrast which we have traced in other lands assumes dimensions which have arrested the attention even of the tourist and the idler. Even *they* have noted with amazement, that under Catholic rulers not a tribe has perished, under Protestant not a tribe has survived; and that while the Indian under Protestant patronage has become a beggar, a menial, or a sot, « the work of the Catholic missionaries, » in the words of Governor Stephens, « is really prodigious, » and *their* disciples « are hardly Indians now! » The Church, they confess, has brought life, unity, progress, and peace; the Sects, as their own annalists relate, have sown only misery, discord, corruption, and death. Which, shall we deem, has been the work of God?

And now we have accomplished our task. We have compared, as we proposed to do, by the aid of Protestant witnesses, the Missions of the Church and of the Sects, in their Agents, their Method, and their Results. The office of the compiler is discharged, that of the reader begins.

Three classes of men, we may perhaps anticipate, will pronounce judgment upon the history which we have attempted to trace. The first, incapable of accepting the lesson which even the barbarian has derived from such facts, and too much absorbed in self-worship to distinguish between the work of God and the work of man; vexed and irritated, but not instructed, by the contrast which their own associates have revealed; will only espouse more vehemently the earthly cause to which their sympathies are given, and nourish a deeper malice towards the apostles whom God has filled with His presence, but whose virtues they hate and whose triumphs they envy, without so much as the wish to emulate the one, or the hope of rivalling the other. To such men, it will be simply intolerable that their ministry should be « reputed for nothing, » and their craft

« in danger to be set at nought; » nor may we reasonably expect from *them* any other argument than that of the silversmiths of Ephesus, « Sirs, you know that our gain is by this trade. » (1)

A second class, more impartial because less interested, but indifferent to the supernatural character of actions which confound their reason while they leave their conscience untouched, will smile with lenient contempt at the tale of Protestant missions, confess with a kind of peevish and fickle applause the sublimity of the Catholic, and then, « caring for none of these things, » will presently forget both the one and the other. Or perhaps, unwilling to admit the whole conclusion which this history suggests, accustomed to regard only the *human* side of the Church, and casting about for some convenient plea which may excuse inaction, they will propose to transfer the discussion to a wider field. We admit, they will say, that the two classes of missionaries cannot be compared; but christian societies are not composed of missionaries alone, and must be judged, not by an exceptional class, but by the whole mass of their members. And this test they will propose with greater confidence, because they know it would reveal nothing, even if it were possible to apply it. Nature can imitate grace, at least in its lower manifestations, with so much apparent success, that ordinary men cannot distinguish between them. The natural virtues which exist in certain races, both pagan and christian, and which even a false religion does not wholly destroy, may easily be confounded with those which

(1) Acts XIX, 25.

are supernatural; and there are countries in which many a man passes among his friends as a model Christian, who has perhaps not even been baptized, and who never performed a good action in his life from a supernatural motive.

Nor would it be possible to estimate how much of the good which may still be found in non-catholic races, — unfed by sacramental grace, and therefore producing only a feeble growth of sickly and stunted virtues, or at best a mournful yearning after the holiness which finds no nourishment in so poor a soil, — is due to the lingering influence of Catholic tradition, and of those fragments of Catholic truth which have not yet wholly disappeared in Protestant nations. In every sect, the real source of such religious life as its members display is found, not in their human traditions, but in the power of some Catholic doctrine which heresy has not wholly defaced. If they « wrest the Scriptures to their own destruction, » they still owe to the Church both the Scriptures themselves, and the pious thought that, to the pure in heart, a special and almost sacramental blessedness attends the study of them. If they preach too often out of vanity and contention, and can only awaken transient emotion, while they exhort their hearers to virtues which they can afford them no aid in acquiring; they are at least right in believing, however unprofitable the conviction may be, the Catholic dogma, that « faith cometh by hearing. » Even in those painful cases, happily few in number, where there is an imitation of the most solemn Catholic rites, and the awful Sacraments of Penance and the Altar are represented in some of their external forms by men whose act would be a sacrilege if it were not a delusion; though this playing with shadows too often leads to spiritual blindness and death, it engenders in particular cases an ardent and insatiable longing for realities, and though it is utterly void of sacramental power, produces in humble minds a certain moral influence of which the final grace of conversion is not unfrequently the blessed sequel. So true it is that all the evil which exists in heretical communities is due to their own errors, while the good which struggles with it is the alien's portion of those lavish benedictions which the Church scatters with divine prodigality over the whole earth. (1)

For these reasons, the test to which we have referred would be sure to fail. It could afford no assistance in penetrating beyond the surface of things. God has given us another and a surer rule. It is in the order of apostles that He warned us to look for the signs of His presence and the evidence of His power, when He said, *By their fruits ye shall know them;* and in making the conversion of the Gentiles the special function of the apostles of His Church, He made it also the supreme test both of *their* mission and of *her* eternal union with Himself. « They shall build the places that have been waste from of old, » was the declaration of the Holy Ghost; « And they shall know their seed among the Gentiles, and

(1) « Jésus les vit tous : il pleura sur ceux qui erraient les yeux fermés autour des jardins de l'Église, *et ne vivant plus que des parfums qui s'en exhalaient.* » *La Douloureuse Passion de N. S. Jésus-Christ*, d'après les Méditations d'Anne Catherine Emmerich; p. 71, 3me édition.

their offspring in the midst of peoples : all that shall see *them* shall know them, that these are the seed which the Lord hath blessed. »

A third class, let it be permitted to hope, will discern at length, by the light of history, the truth which they have often suspected, but which they have hitherto been reluctant to confess. Halting between two opinions, and neither frankly Protestant nor effectually Catholic; urged by a secret instinct to cast in their lot with the Church, yet constrained by lingering prejudice, or the tyranny of habit, or the fascination of domestic ties, or haply by personal interest, to waste their gifts in the service of a Sect; *they* may comprehend at last on which side is God, and hasten to seek in the Church Him who has announced, by acts which even savages have understood, that they shall not find Him elsewhere. If their seeming virtues are real, and they honestly desire to discriminate between things divine and human, they will no longer hesitate to apply that rule of their only true Master, *By their fruits ye shall know them*. Hitherto they have not seen, because they have closed their eyes; or have mistaken purely natural for supernatural gifts; or have misused graces which were designed, not to adorn a Sect, but to lead them out of it, and which, if they die in their schism, will only increase their condemnation. « Comparing themselves with themselves, » and carefully adjusting their vision to the narrow field of their own interests and occupations, they have refused until now so much as to look up lest they should discern what was passing around them, or to turn one glance towards that mournful desert which hems them in on every side, and which represents, more truly than their own imperceptible spheres of action, the real work of their Sect, and the final issue of its unblest career, against which their own is only an unavailing protest. Busy with some local scheme, large enough for their narrow sympathies, but which the next hour may subvert, and which is at the mercy of popular waywardness or arbitrary caprice; taking counsel, neither with the Church triumphant in heaven nor militant on earth, but only with a few kindred associates, whose unfruitful ardour reflects and sustains their own; voluntary exiles, who belong by profession neither to the Church nor the world, but are anathematised by the first because she knows they are her enemies, and suspected by the second because it imagines they are her friends; keeping always on the confines of that Promised Land which they idly deem their own, but never attempt to enter; pastors of a « church, » the least considerable of human sects, of which they are the sole pontiffs and lawgivers, and which itself is only the fragment of a larger sect; having a « priesthood » which no one claims but themselves, and no one admits but their companions; distributing to the hungry a barren feast of bread and wine in which their unconsecrated lips can work no change, and to the guilty a semblance of absolution which absolves nothing; claiming to hold truths which their Sect abhors, but only to use them *against* the Authority which delivered them to the world, and often more self-willed in maintaining than their co-religionists in rejecting them; never so wholly Protestant, in all their thoughts words and actions, as when most they affect to be Catholic; fretfully subject to « bishops » whose heresies they profess to deplore, but always make their own by submission, and feebly loyal to masters who betray them in their need without scruple, ruling them without love and abandoning them without regret; such men, who have every thing to gain and nothing to lose, may perhaps learn at length from the history which we have reviewed the lessons which their own failures and calamities, the phenomena of their age and country, and even the suggestions of conscience, have hitherto taught them in vain. (1)

It is not indeed a new truth which the events of the last three centuries, and the perpetual union of God with the Church and her ministry, have taught the world, though mightily confirmed by a new series of facts. A thousand years ago our fathers were already proclaiming it with admiration, for *they* detected on little evidence what has been announced to ourselves by greater. The first victories of the Church had hardly been gained, when St. Augustine was telling the faithful in Africa, that Christians of his age had this advantage over the disciples of our Lord, that whereas the latter could only look for-

(1) How should they not be taught in vain, to whom the Tempter has artfully suggested, that it is their *duty* to abstain from all enquiry? « There is an essential irreverence, similar to that false devotion which the prophet rebuked in Achaz, when he refused to ask a sign of God, though God through His prophet bade him do so; the irreverence of *not investigating the signs which God gives us for the purpose of being investigated*, as if we knew better than He, and were more delicate and circumspect in our operations. » *Bethlehem*, ch. VI, p. 324.

ward to the promised glories of the Bride of Christ,
the former could already look back to their partial
fulfilment. Fifteen centuries have passed away since
then, and each has only accumulated fresh evidence
of the indefectibility of that Church in which the
Saviour dwells by a kind of second Incarnation,
« which is in fact the world of the Incarnation, »
and whose life is the counterpart of His. « No weapon
that is formed against thee, » was the promise
of her Almighty Founder, « shall prosper, and every
tongue that resisteth thee in judgment thou shalt
condemn. » Who shall say that the promise has been
unfulfilled? What is the history of the world but the
history of her sufferings and triumphs? Perpetually
assaulted, she has outlived every enemy; and though
they have predicted, one after another, her approaching
end, she has chanted her *de profundis* over them
all. « When we reflect, » says the great English
essayist, suggesting truths which bore no fruit in
his own soul, « on the tremendous assaults which
she has survived, we find it difficult to conceive in
what way she is to perish. » What new snare can
men set for her which she has not already baffled,
what new adversary can they bring from the ends of
the earth whom she has not already overcome? Who
has fallen upon this stone, and has not been « broken ; »
upon whom did it ever fall, and did not
« grind him to powder? » In vain the Arian fought
against her, wresting from her whole kingdoms, till
half the Christian world had apostatised, from the
cities of Africa to the shores of the Bosphorus and
the Danube; and when faith seemed about to perish
from the earth, and even Saints deemed the Judg-

ment was at hand, the decree of her assembled Fathers prevailed, the *Consubstantial* was proclaimed by the voice of the Holy Ghost, and Arius and his host were swallowed up in the abyss. In vain the evil spirits arrayed against her the Hun, the Goth, and the Vandal, whose armies humbly laid their spoils at her feet, and finished by adoring the Cross which they had been sent to destroy; and when all else perished and was engulfed in that wreck of nations, she alone remained, like the Ark upon the flood of waters, guardian of the ancient faith and source of a new civilisation. In vain the satellites of the false prophet over-ran Africa, Spain, and half Gaul, blotted out the corrupt churches of the East, made Greece their prey, and set up a throne in Byzantium; for then the cry of her supreme pontiffs was heard, calling the Latin chivalry to arms, and bidding them « tear up Europe by the roots to fling it on Asia, » that so the torrent might be stayed or turned from its course; until even the Moslem understood that faith was more than a match for fanaticism, that christian unity was a more impenetrable barrier than human or satanical confederacy, and that it was time to despair of gaining new conquests over a Power which could so effectually dispute those he deemed already secured. In vain, lastly, did the « Prince of this world, » baffled in so many encounters, head the most formidable revolt against which she has ever contended; for in that sixteenth century in which the gates of hell were thrown wide open, and a legion of unclean spirits received permission to make war upon her, — at the very moment when their loud cry of triumph was heard in half the kingdoms of Europe, and was echoed by the acclamations of a hundred sects, — a new army of apostles came out of the sanctuary, clothed in the armour of God, and charged by Him to gather out of all nations and peoples, in India and China, in Peru and Mexico, and in all the islands of the sea, that vast company of new believers to whom He resolved to transfer the inheritance which Swedes and Saxons, drunk with the enchanter's cup, were now forfeiting for ever.

Such was the latest victory of the Church, of which we have attempted to trace the glorious details in these pages. Yet even this was only the half of her triumph. It was not enough that she should more than repair the losses inflicted upon her, by adding to her communion whole nations in the East and West whose fathers knew not God. A more perfect satisfaction was due both to Him and to her, and therefore she received power to recover millions, by an effort not too great for this mighty mother, even from the apostate races over whom the enemy had begun to reign. This was the last and greatest of her triumphs. In the very hour of her sorest need, a double victory was prepared for her, a double confusion for her enemies : for while they could neither recruit their ranks in the new world, nor maintain their conquests in the old, she did both at once ; and as Moses with one hand had given the Covenant to his people, and lifting up the other had « put Amalec to flight; » so she presented at one moment to a thousand pagan tribes the Gospel of Christ, and the next drove back from the Mediterranean to the Baltic the swarming legions who were arrayed against her.

Let us contemplate for a moment both the victory and the defeat, since in these will be found the true summary of all which has been said in these volumes.

In little more than half a century, Protestantism, gorged with the spoils of the Church, and still breathing out destruction against her, had already begun to dwindle and decay. For a moment it seemed about to triumph, then yielded everywhere before that awful Power which was strong enough both to vanquish heresy in Europe, and to kindle simultaneously the light of faith in China and India, in Canada, Brazil, and Paraguay. Like Arianism and Islamism, the new religion over-ran Christendom, but only to give place to the Church, with whom it vainly disputed the sovereignty of the world.

In *Germany*, as early as 1558, « only a *tenth part* of the inhabitants had remained faithful to the old religion; » and twenty years later, « Protestantism was the dominant creed of all the *Austrian* provinces, whether of the German, Sclavonic, or Hungarian tongues. » Even in *France*, « for some time the whole people seemed to lean towards the Protestant confession, » and in 1600 « there were seven hundred and sixty parish churches belonging to the Protestants of France, all in good order; four thousand of the nobility belonged to that confession. » (1)

Yet how transient was this seeming triumph! In Germany, as early as 1622, « Catholicism poured in a mighty torrent from the south to the north, » and « the work of conversion advanced, » says a well

---

(1) Ranke, vol. I, pp. 364, 412.

known Protestant writer, « *with resistless force.* » (1) Almost the whole of Austria, Poland, Saxony, Bavaria, and half Prussia returned to the Church. « Belgium, which had been half Protestant, was transformed into one of the most Catholic countries of the world. » Even Holland, at a later period, recovered her sacred hierarchy; and after losing by a religious revolution Flanders and Brabant, and every thing south of the Scheldt and the Rhine, has seen one half of her diminished population reconciled to the Church.

In France, in the course of a few years, says Ranke, « the number of Protestants was decreased *seventy per cent.;* » and only twenty years after the new religion had devastated the land with civil war, and sent forth its armed hosts under the command of kings and princes, men were already predicting « the inevitable and final downfall of Protestantism in France. »

In every land, except Sweden and England, — where the state prohibited the freedom of conscience which the new religion was supposed to guarantee, and where the rack or the gibbet supplanted reason and extinguished faith, — the same swift decay commenced, of which Macaulay wrote the pregnant summary when he said, — « Fifty years after the Lutheran separation, Catholicism could scarcely maintain itself on the shores of the Mediterranean; a hundred years after the separation, Protestantism could scarcely maintain itself on the shores of the Baltic. » (2)

(1) Ranke, vol. II, p. 77.
(2) *Essay* on Ranke's *History of the Popes*.

And even these facts only imperfectly resume the historical results of that boasted confederacy which had lost all cohesion before it had been ten years in the world, and whose broken bands were soon busy in those fierce mutual conflicts by which God devoted them to destruction, and which at a later period they were to renew, to the dishonour of Christianity, before the face of the heathen. « Lutherans and Calvinists stood opposed to each other with a feeling of mutual hatred;... Episcopalians and Puritans, Arminians and Gomarists, attacked each other with the fiercest hate. » (1) So quickly did the new religions betray their true origin; and meanwhile the Church looked on with folded arms, and saw her enemies, reeling to and fro like drunken men, hew each other in pieces. She had survived every other combat, and once more the word came to her to « stand by » (2) and see how God would baffle this new foe. She knew what He would do, and He has justified her confidence.

It is not at the close of a work already extended to extravagant dimensions that we can attempt to exhaust the proofs of this consoling fact. Let it suffice to indicate them. They will at least serve to convince us that not one promise which the Sects made to a foolish generation has been kept, even in part. They boasted, that they would restore Christian doctrine to its primitive purity, and everywhere they have revived blasphemies against the Blessed Trinity and the Incarnation which had been almost

(1) Ranke, vol. II, p. 57.
(2) Exodus, XIV, 13.

unknown in the world for a thousand years. « The ancient controversies on the Trinity» observes Mʳ Hallam, « had long subsided,... and Erasmus, when accused of Arianism, might reply with apparent truth, *that no heresy was more extinct.* » (1) A few years after the new religion was preached, it had revived in every land, was diffused like a plague wherever the Reformation found disciples, and now, at the end of three centuries, the Church is found to be everywhere defending against the incessant assaults of the Sects even those fundamental truths of revelation, of which their founders claimed, with eager imprecation and clamorous taunt, to be the exclusive advocates!

They claimed also to be the champions of human reason, and have only generated at last a school of pretended philosophers who have destroyed every thing and created nothing; who grope their way in obscurity, to feel after truths of which they have lost the trace; who weary the world with empty theories without even pretending to confide in their own inventions, and scoff at the faith which they do not share without even the poor merit of believing their own calumnies; who consume their lives, not in adding to the sum of human wisdom, but in refuting themselves and one another; who have substituted doubt for belief, speculation for knowledge, darkness for light; and after wasting every gift and abusing every talent, despising truths which even pagans admit and insensible to virtues which even pagans revere, they die as they have lived, a boast on their

(1) *Introduction to the Literature of Europe*, vol. I, ch. v, p. 507.

lips and doubt in their heart, and fall at last into the dread abyss which they thought they had proved by invincible arguments had no existence.

They promised the world « liberty, » and then made it impossible, by casting away the divine authority whose law is the condition of liberty, and beyond whose limits it has no sphere. When God imposed the law of *obedience* upon every creature, under penalty of eternal death, though he ennobled the compulsory service by becoming Himself its object, He left man only the choice of a master, and made freedom consist in submission. And for this reason every new religion, though it may delude its votaries with « proud words of vanity, » is inevitably an enslaver; because it substitutes a human for a divine authority, a spurious for a legitimate control, the passions of the individual or the caprices of a sect for the fixed and rational precepts of the Church. And thus it has come to pass in many a land, that civil freedom co-exists with spiritual bondage; that men have become the serfs of their own conceits, of a school, a parliament, or a preacher; and the citizen exults in liberties which the christian has ceased either to value or understand. « The whole of the northern people of Protestant countries, » said Lord Molesworth, « *have lost their liberties* ever since they changed their religion for a better. » (1) « Sweden, Denmark, Prussia, and all the Protestant states of Germany, » adds a Scotch Presbyterian, « are at this day, in all that regards freedom in social action, freedom *of mind and opinion*, more

---

(1) Quoted by Laing, *Observations in Sweden*, ch. I, p. 11.

enslaved than they were in the middle of the middle ages. » (1)

Finally, they announced to mankind the overthrow of ecclesiastical thraldom, and from that hour ruled their own followers in every land with such audacious tyranny, that there has been more « priestcraft, » and of the worst kind, in a single week, in the most obscure sect of England, Scotland, or Sweden, than was ever possible in the Catholic Church in the course of centuries. Whole nations have accepted unconsciously the ignominious bondage. There is not in the world, and probably there never was, such a state of society as that which exists in Scotland. The humiliation of « the servile Church of England » was contrasted long ago by M. Guizot with the unconquerable « independence of the Roman Church. » In Russia, as Mr Golovine has told us, « the Church is nothing but a blind instrument in the hands of the sovereign. » Of Prussia and her people we are assured by Mr Laing, that « morally they are slaves, of enslaved minds, » in spite of their « compulsory education, compulsory religion, and compulsory military service. » In 1834, a Prussian monarch, without even the affectation of consulting the nation, could peremptorily suppress, by a stroke of the pen, both the Lutheran and Calvinistic churches, in order to substitute a new one of his own invention; and when the Protestants of Silesia hesitated to obey the royal edict, or to « fall down and worship the golden image which the king had set up, » with the usual accompaniment of « harp, and sackbut, and all kinds

---

(1) Id. *Observations on Europe*, ch. xv, p. 394.

of music, »—« coercion, imprisonment, military force, and quarterings of troops on the recusant peasants, were resorted to, in order to *force* the ministers and people to receive this new service. » And these are the reflections which this characteristic fact suggested to a Protestant observer. « To resist this monstrous tyranny and persecution, *there was no Rome,* no Vatican, no pope or head of the Church to appeal to. How different, in the same country, at the same period, was the exertion of the autocratic power of the same Prussian monarch over his Roman Catholic subjects! *They* had protection at Rome, and consequently in the whole Catholic world, against such arbitrary violence. He could not even appoint to any clerical office independently of Rome, although he could, and actually did, imprison and dismiss Protestant clergymen, for refusing to adopt a new church service, which, as head of the church and state, he composed and promulgated by royal edict! » (1) Is it possible to confess more impressively, because undesignedly, that true liberty has no existence out of the Catholic Church? and that Christ's Vicar, after defending the weak against the strong for nearly two thousand years, is still the only safeguard of ecclesiastical freedom, the solitary bulwark against spiritual oppression? « Catholicism is, in fact, » adds Mr Laing, « the *only* barrier at present in Prussia against a general and debasing despotism of the state over mind and action : » a statement which appears to illustrate the keen observation of M. Guizot in the first volume of his Memoirs, that

(1) *Notes of a Traveller*, ch. vi, pp. 171, 212.

« people who aspire to liberty run the risk of deceiving themselves as to the nature of tyranny; » and to justify the reproach of Father Faber, that « men would rather be enslaved by the state than owe their emancipation to the Church. »

But if the Reformation, which has made the Gospel a jest in Asia and America, has in Europe every where substituted the arrogant and contemptuous tyranny of princes and statesmen, or the still more intolerable rule of sophists and preachers, for the easy yoke of the Church, it has been even more fatal to Christianity than to freedom. It failed, indeed, to teach it to the heathen, but it failed equally to preserve it from the outrages of its own disciples. This is its twofold shame. « Men are doubting, » said Melancthon, with real or affected horror, « about the most fundamental truths ! » — and he foresaw, even in that early day, what the final issue would be. (1) It has come at last.

In 1825, a German theologian, « in recounting the professors who could *any how* be considered orthodox,-i-e. those who *in any way* contended for the doctrines of the Gospel, or its very truth, counted, in all Protestant Germany, *seventeen*. » (2) What more proof do we need that Protestantism in Germany is the negation of Christianity?

In Switzerland, the second conquest of the Reform-

(1) Quoted by Starck, *Theodul's Gastmahl*, p. 246 ; ed. Kentzinger. « Vides *quo tendat* petulantia multorum. » *Thomæ Matthiæ Epist.*, p. 252. Such expressions abound in the writings of Melancthon.

(2) *A Letter to the Archbishop of Canterbury*, by Dr Pusey ; p. 123.

ation, the Gospel was finally dethroned more than a century ago. « O Bossuet, » said the infidel d'Alembert, « where art thou? Eighty years have passed away since you predicted that the principles of the Protestants would conduct them to Socinianism: what gratitude do you not owe to an author who has attested before all Europe the truth of your prophecy! » (1) « To reject the doctrine of the Trinity is necessary on our principles, » said the « Venerable Company of Pastors » thirty years ago; and when a few ministers in the Canton de Vaud claimed to draw from the same principles different conclusions, they were committed to prison! (2) The Saviour is now declared by the University of Geneva to be « a mere man, » and the students for the ministry are told by their professors, « Make any thing you like of Jesus Christ, so that you do not make him God. » (3) Forty thousand Genevans are infidels or Arians; and while the Church once more numbers eighteen thousand faithful in the metropolis of Calvinism, the solitary Protestant advocate of that doctrine which Servetus was burned for denying counts only 150 followers! « You have entirely abandoned the principles of your Church at the Reformation, » said a British Protestant not long ago, addressing

(1) *Œuvres de d'Alembert*, tome V, p. 272.
(2) *Défense de la Vénérable Compagnie*, etc. Cf. *Feuille d'Avis de Genève*, Octobre 7, 1818; *Mélanges de Religion*, tome IX, p. 342; *Genève Religieuse*, par M. A. Bost, p. 12; *Œuvres de M. de Lamennais*, tome VIII, pp. 392-4.
(3) *Sketch of the Religious Discussions which have lately taken place at Geneva*, pp. 4, 5. Cf. Considérations sur la Divinité de Jésus-Christ, par H. L. Empaytaz.

the Genevan pastors, « you have become Arians. »(1)
« The centre of the Calvinistic Reformation, » adds
de La Mennais, « has become the centre of deism,
and there no longer exists in the Protestant Rome, I
do not say any Christian faith, but any faith whatever. »(2) «Geneva, the seat and centre of Calvinism,»
exclaims'a Scotch Presbyterian, « the fountain head
from which the pure and living waters of our Scottish Zion flow, the earthly source, the pattern, the
Rome of our Presbyterian doctrine and practice,
has fallen lower from her own original doctrine and
practice than ever Rome fell. Rome has still superstition, Geneva has not even that semblance of religion. » (3)

More than twenty years ago, Protestantism in
France — where « hardly twenty *pasteurs* confessed
the doctrines of the Trinity and the Atonement » —
was thus described by an English Protestant.
« Christianity must appear to the great majority of
French Protestants to have in it nothing positive or
defined at all... There is in it neither conviction, nor
that venerating and hallowing attachment to a creed
which is its best substitute. On entering a French
temple, one experiences the same sensation as on
entering a Jewish synagogue. Its services appear like
a wretched effort, not to serve, but to keep up the
memory of an abolished religion. » (4)

Of Holland, — where, as Huber remarks, « reliligion, since the Reformation, has never continued

(1) Haldane's Letter to M. J. J. Chenevière, p. 3.
(2) *Histoire des Momiers*, p. 391.
(3) Laing, *Notes of a Traveller*, ch. xiii, p. 325.
(4) *Blackwood's Magazine*, April 1836, p. 470.

the same for thirty years together; » (1) and where, as early as 1655, an English writer could report, « The sect of Socinianism bears great sway, *and is assented to by most there*, » (2) — we have the following account, in 1838, by Dr Candlish, a conspicuous Presbyterian minister. « The four Protestant denominations of Holland differ in their standards of doctrine... It is said that in all of them there has been a great departure from the orthodoxy of their creeds, and a great decline of spiritual life... It is certain that there has been in the Dutch Church a grievous declension and departure from her first faith and her first love. Laxity in doctrinal views has for a considerable time prevailed among a large proportion of her clergy, and even the standard of orthodoxy has been modified. The sentiments of many of the ministers are tainted with the Arminian and Socinian heresies. » (3)

What England has become, her own writers have told us. One of the most eminent of her clergy, noting the gradual retrogression of her masses towards a virtual paganism, described them a few years ago as « a nation of heathens. » The report was probably

---

(1) *Bibliothèque Universelle*, tome XXIV, p. 181.
(2) Thurloe's *State Papers*, vol. I, p. 508; vol. III, p. 50. Cf. Winwood's *Memorials*, vol. III, p. 340; Gerard Brandt, *History of the Reformation in the Low Countries*, vol. IV; Grotius, *Ordin. Holland. et Westfrisiœ Pietas*, p. 123; *Encyclopédie Méthodique*, Art. Sociniens; Vedelius, *De Arcanis Arminianismi*, lib. I; Pluquet, *Dictionnaire*, tome I, p, 78; Bossuet, *Hist. des Variations*, tome IV, p. 510.
(3) *The Scottish Christian Herald*, vol. III, pp. 199, 504. 2nd series.

more injurious to the heathen than to the English, for multitudes of the latter have lost even the belief in the supernatural, and the consciousness of immortality, which the former every where retain; so that a French writer, speaking from actual observation, could describe Protestantism in England as « paganism *minus* its gods. » It is in England that already more than five millions of the population are said to « profess no religion whatever, » and whose great cities have reached such an advanced stage of decay, as an official census not long ago informed the country, that — in spite of the richest establishment in the world, which has at least one representative in every village in the land — in Leeds and Liverpool *forty*, in Manchester *fifty-one*, in Birmingham *fifty-four*, in Lambeth *sixty-one*, and in Sheffield *sixty-two* per cent, of the whole population, neither have, nor profess to have, any religion whatever; so that, speaking generally, « heathenism is fast prevailing over Christianity. » (1)

It is in England, again, that the masses have sunk into such a condition of purely animal existence that, in the words of her chief oracle, « our peasantry are far worse lodged than our beasts of burden ; » while it is no exaggeration to say that in point of morality they have often descended below the heathen. In two important districts of the country, the counties of Durham and Stafford, the Assistant Commissioners employed during the late Education Enquiry report, amongst other almost incredible facts, that « adultery is made a mere matter of jest, and incest also is

(1) See *The Times*, May 4, 1860.

frightfully common; » that even in the schools which have been established to improve this barbarous population, « it is impossible to state the coarseness of manners that prevails; » and that in one county, « it is rather a shame to an unmarried woman not to have had a child. » (1) In no other country in the world, save England, whether christian or pagan, were such scenes ever described by an official pen; and they are found, not only in rural and mining districts, but, as an eminent advocate of the Establishment deplores, in « the fairest portions of this magnificent City. » « Thousands and tens of thousands are living in London, » he says, « to whom the great truths of the Gospel are practically as little known as if the land of their birth were a heathen land, and not the great bulwark of Protestant Christianity. » The Rector of « the important parish of St. Clement Danes, in the Strand, » detects in his nominal flock « a frightful amount of infidelity — infidelity in all its shapes, extending not only to the denying of the Christian revelation, but even to the grossest and darkest heathenism, » and this « actually extends among the better classes. » Again, « there are whole streets within easy walk of Charing Cross, » and « miles and miles » in more obscure places, « where the people live literally without God in the world... We could name entire quarters in which it seems to be a custom that men and women should live in promiscuous concubinage — where the very shop-keepers make a profession of atheism, and encourage their poor customers to do the same. »

(1) Quoted in *The Times*.

Finally, this authority laments what he calls « the well known fact, » that « there never was a time when the temper of the lower orders in this country was less satisfactory than it is now. » (1)

And so universal is the unmatched brutality of which even these are hardly extreme instances, that a learned English writer could thus appreciate, after much travel, in 1856, the comparative civilisation of the British labourer and « the black African or the red American Indian. » « I was compelled to come to the conclusion, » says Dr Shaw, « after fairly investigating the question, that the physical, moral, intellectual, and educational state of the lower orders in England *was the lowest on the scale I had ever witnessed;* and further, that they were more degraded in habits and manners, » and that, « above all, their moral and educational condition was quite on a par with that of the savage, and sometimes even below it. » (2) And this account is confirmed by an Anglican clergyman, who had also gathered knowledge from foreign travel, and who candidly observes; « Bad as the moral effects of the Jewish and Mohammedan religions are, it must strike every traveller that the people are under the influence of religion, such as it is, more than they seem to be in the great towns of England. » (3)

And if the more educated members of the Anglican Establishment, which has brought to this pass a na-

(1) *Quarterly Review*, April, 1861; pp. 432-63.
(2) *The United States*, etc., by John Shaw, M. D., F. G. S., F. L. S.; ch. x, p. 244.
(3) *The Canary Isles*, etc., by the Revd Thomas Debary, M.A.; ch. xxi, p. 255.

tion once known as « the Isle of Saints, » unlike the Prussians, the Swiss, or the Dutch, have nominally maintained, or only partially modified, their original formularies; this is because the English, proverbially inconsequent, and mortally apathetic about questions of dogma, have consented to perpetuate for the sake of tranquillity illusions which would not survive a month in any other European land. Why, indeed, should they refuse to tolerate a so-called « national » standard of belief, which exists only on paper, and even there in ambiguous and contradictory terms; which long experience has taught them is a burden to nobody; and which leaves every one at liberty to defend or attack, to commend or revile, to use or suppress it, according to his private humour? The Church of England — which neither teaches nor rebukes, neither approves nor condemns, and is officially represented at the same moment and with equal authority by Gorham and Philpots, by Hampden and Keble, by Jowett and Wilberforce, by Denison and Whateley, — probably numbers within her undefined precincts eager advocates of *every* tenet, theory, or opinion, which Protestantism has at any time, or by any agency, introduced into the world; while it is lawful within her pale, as we continually see, either to exalt as scriptural, or to execrate as impious, any doctrine whatsoever which man can affirm or deny. She is no longer even a sect, like the Baptists or Wesleyans, though out of her all sects are bred; but simply a religious club, luxuriously furnished and copiously endowed, to which indifference and not partiality is the sole title of admission. « The religion of the Church of England, » said Lord Macaulay, « is in fact, a bundle of religious systems without number;... *a hundred sects battling within one church.* » (1)

Lastly, of Sweden we are told, not only that « the efforts of the Lutheran doctors to refute Socinianism show plainly enough that its impious doctrines are widely spread in that country; » (2) but that « it is evident, from the official returns of crime, that in no Christian community has religion less influence on the state of public morals. » As you stand in the streets of Stockholm, says the same impartial witness, you may make this unusual reflection; « One out of every *three* persons passing me is, on an average, the offspring of illicit intercourse; and one out of every *forty-nine* has been convicted within these twelve months of some criminal offence. » So that even this Protestant writer adds, « the Reformation, as far as regards the moral condition of the Swedish people, has done harm rather than good; » (3) while another assures us that, bad as the state of Sweden is, « the standard of morals is considerably *higher* than in Norway, » where « *general indifference* is manifested for religion. » (4)

Such have been, in every country of Europe, by Protestant testimony, the historical results of the so-called Reformation. Everywhere it has broken every

(1) *Essay on Church and State.*
(2) *Chronique Religieuse*, tome II, p. 495; *De l'État Religieux de la Suède, Memorial Catholique*, tome VI, p. 130.
(3) Laing, *Tour in Sweden*, ch. IV, pp. 115, 125.
(4) *Norway, Sweden, and Denmark*, by H. D. Inglis; part. 2, ch. I, p. 142. (4th edition).

promise which it once made to a credulous world, and has only generated, by the confession of its own advocates, sterile fanaticism in the few, gloomy unbelief in the many; and while it has shamefully failed to propagate Christianity among the heathen, whom it has taught to hate and despise the religion of Jesus, it has been powerless to maintain, even among its own disciples, its most fundamental truths. Such, once more, has been the double ignominy of the Sects.

And meanwhile the Church, which has seen this new judgment of God upon her foes, has continued to live a divine life. The Sects have putrified or dissolved, filling the air with the odour of death, while *she* has remained unmoved upon her eternal foundations, and continues to teach at this hour the same evangelical doctrines which she taught before they came into being, and will still be teaching when they have vanished from the world. Never has the illuminating presence of her Lord been manifested by more affecting tokens than in the years which have elapsed since the great revolt of the sixteenth century. Never have the faithful been admonished by more consoling proofs, that her weakness is mightier than all the unstable powers which the world can array against her; that the arm which ventures to strike her, though it be that which once reached from the Baltic to the Adriatic, plucked kings from their seats, and ruled as a god over Christian France, shall wither away in shameful impotence; that when she seems about to fall, the hour of her triumph is most surely at hand; and that if for a season dark clouds gather round her, and the cross seems to lie heavy upon her, — if her pontiffs are despoiled and her sanctuaries laid waste, and even the Vicar of God becomes the jibe of the infidel and the sport of the assassin, — then is the moment to be filled with dread and compassion, not for her, but for her enemies, because their judgment is at hand, and the Avenger is at the door.

If the sectary could profit by the lesson which eighteen centuries have failed to teach him, and which during the last three has been written on the earth and in the firmament by the finger of angels, that all might read it there, he would cease to plot, or to desire, the overthrow of the Church; not only because it is idle to waste life in « imagining vain things, » but because he would understand that her end, when it comes at last, will be a dark hour for him, since it will involve his own end also. But it is one of the marks of his judicial blindness, that as each of the prophetic seals is opened, and some new apparition reveals the progress of that tremendous drama of which the final scene is approaching, he alone, blinded by vanity and self-love, and empty of faith, is unconscious of portents which have already passed away and uttered their awful warning, before he has even noted them. Whatever be the mystery which follows the opening of the seal, — whether it be the « white horse, » on which a Crowned Rider goes forth to chastise the enemies of the Church; (1) or the « red, » which comes to kindle war; or the « black, » in whose train follow famine and want; or the « pale horse, » which has death for its rider,

(1) Apoc. VI, 2-8; IX, 3.

and plague and pestilence for its attendants; or lastly, the « locusts, » which, as in the sixteenth century, « come out from the smoke of the pit, » to sting the souls of men, « as the scorpions of the earth, » with the poison of heresy; for him there is no instruction in these dread forms, of which he neither sees the coming nor the going away.

Yet there are signs of the presence and of the work of God which even he might understand, and of which the facts reviewed in these pages are perhaps the most impressive in their deep significance. When St. Leo would teach his generation how to distinguish between those mysterious workings of Providence of which man cannot penetrate the secret plan, and the more intelligible operations, clear as the lightning which shines out of heaven, which even a child can mark and interpret, he said; « Non intelligimus judicantem, *sed vidimus operantem.* » This is the truth which it has been our purpose to illustrate in these volumes. *Vidimus operantem!* We have *seen* Him, who knows how to dispense His own gifts, pouring out in all lands the most stupendous graces on one class, and peremptorily refusing them to every other. We have *seen* Him summoning His apostles, not by tens nor by twenties, but by thousands, to bear to the heathen the very message against which the apostate had closed his ears. We have *seen* Him send forth a new Paul or Barnabas, filled with their wisdom, and preaching their doctrine, to every province of the earth, from the populous homes of the East to where the scattered tents of the savage are reared in the distant West, and everywhere charging His angels to prepare their way before them. *Vidimus operantem!* We have *seen* the weak become valiant and the timid strong, so that they could smile at torture and rejoice in death, because His grace was in their hearts, kindling in them the apostle's courage and the martyr's hope. We have *seen* in the cities of China and India, in the islands of the southern ocean, and by the banks of the Plata and the Uruguay, of the Mohawk and the Genesee, the same mysterious sacrifices by which nations live and kingdoms are won to Christ, and which once crimsoned at the same hour the waters of the Rhone and the Tiber, of the Abana and the Orontes, and were offered for the same end, amid the hosannas of astonished angels, in the streets of Lyons, Rome and Jerusalem, and in the capitals of Lydia, Pontus, and Syria.

Lastly, we have seen all these marvels renewed in our own day, by our own brothers and kinsmen, still filled with the Holy Ghost as their fathers were, still accepting the same almost incredible sacrifices, and accomplishing the same divine victories. And while the emissaries of the Sects, — salaried apostles of a mutilated gospel, from which they have excluded all which might disturb their repose or restrain their earthly appetites; to whom even Divine bounty refuses all but purely natural gifts, and deprives even these of their efficacy; who call themselves missionaries, but live like merchants, and vainly invite the pagan to the practice of virtues which they can neither teach him to love nor aid him to acquire, — are everywhere making Christianity a proverb, its cruel dissensions a bye-word, and its ministers a jest among the heathen; the Church is still sending forth, as she did of old, apostles upon whom God is never weary of lavishing a Father's gifts, and of whom He still lovingly proclaims, before men and angels, « *They* shall know their seed among the Gentiles, and their offspring in the midst of peoples : All that see them shall know them, that these are the seed which the Lord hath blessed. »

Vidimus operantem! By the uncreated light of His adorable presence, by the outpouring of His rarest gifts, by the effulgence of virtues which only His love could bestow, and the testimony of actions which only His grace could inspire, we have *seen* where He dwells. It is still in the Church that He lives and acts. She is still the sole sanctuary which He deigns to illumine with the brightness of His glory. Search not for Him elsewhere, for He has announced in a hundred lands, by signs which even the pagan has understood, how vain the search would prove. And now, in that old age which is but the renewal of her vigorous youth, — after saving the world a thousand times by her mighty intercession, and acquiring in each generation fresh titles to its love and gratitude, — arrived at length at the eve of that reign of Antichrist of which the events of the sixteenth century were the dismal presage, and of which the phenomena of our own are the certain harbinger; this royal mother, calm and unmoved while all around her is swaying to and fro in the first throes of approaching dissolution, accepts without fear the coming conflict. Once more she utters her cry of expostulation, both to her children and her foes. Never so loving as when she warns, never so compassionate as when she rebukes, she addresses to her ungrateful sons the tender reproach which Jesus has put into her mouth, « *What more ought I to have done for thee, and have not done it?* » While to others, who have never known her, but seem to ask, before the final catastrophe is upon them, for fresh proofs that she is indeed the true Spouse, she is content to rehearse all that she has done among men since the hour when the Son of God committed them to her charge, and chiefly what He has done in and by her during the last three centuries, — all the nations she has begotten to Him, all the apostles she has nurtured, all the martyrs she has blessed, all the miracles of power and love of which every heathen land bears the luminous trace, and which attest her inseparable union with the Heart of Jesus; — and when the tale is told, and she has unveiled the majesty of that form in which even the barbarians of Asia and America discerned the reflected image of God, she leaves judgment to Him, and only borrows His gentle rebuke, to say, it may be for the last time, to those who still affect to doubt, — « If you believe not my words, *believe the works that I do.* »

TABLE OF CONTENTS.

VOL. III.

Chapter IX. — Missions in America . . . . P.   1
    »   X. — Summary   401